Communicating
IN groups

APPLICATIONS
and SKILLS

FIFTH
EDITION

Communicating
IN groups

APPLICATIONS
and SKILLS

FIFTH
EDITION

Katherine Adams
California State University, Fresno

Gloria J. Galanes
Southwest Missouri State University

Boston Burr Ridge, IL Dubuque, IA Madison, WI New York
San Francisco St. Louis Bangkok Bogotá Caracas Kuala Lumpur
Lisbon London Madrid Mexico City Milan Montreal New Delhi
Santiago Seoul Singapore Sydney Taipei Toronto

McGraw-Hill Higher Education

*A Division of The **McGraw-Hill** Companies*

COMMUNICATING IN GROUPS: APPLICATIONS AND SKILLS

Published by McGraw-Hill, a business unit of The McGraw-Hill Companies, Inc.,
1221 Avenue of the Americas, New York, NY 10020. Copyright © 2003, 2000, 1997, 1994, 1991
by The McGraw-Hill Companies, Inc. All rights reserved. No part of this
publication may be reproduced or distributed in any form or by any means, or stored in a
database or retrieval system, without the prior written consent of The McGraw-Hill
Companies, Inc., including, but not limited to, in any network or other electronic storage
or transmission, or broadcast for distance learning.

Some ancillaries, including electronic and print components, may not be available to customers
outside the United States.

This book is printed on acid-free paper.

3 4 5 6 7 8 9 0 FGR/FGR 0 9 8 7 6 5 4 3

ISBN 0–07–248388–1

Editorial director: *Phillip A. Butcher*
Sponsoring editor: *Nannette Kauffman*
Developmental editor II: *Jennie Katsaros*
Project manager: *Ruth Smith*
Lead production supervisor: *Lori Koetters*
Coordinator of freelance design: *Mary E. Kazak*
Producer, Media technology: *Jessica Bodie*
Supplement producer: *Nathan Perry*
Cover and interior design: *Amanda Kavanagh/Ark Design Studio*
Cover image: *"Blocks" by Tracy McGuinness*
Typeface: *10/12 Garamond*
Compositor: *Shepherd Incorporated*
Printer: *Quebecor World Fairfield Inc.*

Library of Congress Cataloging-in-Publication Data

Adams, Katherine L.
    Communicating in groups : applications and skills.—5th ed. / Katherine Adams and
Gloria J. Galanes.
        p. cm.
    Rev. ed. of: Communicating in groups / Gloria J. Galanes, Katherine Adams, John K.
Brilhart. 4th ed. 2000.
    Includes index.
    ISBN 0–07–248388–1 (alk. paper)
    1. Small groups. 2. Interpersonal communication. I. Galanes, Gloria J. II. Title.
HM736 G33 2003
302.3'4—dc21
                                                    2002020221

www.mhhe.com

We dedicate this book to our students,
who teach us as much as we teach them.

PREFACE

People can be motivated to be good not by telling them that hell is a place where they will burn, but by telling them it is an unending committee meeting. On judgment day, the Lord will divide people by telling those on His right hand to enter His kingdom and those on His left to break into small groups.

Rev. Robert Kennedy

This quote, given to us by a student, expresses precisely how many people feel about participating in groups. In fact, it describes some of our own experiences! But the quote's sentiment focuses attention on the torture that participating in small groups can produce—and it ignores the uplifting, energizing effect that can also occur through group participation. Group participation *can* feel like torture, but it can also be incredibly rewarding and a lot of fun. Both of us have had the experience of being in a group that so excited us, made us feel alive, gave us a way to express ourselves, helped us connect with others, and so enabled us to accomplish a tremendous amount of work, that we didn't want to see the group end. Yes, that is a rare occurrence. But in this book, we hope to give students tools to help them attain those ideals by providing insight about how groups work and practical suggestions for applying those insights.

This book is designed for the first or second year student who may not have had a prior communication course and who may never take a subsequent course—but who *must* work in groups because that is the nature of corporate, educational, and civic participation in this day and age. Two overarching goals guide our writing. First, being able to work effectively in groups is not a luxury—it's a necessity. Our introductory students want to cut to the chase; they want to know what works *right now*. That is the reason for our distinctly *practical* focus of *Communicating in Groups.* Although this text uses the same research foundation as our more advanced text, *Effective Group Discussion,* we strive here to provide information in a way that is both useful and immediately usable. Second, we want students to recognize that effective group work is, to a great extent, a matter of *communication behavior,* not a matter of personality or fate. Thus, it is to a great extent within their own control. We want students to start thinking about their own communicative choices in groups and to have the tools to make wise choices so they can make the groups they belong to as rewarding and productive as possible.

To meet our goals, we have chosen to use an informal writing style and to provide many examples from our own and others' experiences. We also report research findings in much less detail, with more synthesis and distillation of findings, fewer footnotes, and less evaluation of competing theories than in our other text. This allows readers to focus on what is usually more important to them—the practical application of the research. Finally, we refer to ourselves, Kathy and Gloria, frequently throughout the text. We think of our readers as individuals with whom we are on a first-name basis and we encourage you to think of us the same way, as if we were members of the same small group.

Overview of the Text

With each revision, the hardest thing we have to do is decide what to include and what to leave out. We try to focus on what we believe are the most important concepts, particularly those that will be most useful and practical for students to understand. In this edition, we have increased our coverage of technological changes that affect small groups, of generational differences that can impair the ability of group members to work together well, and of the socialization process as members come and go. We continue to use general systems theory as our structural framework because we believe it provides a framework that is easy to grasp. As before, the chapters are ordered in a way that is logical to us but that does not preclude other methods of organizing a small group course. Each chapter is self-contained and can be taken in an order different from what we provide here.

Part One provides basic information students need to understand how groups function. Chapter 1 introduces some basic terms encountered throughout the book, shows how to classify groups according to their major purpose, and introduces the concept of ethical behavior of group members. Chapter 2 presents general systems theory as a framework for understanding the complexity of group communication. We provide specific illustrations of systems concepts throughout the rest of the book as well.

Part Two provides the foundation for understanding communication in groups. Chapter 3, which may present review material for some readers, discusses basic communication theory, including what communication is, what constitutes effective listening, and how people interpret what they see and hear. Chapter 4 discusses the specifics of verbal and nonverbal communication. Chapter 5 discusses the creative and critical thinking skills necessary for effective group problem solving. We believe creative and critical thinking are at the heart of the group problem-solving process and that students should know something about these processes before understanding problem solving in general. Chapter 6 describes the problem-solving process and introduces the Procedural Model of Problem Solving as a helpful guideline to follow.

Part Three focuses on the group's throughput processes. Chapter 7 explains how a group develops into a team from an initial collection of individuals. Leadership concepts are introduced here and expanded on later. Chapter 8 celebrates group diversity, which is group strength but also presents challenges for members who must manage the diversity of member motivation, learning style, personality, culture, gender, generation, and ethnicity. The chapter also offers SYMLOG as a technique for discussing and capitalizing on member diversity. Chapter 9 explains why group conflicts occur and how they can be managed so that the group benefits instead of suffers. Chapter 10 provides a comprehensive picture of what group leaders are expected to do and also gives suggestions for applying leadership principles effectively and ethically.

Part Four presents information about oral presentations, the culmination of much group effort. In Chapter 11, students will learn about the types of oral presentations, how to prepare effective presentations, and criteria for evaluating presentations. We wish to acknowledge the contributions of Dr. Hal Bochin (California State University, Fresno) and Robin McGehee (College of the Sequoias—Visalia, California) to this chapter. Dr. Bochin wrote the original version and Robin McGehee revised the chapter for us. Finally, the **appendix** presents information about a number of techniques a member or outside observer can use to gather information about a problem-solving group and help it improve its performance.

Features

Case Studies: Each chapter begins with a case study that illustrates several of the major points we make throughout the chapter. These studies are based on our own experiences, situations we've read or heard about, and examples our students have given us. Each case study is a story—and stories will help you recognize and remember the chapter's main concepts.

Apply Now Boxes: Practical application of information is one of our main goals, and the Apply Now features provide opportunities for you to apply the concepts in the chapters to the examples found in the boxes.

New! Ethical Dilemma Boxes: Being a member of a group means you have to balance your individual needs with those of the group, and sometimes those needs come into conflict. The Ethical Dilemma boxes invite you to give more thought to typical ethical dilemmas and to think carefully about what you would do.

New! Media and Technology Boxes: Media and technology are changing the world around us and changing our interactions in small group communication. Media boxes are designed to help you discover how the Internet can enhance your group participation by providing information about using the chat room for GSS, socialization in online groups, and online support groups.

New! Running Glossary: Key terms are boldfaced in the text and defined in the margin next to the narrative to help you identify important terms and concepts.

Tables, Figures, Cartoons: We provide numerous summaries, examples, and humorous illustrations. These visual summaries help serve as study aids, provide practical suggestions at a glance, and also help you find the humor in many small group situations.

Learning Aids: Each chapter begins with a list of objectives that highlights the important information in the chapter and concludes with summaries, bulleted points that summarize the most important ideas in the chapter. Exercises at the end of each chapter provide additional ways to think about and apply the information.

New! Online Learning Center and Small Group Supersite: The icons at the end of each chapter and in the margins guide students to additional activities on the Web including interactive quizzes, glossary flashcards, and weblinks.

Resources for Instructors:

Instructor's Manual: This manual provides exercises, sample syllabi, writing assignments, a list of transparency masters, and a test bank to help faculty, from first-time small group instructors to experienced ones, structure the course in ways that correspond with their teaching goals.

Videos: Two videos accompany the text. The first, *Communicating in Groups: Short Takes,* provides numerous brief video examples to help students visualize a number of concepts. The second, *Communicating Effectively in Small Groups,* provides four extended small group scenarios that are appropriate for class discussion or written analysis. Icons in the text guide students and instructors to the video clips.

Web Sites: The *Online Learning Center* and *Small Group Web Site* offer book-specific exercises, quizzes, supplemental content, and up-to-date links to sites with useful information for small group communication for both students and instructors.

Acknowledgments

We wish to thank the reviewers, all of whom did a conscientious job of reading the manuscript and providing helpful suggestions. We appreciate their thoughtful suggestions and have incorporated many of them in this fifth edition.

Hank Flick, Mississippi State University
Amy Bowie Fountain, Mississippi State University
Tim Steffensmeier, University of Nebraska, Omaha
Kathryn C. Jones, Northern Virginia Community College
Mary Helen Brown, Auburn University
Hal W. Fulmer, Georgia Southern University
Pamela McWherter, University of Alaska, Fairbanks
Ellen Arden-Ogle, Cosumnes River College
Bohn D. Lattin, University of Portland
Clay Warren, Washington University

Katherine Adams
Gloria J. Galanes

BRIEF CONTENTS

CONTENTS

PART FOUR
Small Group Public Presentations   287

CHAPTER 11
Planning, Organizing, and Presenting Small Group Oral Presentations   288

FEATURES

Orientation to Small Group Systems

Part One introduces you to the study of small groups. In Chapter 1 we explain why small groups are important to understand and define many of the terms you will need in your study of small groups. We discuss the types of small groups you are likely to experience, and we explain the participant-observer perspective used throughout the book. Chapter 2 presents you with a framework, general systems theory, to help organize the many concepts important to understanding how groups function.

Small Groups as the Heart of Society

After reading this chapter you should be able to:

1. Explain why groups play a vital role in the personal and professional lives of individuals.

2. Describe the two major stages any problem-solving group goes through.

3. List criteria for determining whether a group or an individual should be used to solve a problem.

4. Define a group, a small group, and group dynamics.

5. Differentiate between small group communication, public communication, interpersonal communication, and intrapersonal communication.

6. Explain and give examples of primary groups.

7. Explain and give examples of secondary groups.

8. Compare and contrast the different organizational groups.

9. Describe how an individual can be a valuable group member.

10. Explain the four ethical standards any member of a group should be held to.

11. Explain and give examples of a member being an effective participant-observer.

The El Cajon Book Club

When Estelle Womack, principal of Madison Elementary School in El Cajon, California, retired, she searched for a way to keep in regular contact with her friends and colleagues at the school district.[1] Her solution was to start the El Cajon Book Club. Members, most of them secretaries and teachers, meet once a month to discuss books, talk, and support each other in a kind of self-help group for educators. Members have come and gone—even Ms. Womack no longer attends—but others from the school district have stepped in to take their places. Because of their common interests in education and children, members often find that their book discussions trigger talk about their jobs within the district. For example, Jane Hamilton's book, *A Map of the World,* where a child charges a school nurse with abuse, prompted discussion about how easy it is to make allegations of abuse. Members learn from each other and say participation in the club has helped them do their jobs better. Principals learn to understand teachers' perspectives, media specialists understand some of the problems of principals, and so forth. Started for one purpose—as a way for a retiring principal to keep in touch with people who have similar professional interests—the club continues because it meets a variety of needs of many different individuals.

This story highlights a central premise of this book: Small groups are *essential* to us in every aspect of our lives! Whether we join a group to accomplish something we can't accomplish alone or whether we join a group for the sheer pleasure of getting together with people we like, groups are necessary to our survival and to our enjoyment of life.

The El Cajon Book Club is a voluntary group of members choosing to meet for both social and professional reasons. Many of the groups you belong to, particularly where you work, may not be voluntary. You may be assigned to a group because you have a particular expertise your employer believes is important to the group's task or because you represent a political constituency whose viewpoint must be included. No matter what the reason, you will have to be able to work well in teams, task forces, committees, and all kinds of special problem-solving groups if you want to succeed in the organized world of today. Teams of all kinds, especially multidisciplinary teams, are becoming more common in all areas of American life: business, industry, education, health care, the nonprofit sector, and government. For example, some of the biggest companies in the United States, including every Fortune 500 company, has some version of small groups and teams in place.[2] Companies use teams in a number of ways. For instance, Motorola has more than 5,000 teams operating. Eastman Kodak forms process teams to follow a product through the design, manufacture, and marketing processes. Ritz-Carlton Hotels employees can choose to participate in team-based work in addition to their regular jobs, and 5 percent of the Texas Instruments work force participates in self-directed work teams (described later in this chapter).

But there's a dark side to small group work. In one study of 179 teams, only 13 percent were rated highly effective.[3] A recent *Newsweek* article highlights some of the problems.[4] The article reports that one survey estimates managers spend one to one-and-a-half days in meetings each week—and half of that is wasted time. Some companies, including Nestlé USA and SC Johnson, ban meetings on Fridays. Another study observes that sit-down meetings take 34 percent longer than meetings where members have to stand. One management consultant estimates that the average meeting in a large company costs approximately $15,000. Clearly, meetings are expensive! If meeting time isn't used effectively, that expense can be staggering and wasteful.

Your authors take the position that effective small group work—whether in meetings, on teams, on committees, and so forth—cannot be left to chance. When individuals come together, particularly individuals from differing backgrounds, perspectives, and areas of expertise, teamwork doesn't just happen. Training in *how* to be an effective team member is essential. If you want to succeed as a team member, you must learn how small groups function and what you personally can do to help ensure team success. Chapter 1 helps you start this process by asking you to consider how important groups are in your own life and by introducing you to concepts central to understanding small group processes, the variety of groups you will encounter, and the importance of being a valuable and ethical participant-observer in groups.

Groups in Your Life

Lawrence Frey, a leading advocate for the study of small groups in their natural settings, believes that the small group is the most important social formation: "From birth to death, small groups are interwoven into the fabric of our lives."[5] Small groups usher us in when we are born and out when we die, and they are present at every phase in between. The first group you encounter is your family, and, in many ways, this group forms the foundation for other groups that follow. Think about your family of origin for a moment and consider how much of your identity—who you think you are—was formed by that initial group. Development and maintenance of identity remain important functions that only groups can provide for us. This is obvious when we consider groups such as fraternities or sororities, spiritually based groups (churches, synagogues, or other religious organizations), gangs, book clubs, poker clubs, and so forth. Groups formed at work also contribute to who we think we are. Are you a member of a union, for example? A management group? A neighborhood coalition trying to prevent a zoning change in your neighborhood? Each one of these groups, though not expressly formed as an identity-supporting group, will affect how you see yourself in relation to other people.

Professionally, the higher you go in any organization (government, service, manufacturing, education, communication, the military, or whatever), the more time you will spend working as a member of small groups. No matter what specific group you are in, you need to know how to behave in ways that are appropriate and helpful to the group and to any larger organization to which the group may be attached. If you don't work well in groups, you are more likely to be laid off or frozen at a low-level job. A recent survey of 750 leading American companies asked businesspeople to describe characteristics of the ideal MBA (Master of Business Administration) graduate.[6] The top preference was possession of good oral and written communication skills (listed by 83.5 percent of respondents). The fourth-ranked preference, the ability to work in teams, was listed by 71.4 percent. These communication skills far surpassed even cutting-edge knowledge of the company's field (14.8 percent) and previous work experience (31.9 percent) in importance. Clearly, knowing how to work in a small group can be of practical benefit to you.

Even as a student, you may be surprised to discover how many groups you belong to. For most students, the list goes up to 8, 10, 15, or even 20 or more small groups. Why do most of us belong to so many groups? We humans are social beings with powerful genetic needs to belong to small groups. We need to affiliate with others of our kind, just as do many other animals. A human infant is completely dependent on others for its care for a long time before it develops self-reliance. Plus, one lone adult cannot provide everything a baby needs. This function is provided by different kinds of small groups, sometimes families with father and mother, but also groupings of the "Full House" sort, kibbutzim, extended family groupings that include a grandmother or aunts, or other child care groups. The famous African proverb is right: "It takes a village to raise a child."

GROUPS AS PROBLEM SOLVERS

If you are alive, you are constantly solving problems: how to find a job, where to eat lunch, how to keep your car running on a limited budget, and even how to keep your company on the cutting edge of its industry in a turbulent economic climate. Life can properly be called an unending series of problem-solving episodes. Solving any problem means coming up with a plan (even if it takes only a split second) and executing it. Planning solutions to problems used to be both the privilege and the responsibility of high-status people: generals, kings and queens, dictators, managers, and directors. Carrying out the solutions was usually the work of lower-ranked people: infantrymen, secretaries, workers, and other subordinates. But things are changing. As you can see from the information provided earlier about the number of companies using teams and groups, more and more planning is done by groups—you won't be able to escape it! Even technological problems are not solved by lone rangers but by groups of technical specialists. If you want to participate in planning and not just carry out assignments planned by others, you will need to be able to work effectively in groups.

PARTICIPATING IN GROUPS

We emphasize how groups can become better problem solvers, but that cannot be accomplished by focusing only on the rational side of human behavior. To understand how groups really operate, you must know something about human feelings and behavior. We believe that effective group problem solving depends on how well members understand and manage such things as informational resources, how members feel about each other, how members feel about the task of the group, how skilled they are at expressing themselves and listening to others, and how well they collectively process the information they have to work with.

Group members must make sure they have the materials (information, tangible resources, time, and so forth) to complete the task, but they also must learn to manage their interpersonal relationships effectively enough to complete the task well. Keyton notes that relational communication in groups encompasses the "verbal and nonverbal messages that create the social fabric of a group by promoting relationships between and among members."[7] This function is equally as important as the task-oriented functions of group work.

General Motors recognized this when it organized its Saturn division in the late 1980s.[8] GM had been hammered by Japanese competitors and had seen its market share drop from 46 to 32 percent. In addition, GM's reputation had taken a beating after several fiascoes that revealed poorly designed and defective cars. The company knew that it had to do something drastic, with no room for error. In response, the Saturn division was established as a separate company for manufacturing the Saturn automobile to compete directly with Japanese imports. The car uses teamwork at all stages of the design and manufacturing process. In fact, the Saturn division itself is structured as a series of interdependent teams.

GM invests considerable time and money training the employees. New workers receive five days' training on how to work in teams and how to build consensus. This is followed by 100 to 175 hours of training in every aspect of the business, including conflict resolution and finance. In addition, the Saturn labor agreement calls for workers to continue their education by spending 12 or 13 days each year in class. The Saturn experiment helped GM become profitable during the 1990s. GM, knowing this experiment *had* to work, took no chances that the teams would malfunction. The company focused on both the task *and* relationship aspects of working in teams. When a major corporation recognizes that both work skills and people skills are essential, you can bet that other companies value those skills as well! We hope this book furthers your understanding and your skill in group participation.

When groups solve complex problems, they usually go through two major stages: planning and implementing. The planning stage involves considerable discussion and interaction. This is the stage at which all group members, with their differing viewpoints and opinions, must come to some overall conclusions if the group is to move successfully to the implementing stage, where the group's solutions are put into effect. To be valued by your group, you must become competent at the type of verbal interaction demanded in the group's planning stage. Later, you must demonstrate loyalty to the group by being willing to carry out what the group has planned. While all problem-solving groups engage in planning, only some of them are also responsible for implementation. For instance, Saturn work teams have both the authority to do what is necessary to carry out their work and the responsibility of implementing their decisions.

Participation in a group always requires trade-offs. You give up the total freedom to do what you want when you want for the advantages of affiliating with others to produce the kind of work possible only when several people coordinate their efforts. However, when individuals must coordinate their efforts, tensions always arise. This is true in all small groups, from a tug-of-war team to a task force of engineers designing a rocket. This is what *Communicating in Groups* is about: knowing what produces tensions in a group (both in the individuals and in the group as a whole), and knowing how to manage the tensions so that the group's decisions are the best that can be made, the members gain from the group, and the organization that gave birth to the group is improved by the group's work.

Groups versus Individuals as Problem Solvers

If group work is so tricky and has such potential for problems, why not have individuals plan the solutions to all problems? The benefits of having a group tackle a problem *can* (but not necessarily *will*) outweigh the costs in time and tensions.

Research into the effectiveness of solutions developed by small groups, compared to those planned by individuals acting alone, has shown that groups can be far superior for solving many types of problems.[9] Groups tend to do much better than individuals when several alternative solutions are possible, none of which is known to be superior or "correct." They also are better at conjunctive tasks, where no one person has all the information needed to solve a problem, but each member has some needed information.[10] These are the very sorts of problems most groups and organizations face. For example, which of several designs for a car is most likely to sell well? What benefit options should be available to employees? How can the federal government provide citizens a tax cut and still provide sufficient funds for social programs and the homeland defense?

The following story illustrates how a group's greater resources can help the problem-solving process. Gloria recently participated on a steering committee to help integrate a public television station into the university where she teaches. (This case introduces Chapter 6.) This large committee also included a lawyer, the general manager of the TV station, the general manager of the university's public radio station, the director of development, the vice president overseeing physical plant matters, the vice president for finance, along with several other administrators. This committee had six months to complete its work. The lawyer drew up the documents for the Federal Communications Commission (FCC) to approve the license transfer to the university. The vice president overseeing physical plant worked with others to determine how space needed to be modified to accommodate the station's master control units, other equipment, and personnel. The finance vice president kept track of the budget. The TV station manager served a liaison function with her employees and met with them to determine what new equipment was needed. The radio station manager helped the TV station manager and others rewrite the job descriptions so they would be compatible with the university's human resources designations. Many, many other tasks had to be completed in the time allotted for the transfer. No one person possessed the necessary expertise (to say nothing of time and energy) to accomplish this highly complex, conjunctive task. Also, an enormous amount of coordination had to occur for this task to be accomplished successfully and for that everybody's people skills were needed. To date, the major tasks have been completed, with smaller, more focused committees taking over the remaining tasks.

WHEN A GROUP IS A GOOD CHOICE

For several reasons, groups working on problems with several solutions typically make higher-quality decisions than do individuals (see Table 1.1). Groups usually have a much larger number of possible solutions from which to choose. Group members can help each other think critically by correcting one another's misinformation, faulty assumptions, and invalid reasoning. Several people can often think of issues to be handled in the process of solving a problem that might be overlooked by any one member. In addition, several people can conduct more thorough investigative research than one person working alone. Group members often counteract each other's tendencies to engage in self-defeating behavior.[11] A further advantage is that group members who are involved in planning a job or procedure usually understand that procedure and work hard to implement it. In addition, people are more likely to accept a solution that they have had a hand in designing. These principles have resulted in such small group techniques as quality control circles, self-managed work groups, and other forms of employee participation. But no plan for dealing with a problem or performing a task is better than the willingness to make it work on the part of those who must do the work or live with the results. Satisfaction, loyalty, and commitment tend to be higher when people have a voice.

WHEN A GROUP IS NOT A GOOD CHOICE

On the other hand, not all sorts of problems are suitable for groups, nor is group decision making always a wise or productive use of time. When a problem has a best or correct solution (such as in an arithmetic or accounting task), a skilled person working alone often exceeds the output quality of a group of less knowledgeable people, even if the group includes the highly skilled person as a member. Coordinating the work of several persons when conditions are changing rapidly (as in a weather disaster, battle, or

TABLE 1.1	Why Groups Can Make Better Decisions Than Individuals
	Groups have more information available about the problem and are less likely to omit something important.
	Groups can get more investigative research and other work done.
	Group members can correct each other's misinformation, faulty assumptions, and invalid reasoning.
	Groups can think of more suggestions, ideas, and alternatives from which to create or choose a solution.
	Group participation fosters loyalty to the solution and makes implementation easier and faster.

ball game) may be done best by one person (a commander, chief, or coach). Likewise, if small groups have certain social, procedural, or personality-mix problems, the output may be inferior, even though members may produce it with pleasure and confidence in the results. Much of this book addresses how to apply small group theory—based as much as possible on scientific research—to make sure that groups work on the kinds of problems for which they are best suited, and to do so in ways likely to produce a high-quality solution (see Table 1.2).

Your experiences in task-oriented groups may have been unpleasant ones. In fact, you may dread hearing a teacher tell you that you'll be working on a group project. Unfortunately, this kind of **grouphate** is common, probably because many groups do not function as well as they should. If this is how you feel about group participation, it is especially important for you to become familiar with group processes, ways to handle problems, and what sorts of procedures can help solve group problems.

Thus far we have seen that small groups are commonly involved in problem solving. We now introduce you to the types of small groups that engage in problem solving and the situations that create them. We will first define terms necessary to understand group communication. We encourage you to use our definitions when you think about, discuss, and complete assignments about small groups as you read this book. That will help you understand the terms more completely.

GLOSSARY

Grouphate

Hating or dreading participation in groups

TABLE 1.2	**Problems Appropriate for Groups versus Individuals**
Problems Suitable for a Group	**Problems Suitable for an Individual**
1. The problem is complex; one person is not likely to have all relevant information.	**1.** There is a best solution and a recognized expert is most qualified to determine that solution.
2. There are several acceptable solutions, and one best solution does not exist.	**2.** Conditions are changing rapidly (such as during a fire, natural disaster, or other crisis), and coordination is best done by one person.
3. Acceptance of the solution by those who are affected is critical.	**3.** Time is short and a decision must be made quickly.
4. Sufficient time exists for a group to meet, discuss, and analyze the problem.	**4.** Group members have personality, procedural, or social problems that make it difficult or impossible for them to work as a team on the solution.

"You take two of these at the first sign of the onset of boardroom turbulence."

Many organization members have come to dread participation in groups. (© The New Yorker Collection; 1985 Donald Reilly from cartoonbank.com. All Rights Reserved.)

1.1   Individual or Group?

What would you do if you were president of a university and your governing board approved the acquisition and license transfer to the university of the public television station in your town? As president, you have the power to make this happen by appointing a high-level person to coordinate the many tasks that need to be done, or you can appoint a committee to accomplish the same thing.

1. How would you weigh the factors (time, energy, expertise) in making your decision?

2. What are the advantages and disadvantages of having your appointee placed in charge of this effort compared with having an appointed committee placed in charge?

3. The members of the committee actually in charge of overseeing the project spent untold person hours making sure that no important detail was left undone. What benefits do you think they may have gained by working on this time-consuming project?

Groups, Small Groups, and Small Group Theory

To understand the term *small group communication,* you must first understand the terms *group* and *communication.*

GROUPS

Group has been defined or used by writers in a variety of ways. We use the term in a very specific way. Being a **group** means that people have interdependent relationships, and these relationships are the essence of being a group—no relationships among members, no group. In a group, members are bound together through a common purpose or function. Marvin Shaw, one of the most important writers about small group theory, defines a human group in terms of interaction producing mutual influence: "persons who are interacting with one another in such a manner that each person influences and is influenced by each other person."[12] We add to this that group members strive to achieve a common purpose.

The following example illustrates this. At a recent communication convention, one of us stood waiting for a streetcar with several other individuals, some of whom also wore convention badges. It was late at night and the streetcar was late. This collection of individuals had not yet become a group. However, when we began to talk to each other about how late the streetcar was, how concerned we all were about how we'd be able to get to our respective hotels, and whether there might be an alternative solution, we began to form into a group. Several of us decided to share a cab to our various hotels. Through our interaction, we formed interdependent relationships, developed a common purpose, and became a group—even though it was short-lived and relatively unimportant.

Groups can range in size from very small (three) to very large. In this book, we are concerned only with small groups. The principles that pertain to small groups do not necessarily hold true for large ones, and vice versa. Techniques appropriate for groups of from 3 to 7 members may be disastrous if tried in groups of 30, 70, or more. Likewise, communication techniques and procedures appropriate in large group meetings may be harmful to the effective functioning of small groups. For instance, parliamentary procedures developed for large group meetings (e.g., Robert's Rules of Order) are not meant to help small groups accomplish their tasks efficiently.

SMALL GROUPS

Small as used for human groups has usually been defined either by an arbitrary number or in terms of human perception. We prefer to define it in terms of psychological perception: We use the term **small group** to refer to a group in which individual members perceive each other and are aware of each other as individuals when they interact. This definition is precise only for a given point in time. A committee of five new members may be perceptually large until after each member has had a chance to speak repeatedly, but a seminar of 15 people may be perceptually small after several meetings. At that point, each member could name or describe every other, say who was and who was not at a meeting without taking formal attendance, and say something about what each contributed to the discussion and meeting. That is the idea of small group as we use it.

More practically, small groups usually consist of three to seven members, occasionally more. This seems to be the ideal range, with five as an ideal number if members possess sufficient knowledge and skills to do the job facing the group and have a diversity of perspectives and information relevant to the task. The more members, the more likely there will be inequity and communication overload for some members. We intentionally exclude the dyad (two-person group) from our definition of small group because dyads function differently. For example, dyads do not form networks or leadership hierarchies. Groups have continuity that dyads do not. If one member leaves a dyad, the dyad disbands, but members often leave small groups, sometimes to be replaced by new members, and the group itself continues. You are most likely to study dyadic communication in a book and/or course about interpersonal or family communication.

1.2   How Small Is Small?

APPLY NOW

The steering committee overseeing the transfer of the public TV station to the university discussed earlier consisted of 15 people, all administrators of some kind.

1. What evidence in the story suggests this group is actually a group and not a collection of individuals?

2. Would you classify this group as "small"? Why or why not?

3. What kinds of problems might a group of this size encounter? What kinds of advantages might it have over a smaller group?

4. Why is this story a good example of small group communication?

We are most concerned with continuing small groups, in which the members "meet more or less regularly in face-to-face interaction, . . . possess a common identity or exclusiveness of purpose, and . . . share a set of standards governing their activity."[13] Task forces, work crews, sport teams, committees, quality circles, and military squads are examples of such groups. One-meeting groups in which members have a sense of shared purpose, interact face-to-face, share at least some standards and procedures for governing their interaction, and have a sense of each other as group members also qualify as small groups by our definition.

In addition, although we have mentioned that face-to-face interaction is an important component of small groups, we relax this standard to include many computer-mediated groups whose members may never meet face-to-face. Often, such groups meet all other criteria. Members have a sense of belonging and identity, a shared purpose, and do their work through the exchange of signals—both verbal (mostly) and nonverbal (in the form of punctuation and "emoticons" that we discuss in Chapter 4). More important, members of computer-mediated groups often perceive themselves to be part a group. They find ways to work around computers' limitations in conveying *social presence,* or the extent to which computer-mediated communication is socially and emotionally similar to face-to-face communication.[14] Thus, we include many computer-mediated groups in our definition.

"This is where our trails divide, Luke. You have my E-mail address, right?"

GROUP DYNAMICS

Like all life forms, small groups function lawfully. That is, certain principles have been observed to hold for all small groups, just as other principles hold for all individual humans and other life forms. Group dynamics is the study of ways in which groups form and behave. Like others who study small groups, we use it to refer to that "field of inquiry dedicated to advancing knowledge about the nature of groups, the laws of their development, and their interrelations with individuals, other groups, and larger institutions."[15] Much of this book applies findings from the broad research field of group dynamics to the particular small groups in which you are certain to be involved.

COMMUNICATION

Communication refers to the perception, interpretation, and response of people to signals produced by other people. We develop this concept in detail in Chapter 3, but we introduce it here so you can start to observe how communication functions in a small group setting. The definition states that group members send verbal and nonverbal messages—words, gestures, facial expressions, and so forth—and that the other group members observe, interpret, and respond to these messages. This implies that members of a group pay attention to each other and coordinate their communication behavior to accomplish the group's assignment. It is the members' communication with each other—their perceiving, interpreting, and responding to one another's signals—that creates the interdependence necessary for individuals to be called a group.

GLOSSARY

Communication

The perception, interpretation, and response of people to signals produced by others

SMALL GROUP COMMUNICATION

Small group communication refers to the part of the field of group dynamics that focuses on the exchange of verbal and nonverbal information among group members. Small group communication requires interacting. As members create, perceive, interpret, and respond to messages, they are engaging in small group communication. This is different from public speaking to large groups (audiences), participating in a large assembly (i.e., a legislature or convention), communicating in a more-or-less-intimate dyad, or talking with one other person in assigned roles such as waiter and customer. While basic communication principles are common no matter what the setting, our emphasis in *Communicating in Groups* is communication that occurs within the group.

The communication that occurs in small groups is different from the communication that occurs in other contexts, such as public communication and interpersonal communication. Small group communication is more complex than interpersonal communication, which focuses on the communication between individuals as unique persons, as in a dyad. For instance, in a dyad, only one interpersonal relationship is possible, but in a five-person group 10 unique interpersonal relationships exist. In addition, a main reason people form groups is to get something done, to accomplish a task, which is not usually the main reason for forming interpersonal relationships. Small group communication is more informal and spontaneous than public communication such as giving a speech. In a public speaking situation, usually the speaker's role (speaking) is clearly differentiated from the audience's role (listening), but in a small group these roles are interchangeable. In addition, a public speaker usually has preplanned his or her remarks, whereas a small group member responds relatively spontaneously to the group interaction. Verbal feedback in a small group is immediate but is usually delayed in a public situation, although much nonverbal feedback is instantaneous in both contexts. There are, however, various kinds of public presentations in which group members may find themselves involved and some of these, such as symposiums, involve group member speeches. These will be discussed in Chapter 11. Finally, intrapersonal communication, the communication that occurs within an individual human being (such as thinking and self-talk) is always present in all communication contexts, including small groups.

Classifying Groups by Their Major Purpose

How a specific small group functions in part reflects general laws of group dynamics but also reflects the purpose for which the group exists. We have classified small groups according to the reasons they exist.

PRIMARY OR SECONDARY GROUPS

Many small group writers accept the theory, proposed by psychologist Will C. Schutz, that three major forces motivate human interaction. These are the needs for inclusion, affection, and control. The first two concern needs for belonging and caring from other people. The third, control, refers to the need for power or control over the world in which we exist, including the people we encounter.[16] A group is classified by sociologists as primary or secondary depending upon which of these needs is the major reason it exists (see Figure 1.1).

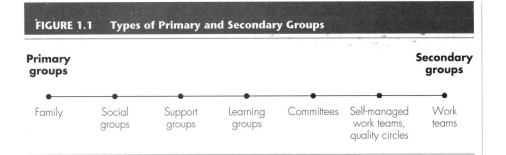

FIGURE 1.1   Types of Primary and Secondary Groups

Primary
groups

Secondary
groups

Family   Social   Support   Learning   Committees   Self-managed   Work
          groups   groups   groups   work teams,   teams
                                                                quality circles

1.3   Meeting Member Needs and Handling Membership Changes

The membership of the El Cajon Book Club changed regularly, as members left and new members were added. The founder of the club left after nearly nine years of participation. Membership changes present unique challenges to a group.

1. Did it surprise you that the El Cajon Book Club's founder is no longer a member? For what reasons do you think a long-standing member might want to leave a group?
2. Why might a new member choose to join?
3. What challenges does member fluctuation present for group members, existing and new?
4. What can current members do to make new members feel welcomed and part of the existing group?

Primary Groups.   **Primary groups** form to meet the first two types of needs, inclusion and affection. They may accomplish work, but that is not their primary objective. Loving, caring, avoiding feelings of loneliness, sharing, feeling cared about—these are the motives for which we willingly give up some freedom as individuals to be members of primary groups. We are all familiar with families, friendship groups (the television show "Friends"), sororities and fraternities, drinking buddies, cliques, gangs, and those many small groups that seem to form spontaneously to meet interpersonal needs for inclusion and affection. As we mentioned earlier, your family is probably your first group and mirrors, in many ways, the many groups you belong to now. The communication patterns you learned in your first group likely affect the way you communicate in groups now.[17] In addition, many of the needs that were met by your first group are now met by other groups you belong to.

Secondary Groups.   **Secondary groups** exist mainly to meet control needs: solving all sorts of problems. They are task groups. A secondary group may create or implement a plan (solution) to provide control. Control, in this sense, may include supplying physical needs for food and water, preventing or controlling disease, coping with insects and other

GLOSSARY

Primary Groups

Groups formed to meet primary needs for inclusion and affection

Secondary Groups

Groups formed to meet secondary needs for control and problem-solving

vermin, or even more mundane matters such as fixing a flat tire or designing a computer program to organize recipes. This book is mostly about secondary groups. Task forces, committees, work crews, quality circles, and learning groups are all secondary.

However, no group is purely primary or secondary in its functioning. Primary groups encounter and solve problems. Secondary groups supply members with a sense of inclusion and often with affection. In fact, sometimes the most productive and satisfying secondary groups have strong primary components, where members feel included, appreciated, and even cared for. Think of the best group you can ever remember. Chances are that not only was this group productive, but you formed close bonds of friendship with the other members. Most likely, a number of your psychological needs—for inclusion, affection, and control—were met. Our motives for joining groups are often mixed; we may want to participate in solving a problem, but experiencing pleasure in the interaction with others is also a main reason for our involvement.[18]

TYPES OF SECONDARY GROUPS

Secondary groups tackle a range of tasks. They may be formed for one specific job or a variety of related tasks. Included are support groups, learning groups, organizational groups (such as committees, work teams, self-managed work teams, and quality control circles), and activity groups.

Support Groups.   **Support groups** exist to help members understand and address personal issues or problems. Support groups may be called therapy or personal growth groups. Regardless of what they are called, their purpose is not to solve a problem *as a group* but to help individual members address or solve personal issues or cope with personal problems. Groups based on the well-known 12–step process developed by Alcoholics Anonymous are examples of support groups, as are groups such as breast cancer support groups, anger management groups for abusive husbands, and so forth. The premise of these groups is that individuals can understand and better cope with their own problems if they interact with others whose problems are similar.

One of our friends, who completed her treatment for ovarian cancer several months ago, has recently started a support group—only the second such group in Missouri—for women diagnosed with the same disease. The treatment prognosis for such women is usually not optimistic, so Joy believed it was especially important for such women to support each other. She felt the need to talk with others who had been through the same experience, particularly those women whose treatments had been successful. But more importantly, she was eager to share her experiences and her message of hope to women newly diagnosed. The group meets once a week, with members offering practical advice and suggestions. But beyond the practical advice, the women receive needed affirmation and belonging. Clearly, both secondary and primary functions are performed by this group. During the aftermath of the World Trade Center attacks on September 11, 2001, police officers, fire fighters, and rescue workers assembled in New York City. Although these people came to help rescue efforts and clean up the devastation, they also provided emotional support to each other and to shocked New Yorkers. Primary and secondary functions were equally important.

The easy availability of computers has made it possible for people to form support groups of members who never meet face-to-face, yet who experience strong support and comfort from their computer contacts. In a recent study comparing online and

GLOSSARY

Support Groups

Groups formed for members to help each other understand, address, and cope with personal issues or problems

1.1 Online Support Groups

MEDIA AND TECHNOLOGY

The Internet is a collection of interconnected computers that allows information to be communicated electronically around the world. Common uses of the Internet include the sharing of information using Web pages, communication among large groups of individuals using bulletin board systems, and personal communication using electronic mail.

Although the Internet was initially formed for task purposes—to facilitate strategic military communication—it has now become a useful tool for creating and sustaining primary groups. Communication researcher Kevin Wright has studied the effectiveness of the Internet as a method of obtaining social support from others—a characteristic of primary groups like families and friends. Wright explains that Internet-based support groups allow 24-hour access, anonymity for participants, and opportunities for connecting with other individuals encountering problems similar to our own. What is your opinion about using online groups for personal support? What advantages or potential disadvantages do you think are most important?

You can search for online support groups by using any of the popular search engines such as Yahoo! or Excite. There are also websites that contain message boards for a variety of self-help topics. One such website is the Mental Health Net site, which may be accessed through the following address:

http://community.mentalhelp.net/forum/newforums.html

SOURCE: K. Wright, "Computer-Mediated Support Groups: An Examination of Relationships among Social Support, Perceived Stress, and Coping Strategies," *Communication Quarterly* 47 (1999), pp. 402–14.

Go to **www.mhhe. com/adams galanes** for additional weblink activities.

For more information on finding groups on the net, go to the on-line learning center.

face-to-face support groups, Wright found that people benefited from both types.[19] Online groups have the advantages of providing 24-hour access, greater participant diversity of experience and information, and freedom to discuss risky topics. The online support networks also tended to be larger, thereby providing members with more resources. Interestingly, the online support groups did not evolve into face-to-face groups. Both online and face-to-face groups met the support needs of their members.

Learning Groups. **Learning groups** of many sorts exist to help members understand or control events in their lives and the world around them. Your class is a learning group (probably a large one) that may be further organized into several small learning groups. Learning groups of people from preschool to retirement age discuss all sorts of interests. Study groups are all types of learning groups. So are cohort groups; many universities group students into cohorts, who enter a particular program together and stay together throughout their course of study. Cohorts are encouraged to study together and to help each other learn. In a recent study of adult undergraduate learning cohorts, researchers found a significant relationship between the level of group development and

GLOSSARY

Learning Groups

Secondary groups of members meeting to understand and learn about a particular topic

the individual achievement, measured by grade point average, of the members.[20] Not all groups achieved equally, which further emphasizes the importance of understanding group communication and development.

Although this book does not specifically focus on support or learning groups, learning is a first step in many problem-solving groups, and personal affirmation and support are crucial by-products of effective group interaction in all kinds of groups.

Organizational Groups.   Organizations such as corporations, schools, agencies, legislatures, bureaus, large departments, hospitals, and even social clubs create problem-solving groups to serve them. **Organizational groups** include any such problem-solving group formed within the context of a larger organization.

Committees.   Most **committees** are created by larger organizations to perform a service for the organization. The organization commits a problem or duty to the small group (committee) created for that purpose. For example, a fact-finding committee may be asked to investigate the scope and effect of cheating on intercollegiate athletic rules, then report its conclusions. Occasionally a special committee is empowered both to select a plan and to execute it, though in most cases problem-solving committees do not go beyond recommending. Instead, they are usually advisory, reporting to an executive or a board that has final authority and responsibility for deciding. A different committee is created to carry out the chosen plan or an individual may be assigned to execute the solution. Committees in organizations may be standing or ad hoc. Another special kind of committee is the conference committee.

A standing committee is a permanent committee. Often, an organization's bylaws include a procedure for creating it and a description of its purpose and area of freedom to act. For example, a membership committee may be responsible for recruiting new members and for screening the applicants' qualifications.

"Standing" implies that a committee continues indefinitely. However, its membership is usually changed by election or appointment on a periodic basis. Usually, some members continue from one year into the next, while others are replaced. A typical term of office for a standing committee member is three years.

Ad hoc committees are created to perform one special assignment, then go out of existence. The end product might be a report of findings or recommended solutions—for example, evaluations of several sites for a new plant or suggestions about how to cut costs. This report is often delivered in writing and orally to the person(s) who created the special committee. A couple of years ago one of us headed a faculty ad hoc committee formed to prevent the loss of a department's graduate program. This committee put together a plan to build the graduate program, which included a newly designed graduate curriculum, a plan for recruitment, and the policy for a newly formed department graduate committee. This plan was presented orally and in writing to the dean of graduate studies. Its work thus completed, the committee disbanded. Later, the written plan was used by the dean as a model for other departments that may have to justify the existence of their graduate programs.

Such groups are often called task forces, with members selected because their knowledge and skills are thought necessary to do the group's work. Presidents have created many task forces to investigate and make recommendations on such national concerns as illegal drug traffic, acid rain, the condition of national parks, health care, waste in government expenditures, and disease epidemics. You are likely to serve on many task forces during a lifetime of work. Knowing how to get a task force organized and working smoothly as a unit is vital to corporate life. *Communicating in Groups* discusses this in detail.

Conference committees are composed of members who represent other groups that must find common ground to accomplish their work. For example, as we write this, the U.S. Senate has passed the Patient's Bill of Rights. However, that bill will not become law as it stands. The House of Representatives will craft its own version of a Patient's Bill of Rights that is likely to differ in key respects from the Senate's bill. A conference committee composed of both representatives and senators will then be formed to reconcile differences in the two bills. The compromise bill will then be sent back to the Senate and the House for discussion and possible approval. When members of a conference committee agree on a plan, they normally must recommend it to their respective parent organizations, which must then decide whether or not to accept the conference committee's recommended plan. We will use the term *conference* to refer only to such groups of representatives, never as a synonym for committee or task force.

Quality Control Circles. American, foreign, and multinational companies, including Xerox, Procter & Gamble, Westinghouse, Ford, General Motors, Dow Chemical, Paul Revere Insurance Group, and countless others, use **quality control circles.** Quality control circle or quality circle is a generic name for small groups of company employees who volunteer to tackle any issue that may affect job performance. Such groups may have different names in different organizations, but in all cases they are concerned with the quality and quantity of their work output and attempt to improve their competitiveness with other organizations. They can be found in all types of organizations, ranging from manufacturing and service organizations to state governments, to school systems, to voluntary organizations, and sometimes to individual families. They help involve employees in the decision-making loops of the organization.

Each circle consists of a small number of people from a department or division who meet regularly during work hours to solve production problems that either they or managers identify. The leader may be elected or appointed. Suggestions are then forwarded to the managers, who decide what action to take.

If instituted properly, quality circles can improve company effectiveness by increasing worker productivity, identifying quality control problems and possible solutions, and enhancing worker involvement. For instance, quality circles helped one international hotel chain cut losses on unused fruit baskets by over $5,500 per quarter.[21] However, for quality circles to produce these kinds of benefits, careful planning is required. The organization must prepare before introducing quality circles and train employees in how to participate.

In addition, a number of consistent problems have occurred with quality circles. Sometimes unions see them as a ploy to increase production without improving wages or benefits. Managers can be threatened if they perceive that suggestions from quality circles sabotage their managerial prerogatives. Quality circle programs stagnate if the company fails to act promptly on suggestions provided by the quality circle or explain why a suggestion is not being implemented. Quality circles often work best in conjunction with an overall organizational development program that supports the concept of employee participation.

GLOSSARY

Quality Control Circles

Organizational groups that address issues of job performance and work improvement

GLOSSARY

Self-Managed Work Teams

Also called autonomous work groups, groups of peers who manage their own work schedules and procedures

Self-Managed Work Teams.   Sometimes called autonomous work groups or modules, **self-managed work teams** are groups of peers who manage their own work schedules and procedures within certain prescribed limits. Members are highly trained and cross-trained—each is able to perform several tasks for the team. The process is similar to having a team of people building a house: "When you need more carpenters, the painters can put down their brushes and pick up hammers for a couple of hours. Or the carpenter goes and helps the plumber when he's behind."[22] Not only is this efficient, but it also helps workers develop a variety of skills and reduces boredom and frustration. Self-managed work teams have been used with great success at such companies as Procter & Gamble, Sherwin-Williams, GM, and TRW.

A self-managed work team elects its own leader, who is a co-worker, not a supervisor or manager. The leader acts as a coordinator, not a boss. The organization establishes the work group's area of freedom, but often these groups have a great deal of latitude in how they operate. Some work groups establish their own schedules and annual budgets, prepare their own reports, develop specifications for jobs and procedures, solve technical problems that occur while completing jobs, and even prepare bids in attempting to attract new company business. For example, at one office furniture manufacturer, the custom-orders team has complete authority to bid jobs under $10,000, custom-design the furniture for the client, and schedule its manufacture. For complex jobs, the whole team goes to the client's office to listen and offer suggestions. The team's success has made the custom-order portion of the business extremely profitable.[23]

Several of the same concerns exist with autonomous work groups as with quality circles. However, companies that have instituted such programs report that self-managing work teams give a 20 to 40 percent edge in productivity over more traditional work systems.[24] They require less supervision and surveillance, produce higher-quality products, have less lost time, and generally produce high morale and job satisfaction.

1.4   What's In a Name?

APPLY NOW

The SC Johnson Company, mentioned earlier in the *Newsweek* article, has a meeting-intensive culture that has spawned its own vocabulary to describe various kinds of meetings. *Generals* are weekly one-on-one meetings that bosses hold with their subordinates. *Nice to knows* are optional informational meetings that employees often skip, and *huddles* are meetings designed to provide quick updates.

1. What kinds of group meetings do you attend?
2. What nicknames would you give to them?

Being a Valuable Group Member

Most of us, when we join a group, want to be a valued member of that group. We want to be liked and respected by our fellow group members, and we want them to think of us as an asset to the group. Certain attitudes and behaviors are especially helpful to a group's process and will contribute to your value as a member. We discuss them here as an incentive for you to evaluate yourself as a potential group member. We especially want you to assess your values and attitudes toward the other members and the group itself.

Egalitarianism is vital if people are to work as equal team members instead of in superior-inferior relationships (such as boss/subordinate). **Egalitarianism** refers to the belief that, as group members, all people should have the same rights. Egalitarian attitudes encourage all members to contribute fully to a group's work and value good ideas, no matter who contributes them. In contrast, authoritarian committee members tend to be bossy when they are in charge but will uncritically follow the leader, even when the leader asks for unethical behavior. They believe that leaders have the right to give orders as they see fit, whereas egalitarian members expect leaders to coordinate members' behavior by exercising just those controls that group members themselves authorize.

A strong sense of personal responsibility for the success of a group is typical of members who make major contributions to group achievement. In an ideal group, every member exerts the effort and time required to accomplish group goals such as winning a hard-fought basketball game in the closing minutes, completing an important written report, producing an outstanding show, or creating a car that will stand up to foreign competition. Such results depend on every person's acting as if success depends totally on him or her, and it does. In small groups, everyone is needed—there is no room for freeloaders. Any member not making such contributions is likely to be deeply resented, regardless of his or her excuses.

Responsible members are highly involved in the activity of the group. They communicate willingly, expressing what they think and hope. And they support group outcomes by doing follow-up work and speaking highly of the group to nonmembers. For example, one of the authors participated in a musical production by a cohesive group of highly responsible members. The members built all the scenery, made their own costumes, sold tickets, and afterwards even struck the set and cleaned the theater. After the production, they met to socialize and plan a subsequent production, speaking often of how "terrific it was to work with such a great, supportive bunch of people."

In most small group communication classes, we have found that one or two project groups are plagued with irresponsible members who want credit for the work but are unwilling to do an equal share. They fail to show up for meetings, they miss deadlines for reports, they disappear with essential data, or they are absent for rehearsals of final presentations. Irresponsible members seem to be the greatest single source of bad feelings among group members and of poor-quality projects. In the business world, such deadwood is weeded out of self-managing work teams and task forces, or the organization is bankrupted.

Those who are appointed, elected, or emerge as leaders of a group, such as a class project group or a committee in student government, should work to supply any needed functions (services) that other members are not providing or at least to see that someone does supply these services. Leaders as completers[25] are responsible for constantly monitoring the group's progress to identify what the group needs at any point in time, deciding whether those functions are currently being performed adequately by other members and, if not, providing needed services or encouraging someone else to provide them. For

GLOSSARY

Egalitarianism

The belief that all group members are created equal

example, if the leader sees that one member has not offered an opinion about an important issue considered by the group, the leader could be the gatekeeper by asking that member's opinion. If the group seems confused, the leader should summarize, clarify, and reorient the group or ask that someone else do so. If tensions are mounting, the leader should try to relieve them before they cause harm, perhaps by cracking a joke or suggesting a 10-minute break.

The notion that leaders are completers requires that they be able to determine what functions are needed as well as be able to supply them. Leaders must constantly be aware of what is happening in the group. The completer concept assumes that people can learn a variety of leader behaviors and that all of us should learn to function as leaders in certain circumstances. Throughout *Communicating in Groups* we will discuss the importance of effective leadership to the functioning of a small group. We will explore the application of particular leadership principles in Chapter 10.

Being an Ethical Group Member

Throughout this chapter, we have emphasized how important it is for you to understand something about small groups so you can be a valuable and valued participant in them. You want to be the kind of member others can count on. You need to know what kind of behavior other members will expect from their colleagues. **Ethics** refers to the "rules or standards for right conduct or practice."[26] In a small group, ethical standards for members concern their willingness to communicate, treatment of fellow members, treatment of information, and commitment to the group.

First, ethical members must be willing to communicate and share their ideas, information, and perspectives within the group. As we said earlier, groups succeed because several heads are better than one. However, this advantage will not be realized if group members are unwilling to speak up in the group. Being silent when you have relevant information, a question, an idea, or even a disagreement deprives the group of your perspective and undermines the potential advantage of group discussion.

Second, group members should treat their fellow members with respect and consideration. As with the first principle, failure to treat others with consideration undermines the potential effectiveness of the group. If other members won't speak or share because they fear an attack from you, you have derailed the group discussion process. More important, treating others with respect is a cultural value embedded deep in our democratic traditions and is the right thing to do. Group members should never do anything that is designed to disconfirm, belittle, or ridicule other members. Even when they disagree with others, they should disagree without being disagreeable or without personalizing the disagreement.

Third, ethical group members should use their best critical thinking skills when they evaluate information, ideas, and proposals in a group, and they should evaluate information in a thorough and unbiased way. Earlier, we noted that group members can correct each other's misinformation and faulty reasoning. In fact, it is unethical for them not to do so because decisions are only as good as the information and reasoning on which they are based. What if jury members, in a hurry to leave the jury room, decided to forgo

GLOSSARY

Ethics

Standards and rules for appropriate member and leader behavior

TABLE 1.3	**Ethical Principles for Group Members**

Be willing to communicate; share your ideas, suggestions, information, and unique perspective.

Treat fellow group members with respect.

Do nothing designed to prevent others from sharing with the group.

Never disconfirm, belittle, or ridicule others.

Use your best critical thinking skills to evaluate information and ideas.

Make sure you have as complete information as possible.

Never lie or falsify information or data.

Credit the sources of your information.

Evaluate all the information you have in an unbiased way.

Demonstrate a commitment to the group.

Complete assignments for the group.

Support group decisions.

Consider leaving the group if the group's actions violate your values and standards.

evaluating the evidence just to speed things up? This ethical principle implies that group members must make a conscientious effort to find and present to the group all relevant information and points of view, must not falsify data or information, and must evaluate all the information in an objective and unbiased way. This is the heart of effective group problem solving.

Finally, ethical group members must demonstrate a commitment to the group. This means that, for as long as they are members of the group, they should place the good of the group ahead of their own individual goals within the group. Some people are unable, or unwilling, to do this and they make terrible team members. This ethical principle implies that group members will complete assignments for the group in a timely fashion and will support the group's decisions, particularly to those outside the group. Sometimes a group makes a decision you cannot support, perhaps one that violates your own personal ethical or moral standards. In that case, it may be better for you to leave the group than to compromise your integrity. If you choose to belong to a group, make sure you can support the group's actions and decisions, even if they aren't necessarily the decisions you would have made on your own (see Table 1.3).

1.1   Would You Falsify Data?

ETHICAL DILEMMA

Your five-member class project group has been given the assignment of serving as consultants to another group. You are charged with observing this group, gathering data about it, evaluating the group's communication, and making recommendations to improve the group's functioning. The problem is that each of your project group members is very busy and you're having a hard time agreeing on a time to observe the other group. Two of you are graduating at the end of the semester and one of you, planning to spend the summer working in Europe, is scrambling trying to get all assignments finished in time to leave. Two members suggest making up data for your final project. The chances of getting caught are slim, and this "solution" would save you all several hours of observation and work. You personally strongly object to this form of cheating. For one thing, you don't want to chance having a plagiarism charge against you. But mainly you object to this form of lying and you don't want to damage your relationship with your professor. What do you do?

1. Do you speak or remain silent?

2. If you speak, what would you say?

3. What would you do if the entire group—except you—was in favor of falsifying data?

4. Would you talk to the teacher? Why or why not?

The Participant-Observer Perspective

Earlier, we asked you to consider all the groups to which you belong. Even as you learn about the principles of communicating in groups from reading this book, you will continue to be a member of these groups. We hope you will want to use the principles and techniques you learn to improve the functioning of your groups. This means that you will be in the role of a **participant-observer,** someone who is a regular member of the group and, at the same time, actively observes the group and adapts to its processes and procedures. This is especially important for the group leader or leaders. Because most group members have not been trained to be effective group participants, it is especially important for us who know something about small group communication to monitor the group's discussions and help our groups perform as well as possible. A skilled participant-observer can help a group by supplying information, procedural suggestions, and interpersonal communication skills needed by the group. This is an important focus of this book—to help you become a more valuable group member as you sharpen your skills in observing small group processes.

We encourage you to become a participant-observer for the groups you are in. As you read the information in this book, try to think of examples from your own group experiences that illustrate the principles described in the text. Start paying attention in a con-

---

GLOSSARY

Participant-Observer (Perspective)

A group member who participates but also observes the group and adapts as necessary

scious way to the processes of small group communication. In addition, use the case study before each chapter and application boxes to improve your awareness of group dynamics. As you learn more about communicating effectively in groups, you will feel more comfortable making suggestions to serve the groups to which you belong. We provide additional information about the participant-observer and other types of observers in the Appendix.

SUMMARY

- People in modern society need to be able to function effectively in small groups if they want to succeed and if they want to be full participants in contemporary organizational life.

- Small group members participating in decisions create and consider more issues, correct each other's misinformation, accept solutions more, and are more loyal to the organization than members who don't participate in decisions.

- Perceptual awareness makes a group "small"; the group must be small enough for each member to participate and for each member to be conscious of and aware of each other member.

- Ideal small group members are egalitarian and feel a strong sense of responsibility to the group.

- Ethical members are willing to communicate, treat others with respect, evaluate information thoroughly, and demonstrate commitment to the group.

- Participant-observers, members who know something about the small group process, can help a group succeed.

EXERCISES

1. List all the groups to which you belong. Be sure to include family groups, friendship and other social groups, activity groups, committees, work teams, athletic teams, classroom groups, study groups, political action groups, interest groups, and every other type of small group to which you belong. Categorize them into primary or secondary groups (recognizing that no group is solely one or the other). Discuss your list with the class or in small groups.

2. Ask several individuals to define *group*. Bring your definitions to class and together or in small groups share those definitions. Report aspects of the definitions that are similar and that are not similar. Compare and contrast them to the one presented in your text. Decide, as a class, your working definition of *group*.

3. Break up into small groups. Devise your own list of ethical standards for group members. You can do this for a general class discussion or you can develop a class list of standards that will be used for all future group work in the class. If the class is structured around a major group project, then individual groups can create their lists relevant to the standards of the group members.

 Go to **www.mhhe.com/adamsgalanes** and **www.mhhe.com/groups** for Self-Quizzes and weblinks.

KEY TERMS and CONCEPTS

Committee

Communication

Egalitarianism

Ethics

Group

Grouphate

Learning Groups

Organizational Groups

Participant-Observer
 (Perspective)

Primary Groups

Quality Control Circles

Secondary Groups

Self-Managed Work Teams

Small Group

Small Group
 Communication

Support Groups

www.mhhe.com/adamsgalanes
Use the flashcards and crossword puzzles on the Online Learning Center to further your knowledge of these key terms.

Groups as Structured Open Systems

After reading this chapter you should be able to:

1. Explain why systems theory is a useful perspective for studying small group communication.

2. Define and give examples of a system.

3. Define inputs, throughput process, and outputs of a group system.

4. Explain why interaction is at the heart of a group's throughput process.

5. Describe the role of the group's environment.

6. Compare and contrast open and closed systems.

7. Describe what interdependence means to the functioning of a small group system.

8. Explain the valuable role of feedback in helping a system adapt to changing circumstances.

9. Explain why all groups, along with other living systems, experience multiple causes and multiple paths.

10. Explain why nonsummativity is a characteristic of groups.

11. Describe the stages in the life cycle of a small group system.

12. Explain how modern organizations are composed of networks of groups.

The Jamaican Winter Olympic Bobsled Team

A Jamaican Olympic bobsled team is about as unlikely as a Popsicle stand in the middle of the Mohave Desert—but that is the true story told in the film *Cool Runnings!* With only three months to find equipment, secure financial backing, and qualify for the Winter Olympics in Calgary, Alberta, Canada, four of the most incompatible, untrained Jamaicans come together to compete for an Olympic gold medal. Sanka is the best pushcart driver in all Jamaica; his friend Derice is Jamaica's beloved track sprinter; Yul is a moody, angry sprinter; and Junior is a wealthy sprinter who tripped both Derice and Yul in the Olympic track qualifiers. Junior's mistake cost Derice his chance to follow his dad's legacy and compete for Olympic gold. Not to be denied, Derice searches for another way to try for a medal. He hears about Irving Blitzer, a former Olympian and friend of his dad. Irv, an Olympic medalist in the bobsled, had tried to talk Derice's father into switching sports because he believed track sprinters would make outstanding bobsledders, but Derice's dad would have nothing to do with the idea. Irv was stripped of both his medals and left the sport in disgrace after cheating. Derice finds Irv in Jamaica and pleads with him to coach the first Jamaican bobsled team. Sanka signs on as a favor for his friend, Yul joins to get off the island, and Junior joins to get away from his domineering father.

This unlikely collection of three track sprinters, one pushcart driver, and a disgraced coach begins with no money, no sled, no ice and snow to practice on, no fan support, skeptical and cruel responses from fellow bobsledders, and animosity between them. Any betting person would predict from these initial factors that they would fail. Not even the Jamaican Olympic committee would give them the money to go to Canada for the bobsled trials. Facing one obstacle after another, these athletes slowly emerge as a cohesive team and find themselves in the Olympics. During the last run for gold, this unlikely Jamaican bobsled team crashes before the finish line because of a loose runner on the sled. Injured but not deterred, they pick up their sled, named "Cool Runnings," and walk over the finish line to the cheers of the other bobsledders and all of Jamaica. What does "Cool Runnings" mean? It translates into "peace be the journey."[1]

The story of *Cool Runnings* illustrates several important aspects of systems theory, the focus of Chapter 2. We will return to the story throughout the chapter to provide examples of what we mean by these various aspects of systems theory and how they apply to the Jamaican bobsled team. First, let's consider an overview of general systems theory and how it furnishes a useful and popular framework for examining small group communication.

Overview of General Systems Theory

General systems theory was developed by a biologist, Ludwig von Bertalanffy, as a way to examine and explain complex living organisms. Because living organisms, including groups, are constantly changing, they are difficult to study. When a biologist describes an organism, the description is out of date as soon as it is written. Only processes and relationships display any constancy. Think for a moment about your own body, one of the most complex of all organisms. Although it appears to operate as a single unit, in reality it is composed of many smaller units that work interdependently to sustain your life. For example, when you walk across the room, your muscular, skeletal, nervous, circulatory, and respiratory systems all cooperate in moving you to your destination. Even if you are sitting still, your body is involved in constant activity—your eyelids are blinking, your heart is beating, you are breathing automatically, and so forth. Your individual cells constantly change as they take in nourishment through the blood, restore themselves, and excrete waste through the cell walls. This complicated, continuous process is hard to study. Fortunately, systems theory provides us with a way of examining and describing how a system's parts are related to each other, even while they are continuously changing. Systems theory reminds us that when we want to understand any living entity we not only study its component parts, but we must also examine the ways in which the parts operate together if we want to understand the organism as a whole.

Systems theory has helped social scientists, family therapists, business professionals, and others by giving them a useful framework for looking at complex human groupings, including small groups. Many individual elements affect the dynamics of a group—the reason the group was formed, the personalities of the group members, the information members have, the type of leadership, how the group handles conflict, and how successful the group has been in accomplishing its assigned task, to name only a few. But no single element functions alone; the elements interact continuously. Systems theory concepts keep us from oversimplifying our description of group interaction. All parts interact to produce the entity called a "small group" we defined in Chapter 1.

The Small Group as a System

Several concepts and definitions are important to understanding a small group as a system. We will use the Jamaican bobsled case study we presented at the beginning of the chapter to illustrate these terms and concepts.

DEFINITION OF A SYSTEM

A **system** consists of elements that function interdependently. The system, in our case a small group, also functions interdependently with the environment in which it operates as part of a larger system. Not only is a group made up of several elements that influence one another, but the group also both affects and is affected by its surroundings.

Think back to that unlikely Jamaican bobsled team (see also Figure 2.1). Several elements and their unique interaction affected the team. Consider first the members themselves, with their various abilities. A winning bobsled team needs a driver and three strong runners to push the sled—and this team has them. Sanka is loyal to Derice and is, after all, the best pushcart driver in all of Jamaica. Yul is strong and fast. Junior is also quick and sharp. Derice was born to compete in the Olympics—he is fast and driven.

A second element is the team's game plan. For example, how should the coach match these abilities with the various positions? Should the pushcart driver be the driver of the sled? The team's first conflict involves this very issue. Sanka thinks he should be the

GLOSSARY

System

A set of elements that functions as a whole because of interdependent relationships

---

FIGURE 2.1   Bobsled Teams as a Small Group System

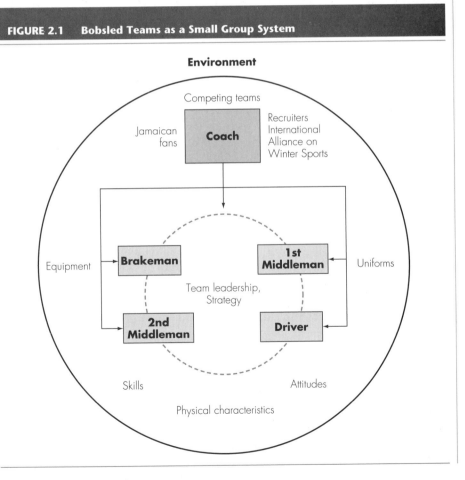

TABLE 2.1	**Examples of Small Group Inputs**

Members	Resources	Environmental factors
Personalities and characteristics (e.g., age, gender)	Information about the task	Physical surroundings
	Knowledge and expertise	Degree of support from parent group or organization
Needs	Time available for group work	
Attitudes	Tangible resources (e.g., money, materials)	
Values		
Abilities and skills	Group computer software systems	

driver, yet the coach points out that the driver has to be focused at all times and is responsible not only for the course but also for the lives of the others. So Derice is selected as the driver and Sanka becomes the brakeman. The other two are the middlemen.

The third element is the leadership within the team. Derice, for instance, has to figure out how to manage the hard feelings between Yul and Junior. In addition, Yul desires to be no one's teammate but instead wants to use the "team" to get off the island.

The fourth element is Irv's ability to assess the team's competency, earn members' trust, and motivate them to find their own style of sledding. Notice also the interaction of the team with its surroundings. The attitudes of the Jamaicans, their families, other Olympic bobsledders and coaches, as well as the media, first thwarted then later inspired the team. In return, the team's success influenced the entire country of Jamaica and the rest of the winter Olympic community.

CONCEPTS VITAL TO UNDERSTANDING SYSTEMS

To understand systems theory, you need to understand certain concepts true of all systems. Four basic concepts are essential. Our explanations of these are based on scholarly work by Daniel Katz and Robert Kahn.[2]

Inputs.   Elements involved in a group's dynamics can be classified into three broad categories: inputs, throughputs, and outputs. **Inputs,** the first of these categories, consists of all the factors—people, information, energies, and other resources such as computer programs designed to facilitate group problem solving—that are brought into the group from the outside (see Table 2.1). Inputs are the "raw materials" from which the group is initially formed and are used by members to perform their work. For example, the abilities of the bobsled players—whether they are smart or not, whether they are relatively fast or slow, how well they can "read" the subtle nature of the course—are all input characteristics that the players bring with them to the group and that influence how well the team performs during a run. Other inputs include the instructions on how to synchronize the movements of all four bobsledders and their sled, the continuous

2.1   The Internet as a Source of Input

MEDIA AND TECHNOLOGY

Input can be any "raw material" used by a group to perform work. Although input can include instructions given to the group, group members' attitudes toward the group's task, and resources available to the group, an important form of input for any group is information.

One hallmark of the Internet and World Wide Web (WWW) is the vast amount of information available. Web databases, accessed by search engines, are used to locate Web pages on specific topics. By typing phrases into the search engine you can find Web pages on topics ranging from aardvarks to xylophones. Using the Internet to find information is perhaps more common today than the use of encyclopedias was 20 years ago.

To illustrate the power of the Internet, assume you are the coach of a new bobsled team wanting to rival the famous Jamaican team. Where would you begin? If you use the Internet effectively, you can be well on the way to the gold. Try using Yahoo! to search for the phrase "Olympic bobsledding." When we tried this we found over 1,300 Web pages with information on the topic.

A variety of search engines exist that can help you find information. Some of the most popular include:

Yahoo.com
Google.com
Metacrawler.com

OLC

Go to **www. mhhe.com/ adamsgalanes** for additional weblink activities.

stream of information that Irv gathers about the strengths and weaknesses of opposing teams, the three-month time limit they have to qualify for the Olympics, and the beliefs and attitudes of the team members toward each other, the sport, and their coach.

Perhaps your class has been divided into groups to complete a group project. Examples of inputs to your project group include the group's purpose (beginning with the assignment your instructor gave you), the members' attitudes toward the project, the abilities and experiences of the members, the information members have or are able to find about the topic, and the physical or social features of the environment that may affect the group, such as classroom noise that makes it hard to hear other members.

Throughput Processes.   The **throughput processes** of the group are the activities within the group as it goes about its work (see Table 2.2). These include such processes as how roles, rules, and leadership develop; how members handle conflict; and how members evaluate the information they receive. Throughput processes are the "how" of the group, including all the verbal and nonverbal behaviors that occur within the group. In our bobsled team example, the coach's placement of Derice as the driver instead of Sanka, the obvious choice, is an example of a throughput process. The informal leadership of Sanka, whose enthusiasm motivated the other members, is

GLOSSARY

Throughput Processes

Influences on the system that result from actual activities within the group as it goes about its business

TABLE 2.2	**Examples of Small Group Throughput Processes**

MEMBERS' BEHAVIORS

Degree of encouragement for presenting ideas

Demonstration of members' willingness to work

Dogmatic or otherwise stifling behaviors

Methods of expressing and resolving disagreements

Degree to which cohesiveness is expressed

GROUP NORMS

Support for using critical thinking skills to test ideas versus uncritical acceptance of ideas

Support for open disagreement versus suppression of conflict

Support for relative equality among members versus a strict hierarchy

COMMUNICATION NETWORKS

Extent to which each member talks to every other member

Extent to which participation is distributed evenly

STATUS RELATIONSHIPS

Type of leadership

Degree to which power and influence are shared

PROCEDURES

Communication

Decision making and problem solving

Method for implementing solutions

GLOSSARY

Interaction

The heart of group processes revolving around communication among the group members

also part of the team's throughput processes. Significant for this team was how Yul and Junior reconciled their differences and developed a mutual respect across their socioeconomic lines.

In another example, members of your classroom group may have developed the habit of examining critically all the information they bring to meetings and arguing openly before they reach any decision. This style of handling conflict is an example of a throughput process. This will have a different effect on the group's decisions than if the members uncritically accept any and all information.

The heart of the group's throughput process is **interaction,** or the mutual influence that occurs when people communicate with each other. You may be accustomed to thinking of interaction as just the talk that occurs within a group, but it actually involves more than that. Interaction includes all the verbal and nonverbal behavior in the group

| TABLE 2.3 | **Examples of Small Group Outputs** |

Tangible Outcomes	Intangible Outcomes
Reports	Feelings among members (cohesiveness, trust; disharmony, dislike)
Recommendations	Personal growth of members
Solutions and decisions	Personal satisfaction of members
Physical objects (e.g., table decorations, assembled cars)	Modifications in throughput procedures (e.g., alterations in the status relationships, use of different conflict resolution strategies)

and implies that members of the group are open to each other's persuasive attempts. Interaction assumes that members are aware of one another; are simultaneously sending, interpreting, and receiving messages designed to influence; and are affected by one another. Interaction is the key focus of Part 2 of our text.

Outputs. **Outputs** are the "results," the products of the group's throughput processes (see Table 2.3). They include tangible outcomes, such as decisions the group has made and written reports. However, they also include less obvious results, such as cohesiveness, member satisfaction, personal growth of individual members, and changes in the group's structure. In our bobsled example, a clear result of the team's respect for each other was not a gold medal but instead pride in themselves and from their country. Other outputs included the sledders' increased cohesiveness and new skills, Junior's independence from his father, Yul's team pride, and Derice's realization that a gold medal does not make one a whole person.

Although we hope that the outputs of a small group's interaction are positive and helpful, some outputs are destructive to both the group itself and the organization that established the group. Hasty decisions, dissatisfaction of group members, and shoddy products are examples of destructive outputs. Harmful group outputs are like toxic waste, dangerous to everyone involved, including the organization to which the group belongs.

Environment. A group does not exist apart from its surroundings, or **environment,** which consists of everything outside the group that affects the group. In our example, the Jamaican fans and the other bobsledders influenced the team's morale and enthusiasm. Notice that the team affected its environment as well. When the other bobsledders discovered the courage of this Jamaican team, their disrespect turned into support, and those who had rejected the coach for his past cheating accepted him back into the bobsled fraternity.

Your classroom group's immediate environment is the classroom. Your group is affected by whether the classroom is pleasant or ugly, noisy or quiet. In addition, what your friends in other classes say or do may cause your group to change a procedure, a topic, an approach, and so forth. These friends and their classes are part of your group's environment, too.

GLOSSARY

Outputs

Those tangible and intangible products or achievements of the group system emerging from throughput processes

Environment

Systems do not exist in a vacuum but are embedded in multiple surroundings or contexts

2.1 Bona Fide Groups: The Jamaican Bobsled Team

The Jamaican Olympic bobsled team is not an isolated group, separate from its environment. As a bona fide group it is connected to its environment and vice versa. Four reasons explain the interdependence between this bobsled team and its environment. Using the information from the case study at the beginning of the chapter, surmise possible answers to the following questions:

1. For each member of the team (sledders and coach), what are all the possible groups these individuals may belong to while they are members of the team (e.g., the coach is a banished member of the Olympic bobsled fraternity)?

2. Bona fide groups are faced with coordinating their actions with other groups. Considering the list of groups for each member of the team, what actions will have to be coordinated (e.g., Junior is supposed to leave the country and attend school to be an accountant)?

3. What kind of internal and external communication about team goals, team authority, and support exists for this team (e.g., the governing body of winter sports disqualifies the team after it successfully qualifies)? With each example, discuss how the communication impacts the group.

4. How might this team vary according to interests, ways of speaking, and past experience on athletic teams?

Once you have compiled some of the information from these questions, examine the complicated manner in which this bobsled team is interdependently connected with its environment.

The effect of a group's environment, or the context within which the group operates, is an important but understudied factor in how well a group operates.[3] The small group system is linked to its environment, which in turn affects communication processes within the small group itself. To understand a small group, it's important to consider the group's environment. Linda Putnam and Cynthia Stohl, two leading scholars in the study of group communication, call this a bona fide group perspective.[4] They emphasize that groups are not only influenced by their environments but also help shape those same environments. This interdependence occurs for several reasons. First, members of groups often belong to other groups that simultaneously influence and are influenced by them. Second, groups typically have to coordinate their actions with other groups within the same parent organization or across organizations. Third, there is frequent internal and external communication over interpretation of group goals, the extent of the group's authority, and support for group actions that helps define a group's accountability for its task. Finally, members bring to their groups a variety of interests, ways of speaking, and mental models of effective group problem solving. This in turn affects how members create their sense of "group."

All group interaction directly and indirectly reflects this back-and-forth relationship between the group and its environment. For example, one of our colleagues is a member of the College of Arts and Humanities' general education subcommittee. This subcommittee is composed of members from all of this college's departments. Members are accountable not only to each of the departments in the college but also to the university's general education committee. The college's committee is influenced by the priorities of all those departments as well as by the biases developed within the college committee. The actions of the college's committee are reported to the university's committee and can change how that committee operates. Nowhere is this complexity of interlocked groups and multiple membership seen more clearly than in the modern organization, which we discuss later in the chapter.

CHARACTERISTICS OF SYSTEMS

The concepts that follow describe several important characteristics of living systems. These characteristics help explain how a system functions, both internally and within the surrounding environment.

Open and Closed Systems.   Whether a system is relatively open or closed is determined by the amount of interaction the system has with its environment. A **closed system** (we know of no completely closed human system) has little interaction with its environment, whereas an **open system** has a great deal (see Figure 2.2). The fact that the United States is an exceptionally open system made it easier for the World Trade Center terrorist pilots to enter the country, train as student pilots, and travel freely from state to state. Groups are open systems, too, experiencing varying levels of interchange with their environment. Our bobsled team had a moderate amount of interaction with its surroundings. The team was affected by the fans' reactions, and the fans and general public were influenced by the team's successes as well.

Each position has advantages and disadvantages. For example, the influx of drugs from other countries into the United States, an open system, is hard to control because its borders are so open. On the other hand, some restrictive countries experience a shortage of basic goods and technology developed outside their territories. Some American companies, resisting the changes brought by "outsiders," prefer to stay as closed to outside influence as possible. This enables managers to maintain more control over what happens internally, but it also cuts off the company from what could be helpful information that might improve its operation and profits.

Openness and free interchange with the environment are distinct advantages for most groups. For example, the Ford Motor Company groups that were responsible for the design of Ford's successful Taurus automobile made a point of seeking input (information, ideas, suggestions) from the factory workers who would build the Taurus and many of whom could be expected to buy it. The workers supplied numerous suggestions, which were adopted. If the Taurus engineering group had remained closed to opinions from workers and others outside the immediate group, the Taurus might not have been so well designed and sought after by the car-buying public.

Interdependence.   **Interdependence** refers to the fact that each element of a system influences and is influenced by the other elements. Just as the system as a whole is affected by its environment, so are the system's individual components affected by each other. Have you ever set up a row of dominoes, then tipped over the first one and

GLOSSARY

Closed System

Such systems have limited flow of information between themselves and their environment

Open System

Such systems have a free exchange of information with their environments; that is, inputs and outputs flow back and forth between the system and its environment

Interdependence

The elements of a system are related interdependently such that all elements mutually influence each other

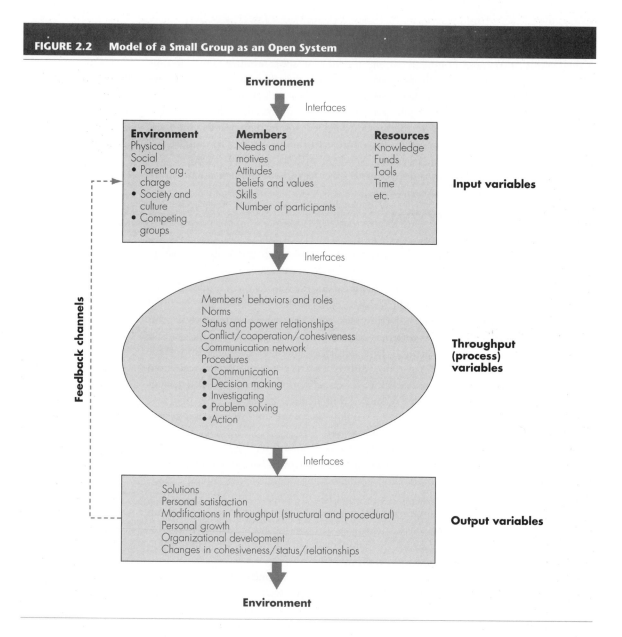

FIGURE 2.2   Model of a Small Group as an Open System

Environment

Interfaces

Environment	**Members**	**Resources**
Physical	Needs and	Knowledge
Social	motives	Funds
• Parent org. charge	Attitudes	Tools
• Society and culture	Beliefs and values	Time
• Competing groups	Skills	etc.
	Number of participants	

Input variables

Interfaces

Members' behaviors and roles
Norms
Status and power relationships
Conflict/cooperation/cohesiveness
Communication network
Procedures
• Communication
• Decision making
• Investigating
• Problem solving
• Action

Throughput (process) variables

Interfaces

Solutions
Personal satisfaction
Modifications in throughput (structural and procedural)
Personal growth
Organizational development
Changes in cohesiveness/status/relationships

Output variables

Feedback channels

Environment

watched the others fall in turn? That's interdependence. Within small groups, one element, idea, behavior, or person can change the functioning of the entire group. In our bobsled story, we saw how the sledders' abilities determined, in part, the coach's strategy, and how the personality of individual players like Sanka, the eternal optimist, could spur a team to greater effort, which in turn increases the likelihood of team success. Each of these separate elements affects the others.

Another characteristic of interdependence among elements of a small group is the interdependent goal toward which all group members work. The members of the group rely on each other as they strive to reach their objective; one member cannot reach the objective alone. As with the bobsled team, group members win and lose as a group. Sports teams cannot have one member win and the rest of the team lose. So it is with most small groups as they work to accomplish a task as a group. If one member is to achieve the goal, then all members must achieve it. For example, if your project group is required to give a presentation to the rest of the class, the goal is reached for all members when the presentation is completed in a manner satisfactory to all. Interdependence is one key characteristic to look for in determining whether a collection of individuals have become a group.

Feedback. One valuable feature of human systems is that they are able to adapt to changing conditions and circumstances. In part, they can do this through the use of **feedback,** the part of the system's output that is returned to the system as input. Feedback enables the system to monitor its progress toward the goal and make corrections when needed.

An example of feedback occurs when you drive a car. If the car veers to the left on a straight road, you know you must steer it to the right to get it back on course. Seeing the car veer left is a type of visual feedback, based on the car's performance (output), that is given back to you in the form of information (input), showing you the car isn't traveling straight. In our bobsled story, Irv saw that his arrangement of sledders was successful. This feedback indicated that what he was doing was working, so he didn't need to change their positions. In another example, during practice runs and by studying pictures of the course, Derice could make adjustments in the team's movements for more successful runs.

Multiple Causes, Multiple Paths. One feature of all living systems, including small groups, is complexity. Usually, many factors combine to produce a single outcome, indicated by the concept of **multiple causes.** As an example of multiple causes, the Jamaican bobsled team had high morale at the end of the Olympics. This occurred for several reasons: They became medal contenders, the country supported them, they had a leader who was well liked and effective, all the members contributed to the team's success, and other factors that are not readily apparent. Too often, individuals try to pinpoint a single cause for a group outcome. For example, you may have heard someone say, "We would have come up with an excellent proposal if our chair had listened to our suggestions. As it was, everybody hated the group." Well, the behavior of the group's chair definitely contributed to the group's low morale, but other factors probably had an impact as well. Perhaps members did not like each other, the task was not an interesting one, or the group did not have sufficient time or information to do its best. All these factors could have interacted to produce the dissatisfaction.

A related principle of groups is that there is usually more than one appropriate way to reach a particular objective. This principle is indicated by the concept of **multiple paths.** For example, there are a number of ways to plan a fun party, and a variety of ways to develop a respectable undergraduate curriculum for communication majors. Which is the "right" way? All the ways are right—the most effective approach depends on the characteristics of all the participants. Also, the concept of multiple paths implies

GLOSSARY

Feedback

The return of system outputs as system inputs, which allows the system to monitor its movement toward goals and make necessary changes

Multiple Causes

No single system input determines system outputs; instead system outcomes are the result of numerous, interdependent factors

Multiple Paths

System objectives can be reached in a variety of ways

For more information on multiple paths in a tangled web, go to the on-line leaering center.

GLOSSARY

Nonsummativity

A system's ability to take on an identity separate from its individual elements

that two or more groups could come up with similar solutions to a problem, even though each group had members with different abilities and areas of expertise, leadership styles, and ways of resolving differences of opinion. Like multiple causes, the concept of multiple paths encourages us to recognize the complexity of small groups.

Nonsummativity.   **Nonsummativity** refers to the concept that a system is not the sum of its parts. Sometimes, as with the Jamaican bobsled team, a small group performs better than the sum of its parts, and sometimes it performs much worse than expected.

2.2   CNN's Reporting Disaster: What Happened?

APPLY NOW

CNN, during its premiere of "NewsStand: CNN & *Time*," a television news venture with *Time* magazine, reported in the lead story, "Valley of Death," that the United States had used lethal nerve gas in 1970 as part of a Laotian secret mission to kill American defectors. This report was broadcast June 7, 1998, on "NewsStand: CNN & *Time*" and reported in *Time* despite several oral and written complaints from journalists in both news organizations questioning the validity of the story. A military consultant resigned in light of his concerns. On July 3, 1998, the *Fresno* (California) *Bee,* reported CNN's retraction of the story by Tom Johnson, CNN News Group chair, president, and CEO. Mr. Johnson admitted to serious faults with the broadcast and apologized, saying that CNN was not able to confirm the story. *Time's* managing editor admitted it too could not confirm the story.

A group of television producers and print journalists conducted 200 interviews as they worked together for eight months on the story. The group was headed by two successful producers and included an award-winning documentary producer and a Pulitzer prize–winning journalist. An independent investigation into the validity of the story concluded that the group members had not intentionally made up the story. Instead, the reporting team drew conclusions based on questionable evidence, led sources into thinking that their suspicions could be supported in unseen evidence, and made decisions based on interview responses to a variety of hypothetical questions. The CNN investigation concluded that those involved in putting together the story so firmly believed what they were reporting they ignored information contrary to what they were finding.

How could a team of talented individuals, after an eight-month investigation and in the face of cautionary criticism, produce a report that ended in people being fired, resigning, and facing reprimands—not to mention embarrassing two highly respected news organizations? Using the system concepts open and closed systems, interdependence, feedback, multiple causes/paths, and nonsummativity, develop your own "systems" explanation for this reporting disaster. You can do this in groups or as a class.

On any college football Saturday, you'll be able to find a team that beats another team with better player statistics and overall record. Why? Because a group is an entity of its own and takes on a life of its own, so it performs better—or worse—than anyone can predict. A so-called superior team can have an off day, and a so-called inferior team can become inspired and take off.

Small group researchers have long been aware of this phenomenon. Groups often achieve an assembly effect, or a positive synergy, in which the output is superior to the averaging of the outputs of the individual members. For instance, we heard a television story about a Tucson, Arizona, Little League team called the Diamondbacks who won the 1998 championship, 26–0. What is so unusual about this team winning the championship? The team was made up of all the kids who were not picked for the other teams, the "leftovers"! On the other hand, groups can often experience what some have called process loss, or negative synergy. For example, even groups of intelligent, knowledgeable individuals can make an extremely poor decision, such as the scientists and managers who decided to launch the space shuttle Challenger on its fatal trip.

Although no one knows exactly why one group experiences positive synergy and another negative synergy, it may have something to do with the level of ambiguity that faces the group, whether the group encounters obstacles during its problem-solving process, and how it deals with those obstacles.[5] The Jamaican team faced numerous obstacles: a short time in which to train and qualify, little money, finding a sled for less than $5,000, members with no experience, a country with no snow, a coach lacking respect, ridicule from others, being ousted from the Olympics and getting back in, possible loss of one member, and the list goes on. Yet the team members did not quit and worked together to overcome each obstacle, finding new pride in themselves and their own style of sledding. Communication among members is the key to making the most, instead of the least, of group members' abilities. Group members must understand the problem-solving process and be taught how to use communication that facilitates effective discussion and problem solving.

Life Cycles in the System

A living system's primary objective is survival, but at some point this may be difficult or impossible. Even a casual look at nature tells us that the natural **life cycle** for any living system includes conception and birth, growth and development, maturity, decline, and finally death (see Figure 2.3). But living organisms fight their eventual deaths as long as possible by adapting to changing conditions. Human groups usually do everything in their power to help ensure their own continuation. The Jamaican bobsled team did not abandon its goal of winning a gold medal when members could not find sponsorship money. Instead, members worked hard to raise the money themselves. They did not quit when they first saw the condition of their sled; instead, they fixed it and gave it some new paint—in other words, they found new inputs to replace old outputs.

When members first come together as a new group, they must sort out a variety of factors before they can become a fully functional group. For example, they must get to know each other's strengths and weaknesses. A stable leadership structure must emerge, and a set of rules and norms must be established that all members agree to follow. When

GLOSSARY

Life Cycle

Systems are dynamic processes with inherent moments of stability and change

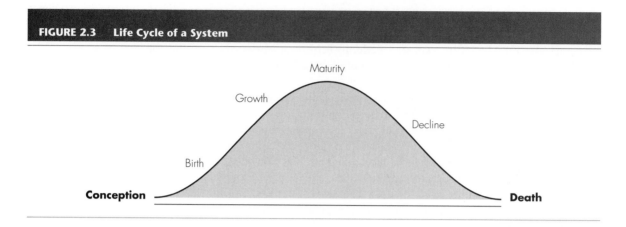

FIGURE 2.3   Life Cycle of a System

this has happened, the group can begin to mature and become productive. Individual members may leave and be replaced by new members, but the group can continue indefinitely as a functioning, successful unit. However, as with any living organism, the small group system will eventually decline and disband, perhaps when it no longer has a purpose, when no new members replace those who leave, or when a competing group destroys or absorbs it. At this point, the group has completed its usefulness and is appropriately laid to rest.

We hope that you see from this discussion that groups, like all other living organisms, are complex, dynamic, ever-changing systems that conform to the natural order of the universe. Although the complexity of small groups makes it difficult to study them, systems theory provides a framework for doing so. It also supplies a perspective for examining how groups exchange inputs and outputs with the environment and how several small group systems link to form a complex network.

Organizations as Systems of Groups

Much of the work of both corporate and nonprofit America is done in and by small groups. Most organizations are interlocking systems of groups (see Figure 2.4). Think for a moment of how the automobile companies design, build, and market their cars. Although many individual engineers are involved in the design of specific car parts, an engineering team is typically responsible for seeing that the individual parts come together into a car that works the way it is supposed to. Decades ago a single manager could oversee the production of cars, but today manufacturing teams have that responsibility. Marketing, too, is a complex activity that usually involves a team of researchers, artists, copywriters, photographers, and other specialists.

In a company such as Saturn, for example, self-managed work teams create major components such as engines and transmissions, while other teams assemble the units into completed cars. In addition, quality control circles and special project teams are composed of individuals from numerous departments and divisions. Many other products could not be manufactured and many types of services could not be offered without the functioning of large systems composed of interdependent small groups.

FIGURE 2.4   An Oranization as a System of Interlocking Group Subsystems

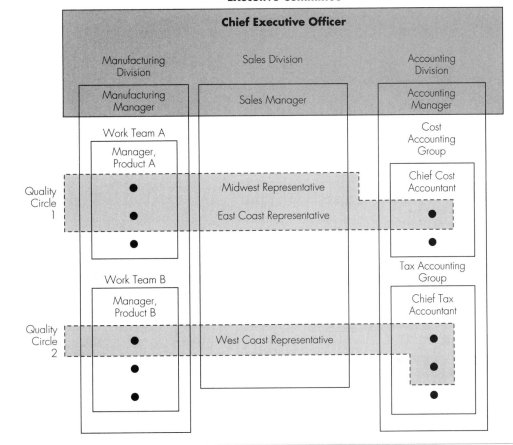

You can see from these examples that complex organizations have small groups as primary components. The principle of larger systems being composed of many subsystems (progressively smaller groups) has many important implications. First, knowing something about how groups function and how to be an effective group member is essential if you hope to survive and prosper in modern society. Second, because there are so many parts to a system, careful coordination and extensive communication among the parts are essential. The individual groups within an organization must find ways of sharing information with each other in order not to duplicate effort or allow important matters to "fall through the cracks." This spotlights the central role of communication, both within each group and among groups, in the effective functioning of modern organizations and society. This extra-group communication has received relatively little attention from researchers, even though it is very important to the long-term survival of the group.[6]

2.3   CNN and *Time* as a System of Groups

The previous application example describes the rather complex system of groups that can make up the modern news organization. CNN, or the Cable News Network, together with *Time* produced "NewsStand: CNN & *Time*." Both CNN and *Time* are owned by Time-Warner. Using this information, and the information in the previous application example, construct your own diagram of the system of interlocking group subsystems. Then discuss the role of "extra-group" communication in this example. What went wrong? At which level? What could they have done differently? Is there a way to guarantee a valid, successful story all the time?

The usefulness of the systems perspective should be clear. We can use that perspective to help us identify and describe the individual components of groups, as long as we remember that each part functions in relation to all the other parts of the system; what affects one part affects all the other parts. This is true whether the system being studied is a person, a single group with several members, or a large organization composed of numerous interlocking groups.

- General systems theory is a useful framework for studying small groups because it reminds us that systems are complex, with all parts of a system being interdependent.

- All systems use inputs to engage in throughput processes and produce outputs. Feedback helps systems monitor their performance, which cannot be predicted by summing the individual performances of the components.

- All systems try to survive by adapting to changing conditions. Open systems freely exchange resources with their environments, but closed systems do not.

- Modern organizations can be pictured as complex systems of interlocking and interdependent small groups.

1. Bring to class a box of toothpicks and glue. Take out 12 toothpicks and use the glue to create some form out of the toothpicks. After you have finished, display your "creation." Discuss all the creations and the concept of nonsummativity. Then move from discussing toothpicks to behaviors and from creations to small groups.

2. Select classmates to form one primary group: a family. Select parents, children, and any other members you want. Then select members of the class to be other individuals who may be involved in the family's life such as a pastor, professor, and boss. With a ball of string, loosely connect all of these individuals to relevant individuals and as you do so create a story about them. For instance, only one spouse may work and so is connected to the boss, the other spouse, and a parent. A child may be connected to only one parent, and so

on. Then instruct the various individuals to role-play their parts by periodically pulling on the strings and requesting something of the individual. Use this activity to "show" the concept of interdependence.

3. Bring a large muffin to class. Use the muffin to discuss inputs, throughputs, and outputs. Make a list of the inputs for making the muffin. Discuss the kinds of throughputs necessary for the creation of the muffin, and then

point out the output. Discuss how the environment may influence the muffin. After this discussion, compare the making of a muffin, as a relatively closed system, to the creation of a group, a relatively open system. How are they similar and how are they different?

Go to **www.mhhe.com/adamsgalanes** and **www.mhhe.com/groups** for Self-Quizzes and weblinks.

KEY TERMS and CONCEPTS

Closed System	Interdependence	Open System
Environment	Life Cycle	Outputs
Feedback	Multiple Causes	System
Inputs	Multiple Paths	Throughput Processes
Interaction	Nonsummativity	

www.mhhe.com/adamsgalanes
Use the flashcards and crossword puzzles on the Online Learning Center to further your knowledge of these key terms.

Foundations
of Small Group
Communicating

For groups to function effectively, they must create and sustain a solid foundation that supports members' efforts. Part Two focuses on this foundation, the communication process itself. As discussed in Chapter 2, communication is at the heart of group throughput processes, so your understanding of this process is essential. Chapter 3 presents basic principles of interpersonal communication you should understand to be an effective group member, and Chapter 4 focuses on verbal and nonverbal messages that comprise member interaction.

Interpersonal Communication Principles for Group Members

CHAPTER OBJECTIVES

After reading this chapter you should be able to:

1. Define *communication.*

2. List and explain the six major characteristics of communication.

3. Explain the three major implications derived from the six major characteristics of communication.

4. Describe the difference between listening and hearing.

5. List and explain the seven habits of poor listeners.

6. Explain why listening is active behavior.

7. Describe paraphrasing as a technique for active listening.

8. Define focused listening and explain how it is a part of active listening.

The Lake Area Wellness Council

The Lake Area Wellness Council is a nonprofit organization of people interested in alternatives to traditional Western medicine. Each month, the council sponsors a seminar, open to everyone, where the featured speaker is a practitioner of some form of alternative medicine. The council operates with a small budget and usually relies on volunteers to present the seminars; volunteers are given a token gift, such as a T-shirt with the council's logo, but are generally not paid an honorarium. The council's executive committee is responsible for scheduling and publicizing speakers.

At one meeting, committee member Rhea suggested they invite Chief Robert, a Cherokee medicine man, to address the group. She further suggested that, as compensation for his talk, they buy Chief Robert a piece of equipment he wanted for his work. Members agreed that Chief Robert, a prominent local healer, deserved a substantial gift, but the equipment was expensive ($200) and paying him would set a precedent for future speakers, which the council could not afford. Norm, chair of the executive committee, said, "I don't know how we'll be able to afford something like that, though I agree that he's certainly worth the money." Rhea then said, "OK, that sounds good to me." The council went on to discuss other matters and Chief Robert was forgotten. At the next council meeting, Sonya reported that publicity for Chief Robert's seminar was proceeding well, and the upcoming Sunday paper was planning a feature story on him and the seminar. Rhea noted how pleased she was that the council had agreed to buy the chief his equipment and especially how grateful he was for their generosity. At that point, the meeting exploded into cries of "What? What do you mean buy his equipment? We didn't agree to buy that for him!" Committee members had misunderstood each other, and as a result Rhea had obligated them to a $200 gift that would come close to wiping out their savings. However, at this point, members believed they couldn't back out. It took the committee members several meetings to overcome their anger and begin to trust each other again.

S cenes like this occur every day and illustrate what can happen when people fail to understand each other. To function effectively as a team, members must learn to put their thoughts and feelings into signals that other members can interpret and respond to. However, glitches can (and often do) occur in this *creating–sending–receiving–interpreting–responding* cycle called *communication*. In our

An object represented by a variety of symbols (words). (Reprinted by permission of Johnny Hart and Creators Syndicate, Inc.)

example, Norm said, "He's certainly worth the money." He meant, "It would be great to pay him and all of our speakers—they do such a wonderful job—but there's no way our budget can handle it, so let's stick to T-shirts." Rhea heard his words yet interpreted them to mean, "We don't have money to pay all our speakers, and it will be hard to come up with that amount for Chief Robert, but, of all the speakers we've had, he is certainly worth the expense, so we'll figure out some way to pay him." She said, "OK," meaning "Great, I'll tell him we'll make an exception in his case." Norm heard her, yet he *interpreted* her meaning as "I see what you mean about the expense, and I agree with you." These collective failures in the messages occurring between group members cost the Lake Area Wellness Council time, money, and energy. Unfortunately, this misunderstanding within a small group is not unusual. We know you can think of numerous instances you have experienced in your own group experiences!

The primary purpose of Chapter 3 is to help you understand the communication process so you can think analytically and critically about communication in your groups. A secondary purpose is to help you improve your own participation in your group's communication. Communicating effectively takes conscious thought and hard work. In this chapter and the next, we focus both on the process and on how you as a group member can communicate more effectively.

Communication: What's That?

The word *communication* has been used in dozens of slightly different ways by different writers. We use **communication** to refer to the *perception, interpretation, and response of people to signals produced by other people.* There are six major characteristics to this seemingly simple definition.

GLOSSARY

Communication

Process of creating, sending, receiving, and interpreting signals between people

Symbols have no natural connection with what they represent. (©1991 by King Features Syndicate, Inc. World rights reserved. Reprinted with special permission of King Features Syndicate.)

First, **communication is symbolic.** Two major categories of signals are involved in communicating with others: signs and symbols. A **sign** is a stimulus that indicates the presence of something else. For example, a blush is a sign of personal tension called *embarrassment,* and a rabbit track in the snow is a sign that a rabbit has passed. Signs closely match that which they signify.

A **symbol,** in contrast to a sign, is a *person-created* signal that arbitrarily represents something with which it has no natural or direct relationship. For instance, there's no natural reason we call something we sit on a *chair* instead of a *pig,* a *snorkel,* or *une chaise.* In addition, a symbol may stand for something that has no tangible form, such as a relationship, an abstract concept such as love, or an idea that cannot be observed, such as democracy. All words are symbols.

There is no inherent or direct relationship between any word and what it represents. For instance, even within a single language, the same food might be called *dinner, supper,* or the *evening meal* by different people. B.C., in our first cartoon, proves his point that no one will ever master the art of communication because of the variety of words or symbols that can arbitrarily represent the material he held in his hand. New symbols are constantly being created to represent new things or ideas: *bioterrorism, interface, surfing the net,* and *user-friendly.* There is no limit to how many symbols we can invent and use to communicate. Even Homer Simpson, Bart's dad on the popular American cartoon "The Simpsons," can have his expression (symbol) for something gone wrong or doing something really foolish, *d'oh,* selected for official entry into the *Oxford English Dictionary.*

Symbols are convenient for thinking and communicating because we do not need to have the items present to represent them to other people. In addition, we can encode great amounts of information in small packages of signals. There is no limit to how many symbols we can invent and use to communicate. Further, symbols allow us to

GLOSSARY

Sign

Any signal that indicates something else and closely matches that which it represents

Symbol

Any signal that arbitrarily stands for something else

communicate through space and time. Did you know that www.symbolics.com was the very first website to go live March 15, 1985? And now there are approximately 30 million registered Internet names or symbols!

Symbols can take a variety of forms. Words are the most common, but we also use numbers; pictographs (such as the international signs for cars and restrooms); Morse code; emoticons such as those used in computer e-mail to convey feelings, gestures, or objects; and gestures like those we use for OK.

As convenient and helpful as symbols are, they also have liabilities. Because symbols are arbitrary, their meaning must be *interpreted.* Dangers come from misuse and misunderstanding symbols. Two people can use a symbol to represent different concepts and therefore misinterpret each other without knowing it, as Rhea and Norm did. For example, when you say, "I love you," do you mean the same thing as your boyfriend or girlfriend does? A person may believe that there is a relationship between symbols and tangible events when none really exists. A symbol can evoke different responses than a communicator intended. Liars can manipulate us even more easily with symbols than with signs. In what some called "tortuous linguistic negotiation,"[1] the United States in the spring of 2001 sent a carefully worded letter to China in hopes of securing the release of the crew of the downed U.S. EP-3E surveillance plane from China's Hainan Island. The Americans attempted to offer regrets to China without offering a formal apology for an incident the United States considered an *accident.* Thus, in the letter, U.S. officials used the phrase *feichang wanxi,* or *extreme sympathy,* which the Chinese interpreted as *shenbiao qianti,* or *deep apology.* Misunderstandings and multiple interpretations are likely in small group communication, which makes it necessary to monitor the communication processes in our groups more thoughtfully than we normally do our everyday conversations.

The second characteristic of communication is that **communication is a process, not a thing or state.** Communication is an extremely complex process involving human senses, feelings, meanings, and cultural experiences, not just a simple matter of nouns and verbs. During the process with no clearly marked beginning and end, one person experiences a perception or feeling and expresses this experience by putting it, consciously or not, into words and/or nonverbal signals, which others can perceive and respond to. This process is diagrammed in Figure 3.1. We won't try to explain all that happens, partly because not all of it is yet understood. However, many sources of distortion and error can creep into the circuits linking a small group of humans. Talking about communication as if it were a simple signal–response event, with nothing likely to go wrong, is naive. It is more complex than any computer circuitry. Signals from a person start as feelings or thoughts, and no one can say when their impact on others ends.

Third, **communication is personal.** Because communication is symbolic, meanings are in people, not in the words themselves. Words can and do have different meanings to different people. Even when two people agree on the dictionary definition of a word, they may disagree vehemently about what that word means to them. For instance, an *excellent* paper to you may mean one that is free of typographical errors and turned in on time. To your teacher, *excellent* may be reserved for a paper that is not only grammati-

FIGURE 3.1   Communication Process (arrows indicate places where mistakes can occur)

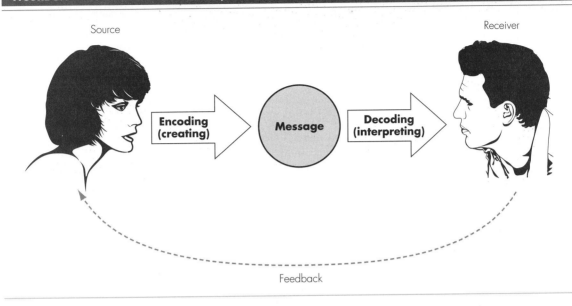

cally perfect but also shows considerable insight and creativity. You both are using the same word, but not meaning the same thing at all. This fact leads directly to the next principle of communication.

Fourth, **face-to-face communicating is a transactional process.** The communication process is often modeled with components that include a source, message, channel, receiver, and response (or feedback). This implies that communication is a one-way or linear process, with feedback similar to a tennis game. The server sends the message, and the receiver lobs a response back. This is misleading because communication is a *multidirectional transactional* process.

Transactional has two major meanings relevant to face-to-face communication among members of a small group. First, communicating is a simultaneous, multidirectional process. That is, regardless of who is speaking at any given moment, *every* member is simultaneously sending signals that every other member (including the speaker) could potentially receive and interpret. Most of these signals are unspoken (nonverbal), and most of them are signs (for instance, the expression you may make when you don't like an idea a speaker is presenting). The implication is clear: to be most effective as a group member, you must be aware of signals from all members, even when you are speaking. For example, a speaker may notice from facial expressions that group members are reacting negatively to her suggestions and thus modify her ideas as she speaks. Communication is not a linear, one-way process but occurs among all members simultaneously. This illustrates the complex, transactional nature of communication.

GLOSSARY

Transactional

While communicating, all interactants mutually and simultaneously define both themselves and others

Second, *transactional* implies that members must work together to create mutual understanding for what words and concepts mean and that members can consciously help each other in this process. For example, consider the following exchange between a friend of ours upgrading his computer system and the computer salesperson "helping" him:

Salesperson: You'll want to upgrade to Windows so you won't have to go directly through DOS.

Noah: What's Windows?

Salesperson: It's a graphic interface that makes computing a lot easier.

Noah: Graphic—does that mean it works with pictures?

Salesperson: Right. We call them icons. Windows interfaces between the user and the computer.

Noah: But why would you want something between you and the computer?

Salesperson: Well, instead of having to talk to the computer in a difficult language that doesn't seem logical to get it to do what you want, you use pictures to talk to the computer. It's more natural, more like the way people actually think.

Noah: Oh, I see now. Windows is like a translator between me and the computer and, because it works with icons, it will be easier for me to use.

In this instance, Noah was able to get the computer salesperson to explain the concepts in ways that would make sense to Noah. However, it took some careful listening on his part and a considerable amount of *transacting* for the salesperson's intended meaning to become clear to Noah. Meanings are not so much *re*ceived intact from each person, but instead *con*ceived or created in context between persons.

Fifth, **human communication is both a sender and a receiver phenomenon.** Of course, something must be sent, but if there is no receiver, there is no communication. Talking makes no sense unless listening is understood and vice versa. If you are talking while no one is listening, no communication has occurred. Neither does it occur if you are listening for something that has not been sent. Many people believe that communication means only the sending of messages, so the best way to improve communication is to improve the quality of the messages we send. However, paying attention only to the sending part of communication overlooks the transactional nature of communicating, especially how a person receives and interprets signals. Thus, *both* the sender and receiver are responsible for the effectiveness of any particular communication. The sender is responsible for being as clear as possible, and the receiver is responsible for attending to the sender, trying to understand what the sender means and asking questions to help the sender clarify the message. The communication problems between Norm and Rhea in Case 3.1 resulted from messages that were unclear as sent but were also never clarified by the receivers and thus were interpreted according to what the receivers *wanted* to believe.

The sixth characteristic of communication is that **all messages involve content and relational dimensions.**[2] The **content dimension** of a message involves the message's ideas or the *what* of the message. When you listen to a teacher's lecture, the content of her or his messages is what you record in your notes. When you listen to a research report from a group member, you often attend to the ideas the member is summarizing for the group. These may be recorded in the group's minutes. The **relational dimension** of a message is *how* the message is expressed and recognizes that content is never expressed in a vacuum. Every time you express a message, you express ideas, and you simultaneously express how you perceive the relationship between yourself and others present. For instance, the teacher's lecture can be given in a variety of ways: boring, passionate, exciting, straightforward, authoritatively, equally, and so forth. Does the teacher talk down to you as if you are a child who must be told what to think, or does the teacher share the information with you as if you are someone with your own valid experiences and knowledge? You usually do not write this dimension in your notes, yet you may talk about it to your friends during and after a lecture: "I really like how Professor Jones treats us like we have something to say, too," or "Man, I am insulted by the way Professor Jones treats us like we are children with no opinions worth listening to!" These same messages are processed in small groups as members always offer how it is they see themselves in relation to each other through their messages. We often focus more explicitly on the content of messages but, as you will see, the relational aspects of messages are constant and just as integral to the communication dynamics of groups.

3.1 Synchronous and Asynchronous CMC

MEDIA AND TECHNOLOGY

Businesses and organizations are increasingly using CMC as a method of communication. One way to classify types of CMC is to determine whether the communication is synchronous or asynchronous. With *synchronous communication* members interact in real time, and each participant is simultaneously a sender and a receiver. With *asynchronous communication* delays occur in the communication interaction, and each participant must take turns being the sender and receiver. What are some reasons groups might use both synchronous and asynchronous communication?

A common form of CMC used by many organizations is electronic mail, or e-mail. E-mail is asynchronous communication because this medium does not allow for interactive, real-time communication between people. Although e-mail does not have the advantage of being synchronous communication, e-mail is a cheap and efficient method for communicating with other Internet users. A study conducted by communication researchers at UCLA found that on average, 76 percent of people with e-mail capability check for messages on a daily basis.

E-mail is quickly becoming one of the most cost-efficient methods of communication. Most colleges and universities provide students with free e-mail accounts. In addition, those with access to the Internet may obtain free e-mail accounts through any number of online services. Examples of free e-mail providers include:

Hotmail.com
Yahoo.com

SOURCE: "Surveying the Digital Future" [Internet], *UCLA Internet Report,* UCLA Center for Communication Policy, 2000. Available: http://www.ccp.ucla.edu.

Go to **www. mhhe.com/ adamsgalanes** for additional weblink activities.

Our discussion thus far has focused on communication in traditional, face-to-face groups, but the growing use of computers for small group problem solving continues to change the nature of communication in small groups. With the help of computers, members can get messages to each other during meetings or outside meeting times. Members do not have to hold meetings face-to-face. They can be in different places and "talk" to each other simultaneously or receive their messages at their leisure. Using computers to interact with others inside or outside the group is called *computer-mediated communication,* or CMC. We introduced computer-mediated support groups to you in Chapter 1 and we continue to explore CMC in subsequent chapters. CMC is a symbolic, personal, and transactional process, yet there is much we still must learn about its nature in comparison to face-to-face communication.

Although skills in both sending and receiving are essential to effective small group communication, most small group members need to pay closer attention to how they *listen* and *interpret* and *how* they express themselves. This is true whether they are communicating face-to-face or doing so through computers. Usually, the *receiving* as well as the *relational* aspects of communication fail to get adequate attention.

Implications for Small Group Communication

The six communication principles just described have several implications that are particularly relevant for small groups. We explain three of the most important ones here, and they are summarized in Table 3.1.

1. **Making group communication productive is the responsibility of every member.**

   There is a great tendency to blame another person when a statement is ignored, misunderstood, forgotten, or not heard. "If he had just listened to me," or "If she weren't so (boring, arrogant, dominating, nasty, prejudiced, ignorant, etc.) I'd

TABLE 3.1	**Communication: Implications for Small Group Communication**

- Making group communication productive is the responsibility of every member. Because communication is both a sender and a receiver phenomenon, clear sending and careful listening are both needed.

- Perfect understanding among group members is impossible. Since communication is symbolic and involves both content and relational components, perfect understanding can never occur, but group members can understand each other well enough to coordinate efforts toward a common goal.

- Disagreement and conflict are not necessarily signs of a breakdown in communication. Sometimes group members understand each other very well but differ in values, beliefs, and goals. Not all such conflicts can be resolved or ended

have paid more attention" are typical statements group members use to blame others and disclaim any responsibility for miscommunicating. But communication is a groupwide multidirectional activity. For example, the responsibility for glitches in the Lake Area Wellness Council's meeting was not Norm's or Rhea's alone. If you don't understand, you can (and should) say so. If you can't hear, you can ask the others to talk louder. If you failed to note an assignment for which you are responsible, you have the obligation to ask. Do not expect others to read your mind and supply you with information you are missing. In short, everyone must constantly monitor how the communication process is working and correct problems as needed.

2. **Perfect understanding among group members is impossible.**

Because of all the communication characteristics we discussed earlier—that it is symbolic, personal, transactional, multidimensional, and so forth—perfect understanding cannot occur. Since we have different words in our vocabularies and different experiences with words, our associations with words and signs

3.1　Communication and the Lake Area Wellness Council

APPLY NOW

The Lake Area Wellness Council is composed of people with a common interest: alternatives to Western medicine. It is an organized, productive council. However, even groups composed of members with a common interest can encounter communication problems. Perfect understanding is never possible in small groups. Reflecting on the six characteristics of communication in small groups, consider the following:

1. Were any signs mentioned in the case study?
2. Which symbols do you think were the most problematic for the council? Why?
3. What different forms did the symbols take in this case study?
4. Explain how there is no definite beginning and ending to the Lake Area Wellness Council story.
5. How is the communication among the members of the council transactional?
6. How did the members of the council work together to create the misunderstanding?
7. Change the script of the council meeting and show how the members together could have produced a better outcome.
8. List what you think are the content issues and then list what you believe are the relational issues expressed in how the messages may have been expressed.
9. Was the conflict between Norm and Rhea a breakdown in communication? If so, how might the conflict have looked if it wasn't from a breakdown in communication?

differ. Hence, some degree of difference in meaning always exists between two or more people responding to each other's messages. Fortunately, perfect understanding isn't necessary. In a group, we need only communicate well enough to coordinate our behavior toward a common goal. When we can do this, we are communicating well enough for group success, even though we haven't achieved perfect understanding.

3. **Disagreement and conflict are not necessarily signs of a breakdown in communication.**

    People often say that conflicts can be avoided if people would communicate better. Nothing could be further from the truth. Some small group conflicts are due to misunderstandings or lack of information that might be solved through communication, but many conflicts result from group members having different values, goals, beliefs, or personal objectives. (We elaborate on several of these in Chapter 9.) In addition, conflict may occur not over the ideas expressed but rather over *how* they were expressed. Thus, no breakdown or misunderstanding occurs—members are quite clear about what the conflict involves; in this case, matters are made worse if miscommunication is blamed while the gist of the conflict is ignored.

Now that we have explained the concept of *communication* as we use it, we turn to one of the most important processes in small group communication: listening.

Listening: Receiving, Interpreting, and Responding to Messages from Other Group Members

Coordinating the efforts of group members in a functioning system is more dependent on good listening than on good speaking skills, although we often concentrate on speaking. No matter the skill of the speaker, it is the listener who determines whether listening will happen. A beneficial group member must be able to synthesize group sentiments and summarize a discussion cogently. But that is not possible if members were not listening well enough to recall what others said or to think carefully about what they mean. For example, at one time it was estimated that 15 million meetings occurred in the United States every morning. In just one six-person group, 30 minutes of time is wasted every time 5 minutes of information is repeated.[3] Imagine the total waste in all these groups! You can probably see why a national survey of 1,000 personnel managers identified listening as the second most important skill that influences their hiring decisions.[4]

If a small group is to operate effectively, members must understand each other. Listening is the central component of this process.[5] It is an important skill for both members and leaders of small groups. Members who are perceived as poor listeners are not likely to be chosen as group leaders, but leaders usually are perceived as good listeners.[6] Thus, as a good listener, you will not only be helpful to your group, but you will be influential as well. The following section describes what constitutes good listening.

LISTENING DEFINED

Many people use *hearing* and *listening* as if they were synonyms, but we agree with Steil, Barker, and Watson that **listening** is a four-step process that begins with perceiving a message, then interpreting it, deciding what it means, and finally responding to it.[7] Such listening is not passive; it requires activity. Listening is behavior over which we can exert considerable control.

Most people do not listen well. The majority of participants in half-hour discussions we observed could not list the ideas proposed as possible solutions, the major issues discussed, or the decisions reached. When we ask students to paraphrase previous speaker's ideas, more than half the time they cannot do so (and we expect that college students are not much worse at such listening than are other people). In short, most of the time we listen rather badly. As respondents, we often give the speaker little or no overt feedback. This gives the speaker little opportunity to assess whether we understood the message as intended. This also implies what the speaker said wasn't worth a response.[8]

Effective listening requires that the listener hear what the speaker said, interpret it accurately, and respond appropriately. Usually, hearing what the speaker said presents little problem. Group members are accustomed to asking a member to repeat a statement they weren't able to hear. However, the interpretation and response steps can be tricky because of the nature of symbolic communication we discussed earlier. Different people mean different things with the same words and actions. Major factors that influence what words and actions mean to us include our culture, gender, age, sexual orientation, learning style, and personalities. We take a closer look at such diversity in small group interaction in Chapter 8.

Steps can be taken to become a more competent listener in small groups. In the next sections, we describe four listening preferences and several of the bad habits of poor listeners, as well as provide suggestions for improving your listening behavior.

LISTENING PREFERENCES

Over time and in a multitude of conversations we all develop listening preferences. When do you enjoy listening? When is listening difficult for you? Who are the people you like listening to? What do you focus on when you listen? Why do you choose to listen? Our preferences can greatly affect the quality of communication in a small group.

There are four general listening preferences: people-, action-, content-, and time-oriented.[9] No one preference is right or wrong; each has its advantages and disadvantages. Being an effective group member means identifying your own preference and those of the other members. It also means shifting your preference to meet the needs of the group.

People-oriented listeners are focused on how their listening behaviors affect relationships. These are members others go to when they want someone to listen. They are attentive and appear nonjudgmental. Their listening behaviors may include the use of *we* more often than *I,* and they incorporate emotional appeals into their discussions. For instance, they might be heard telling a human interest story to calm members who are upset. Showing concern for others is their priority, but people-oriented listeners can attend too much to others' moods and get distracted from the group's task.

The **action-oriented listener** is focused on the job at hand. Such listeners help the group stay on task by paying attention to the details and giving feedback about the goal and how the group may achieve it. They enjoy listening if material is presented in

3.2   Lake Area Wellness Council and Listening

Earlier you met three members of the Lake Area Wellness Council's executive committee: Norm, Rhea, and Sonya. Now let's meet two other members: Bob and Eric. Each of these members has his or her own listening preferences, some of which may be seen in the case study. Rhea is a people-oriented listener, Sonya is a content-oriented listener, and Norm is an action- and content-oriented listener. Bob is a time-oriented listener, and Eric avoids listening situations but is required to show up and vote. Norm and Rhea do not get along at most meetings, often arguing over who should be supported by the council. Norm thinks that Rhea gets too upset when others are upset, and Rhea thinks that Norm is overly critical. Sonya is close friends with Eric, who often votes with Sonya. Bob contributes to the council only when he has something worthwhile to say and does so in a very precise fashion. He gets along well with Rhea and Sonya.

Imagine you are a community member who is interested in bringing Dr. Jessica McGehee, a leading practitioner of holistic medicine, to the attention of the council. You would really like the council to sponsor a seminar with Dr. McGehee. You also know the council is low on funds due to the most recent expenditures, but Dr. McGehee will be in town and will be available. You know a generic presentation to the council will not work, so you decide to tailor your presentation to the listening preferences of the council.

1. Whom would you select as the target of your presentation and why?

2. What specific strategies would you use in your presentation to appeal to those you believe you need to convince most?

GLOSSARY

Content-Oriented Listener

A listener who prefers information from perceived credible sources and is drawn to analyzing the information she or he hears

Time-Oriented Listener

A listener who values time and is focused on efficient discussion

an organized fashion. Sometimes these listeners may appear overly critical, may tune out when the discussion seems aimless, and interrupt too much if the discussion gets off track.

The **content-oriented listener** is drawn to the highly credible source and enjoys analyzing the things she or he hears. These listeners dissect information and can show a group the many sides to an issue. At times, though, they can be seen as overly critical and intimidating. In addition, their listening preference slows the group's problem solving because they like to spend considerable time analyzing information. They also minimize nontechnical information such as anecdotes and devalue information from unknown sources.

The **time-oriented listener** is the member who sets meeting times, reminds members of their time constraints, and discourages wordy discussions. These members value time. They discourage discussion as the time nears for the meeting to end and grow impatient with the more creative, spontaneous activities in groups.

TABLE 3.2	**Listening Preferences**

PEOPLE-ORIENTED LISTENERS

Advantages:	Focus on relationships.
	Show concern for others.
	Inclusive and nonjudgmental.
Disadvantage:	Can become distracted by others' moods.
Example:	"Tell me more about how you would feel if we went ahead with that option."

ACTION-ORIENTED LISTENERS

Advantages:	Focus on the job.
	Help the group stay on task.
	Help the group stay organized.
Disadvantage:	May sacrifice relationships in favor of task.
Example:	"I know you're upset, but we have a lot of work to do so we'd better get down to business."

CONTENT-ORIENTED LISTENERS

Advantages:	Help the group analyze information.
	Look at issues from many sides.
Disadvantages:	Seem overly critical.
	Dismiss anecdotal or nonexpert information.
Example:	"We aren't ready to decide yet because we haven't really heard every side of the issue."

TIME-ORIENTED LISTENER

Advantages:	Help the group stick to schedule.
	Discourage rambling discussions.
Disadvantage:	Impatience with spontaneous discussion may stifle creativity.
Example:	"Let's make up a schedule so we know we can get done by our deadline."

No preference is the best. Our preferences are influenced by many factors, including the nature of the relationships among group members and time constraints. Each one has positive and negative tendencies that are summarized in Table 3.2. Use them productively and curtail the negative characteristics of each one. Do this by knowing your own and the others' preferences and encouraging the productive use of each preference.

HABITS OF POOR LISTENERS

The irony of being in a small group is that you spend more time listening, yet because you are in a small group, the pressure to listen is not as strongly felt as it is when you are interacting with only one other person.[10] The more people held accountable for the success of the group, the easier it is to get away with poor listening. We all develop poor listening habits, yet effective group discussion is built around recognizing the challenges of good listening. You can do that by recognizing the listening preferences of your group and understanding some common poor listening habits, summarized in Table 3.3.

Pseudolistening occurs when a listener fakes active listening by giving the speaker many of the signs that good listeners give, while actually thinking about something else. The pseudolistener nods, smiles, murmurs, and often looks the speaker in the eye. However, he or she may be daydreaming, thinking up an argument instead of trying to understand the speaker's perspective, or working on a personal problem. It is better to say you are uninterested than to pretend interest.

Silent arguing means the listener forms a quick judgment about the speaker's idea, rejects it without listening to the rest of what the speaker says, and then begins a silent mental search for arguments about what is wrong with the idea. We tend to listen to that which supports our previous beliefs and to ignore or tune out what contradicts them. You cannot listen well while silently arguing.

TABLE 3.3   Habits of Poor Listeners

Pseudolistening: Pretending to listen while thinking about something else or while daydreaming.

Silent arguing: Failing to understand what a speaker is saying, then mentally rehearsing objections to the misunderstood notion of the speaker's idea.

Assuming meaning: Interpreting the speaker's behavior by using the cultural rules appropriate for the listener.

Mind assault: Insistence by poor listeners that they understand better than the speaker what the speaker meant, even though the speaker protests.

Focusing on irrelevancies: Becoming distracted from a speaker's message by unimportant details such as dress, accent, physical appearance, or environmental distractions.

Sidetracking: Changing the topic because you weren't paying attention to the speaker; not connecting remarks to statements of the previous speaker.

Defensive responding: Failing to listen or failing to try to understand what a speaker is saying because poor listeners feel psychologically threatened by something the speaker said or did; responding with "chips on their shoulders."

Assuming meaning occurs when the receiver interprets what the sender said or did through the filter of the receiver's culture, then proceeds to make a judgment about the sender. For example, a Native American may answer a question from a European American without looking the questioner in the eye; the European American concludes that the Native American is hiding something or lying. However, looking down is a sign of respect in many Native American cultures. The European American's conclusion is in error because it is based on what middle-class European Americans do when answering questions. In other words, the Native American's behavior is being interpreted by the wrong set of rules, and a serious misunderstanding has occurred.

Mind assault, a stronger form of assuming meaning, is insisting that a speaker meant what the listener would have meant by a statement and continuing to insist on this meaning despite protests from the speaker.[11] For example, "I know what you really mean. You don't think our professor will object to our topic. You just want to do something else!" assumes that the listener knows better than the speaker what the speaker meant. This behavior attempts to dominate or reject the speaker. Instead, good listeners try to understand another as that person wants to be understood, and only then evaluate the other's ideas and motives.

Focusing on irrelevancies occurs when a listener pays attention to something other than what the speaker is saying. Some people pay so much attention to dress, word choices, grammar, face or body details, accent or dialect, or things in the environment that they have little energy to give to the ideas of a speaker. For example, one of our students mispronounced a word during a group presentation. A faculty member smirked and rolled her eyes. She didn't listen to another word the student said, even though the information was valuable, because she had focused on the speaking mistake the student had made. If you are guilty of this bad habit, constantly remind yourself to concentrate on understanding the speaker and not being distracted.

Sidetracking takes several forms, all of which result in going off on a tangent. The listener makes a statement that is not connected to what was previously said, thus sidetracking the discussion by starting a new topic. In the student discussions David Berg analyzed, the topic was switched on the average of about every minute.[12] The following example illustrates sidetracking by switching issues, thereby giving irrelevant responses to previous remarks:

Pete: We can use our time better if we split up the work. Why don't we each pick the section we want to research?

Jean: Did any of you guys happen to see *Pearl Harbor* last weekend? [a sidetrack]

Defensive responding is likely to occur when a listener perceives a threat from another's remark—someone's "hot button" has been pushed. For example, you may be sensitive to attempts of others to control or dominate what you do (shown in how the message is expressed), so, when Tony says, "Get me a Coke while you are at the machine," you reply, "Get your own blankety-blank drink!" People who listen and respond defensively usually quit trying to understand the other's point of view and thus may miss important qualifications or statements that clarify the speaker's meaning. It is especially important to guard against defensive responses when highly emotive words such as *abortion, right to life, gun control, welfare state,* and *liberal* are used. When you feel yourself getting tense and emotionally aroused, sit back, take a deep breath, and try to para-phrase what the other meant before you express either support or opposition. That will keep you from listening or responding defensively.

In all the bad listening habits, the listener is not focusing attention on the ideas of the speaker but on something else—a physical characteristic, a habit of speech, a personal belief, a different topic, a personal definition of a symbol, a private relationship with the speaker, a personally held value, or how the message was expressed. Where and how to focus attention are consistent problems for many, including those who are generally good listeners in other contexts.

LISTENING ACTIVELY

Listening is active, not passive, behavior. Listening requires as much concentration as speaking does. When you pay close attention in an effort to understand what another means, your heart speeds up as your metabolism rate rises. In contrast, heart rates of pas-sive listeners who take no personal responsibility for understanding another slow down. Active listening is partly a matter of choosing to focus on the other and of selecting what parts of a message to focus on and try to recall.

A good test for **active listening** is to paraphrase (put in your own words) what you think the other person meant. Merely repeating another's words, like a parrot, does not demonstrate that you understood. An accurate paraphrase requires the listener to process the information cognitively. When you paraphrase what you thought the speaker said or the relational message you inferred from how it was expressed, you give the speaker a basis for deciding whether or not you understood the original message ad-equately or whether you missed or distorted parts of it. The original speaker, after hear-ing the paraphrase, should accept it if it is accurate or correct the parts that were dis-torted or omitted, then ask you to try paraphrasing again. Only when the original speaker is completely satisfied that you have understood adequately should you proceed to agree, disagree, elaborate, or change topics. Here is a bit of dialogue that illustrates active listening:

Karla:	Medical costs are incredibly high. On the average, it costs about $1,500 per day in the hospital. No wonder 37 percent of our citizens lack hospital insurance! Too many people are making too much money off the illnesses of others. We gotta stop that!
Jeannie:	You're saying that the reason so many people lack hospital insurance is that hospital costs are high, and they are so high because a lot of people are paid too much in the health care business. Is that right? [Jeannie attempts to paraphrase Karla's statement to understand what Karla meant, especially to clarify the content of her reasoning.]
Karla:	Well, basically, but I really don't mean people don't have insurance because the hospital costs so much, but because they can't afford it. That may be partly because it costs a lot for the insurance—like $350 a month for a young husband and wife with no kids—and partly because the insurance companies have to pay such high hospital and other medical bills. [Karla corrects the paraphrase and clarifies her own reasoning.]

GLOSSARY

Active Listening

Listening first to understand another's message before critically judging the message

Jeannie: Now let's see if I understand your thinking: 37 percent of our citizens lack hospital insurance because they feel they can't afford it. Part of the reason they can't afford it is that high medical costs have made premiums very high, like $200 a month for a young person. And a lot of people are making more money than you think they should out of the illnesses of others. [Jeannie's second attempt at paraphrasing Karla's statements.]

Karla: Right. [Karla's confirmation of second paraphrase as accurate.]

Jeannie: I partly agree and partly disagree. I think . . . [The paraphrase accepted, Jeannie now begins to explain her position on the issue about why so many people lack hospital insurance.]

Active listeners confirm their understanding *before* they state evaluations. Then, confident of what the speaker meant, active listeners evaluate what they have understood. They may respond by agreeing or disagreeing, saying that the idea is irrelevant to the issue being discussed, that it is logically unsound, that there is no evidence to support it, and so on. In the above example, the group members are focused on clarifying the content of their messages. They could have also been focused on their interpretations of how the ideas were expressed. For instance, if Jeannie expressed herself as someone who felt superior to the others, they may have asked if she was trying to tell them what to think or just thinking aloud with peers.

One effect of active listening is that the discussion slows. Most of us are our own best listeners—we like to talk and, given half a chance, we will. We may become impatient, not taking time to paraphrase even when we should. You should listen actively all the time but paraphrase only part of the time—when a controversial issue is being discussed, when you can see some possibility that the speaker has a different meaning from what you think, when you are confused by what the speaker has said, and when there has been a lot of topic switching or misunderstanding. Be on guard against pseudolistening. If you realize you didn't really listen, apologize and ask for a restatement.

FOCUSED LISTENING

Many studies show that most listeners remember only half of new information immediately after a lecture. In a couple of days people have forgotten at least half of what they remembered at first. The question is, How can you learn to recall selectively?

Focused listening means listening so you can select the main points you want to recall later and let the nonessential points go. It is associated with action- and content-oriented listener preferences. In a meeting, it may entail writing notes so you can later recall what occurred. Recall is important because a problem-solving discussion can go on over a long time. For example, a group of security experts trying to improve procedures for detecting terrorist activities on airplanes would need many meetings to report and interpret their continuing research. But even in single-meeting discussions, many participants cannot summarize the issues raised, the important information presented, all decisions reached, and assignments made. This lack of functional group memory wastes time.

Two things can improve a group's memory and thereby its functioning. The first is focused listening; the second is carefully maintained reports (i.e., minutes) of all group meetings. Focused listening means you focus on the major points of the discussion, but not all the details of examples, stories, statistics, and comparisons. The skilled listener

GLOSSARY

Focused Listening

Listening that involves concentrating on relevant main ideas for later recall

3.3   Poor Listening Habits and Misunderstandings

APPLY NOW

Reconstruct the Lake Area Wellness Council's meeting. Your agenda item is the discussion of whether or not to sponsor a seminar featuring Chief Robert, a Cherokee medicine man and prominent local leader. Get together with six other members of the class to role-play council members. Before your discussion, hand out envelopes to each member. Four of the envelopes will contain a description of one poor listening habit (pseudolistening, silent arguing, assuming meaning, mind raping, focusing on irrelevancies, and sidetracking). The other three envelopes will instruct the member to practice active, focused listening. Allow yourselves to role-play the meeting for about 25 minutes. Ask your classmates to watch the meeting and take notes on the listening behaviors. After the meeting discuss how the poor habits were displayed and their impact on the discussion.

1. Were any behaviors particularly destructive? Why?

2. How well were the members practicing active, focused listening, and did they reduce the effects of the poor habits? How typical are some of these poor habits?

3. How was the role-play of the meeting different from a real meeting?

keeps the major issue of the moment in mind, notes and points out when someone gets off the issue, and can readily summarize the major arguments or positions on the issue. Once the issue has been settled, this listener can state the decision and the reasons for it—that is what the listener will remember, not all the specific facts, anecdotes, or positions taken by various individuals as they worked toward agreement. Focused listeners jot down brief notes about all the points they want to recall and run brief mental summaries such as the following:

> Let's see, now. We decided that there are likely to be more and more injuries of pedestrians in front of campus unless something is done to prevent them. An unacceptably high accident rate has been going on for years. We considered four options: added crosswalks, underground crossing, overhead crossing, and overhead crossing with pedestrian barriers in the median. We decided that an overhead crossing with barriers would be effective, affordable, and acceptable to both campus and city officials.

Practicing such mental summaries during a lull in discussion will greatly sharpen your skill in focused listening. So will volunteering to write your group's reports and minutes.

SUMMARY

■ Communication is the process by which we create, receive, interpret, and respond to signals from others; this makes communication an ongoing, transactional, sender-and-receiver-oriented phenomenon for which every group member is responsible.

■ Signs have a natural connection with what they represent, but symbols, including words, are arbitrary, which makes perfect understanding among group members impossible.

■ Listening involves hearing a message, interpreting it, deciding what it means, and responding; group members, who typically display a number of bad listening habits, need to improve this skill the most.

■ Active listening, especially paraphrasing, helps members understand others more clearly; focused listening helps members keep track of important points during a discussion.

EXERCISES

1. This exercise is designed to help you distinguish between viewing communication as one-way, linear communication or as transactional communication. Divide into two large groups. Turn to the Karla and Jeannie dialogue in the text. One group should examine the dialogue from a linear approach to communication. The other group should examine it from the transactional approach. Each group can focus on the following questions:

   a. When does communication occur in the dialogue?

   b. What is the message in this dialogue? Where does the message come from?

   c. Who is responsible for clarifying the meaning of the message? How is clarity created in this dialogue?

   d. Who is the communicator and who is the listener?

   With your classmates discuss how different the answers are to these questions depending on the approach used to answer the questions. Remember, although the approach changed how the communication/dialogue was understood, the communication/dialogue did not change.

2. Recall three recent conversations you have had. (If you are taking part in a major group project think about three recent conversations in your group meetings.) For each conversation write down whom the conversation was with, what you talked about, how well you listened (on a scale of 1 [not well at all] to 10 [very well]), and what some of the reasons were for your good or poor listening (e.g., time of day, boring topic, preoccupied with something else). During class discussion, look for factors common to good and poor listening.

   (If you apply this exercise to your group project, create a list of steps you will take to improve your listening in your next meetings.)

3. This exercise is designed to help you apply and practice active listening. Divide into groups of five or six members. Select a controversial topic and practice active listening as you discuss the topic. Remember that paraphrasing is not simply restating the previous remarks. Each group should use the following rules:

   a. A discussant may not have the floor or add anything to the conversation until she or he paraphrases what the previous speaker has said to that speaker's satisfaction.

b. If the paraphrase is not accepted, the discussant may try again until the speaker accepts the paraphrase.

c. Have one member of the group keep track of the number of times paraphrases were accepted or rejected. Each attempt should be recorded.

After the activity, discuss the difficulties encountered in active listening. Look for the benefits of paraphrasing and the problems that may be encountered. Discuss why it may be so hard for group members to understand others before contributing to the discussion.

 Go to **www.mhhe.com/adamsgalanes** and **www.mhhe.com/groups** for Self-Quizzes and weblinks.

KEY TERMS and CONCEPTS

Action-Oriented Listener	Focused Listening	Sidetracking
Active Listening	Focusing on Irrelevancies	Sign
Assuming Meaning	Listening	Silent Arguing
Communication	Mind Raping	Symbol
Content Dimension	People-Oriented Listener	Time-Oriented Listener
Content-Oriented Listener	Pseudolistening	Transactional
Defensive Responding	Relational Dimension	

 www.mhhe.com/adamsgalanes
Use the flashcards and crossword puzzles on the Online Learning Center to further your knowledge of these key terms.

Verbal and Nonverbal Messages

After reading this chapter you should be able to:

1. Define the concept *message*.

2. Describe structuration theory and explain its relevance to small group communication.

3. List and explain five ways to use language appropriately in small group interaction.

4. Explain how to use abstract words effectively.

5. Describe how group members can organize their remarks.

6. Compare and contrast questions of information, interpretation, value, policy, action, procedure, and relationship.

7. Explain how best to phrase questions in small group interaction.

8. Describe the principles of nonverbal communication.

9. List and explain the functions of nonverbal signals.

10. Discuss the significance of the major categories of nonverbal signals to small group communication.

The Search for the New Library Dean

It was the first meeting of the committee charged with managing the search process for a new library dean at Southwest Missouri State University (SMSU), where Gloria teaches. As was customary, there was a student representative on this search committee in addition to faculty members, administrators, and library staff. Gloria chaired this committee and used this organizational meeting to let people talk in an unstructured way about what they wanted in a new library dean.

The committee discussed diversity issues and brainstormed ways that qualified minorities and women could be recruited to apply for the dean's position. Several members talked about what they perceived as a general need to increase diversity on campus because of the very small percentage of minority and international students and administrators currently at SMSU. Suddenly Peter, the student, said, "I don't think that's a big issue because our campus is already very diverse." Simultaneously, two faculty members and one administrator exclaimed, "What?"

Feeling somewhat attacked, Peter became defensive and the meeting threatened to degenerate into a "Yes, it is/No, it isn't" argument. When one member encouraged Peter to explain what he meant, he said, quite reasonably, that the only other campus he had ever visited was a small, church-related school in Tennessee that had an even more homogeneous student population, with a smaller percentage of minority students, than SMSU. The committee members readily agreed that, from Peter's perspective, the SMSU campus was more diverse than his comparison school. Peter, in turn, agreed that the SMSU campus was less diverse than the schools, such as UCLA, Ohio State, and University of Maryland, the other committee members were using for comparison.

This brief episode ended well and set the stage for the rest of the committee's meetings, but it could just as easily have alienated Peter and caused the faculty and administrative members to tune him out.

This story, so typical of many small group discussions, illustrates several important points discussed in this chapter. First, many words can be taken in several different ways. For instance, Peter initially responded defensively to the word *what*. He heard the word *what* as meaning, "What on earth are you saying, calling this a diverse campus?" In fact, that is what two of the members *did* mean when they said *what.* However, the third member, as she explained later, simply hadn't heard Peter, so she said, "What?" as a question, meaning, "Could you please repeat what you said?" Second, verbal and nonverbal signals together contribute to our interpretation of what words mean. For example, how did Peter correctly interpret that two of the committee members intended to challenge his opinion about campus diversity? Probably because of the sharp, disbelieving tone of voice they used and the fact that they both whipped their heads around to look at him when they said it. Peter felt attacked because, in a way, he *was* attacked. In another example, the popular phrase "waazzzup?" only makes sense in how the phrase "What's up?" is said and its use in the appropriate context. Finally, this dean search committee story illustrates the most basic principle of all—*communication creates a group.* The verbal and nonverbal messages all group members send create the working atmosphere in the group. The type of verbal and nonverbal messages members allow determines whether the group will be cooperative or hostile, will think carefully or rush to judgment. In our story, members' basic goodwill and effective listening skills were able to undo the potential harm done by their reaction to Peter's comment. The group went on to be highly productive, cooperative, and cohesive—and it was the members' communication behaviors that made this happen.

In this chapter, we will focus on messages group members exchange and the verbal and nonverbal components of these messages. This chapter examines the complexities of group messages and thus helps improve your sending and interpreting of messages in a group.

Creating Messages in a Small Group

A **message** is any set of signals that is interpreted as a whole by a receiver or receivers.[1] Messages may be entirely nonverbal or a mixture of verbal and nonverbal signs. For instance, a nod of the head may be interpreted as a message of agreement or disagreement. If a member expresses her doubts about a proposal while she simultaneously frowns and begins to speak louder and faster, others will probably see these behaviors collectively as disagreement.

In this chapter we first explain how communication structures and maintains a group. We then look at the impact of both verbal and nonverbal messages in the group's face-to-face interaction.

How Communication Structures the Small Group

We said earlier that communication, the verbal and nonverbal messages members exchange, is the essential throughput process within a small group. The way members create and maintain this exchange of messages is called **structuration.** The theory of structuration, applied to small group communication by Marshall Scott Poole, David

Siebold, and Robert McPhee, is complex, but the main point is this: verbal and nonverbal communication among members creates the group norms and operating procedures and maintains them once they are established.[2]

The theory contains three important assumptions. First, group members do not come to a group with a clean slate about how to behave. They have been taught what is appropriate by their general culture, by their participation in other groups, and by the organizations they belong to. For example, the faculty and administrative culture at SMSU encourages people to treat each other politely and with respect. Thus, when members of the library search committee realized that Peter felt attacked, they were motivated to undo the harm they believe they had created.

Second, although people pick up rules and standards for behavior from the general culture, there is no law that forces them to follow those rules. Individuals may choose to ignore norms and rules for behavior. For instance, even if the library search committee members knew Peter felt attacked and that norms of politeness required them to try to heal the breach, they could have decided just as easily that his opinion didn't matter: "Well, he's just a student. He hasn't seen any of the world, so who cares what he thinks."

4.1   The Symbolic Nature of Emoticons

MEDIA AND TECHNOLOGY

Most computer-mediated communication is text based. That is, communication with other people takes place by typing messages on a computer keyboard. Because CMC relies on text for meaning, much emotional content normally expressed nonverbally (e.g. happiness, sadness, confusion, etc.) is not present in CMC interactions.

To adapt to the CMC medium, Internet users have developed a symbolic code to express emoticon. Known as "emoticons," certain combinations of characters are used to indicate relational messages in e-mails, online chats, bulletin board messages, and other CMC channels. Examples of emoticons include:

:) A basic smiley face

;) A smiley face with a "wink." Used to indicate playfulness or sarcasm.

:') A smiley face indicating "I'm so happy I'm crying."

The popularity of emoticons has led to other text-based symbols finding their way into the common written vocabulary of Internet users. For examples, LOL means "I **L**aughed **O**ut **L**oud at what you wrote." And IMHO means "**I**n **M**y **H**umble **O**pinion," which is often used to precede a controversial opinion. The following websites provide dictionaries of emoticons and other text symbols used in CMC:

http://members.aol.com/bearpage/smileys.htm
http://www.techdictionary.com/chat.html

How do you think emoticons and other online lingo illustrate the notion of structuration discussed in this chapter?

Go to **www.mhhe.com/adamsgalanes** for additional weblink activities.

The third important assumption of structuration theory is that the group is never finally created; instead, it constantly re-creates itself through communication so that it is always in a state of becoming. That suggests that change usually happens incrementally. The library committee's meeting where Peter felt attacked was the committee's first meeting, but what if the meeting had been the 10th meeting, with the norm of attacking members well established? Because group members would have been more set in their communicative ways, it would have been much harder (although not impossible) to move the group to a respectful path. That's what structuration is all about—how communication creates and maintains the group over time.

We especially like the communicative focus of the theory of structuration; it reminds us to look at members' communicative behavior—what they say and do in the group. For instance, Peter didn't feel attacked because he had a paranoid personality. He felt attacked because of the communicative behavior of the other members. Similarly, the other members attempted to rebuild bridges with Peter when they said things such as, "I'm sorry, Peter; I didn't mean to sound so sharp. Why do you think SMSU has a lot of diversity? Tell us about the other campus you visited." Again, it was the communicative behavior that changed a developing norm into a more productive one. We now turn to a discussion of the verbal communication the language group members use.

Using Language to Help the Group Progress

Language, as we explained in Chapter 3, is symbolic. Human language consists of symbols, verbal and nonverbal, and rules for using them. The verbal code is the vocabulary, or the set of words, available to the person who uses the language. In print, nonverbal elements include punctuation marks, underlining, CAPITALIZATION, **boldfacing,** and s p a c i n g. The rules are the spoken and unspoken guidelines for arranging words: what to capitalize, how to space, where to place punctuation marks, and so on. Collectively, these are the rules of syntax and grammar. Both the codes and rules vary according to social contexts; communication rules differ for an on-line chat group, a formal meeting of a city council, a Jamaican bobsled team, or a church building committee. Suggestions for using language effectively are detailed in the following section and summarized in Table 4.1. The suggestions in the table and the discussion that follows are appropriate generally for most task groups in the United States. As we will note in Chapter 8, however, different rules apply in different cultures.

FOLLOW THE RULES

Because different groups and cultures have different rules for communicating, you will increase your chances of being accepted and understood if you follow the rules for the groups you are participating in. For example, some academic groups are formal: Members address each other by title (e.g., Dr. Adams or Ms. Galanes) and use many abstract words with a complex sentence structure. However, these rules would be inappropriate in a self-managed work team in an auto factory, where concrete language with a clear and concise sentence structure is more effective. In some groups, using *ain't* and *he don't* might be acceptable; in others, it would not. Be aware of and adapt to appropriate standards of behavior *for the particular group.* For example, Rick Ayers' communication arts and sciences class at Berkeley High School in California has created its own slang dictionary.[3] Each entry in the dictionary contains its etymological source, a pronunciation key, and a sen-

TABLE 4.1	**Use Language Appropriately to Help the Group Progress**

FOLLOW THE RULES OF STANDARD ENGLISH
- Use standard sentence structure and vocabulary.

- Use correct grammar.

- Avoid jargon, excess slang, and profanity.

ADJUST TO THE SYMBOLIC NATURE OF LANGUAGE
- Guard against bypassing.

- Be as precise and concrete as possible (e.g., an *adjustable crescent wrench* instead of a *tool*).

- Give specific examples of what you mean when you have to use an abstract term, or use synonyms.

USE EMOTIVE WORDS CAUTIOUSLY
- Recognize words that are likely to trigger strong emotional responses in others (e.g., *chick, pig*) and substitute with neutral words (e.g., *woman, police officer*).

- Never use name-calling.

ORGANIZE YOUR REMARKS AND THE GROUP'S DISCUSSION PROCESS
- Relate your statement to the preceding statement.

- Make one point at a time, not a multipoint speech.

- State your case directly and concisely.

- Keep yourself and other members on the topic.

BE SURE THE DISCUSSION QUESTION IS CLEAR AND APPROPRIATE
- Use open-ended questions instead of either–or ones.

- Word questions clearly and concretely.

- Don't give the answer in the question.

- Make sure all group members know what question or issue is being discussed.

tence with the entry—the students have laid out the word or phrase and the rules for its use. "Off the hook" was appropriate for 1999, "off the heazie" for 2000, and now the phrase is "off the hizzle." The purpose of this slang dictionary project was to give students an opportunity to use their own rich home language as a viable avenue for creativity.

Even as we advise this, however, we note that many of the secondary groups you participate in will take place in the mainstream of the U.S. business, professional, and educational communities. In such cases, you are well-advised to conform to the vocabulary and grammar rules of standard English. This will help other people understand you and increase your influence because numerous studies have shown that nonstandard dialects and usage lower the credibility of speakers with a variety of listeners. As teacher Rick Ayers recognized, "I want to make them aware of their brilliance, that the way they speak is not wrong, it's just another form of discourse . . . The trick is teaching them how to translate it into standard English when they need to."[4]

4.1   When to Code Switch and When Not to?

ETHICAL DILEMMA

We have proposed the necessity of adopting to the different rules for communication, or code switching, when the context of the social system changes. A characteristic of communication competence is being aware that different groups use different rules of communicating and changing to meet the expectations and obligations of those different groups. However, the various ways we use language to communicate is highly personal and often resistant to change.

1. When you move from group to group how easily do you adopt the rules of communicating in that group?

2. Are there times when your personal way of communicating should never be given up?

3. Are there appropriate ways of blending both your own personal style and that of the group?

4. Is adapting to the rules of communicating in a particular group a violation of personal language use?

ADJUST TO THE SYMBOLIC NATURE OF LANGUAGE

People who use language effectively in group discussions are keenly aware of its symbolic nature. They realize that words do not have meanings in and of themselves, so they strive to express their ideas in words likely to evoke similar meanings in listeners.

As listeners, they try to interpret accurately by asking themselves, "What does the speaker mean?" rather than, "What do those words mean?" or "What would I mean if I said that?" They are on guard against **bypassing,** in which two or more people have different meanings for a word but do not realize it. Bypassing can lead either to a false agreement or to the perception that a disagreement exists when it really doesn't. For example, members of a faculty group agreed to meet in the Academic Affairs Conference Room. However, there were two conference rooms belonging to Academic Affairs, on two different floors of the same building, and part of the group showed up in each place. No one had bothered to ask, "Do you mean the one on the third floor or the one on the second floor?" Finally, someone thought of that and found the other group members on the second floor. The words had been the same, but the meanings the members gave to the words were different.

Words vary from highly concrete to highly abstract. For example, the terms in the following list become more abstract (more vague) as you proceed down the list:

Maria Thomas

public relations major

"*Can you cut it a little finer, Mergeson, than 'umpteen'?*"

Quantify precisely whenever you can. (© The New Yorker Collection; 1985 Donald Reilly from cartoonbank.com. All Rights Reserved.)

California State University, Fresno student

college student

female

young person

human

Efficient communicators know that many words, especially abstract ones, will be interpreted differently by different people. The most concrete forms are those that refer to one and only one thing: *Dr. Galanes' desk, Lora Croft of Tomb Raider* or *Golden Retriever number PD736251.* However, abstract words and phrases such as *liberal, effective, spiritual democracy,* and *love* are highly ambiguous and likely to be understood quite differently by different group members.

The level of abstractness matters a lot during discussions. With concrete terms, little misunderstanding will occur, but confusion can be rampant when highly abstract words are used. Highly abstract statements (such as "Don't you think this is a matter of historical dialecticism?") consistently disrupt discussions among college students, and the amount of confusion and disarray increases as the statements are made more abstract.[5]

Using abstract words is OK; in fact, having a meaningful discussion without them would be impossible. Many of the ideas group members discuss must include fairly abstract words such as *criteria, equal opportunity, cost effective,* and *fair.* In addition, we sometimes may choose to be ambiguous in an effort to allow for multiple interpretations while exploring an idea. However, you can take steps to help make your remarks more specific and thus clearer. First, speak as concretely as possible to express what you mean. Don't use jargon to show off. Help others understand you by referring to "an adjustable crescent wrench" instead of a "tool," or to "Word 2000" instead of "a word processing program."

Second, whenever you use a highly abstract term that may be problematic, use concrete examples of what you mean—for instance, "He was a really domineering chair [abstract concept]. He decided, by himself, when the group would meet, what would and would not be on the agenda, who could and could not speak at the meetings, and what the committee should recommend to the president of the fraternity" [concrete examples of the abstract idea of *domineering*].

Third, define highly abstract terms by using synonyms or descriptive terms or by explaining an operation the term refers to. Thus, you might define *drunk driving* as "having a level of .08 percent alcohol in the blood as measured immediately after driving by a machine called a Breathalyzer," which is the DWI definition used in many states. This definition combines both a procedure (i.e., measured by a Breathalyzer) and precise quantification for the term (i.e., .08 percent alcohol in the blood).

Fourth, quantify when possible. Frequently, groups use relative terms for comparisons when precise quantification is possible. For instance, instead of saying, "The chances of developing lung cancer are *higher* [a relative term] if you smoke a pack of cigarettes a day than if you don't smoke," you can state quite precisely what the increase in percentage of people developing lung cancer will be.

Listeners are also responsible for helping to clarify group messages. As a listener you can ask speakers who use highly abstract language to quantify, give examples, or define their terms with less abstract language. You can paraphrase in more concrete terms, then ask the speaker to accept or revise the paraphrase. This will help you interpret the speaker's meaning more accurately.

USE EMOTIVE WORDS CAUTIOUSLY

Emotive words are terms that call forth strong feelings. Often these are called *trigger words* because they evoke almost instantaneous emotional responses that could interfere with good listening.

4.2   What Do You Do When Emotive Words Are Offensive?

For more information on defining words with precision, go to the on-line learning center.

ETHICAL DILEMMA

Two African-American members of your group refer to each other as "nigga" when they greet each other at the beginning of group meetings.[6] You and one other member find the use of the term highly offensive and do not believe any person, no matter her or his color, should use the term. One other member really does not care and does not see the point in making a big deal out of it.

This racial epithet is a highly emotive trigger word in the American culture, and people weigh in with all sorts of opinions on its use. As a group what do you do? How would you discuss this issue? When do the references in personal member greetings become an issue for a group? What new rules might this group create to allow for emotive words yet avoid the consequences of their use?

GLOSSARY

Emotive Words

Words that trigger strong emotional responses

"Sorry, Chief, but of course I didn't mean 'bimbo' in the pejorative sense."

Don't use trigger words that may offend others. (© The New Yorker Collection; 1987 Lee Lorenz from cartoonbank.com. All Rights Reserved.)

For instance, for some people, *feminist* conjures up a very negative image of a bra-burning woman who hates men and is destroying the American family because of her selfish goals. Among the worst trigger words are sexist terms and racial epithets (such as *wet back, feminazi, faggot*). Recall the highly controversial use of *nigger* in the televised O. J. Simpson murder trial. Again, we are calling attention to the importance of monitoring your linguistic choices in group interaction. The nature of your communication is not only reflective of the kind of communicative climate in your group but, as we pointed out earlier, it also re-creates that climate over the course of your group's time together.

You can improve the quality of thinking during group discussions by avoiding such words yourself and suggesting alternatives when someone else uses one of them. Consider the following two lists. The first has negative emotive terms; the second, neutral ones that denote the same things.

Negative	Neutral or positive
broad	woman
jock	athlete
Ay-rab	Arab
Jew-them-down	negotiate or haggle
ree-tard	Down's syndrome
hillbilly	native of the Ozarks
bonehead	remedial

"*That's bass with broccoli and mushrooms. Stop calling it animal, vegetable, and fungus.*"

What you call it does make a difference. (© The New Yorker Collection; 1985 Warren Miller from cartoonbank.com. All Rights Reserved.)

If someone said to you, "He's just a career politician from a podunk state, where most of the people sign X on their welfare checks; why should I vote for him for president?" you could paraphrase as follows: "So you think he would not be a good president because he has held many elected offices and is from a small state with a high illiteracy rate?" This will defuse the trigger words so that the group can begin a more objective, less emotional evaluation of the person's qualifications.

ORGANIZE REMARKS

Organization of the discussion in general and of your own remarks in particular is affected by what you say and how you say it. Frequently, discussions jump almost aimlessly from topic to topic, with no one responding to prior comments. It is often hard to tell exactly what issue or question a speaker is addressing, or even what the point is of some remarks. Good organization can do a lot to overcome these communication problems.

Consider the following discussion of a group of students planning publicity for an upcoming career day seminar:

Lori:	OK, the seminar is planned, so now it's time to start working on the publicity. Any ideas?
Deidre:	We forgot to include a session on portfolios.
Tony:	One of the things we could do is send a memo to all the people in the dorms. That worked well last time.
Chris:	I know someone who would do a great job with portfolios, and I'll be glad to call her.

Kevin: I think a memo is a really tacky idea, and we ought to do something more professional.

Lori: I don't like memos either. I'd be happy if we didn't do one.

It's hard to tell from that discussion who is responding to what question, or even exactly what is meant. Let's help the individuals organize their remarks so the discussion is more organized as a *group* process:

Lori: OK, the seminar has been planned, so now it's time to start working on publicity. What ideas do you have for how we could promote the career day seminar? [Not a big change here, but Lori's question to the group is more focused than before.]

Deidre: Lori, could we postpone our discussion of publicity? I'd like to talk first about something we overlooked in the planning. We forgot to schedule a portfolio session. [First, Deidre responds directly to Lori and Lori's question before suggesting a different initial topic.]

Lori: That's a good idea, Deidre. OK, guys, let's spend time making sure the plans are finalized before we talk about publicity. What did you mean by a portfolio session? [Direct response to Deidre, acknowledgment of the legitimacy of her request to postpone discussion of publicity and request for clarification]

Deidre: That was the session where someone showed us how to put together a public relations portfolio so that when we apply for jobs we'll be able to show people what kinds of assignments we've completed. It's like a résumé with specific examples of your work. [Direct clarification response from Deidre]

Lori: You're right; we need that. Big oversight. Glad you thought of it. [Affirming Deidre's good thinking on behalf of the group's project]

Tony: One thing we could do is send a memo to all the people who live in the dorms to let them know about the seminar. [This remark seems to be about publicity and does not appear to respond directly to the portfolio topic.]

Chris: That might be a good idea, Tony, but I'm not sure we're ready to go on to that yet. Were we finished with the portfolio session planning? [Chris doesn't ignore Tony or put him down, but he does help the group keep focused on the topic, and he makes it a group issue by using we.]

Tony: Sorry! I thought we were ready to move on. What do we need to do yet with portfolios? [Apology and direct acknowledgment of the topic under discussion]

Chris: Well, for one thing, we need to figure out who would be a good person to handle that session. [Direct response to Tony and moves the discussion forward]

Kevin: I know someone at Walker, Beard, and Korma Public Relations. I'll call and see if she's available, and, if she isn't, maybe she can suggest somebody else. [Direct response to Chris]

Lori:	OK, Kevin, do I understand you right? You'll take care of getting someone to handle the portfolio session and let us know who that is by next week? [Lori has detected an ambiguity in Kevin's earlier remark ("maybe she can suggest somebody else"), so she helps him clarify.]
Kevin:	Yes. [Direct answer clears up the ambiguity.]
Lori:	OK, Kevin will find someone to handle the portfolio sessions. Now, are we ready to turn to publicity? [Group members nod.] That's great. What ideas do we have for publicizing career day?

In the second version, each comment begins with confirmation of the prior speaker, often using the other member's name. No one switches topics abruptly. Statements are right to the point. In almost all cases, the speaker stays with one point. The following is a list of guidelines to facilitate coherent, orderly, and clear discussion:

1. **Relate your statement to the preceding statement.** Sometimes this will have to be done explicitly in a statement; sometimes it can be done with a word or phrase (e.g., Lori—"That's a good idea"; Tony—"Sorry.")

2. **State one point, not give a multipoint speech.** If you talk about two or more issues, the discussion is likely to go off track because no one can predict which issue the next speaker will pick up on, even if she responds directly to your remarks. The one major exception to this rule occurs when you present an initial description of a problem or make a planned report that has more than one point. In that case, preparing a handout that includes the main findings, facts, statistics, quotations, formulas, and so on, is a good idea.

3. **State the point as directly, concretely, and concisely as possible.** In the dominant culture of the United States, simple declarative sentences are preferable to flowery language and emotive terms. Phrases such as "My point is that . . ." and "This is the idea: . . ." may help focus listeners.

MAKE SURE THE DISCUSSION QUESTION IS CLEAR AND APPROPRIATE

Verbal exchanges among members are about an issue or a point that has not yet been settled or decided on by the group. It may be a matter of controversy or just a matter of information still under discussion. During effective discussions, all members should be able to state the **discussion question,** the central question a group must answer.

Unfortunately, group members often cannot do this. A careful analysis of remarks will show that different members are attempting to answer different questions at the same time. For example, Mary may be trying to evaluate a suggestion Thuy has proposed—to solve the lack of parking spaces on campus—while Sonya is explaining how student parking fees are being spent and LaShonda is presenting her proposal to solve the parking problem. This is certainly a sign of poor listening and disorganized discussion. The result is the kind of confused topic switching described earlier.

Establishing the most effective question is crucial and can determine whether the group produces a good or poor solution. For example, consider the following two discussion

---

GLOSSARY

Discussion Question

The main question or issue that a group must answer

questions: *How can we raise money to build another classroom building?* versus *How can we relieve the overcrowding in classrooms?* The first question focuses on an already-decided solution, which may or may not be the best solution to the problem. The second focuses on the problem (overcrowding) without biasing the solution in advance. Building more classrooms may work, but perhaps the problems are due to poor scheduling of existing facilities. Maybe holding classes at off-campus locations such as shopping centers, factories, and offices throughout the city would be more effective in reducing the overcrowding as well as provide better service to students. However, these options will never be discovered if the group is determined to solve the problem by building more classrooms. Thus, how a group states its discussion question influences the entire progress of the group's discussion. As an input, it has a far-reaching effect on the system's throughput process and its subsequent output.

Anytime you feel confused about what is going on during small group meetings, ask yourself or the group what question is being discussed. Get an answer to that question before you proceed, and help the entire group become oriented toward the same goal at the same moment. When you ask a question, be sure the type of answer you seek is clear from the phrasing of the question. Seven types of questions, classified on the basis of the type of response requested, with examples of each type are described in Table 4.2. These examples should help you appreciate the number of different types of questions you have to choose from and their functions or the kind of information they can solicit from other members.

When you reply to a question, be sure you give the kind of response sought by the questioner. The following are a few guidelines to help you phrase questions that focus and facilitate group interaction.

1. **Unless the group has already narrowed a list of alternatives to two, avoid either–or questions.**

   Usually these grossly oversimplify the issue by treating questions of interpretation, value, or policy as if there were only two legitimate answers instead of a wide range. In the list that follows, the first question of each pair is poorly worded in either–or terms; the second version is worded as a matter of degree:

   Is this a fair way to treat our secretary? (Implied is a yes or no answer.)

   How fair will this be to the secretary?

   Shall we ship this by Federal Express or UPS? (Provides only two options)

   How shall we ship this package?

   Instead of either–or questions, use open-ended discussion questions.

   Leave room for any sort of appropriate response, not just a few responses like the kind supplied in multiple-choice tests.

2. **Word questions as concretely as possible.**

   Double-barreled questions that combine two questions in one are confusing. For example, "Do you think we should increase funding to the public schools by instituting casino gambling in the state?" is a double-barreled question. Listeners may want to respond differently to each part. For example, maybe

TABLE 4.2	Types of Discussion Questions

INFORMATION QUESTIONS

Ask for specific information or facts, but not interpretations or opinions.

Examples

1. Why was this meeting called?

2. How many thefts were reported on campus last year?

3. Where did you learn that?

4. What did Jim say was his reason for missing the meeting?

INTERPRETATION QUESTIONS

Ask for personal opinions, interpretations, judgments; they invite discussion.

Examples

1. What might have caused this increase in the rate of theft?

2. What connection might there be between college grades and whether a student has a computer?

3. Do you think our presentation should emphasize the need to reduce the deficit or the need to keep down inflation?

VALUE QUESTIONS

Ask how good, important, significant, or worthwhile something is in the opinion of the responder. A value question is a type of interpretation question.

Examples

1. How good a president do you think Ronald Reagan was?

2. Is this question important enough to take up the group's time?

3. What are the pros and cons of this alternative?

4. How good a case does the prosecuting attorney have against William Roberts?

5. Which of these suits do you think looks best?

6. How much do you like this painting?

POLICY QUESTIONS

Ask what should be done about an issue; the key word is *should*. Usually, groups have discussed a number of information and interpretation questions before they begin to discuss and decide what policy to take.

Examples

1. What should the U.S. government do to reduce the federal deficit?

2. What should our school's attendance policy be?

3. What kinds of skills should be required of all "med tech" graduates?

4. What should the Washington, D.C., police do to reduce drug-related crimes?

ACTION QUESTIONS

Ask how to implement a decision or policy already decided by the group.

Examples

1. How will we make this recommendation to the student senate?

2. Now that we've decided what food to serve at the banquet, who will see to it that it is prepared and served?

3. How can we guarantee that all pilots know about this policy and follow it?

PROCEDURE QUESTIONS

Ask how the group, or an individual member, does something; what procedure the group will use.

Examples

1. Should we vote or try to come to consensus?

2. What would be the best way to present our proposal to our client?

3. What sequence should we use to organize our discussion of this issue?

4. How can we divide the work of the committee in a way that's fair to everybody?

RELATIONSHIP QUESTIONS

Seek information about how members feel toward each other, the group, their responsibilities to the group, the relative status of members, and sometimes what members expect from each other.

Examples

1. Do we need some introductions, or does everybody know everybody else?

2. How do you all feel about our assignment to select an insurance carrier for our medical programs?

3. How did you get the authority to decide when we meet?

4. Paul, something seems to be bothering you. Is there something that's made you upset?

someone wants to increase funding to the schools but doesn't want to allow casino gambling in the state. Perhaps both issues need to be addressed but, if so, each question should be asked separately: First, do you think funding to the public schools should be increased? Second, should we approve a measure to allow casino gambling in our state?

3. **Avoid suggesting the answer in the question.**

   A question that suggests an answer is not an honest question but an indirect way to make a point. For instance, "Don't you think we should tell Sol we will expel him from the fraternity if he ever takes a brother's clothes without first asking for them?" suggests a solution.

4. **Apply critical-thinking skills to questions you ask.**

   Guidelines for evaluating information and detecting errors in reasoning are explained in Chapter 5. Use them to evaluate and improve the questions you and others ask during discussions.

Up to now we have been emphasizing the importance of words to the messages processed in small group interaction. However, you will recall from our earlier discussion that nonverbal signals also carry a significant communicative load in a group.

4.1 What Are Our Questions?

In Case 4.1 we described the events of the first meeting of SMSU's library dean search committee. During this meeting members talked freely about what they wanted in a new library dean. The search they were about to undertake would be a complicated one that would entail developing a recruitment plan, establishing screening and selection criteria, scheduling on-campus interviews, and so forth. Each phase would require a series of questions. For example, during the recruitment phase, members would have to consider how to recruit a diverse and qualified pool of applicants.

Imagine you are a member of this committee and are helping plan the discussion for subsequent meetings.

1. Think of the phases this committee will experience in the course of its work.

2. Compose a list of discussion questions, including questions of information, interpretation, value, policy, action, procedure, and relationship, that might be asked to guide the group's discussion in each phase.

You can do this by yourself or you can get together in a group. Once the questions have been written critically, go over the examples looking for any questions that may be either–or questions, may not be worded concretely, or may inadvertently suggest an answer.

Nonverbal Signals in Small Group Communication

Nonverbal signals are all the signals contained in a message except the words themselves. They may be signs or symbols and include such things as tone of voice, gestures, and appearance. They serve a number of purposes. In this chapter, we explain several important principles of nonverbal behavior, examine key functions performed by nonverbal signals, and finally look briefly at the categories of nonverbal behavior that have the most important influence on small group communication.

PRINCIPLES OF NONVERBAL COMMUNICATION

Most of the time in a small group, only one person is speaking, but *all* members are sending nonverbal signals *all* the time. Understanding something about nonverbal signals is crucial to understanding what is happening in your groups. However, interpreting nonverbal signals can be trickier than interpreting verbal signals. Table 4.3 summarizes principles of nonverbal communication.

1. **Nonverbal signals are ambiguous.**

   Do you think that a smile means someone is happy? Well, in many cultures that is usually the case, but in Japan, someone who is feeling quite miserable may smile to avoid upsetting the person to whom he is speaking. Do you think that someone who

TABLE 4.3	**Principles of Nonverbal Communication**
Nonverbal signals are ambiguous.	Nonverbal behaviors can be interpreted in a number of ways. Both context and culture are important in determining what a particular nonverbal behavior means.
People cannot stop sending nonverbal signals.	Group members cannot choose to stop communicating because they send nonverbal signals even when they aren't talking. You cannot NOT communicate.
Nonverbal signals are more believable than verbal signals.	It is easier to control words than nonverbal behaviors. When there is a discrepancy between nonverbal and verbal signals, most people believe the nonverbal signals.

has her arms folded across her chest is uninterested in hearing what you say? Maybe. But maybe she is merely trying to keep warm. Many factors influence the meaning of nonverbal signals, including cultural differences. Nonverbal signals should be interpreted in context and in conjunction with the words group members are using.

2. **People cannot stop sending nonverbal signals, even when they are not talking.**
   As mentioned earlier, only one person in a group usually speaks at a time, but all members continuously process nonverbal signals. Even if you choose to be quiet in a group meeting, you will likely leak your feelings nonverbally. For example, a church board member unhappy with the way the church secretary was handling office business chose not to say anything when personnel matters were discussed. However, after the meeting the board chair asked him what was wrong and why he had seemed uninterested at the meeting. This example points out two features of nonverbal behavior. First, even though the member chose not to say anything, he certainly was sending something nonverbally. Second, nonverbal signals are easy to misinterpret. The emotion he was feeling was anger at the church secretary, but the board chair thought he was uninterested in the meeting. Thus, we shouldn't jump to conclusions without first checking them out.

3. **When verbal and nonverbal messages clash, most people believe the nonverbal signals.**
   In fact, when a person is trying to interpret what someone else means in a face-to-face interaction, the nonverbal part of the message counts almost twice as much as the verbal.[7] When the verbal and nonverbal signals don't fit, most people trust the nonverbals because they are less subject to deliberate control. Many nonverbal behaviors, such as sweating, blushing, and shaking, are controlled by primitive

structures of the brain over which we have little or no conscious control. You can choose your words, but your nonverbal behavior often gives you away. When you clench your fists, turn red, and scream at another group member "No, I'M NOT Mad!" no one will believe you.

FUNCTIONS OF NONVERBAL SIGNALS

Nonverbal signals perform a variety of functions, most importantly to express how we feel and to indicate how we perceive our relationships to other people. Nonverbal signals modify the verbal component of messages exchanged among group members. They can supplement the words we utter by emphasizing them or in effect repeating them, just as underlined or **boldfaced** words in a text are emphasized. Thus, nonverbals can call special attention to the words they accompany. For instance, a person may say, "Look at the part of our income that comes from user fees" while pointing at a segment of a pie chart.

Nonverbal signals can *substitute* for spoken or written words. In this case, a gesture becomes a symbol, substituting for the more conventional words. For instance, a circled thumb and index finger can express "OK," or a beckoning finger can indicate you want someone to lean closer to you. Kathy and some of her graduate students bring their two forefingers together when indicating a "shared moment," a gesture they picked up from the movie *Chasing Amy*. Much of the communicating among members must be with unspoken substitutes for spoken words. If you aren't conscious of these signals and don't look for them, you will miss many important messages among group members and misinterpret other nonverbal messages. In a sense, you will be only half-listening.

Another major function of nonverbal messages is to *regulate* the flow of verbal interaction among members. The coordinator of a discussion group may use nods, eye contact, and hand signals to indicate who should speak next. Direct gaze from listeners indicates "continue," whereas looking away is a nonverbal way of saying, "Shut up!" People who want to speak lean forward, slightly open their mouths, extend a hand or finger, and may even utter a sound such as "um." Speakers who ignore such cues are judged inconsiderate and rude. One of us observed a group that contained a blind person who obviously could not see such regulating cues. Other members began to judge this member as arrogant and self-centered for "talking out of turn." Some discussion of visible regulatory cues increased the members' sensitivity to the communicative problem experienced by their blind member and helped the group pull together.

Finally, as noted earlier, nonverbal signs can *contradict* words we utter. A person who says, "I agree" hesitatingly, with a rising pitch at the end of the words, may be perceived as having reservations, or even as disagreeing. A person who says, "I heard you" but will not attempt a paraphrase has indicated nonverbally that he probably was not really listening. When you observe nonverbal signals that seem to contradict what a person has just said, and it matters to you what the person really thinks, try saying, "I heard you say . . . , but the way you said it bothers me." Then explain the apparent contradiction you perceived and ask the person to clarify it for you.

CATEGORIES OF NONVERBAL SIGNALS

Several categories of nonverbal behavior are especially important to your understanding of small group communication. Personal appearance, space and seating, facial expression, eye contact, gestures and body movement, voice, and time cues are among the major types of nonverbal signals most relevant to small groups.

4.2   What If . . .

Earlier you met a group of students planning publicity for a career day seminar. In their meeting they discussed adding a portfolio session and then how best to publicize the seminar. Recollect the following dialogue:

Lori: You're right; we need that. Big oversight. Glad you thought of it.

Tony: One thing we could do is send a memo to all the people who live in the dorms to let them know about the seminar.

Chris: That might be a good idea, but I'm not sure we're ready to go on to that yet. Were we finished with the portfolio session planning?

Tony: Sorry! I thought we were ready to move on. What do we need to do yet with portfolios?

Chris: Well, for one thing, we need to figure out who would be a good person to handle that session.

The goal of this application is to show you how much the context and nonverbal behavior influence the meaning of what we say. Select four trios. Each trio is to role-play the dialogue but from a different relational context. The first trio is composed of close friends who have worked together on several committees. Members of the second trio have never met before and one member is not sure he or she even wants to be on this committee. The third trio has a highly aggressive member who believes he or she knows how to run this group. The fourth trio is composed of individuals who really dislike each other but are trying to be civil.

During the role-plays, have audience members take notes. Ask them to observe the nonverbal behavior and how it changed the meaning of the conversation. When the trios are through, discuss the principles of nonverbal behavior and the functions of nonverbal behavior. You can even discuss how the trios used such things as gestures, facial expressions, movements, and spacing to create the relational context.

Appearance.   Members of a group form impressions of each other, accurate or not, long before anyone says anything. Sex, race, height, build, dress, grooming, and other visible cues have been shown to influence responses. Cues such as sex, body shape, and ethnicity particularly affect how group members interact with each other initially.[8] Such personal characteristics as status and wisdom may be associated with a member's age and sex. Members also create impressions of each other's physical characteristics including impressions of member clothing, makeup, and other body "artifacts." These impressions may very well impact whether a group member even interacts with another member and

GLOSSARY

Group Ecology

A group's space as created by seating choices and furniture arrangements

if so the character of that interaction. For instance, violating societal norms about dress, grooming, makeup, and accessories can arouse suspicion or even mistrust. Dressing noticeably differently from other members will almost certainly be interpreted as a sign that you do not identify with them. You may have to prove yourself in other ways to be accepted. To date, no research has examined the impact of the relative physical attractiveness of group members on group throughput and outcome variables.[9] This is surprising given how much attention is placed on physical attractiveness in the American culture at large and in interpersonal communication research specifically.

Space and Seating.   Many scientists have examined how people use space to communicate. The amount of space people prefer between them depends on a variety of factors, including culture and gender. For example, in the United States, most business transactions are conducted at what Hall calls *social distance,* which is between four and eight feet.[10] We are comfortable allowing only our intimate friends within a foot or two. However, four feet is much too far for someone from the Arab world or from Latin America. In these countries, people transact business at what we consider close personal distance, which often makes Americans very uneasy. In the dominant culture of the United States, females tend to sit closer together than males, as do people of the same age and social status and those who know each other well.

The seating arrangements in groups and even the way furniture is arranged is called **group ecology.**[11] In a group, sitting close together, especially if the room is large enough for members to spread out, indicates that members like each other and there is a sense of cohesiveness. A person who sits apart from the others may be signaling that he or she does not feel a part of the group.

The nature of a group's ecology and group processes such as status, leadership, power, and member participation are linked to each other. Dominant people often claim more than their fair share of space, and a group's leader usually is given more space by the other members than they claim, as is shown in Figure 4.1. In addition, group leaders generally sit in a central position, such as at the head of a rectangular table, where they can see as many of the other members as possible. Quite simply, the most central place in a group's ecology allows members who occupy that space more influence, participation, domination, and opportunity to foster attributions of leadership.[12] People who sit across from each other respond to each other more than people sitting side by side or on the edges of each other's vision. The ideal table for most small group discussions is a round table, where members have easy eye contact with each other. If that is not possible, group members are advised to position themselves around the table, whatever shape it happens to be, in something close to a circle or oval.

Altering seating arrangements may appear nonconsequential; however, the seating choices you and your group members make indicate how socially accessible you have made yourselves to each other. Social accessibility is important if members are to promote social contact and enhance the more relational group outcomes such as respect and cohesiveness.[13]

Facial Expressions and Eye Contact.   Sitting where you can see every other member of the group is important because it allows you to make eye contact with other members. Eye contact and facial expressions are among the most important nonverbal signals for group members. For Americans, making eye contact signals that the channel for communication is open. This is why many students look down at their notebooks

FIGURE 4.1   A Group's Leader May Sit Apart from Other Members

when a teacher asks a question—they avoid eye contact so they won't be called on to answer. Prolonged eye contact can signal cooperativeness or competitiveness, depending on the circumstances. Most Americans establish eye contact before speaking and continue it intermittently when talking to someone they like. However, people from other cultures are sometimes offended by Americans' direct gazes, while others prefer to maintain an intense, unbroken stare when conversing, which is uncomfortable for Americans. As with other nonverbals, numerous cultural factors influence what a person considers to be appropriate eye contact. In unified and cohesive groups, members tend to look continuously at each other during a discussion. In hostile or tense groups, members avoid eye contact.

People can accurately determine the type of emotion someone in a photograph is experiencing from looking just at the face and eyes. Anger, sadness, happiness, support, disagreement, interest, liking—all are indicated by facial expressions.[14] Some people have "poker" faces; their facial expressions change very little. They tend to be trusted less than those whose faces express their feelings more openly. Most of us monitor the facial expressions of others because they provide clues about what is going on in the group. Even if a group member isn't saying anything about your proposal, you can tell by her spontaneous frown and grimace that she doesn't think much of it. That gives you information about what your next steps should be—drop the proposal, modify it, ask the other member directly what she thinks, or speak with her privately after the meeting.

Movements.   Movements of the hands, arms, and body signal many feelings and at-titudes. For example, people turn directly toward others they like and away from those they dislike. Leaning toward each other indicates a sense of mutual inclusiveness, whereas leaning away signals rejection.[15] When group members feel a sense of unity with each other, they tend to imitate each other's posture and body movements. This takes place automatically, without conscious awareness. Mabry found that body orienta-tion changes significantly from one meeting to another.[16] As group members get to know, like, and trust one another more, they tend to increase their eye contact and angle their bodies more directly toward each other.

Both tension and status can be revealed with movements. Members who are swing-ing a foot, twisting a lock of hair, or tapping a pencil may be indicating tension. It may be hard for the other members to know whether the movements indicate frustration, impatience, or annoyance with the group's progress. Movement can also indicate who has high status in the group. High-status workers tend to be the most relaxed, so they lean back and look around.[17] Members are more likely to imitate the movements of high-status members than those of low-status members.[18]

Voice.   Vocal cues include such factors as pitch, speed, fluency, loudness, and pauses. We rely on tone of voice to interpret someone's mood. Someone who says, "Yeah, I could live with that" softly in a questioning tone of voice is not likely to be believed. In addition, listeners tend to judge the status, educational level, ethnicity, and attitudes of speakers on the basis of vocal cues.[19] In the United States, people who speak in a mono-tone have less credibility and are less persuasive than those who speak in a more ani-mated tone of voice. However, those who are extremely animated may appear to be ir-rational or hysterical.

Those nonverbal signals that regulate interaction express group member involvement, dominance, competition, and cooperativeness.[20] For instance, nonverbal backchannel sounds, such as "mm-hmmm" and "uh-huh," are sounds that people make to indicate involvement and understanding when listening. Interestingly, cultures vary in the use of the backchannel. Most people from Western European backgrounds use the back-channel less frequently than African Americans, Hispanics, or people with Southern Eu-ropean backgrounds. We discuss backchannel differences between African Americans and European Americans in Chapter 8. Backchannel sounds also may be interpreted differently; seen as either showing interest in or acceptance of what is being said. These differences can cause misunderstandings in a group if members are not aware of them and thus influence how smoothly members can agree on issues. If, for example, you be-lieve group members agree with your ideas based on their "uh-huhs," only to discover later that they were just trying to show you their interest in your idea, you'll probably be upset!

Timing.   Time cues are both culture-related and relational. In some other cultures and in subcultures of this country, no one would expect to get right to work in a group meeting; first, one must get the feel of the other people. Most rural people tackle busi-ness at a slower pace than their urban counterparts. In the fast-paced U.S. business world, people who come late to meetings are judged inconsiderate and undisciplined. North Americans will allow only about a five-minute leeway before they expect an apol-ogy from someone who is late.[21] In the predominant culture of this country, coming late and leaving early indicates to fellow group members that your time is precious but it's OK to waste theirs. In dozens of case studies of student groups, one consistently late member was the subject of bitter complaints by the others.

Time is a vital commodity during meetings. People who talk little and those who talk excessively have little impact. Excessive talkers are considered rude and selfish. Although they did not protest at the time, many students have complained about fellow project group members who waste time by chattering at length about social matters or other topics irrelevant to the group's purpose. On the other hand, those who talk somewhat above average are judged favorably on leadership characteristics.[22] In fact, talkativeness, or speaking time, is considered a strong factor in determining how much a group member is perceived as powerful.[23] Likewise, people who structure the group's time so that every item on an agenda can be discussed are appreciated. If you are insensitive to time cues in your group, you will have little influence and will not be completely accepted by the others.

No type of nonverbal communication can be overlooked if you want to understand what is going on in a group. Even small group researchers must broaden their efforts to understand the importance of nonverbal signals in small group interaction. Relatively little, for instance, is understood about the influence of member touch behavior, artifacts like clothing, emotion, and different kinds of group contexts (e.g., groups in submarines) on group behavior.[24] Remember also that you cannot state with confidence exactly what someone else is thinking or feeling from nonverbal cues alone. We hope the list of nonverbal signals presented here encourages you to increase your awareness and sensitivity, but you should not consider this list exhaustive.

Computer-Mediated Communication and Group Messages

Our discussion so far has centered around verbal and nonverbal messages in groups that meet face-to-face. However, group members increasingly use computers to communicate with each other during and between meetings. Some groups, such as online chat groups, may communicate with each other only via computers. In business the teleconference is often used because it is ideal for meetings of individuals who are geographically separated.

A **teleconference** is an electronically mediated meeting that can take several forms. In a *videoconference,* participants can both see and hear each other. In an *audio conference,* which can be as simple as a telephone conference call, participants can hear but not see each other. In a *computer conference,* participants can send messages that appear on computer terminals. Currently, these techniques vary in expense and usefulness, but as the expense of travel for executives to attend face-to-face meetings continues to increase, even expensive video teleconferences will eventually pay off. In addition, a number of companies are starting to develop specialized computer software designed especially for employees who are linked to a network to work simultaneously on a variety of tasks. Such software is becoming increasingly easy to use and cost effective.

Most companies now have the capacity to conduct conference calls via telephone. The advantages—lowered travel costs, including money and time—are somewhat offset by the fact that many nonverbal cues (such as facial expressions and body language) are

GLOSSARY

Teleconference

Electronically mediated group meeting

CHAPTER 4

GLOSSARY

Social Presence

*The degree to which
a person feels that
another is actually
present during an
interaction*

missing. Also, the sense of sharing, involvement, and team spirit can be low. For instance, immediate verbal and nonverbal feedback usually does not occur. This could be harmful to the group if members are trying to build consensus about something, but it may not matter if members are only trying to generate a list of ideas.[25] Videoconferencing solves some of these problems, but costs are high.

With current technology, computer conferencing can be used relatively inexpensively. The preferred computer conferencing method allows each participant to view on a personal computer terminal the responses of all other participants simultaneously. This window method is more similar to face-to-face interaction and produces higher-quality decisions than a different system characterized by asynchronous communication, where the receiver picks up the message later than when it was sent.[26]

The use of computer-mediated communication in small groups brings up the issue of **social presence,** or how much group members perceive the communication medium is like face-to-face interaction socially and emotionally. This perception is associated with the degree to which members feel that other members are actually there during interaction.[27] Asynchronous communication promotes less social presence than simultaneous communication. One factor that can influence social presence is task complexity. The more complex the task, the less adequate some computer-mediated communication can become because the medium's channels are not adequate. However members in CMC

4.3   The Public Affairs Web Page Committee

APPLY NOW

At Southwest Missouri State University, where Gloria teaches, a six-member committee has been created to establish policies and review materials for the university's public affairs Web page. Initially, their Webspinner drafted the first version of their report, and committee members commented on the draft from the website. After some discussion the committee has decided it will conduct most of its business over the Web due to difficult schedules. In addition, members need to conduct private discussions, so they each have a password accessing the committee's Web page at their convenience.

Pretend you are the Webspinner for this committee. You are familiar with the different kinds of teleconferences. You also have extensive knowledge of the advantages and disadvantages of using computer mediated communication to conduct business as compared to meeting face-to-face. Given that your committee wants to conduct all business over the Web, what would you recommend? Draw up a description of how the Web is to be used by this committee given your expertise. Your suggestions and guidelines will be given to all the members.

groups are very creative when it comes to creating interaction that relationally approximates face-to-face communication. Social presence is important for any group, and much more needs to be learned about the impact of technology on the felt social presence of group members.[28]

Several factors can improve the effectiveness of teleconferences, and each factor is somehow related to perceptions of social presence.[29] Face-to-face meetings of participants before and after the teleconference enhance the sense of groupness. Using a trained moderator improves the process. So does making sure that participants are aware of the rules and guidelines for speaking, and they agree to abide by specified time limits. Teleconferences are most useful for certain types of tasks, such as routine meetings and information sharing. For complex tasks in which many disagreements are likely to occur, face-to-face meetings are still preferable, although computer conferences have been used effectively to help conflicting group members achieve consensus. Table 4.4 compares the strengths of face-to-face and teleconference meetings.

TABLE 4.4	**Comparison of Strengths**
Teleconferences	**Face-to-face meetings**
• They can be useful for information sharing, routine meetings.	• Face-to-face meetings are better when group cohesiveness and interpersonal relationships are important.
• Quantity and quality of ideas are equal to face-to-face meetings.	• Group organization is easier to maintain.
• In negotiations, evidence is more persuasive than personality.	• Participants can exchange more messages more quickly.
• Participants may pay more attention to what is said.	• Important nonverbal information (facial expressions, uses of space) is available.
• In conflict, more opinion change may occur than in face-to-face meetings.	• People generally prefer face-to-face meetings.
• Audio conferences/computer conferences are cost effective.	• Participants are more confident of their perceptions in face-to-face meetings.

SOURCE: Adapted from Gene D. Fowler and Marilyn E. Wackerbarth, "Audio Teleconferencing versus Face-to-Face Conferencing: A Synthesis of the Literature," *Western Journal of Speech Communication* 44 (Summer 1980), pp. 236–52.

SUMMARY

- Group members communicate via messages, verbal and nonverbal signals they send and interpret; these messages, as noted by the theory of structuration, both create and maintain the group.

- More accurate interpretation of verbal signals occurs when members use standard English, clarify abstract language, organize their remarks, and use clear and appropriate discussion questions.

- Nonverbal signals, more believable because they are harder to control, are especially hard to interpret accurately; they supplement or substitute for verbal communication, regulate the flow, and express feelings.

- Nonverbal categories especially important to understanding small group communication include appearance, use of space, facial expression, eye contact, movements, vocal cues, and timing.

- Group members increasingly use computers to communicate, and computer use dramatically influences the nature of verbal and nonverbal messages exchanged by members.

EXERCISES

1. Browse through several magazines for interesting advertisements. Cut out a variety of advertisements and bring them to class. Discuss with your group or with your class each of the advertisements. Identify the audience for each ad and how the language of the ad is designed to appeal to its audience.

2. Generate a list of words with a positive connotation and a list of words with a negative connotation. Look around at the lists of your classmates and see if any words appear on the same list or different lists. Compile two lists on the board and discuss why some words are on each list and why some words may be on both lists. Where

do these connotations come from? What kinds of experiences contribute to these connotations?

3. Tape record a group meeting. Watch the tape and note the group's seating arrangements and the space between members. Examine the facial expressions and eye contact. Note their voice qualities and timing. When you are finished, discuss your observations. How do you think these nonverbal behaviors contributed to the overall communicative character of this group?

Go to **www.mhhe.com/adamsgalanes** and **www.mhhe.com/groups** for Self-Quizzes and weblinks.

KEY TERMS and CONCEPTS

bypassing	group ecology	social presence
discussion question	message	structuration
emotive words	nonverbal signals	teleconference

www.mhhe.com/adamsgalanes
Use the flashcards and crossword puzzles on the Online Learning Center to further your knowledge of these key terms.

Creative and Critical Thinking in the Small Group

After reading this chapter you should be able to:

1. Define creative thinking and explain why it is important to small group problem solving.

2. Describe both brainstorming and synectics and explain how they can be used to help enhance group creativity.

3. Define critical thinking and explain why it is important to small group problem solving.

4. List and describe the attitudes most conducive to critical thinking in a group.

5. Explain how group members should use critical thinking during the information gathering stage of problem solving.

6. Describe and give examples of each of the five steps crucial to evaluating information.

7. Define and give examples of each of the five reasoning errors described in the text: overgeneralizing, attacking a person instead of the argument, confusing causal relationships, either–or thinking, and incomplete comparisons.

8. Give examples of probing questions critical thinkers should ask when they evaluate information.

The Springfield Greenway Project

In Springfield, Missouri, a group of committed citizens has been working for the past several years to acquire land and access rights for a greenway, a hiking and bicycle path in and around the city. One section of greenway will connect the center of Springfield with a Civil War battlefield 10 miles away. A major challenge for the greenway project was what to do about crossing Kansas Expressway, a major highway between the battlefield and the city proper. The most obvious option was to reroute the greenway to have it cross at a traffic light. This would mean rerouting it along two highways—always a danger to bikers. In addition, this would force acquisition of additional land and access rights, which would be difficult. The greenway committee hoped the route could avoid travel on major highways and stoplights that create long waits. The committee's conclusion was to stick to the original route. Thus, the problem members faced was this: How can the path cross Kansas Expressway safely and without forcing long waits for a light? A creative solution was needed and would have to be tested against the main criteria of the greenway committee: safety, cost, and ease of use.

This chapter examines two processes essential for problem solving in small groups, creative and critical thinking. Both creativity and critical thinking are necessary for effective discussion groups, but neither one alone is sufficient to ensure effective solutions. Also, creative and critical thinking cannot be done simultaneously; that would be like trying to drive a car with one foot on the accelerator and one foot on the brake! Group members must learn when to be creative, when to be critical, and what kinds of procedures help the group do both.

What Is Creative Thinking?

Sometimes a group faces a difficult impasse and must come up with an innovative or unusual solution. Creating is the process of bringing into being something unique that would not evolve naturally from ordinary processes.[1] **Creative thinking** in small groups encourages the use of imagination, hunches, intuition, insight, and fantasy to devise unusual or innovative solutions that are not obvious and would probably not evolve from ordinary group discussion. Contrary to the popular myth of the solitary figure working alone, groups are major sources of creative ideas and innovations.[2] This makes group creativity an important topic for you to understand.

GLOSSARY

Creative Thinking

Encouraging use of hunch, intuition, insight, and fantasy to promote creativity

Americans pride themselves on creative thinking, particularly in business. Our economy is fueled by the ongoing drive to invent better, newer, less-expensive products and services that enhance our lives. Creative thinking, often in groups, is the way we originate innovative ideas. Consider an organization's fund-raising committee that may need to come up with a new type of fund-raiser because all the usual methods—garage sales, golf tournaments, door-to-door solicitations, and so forth—have lost their effectiveness. Somehow the committee must come up with something unusual and appealing to raise money.

Creative thinking is always appropriate, but it is especially useful at the beginning of a problem-solving process. When group members have learned something about the problem but before they have gotten bogged down in details is an ideal time for creativity-

5.1   Creative Fund-Raising for the College

APPLY NOW

Several years ago, members of the Advisory Council of the College of Arts and Letters where one of us works met to discuss creative fund-raising ideas to enhance the college's endowment for student scholarships. One council member mentioned a combination lecture/dinner fund-raiser a museum in New York City had initiated, which had become a highly successful event. Members began to talk about ways that event could be modified to work in Springfield, Missouri. They decided to have faculty give presentations or performances based on their expertise, combined with a dinner at one of the council member's homes. For instance, a film professor followed his lecture about a particular film director with a special showing of one of the director's lesser-known films, followed by dinner. Another professor gave a brief piano concert followed by an elaborate dessert. These events, known as the A La Carte Series, have become so successful that the college has a long list of volunteers wanting to host one of the dinners. In addition, the events sell out quickly, sometimes the first day that tickets become available. This is an example of how a group can modify an existing idea to arrive at something unique. Before you read further in this chapter, address the following questions:

1. What kinds of communication behaviors and skills would group members have to demonstrate to encourage the kind of creativity demonstrated by the advisory council?

2. What kinds of member behaviors would interfere with this kind of creativity?

3. What kinds of group rules, norms, and procedures would support this type of creativity?

4. What kinds of group norms would interfere?

enhancing procedures. Group members can then create a number of innovative ideas that they later can examine before choosing one. However, creativity may take extra time, which may not be worthwhile for relatively unimportant decisions. Group members who want to focus on devising creative options should make sure they have the time to devote to the creative process because abandoning a creative process for lack of time is demoralizing.

Certain conditions must be present for groups or individuals to be fully creative. For instance, group members who have a high tolerance for ambiguity, possess low levels of communication apprehension, and aren't afraid of violating societal norms and rules (think of the student whose hair is dyed purple) are more likely to embrace creative thinking.[3] Table 5.1 summarizes member qualities that promote creativity. It's impossible to be creative when your internal critic is actively evaluating and criticizing your ideas. In one recent study, members remained anonymous during an electronic problem-solving session while the leader gave individualized feedback designed to be intellectually stimulating. However, even this feedback, given anonymously and intended to motivate, was likely to be interpreted as critical and hurt group creativity.[4]

To create, your mind must be given the freedom to wander, to make unusual connections between different elements, to fantasize, and not to worry about what others think. Creative thinkers in a small group must also give themselves time to let ideas incubate and to create a group climate where members are comfortable having fun. Creative groups have flexible norms or are willing to discuss openly norms that interfere with creativity; they also are willing to collaborate with each other and to support, rather than mistrust, the creative people in the group.[5] Table 5.2 summarizes these characteristics. These features of creative thinking differentiate it from critical thinking, which we will discuss later.[6] Many techniques can help groups enhance their creative thinking. We describe two of them here.

TABLE 5.1	**Member Characteristics that Promote Creative Thinking**
Willing to communicate and participate in a group.	
Willing to be unconventional and to think outside societal norms.	
Not afraid of rejection.	
Confident in his or her own creativity; willing to risk failure.	
Not thinking there is one right answer to a problem and not relying too heavily on past experience.	
Willing to play and have fun in the group.	

TABLE 5.2	**Group Characteristics that Promote Creative Thinking**

Willingness to examine and change norms that interfere with creativity.

Establishment of norms that encourage exploration and freedom of expression.

Willingness to use procedures (such as brainstorming and synectics) that promote creativity.

Willingness to collaborate with each other, even when members have different working styles.

Enhancing Group Creativity

Sometimes a group needs to be shocked out of its habitual ways of thinking to come up with a creative, innovative solution for a problem. That might be an idea for a new product, an eye-catching print advertising campaign, or a novel way to build a safe greenway across a busy expressway. Brainstorming and synectics help groups tap their creative potential.

BRAINSTORMING

For more information on using the Internet to brainstorm, go to the on-line learning center.

Many groups use **brainstorming,** a procedure designed especially to release a group's creativity.[7] Brainstorming is used most often in the idea-generation stage of problem solving, but it also can be used in other stages. We have noted that it is impossible to be creative and critical at the same time. Brainstorming consciously separates idea creation from idea evaluation by not allowing any criticism to occur while the group is generating ideas. Later, the group evaluates the ideas, combines or modifies them, and selects the best ones. The basic procedure is described below. Figure 5.1 presents a summary of these brainstorming guidelines.

1. The group is presented with a problem to solve. The problem can range from something specific and concrete ("How can we raise more money for student scholarships?) to something abstract and intangible ("How can we improve the quality of work life for employees?").

2. Members are encouraged to come up with as many solutions as possible to the problem. Quantity is the goal here and several rules must be followed. The first and most important is that no evaluation is permitted during brainstorming. With judgment temporarily suspended, members are encouraged to turn their imaginations loose, to encourage wild and crazy ideas to surface, to build on each other's ideas, to combine ideas, and to strive for more and more suggestions. Second, you do not want to stop generating ideas too soon. Often, the best ideas—the ones a group eventually selects—were listed during the latter part of the brainstorming session.[8]

FIGURE 5.1   Guidelines for Brainstorming

| Group is presented with a problem to solve. | → | Members generate as many solutions as possible, without any criticism. | → | All suggestions are recorded for group to see. | → | Ideas are evaluated at another session. |

3. All ideas are recorded so that the whole group can see them. Usually the group's recorder will write ideas on a large pad of paper. As the top sheet is filled, it is posted on the wall so that all ideas are clearly visible at all times. Seeing the previous ideas often triggers new ideas.

4. The ideas are evaluated at another session. Just because brainstorming requires temporarily suspending critical evaluation does not mean the critical thinking function is unimportant. Also, incubation is an important feature of creative thinking. After brainstorming has generated a lot of ideas and the group has had a chance to let the ideas sit for a while, critical thinking is used to evaluate each idea and to modify or combine ideas into workable solutions to the problem.

The basic brainstorming technique has several variations. Often groups have one or two vocal people who are highly creative, share many innovative ideas, and may intimidate others from participating. In this case, it may be more productive for each person to brainstorm silently rather than openly in a group. In this form of brainstorming, called brainwriting, each person quietly writes as many new and different solutions as possible on a notepad. Then each person shares one new idea, round-robin fashion, as the facilitator posts it on a chart for all to see. The sharing continues until all ideas have been posted. Members are encouraged to add to the list as new ideas occur to them.

Electronic brainstorming, another variation, takes advantage of the fact that anonymity may remove inhibitions. In this variation, each group member sits at an individual computer terminal (all of which may be in the same room) and types out his or her ideas. The ideas are combined onto a large screen visible to everyone. Because no one knows who contributed what, electronic brainstorming, especially with 8- to 10-member groups, often generates more and better ideas than traditional brainstorming.[9]

SYNECTICS

Synectics is a technique that stimulates metaphoric or analogic thinking.[10] This technique encourages members to look for similarities in different things, or to use a metaphor to gain insight into the problem. For instance, a mini laptop computer developed by IBM was designed this way.[11] Its inventor, John Karidis, was trying to figure out how he could get a typical, full-size rectangular keyboard to fit into the small, square case consumers wanted. One day, watching his small daughter play with blocks, he got an intuitive flash that the keyboard could be broken into movable parts (like the blocks). He designed a laptop that pulls out to make a long keyboard but pushes in to make a compact unit for storage. The blocks served as the analogy, or metaphor, for his real problem, the keyboard.

GLOSSARY

Synectics

A procedure designed to stimulate creative thinking through use of metaphor and looking for similarities in different things

5.2   Creating Suggestions for Crossing Kansas Expressway

The Springfield Greenway Committee must come up with a solution to the following problem. Land has been acquired on either side of busy Kansas Expressway for a greenway, a bicycle and hiking path to join Springfield with Wilson's Creek Battlefield. However, there is no traffic light where the land reaches the expressway and the city has no plans to put a light there. Your task is to come up with a solution for the greenway that will keep bikers and hikers moving and that will be safe and inexpensive.

Divide the class into groups of five or six. Appoint a facilitator to record suggestions and make sure the group follows the "no criticism" rule. Ask each group to brainstorm a list of suggestions for the greenway problem. The groups should brainstorm for 10 minutes and should think of as many suggestions as possible. At the end of the period, all the suggestions should be posted at the front of the class so that all can see. The class should then address the following questions:

1. Was it easy or difficult to follow the brainstorming rules? What was the hardest to do?
2. How did members feel during the process?
3. What do members remember thinking during the process?
4. Did anything stand in the way of being imaginative and having fun? If so, how might the process be modified to encourage more imagination and fun?

As an alternative to this exercise, some groups can be instructed to brainstorm in the traditional way while others are instructed to use brainwriting. If this is done, class members can compare the efficacy of each technique. Groups can also use a facilitator to help members stick to the brainstorming rules.

Synectics encourages such linking of apparently unrelated elements. A group follows certain procedures to encourage helpful analogies. First, the group identifies the essence of the problem. For instance, "shape changing" could have been the metaphor for the laptop example: How can we change the shape of the keyboard so it's full size when in use and compact when in storage? Then the group creates an analogy that captures that essence. For example, group members might ask, "Where in everyday life do we find things that can change shape?" Answers could include things like clouds, amoeba, or butterflies, whose shape during flight is different from when they fold their wings to rest on a flower. Finally, members look for metaphors that seem unrelated or that use a different sensory perception. For example, if the analogy is visual, members might search for a hearing or touch metaphor. The visual "shape change" metaphor connected to the touch metaphor of the little girl playing with the blocks to create the "aha" insight. Asking a group to consider the following questions helps trigger such insights. The leader may even lead the group in a guided meditation to stimulate insights.

1. **Change your perspective.** Sometimes, changing the angle from which you view a problem gives you a different insight. For example, if you are the greenway committee, imagine that you are Superman and can view the city's streets from above.

2. **Look for a direct comparison.** Look for something from another field that might help. For example, the man who created Velcro noticed, after taking a hike in the woods, that burrs stuck to his pants and socks. He took that event from one arena—nature—and translated it into another—the manufacturing of a different type of fastener.

3. **Temporarily suspend reality to use fantasy and imagination.** Ignore objective reality for a moment to learn what you can discover. Imagine that your bicycle has wings and can fly over Kansas Expressway to solve the greenway problem.

Synectics may seem strange at first because it forces group members to jump out of their self-imposed conceptual boxes. It feels uncomfortable to group members because it is designed to create rather than reduce ambiguity, but that's exactly why it works. Some corporations, such as General Electric, deliberately send groups of employees away from their normal work settings to jolt them out of possible ruts so they can come up with new ideas.[12] In one such group meeting between GE middle managers and colonels from the Army War College, a long-standing GE rule was challenged. One of the colonels asked whether GE's stated policy of being number one or number two in every business it entered or product it produced was perhaps causing the company to miss out on profitable opportunities. His statement produced an instant "aha" reaction from the GE managers, who recognized that they dismissed good ideas if those ideas wouldn't lead to a top market share. Upon their return, the managers were able to persuade CEO Jack Welch to rethink the "GE must be Number 1 or 2" rule. The limitations of this rule would never have been recognized or questioned from the safety of GE home base—the executives needed to be in a new setting to see things from a different perspective. This is exactly what synectics promotes.

Creative thinking plays a significant role in group problem solving. Groups trained in creative thinking have been found to show more humor and participation than those not trained to think creatively. Members of such groups support more ideas and criticize less, both of which are important to creative thinking.[13]

Creativity is important, but it is not a sufficient process for small groups. Once a group has come up with creative options for solving problems, its work isn't finished! Now members must carefully and critically examine those options to evaluate which ones are best. Surprisingly, groups have more problems being critical than being creative. In addition, failure to be critical is more dangerous than failure to be creative. Group problem solving can be effective because several heads are potentially better problem solvers than one, but many groups do not achieve this advantage. Members are not as vigilant or critical in their discussion of information because they avoid challenging each other's ideas and developing their own arguments.[14] The implications and consequences can be considerable if a group doesn't think things through carefully, as the following case example will illustrate.

In the remainder of this chapter, we examine how groups can help ensure good decision making and problem solving to complement their creativity.

GLOSSARY

Critical Thinking

Systematic thinking using evidence, reasoning, and logic to promote soundness

Evidence

Facts, data, opinions, and other information that back a claim or conclusion

Arguments

Claims supported by evidence and reasoning

What Makes Thinking "Critical"?

We have seen that creative thinking is intuitive, unsystematic, and spontaneous. In contrast, **critical thinking** involves using information that is supported by evidence and reasoning and examining both the evidence and the reasoning systematically and logically to ensure that they are sound.

Two principles differentiate critical from creative thinking: (1) the use of **evidence** (facts, data, opinions, and other information backing a claim or conclusion) and (2) the logical **arguments** speakers and writers make with that evidence to support what they

The *Challenger* Explosion

CASE 5.2

On January 28, 1986, the space shuttle *Challenger* exploded shortly after takeoff, killing all seven members of the crew. The Rogers Commission, charged with discovering the reasons for the disaster, identified the primary cause as a malfunction of the O-ring seals on one of the solid rocket boosters. The commission revealed that this was an avoidable accident. Because National Aeronautics and Space Administration (NASA) officials and the manufacturers of the rocket boosters knew about potential problems with the O-rings in cold weather, the disaster was predictable. The real problem, according to the Rogers Commission, occurred in the procedures used to make the launch/no launch decision. This decision-making procedure involved many knowledgeable individuals and groups and should have produced the type of high-quality decision for which groups are noted, one that utilized all relevant available information. How could the experts have allowed such a poor decision to be made?

Communication scholars who analyzed the *Challenger* decision making concluded that the procedure was flawed in several ways.[15] Because the launch had already been postponed three times, NASA officials were biased in favor of launching. In addition, the engineers were reluctant to bypass their normal reporting channels and demand that superiors pay attention to their concerns. Several decision makers discounted the relevance of pertinent technical data. Worse, they rejected an interpretation of the data by those people who disagreed. Serious consideration of those data would have canceled the launch. But the engineers, too, share some blame; they used ambiguous language rather than stating their concerns simply and clearly. So even a group of highly trained experts can ignore or reject important information and accept seriously defective information.

believe are valid reasons to accept their claims and assertions. This means that, for critical thinking to occur, a problem must be analyzed thoroughly, with as much relevant information as possible examined during that analysis. Then the solution must be developed on the basis of all that information and the best reasoning and logic you can use.

Although thinking critically is necessary, it is time consuming. You should be able to determine when you need to take the extra time that critical thinking demands and when you can make a decision that is just "good enough" without analyzing all your choices. For example, suppose your committee is charged with deciding whether to give coffee mugs or comparably priced pens with your organization's logo as souvenirs at your annual banquet. Does it really matter which favor is selected? Will anyone be hurt by your choice? Such a decision probably does not warrant taking the time to agonize over every aspect of the choice. However, with such decisions where human lives are at stake, such as whether or not to launch the *Challenger,* critical thinking is essential.

Enhancing Critical Thinking in a Group

Critical thinking in a group is not just one thing that members know or do. Critical thinking involves a number of factors, including the attitudes members have toward information, the way they gather information, how careful they are in evaluating information, and how skilled they are in making reasoned judgments on the basis of that information. Table 5.3 summarizes several characteristics of critical thinkers.

ATTITUDES

The most important "technique" to help groups do a good job of critical thinking is not a technique at all—it is the attitude of the members. Ideally, critical thinkers have the desire to make the best possible decision, are skeptical when they receive information, and are active in the information gathering and evaluation process.

The most important attitude necessary for critical thinking in groups is the desire to make the best possible decision. You have to want to make a good decision because doing so takes a great deal of time and effort. Your desire is what gives you the energy to engage fully in the critical thinking process. Critical thinkers are **open-minded,** which means they are willing and eager to consider new information and ideas, even if that

TABLE 5.3	**Characteristics of Critical Thinkers**

- Curious.
- Willing to take responsibility for decisions.
- Aware of gaps in their supply of information.
- Systematic in their search for information.
- Open-minded; attempt to find information supporting a wide variety of opinions.

information contradicts what they previously believed. They go out of their way to look for relevant information and tap a wide variety of sources in their attempt to gather information that supports all sides of an issue. Finally, they pride themselves on being objective and fair about evaluating information. The NASA officials involved in making the *Challenger* launch decision were apparently prejudiced in favor of the launch. This lack of objectivity biased their search for information, so they did not work as hard to find information that opposed the launch as they did to get information that supported it. They evaluated that information in a biased way—they uncritically accepted prolaunch information but were hypercritical of antilaunch data.

A second important attitude is a "show me" skepticism that indicates members want to think for themselves rather than being told what to think by others. Critical thinkers do not assume that anything they read or hear is true or accept something as true just because a parent, friend, or teacher "said so." They are willing to challenge any information, even information presented to them by experts, high-status individuals, or the group's majority, by raising questions about it.[16] This also means they are willing to hold off making a decision until the facts are in, which suggests they can tolerate ambiguity, at least for a while, so that they don't reach a premature conclusion just to get a difficult decision-making process over with. They know that better decisions result from applying the same skeptical approach to all claims, including their own.

Skeptical decision makers try to test information and opinions as well as the sources of such information. To do this, they ask lots of **probing questions** to determine the adequacy and quality of evidence and reasoning supporting a claim or decision. Table 5.4

"What we didn't have but obviously needed was an alarmist."

provides examples of probing questions. Asking the engineers probing questions about the safety of the launch is exactly what officials of the company that manufactured the *Challenger* rockets did not do. Instead, these managers were confident they knew what their subordinates were thinking, so they didn't ask directly.

Finally, critical thinking is an active (rather than passive) process of testing information. It demands hard work to find the information necessary to understand the problem and subject solutions to the most rigorous tests possible. Mentally lazy group members object to this hard work, but critical thinkers look forward to it.

The information just presented describes attitudes essential to critical thinking in a small group. Several attitudes and behaviors make it difficult for group members to engage in critical thinking, and these are worth looking at briefly. It is just as important for you to know what not to do as to know what to do, so we summarize these counterproductive behaviors in Table 5.5.

TABLE 5.4	**Probing Questions to Evaluate Evidence and Reasoning**

- What evidence do you have to suggest that statement is true?

- Where did that evidence come from?

- Does anyone have any evidence to contradict the statement we just heard?

- If we make that decision, what will it lead to?

- What might the consequences be if we are wrong?

- How much danger is there that we have reached the wrong conclusion?

- How did you arrive at that conclusion?

TABLE 5.5	**Attitudes and Behaviors Counterproductive to Critical Thinking**

- Oversimplifying the thinking process; evaluating information and ideas in either–or, black–white terms.

- Impulsiveness; jumping to premature conclusions.

- Overdependence on authority figures; waiting for someone else to tell you how to think, what to conclude, or what to do.

- Lack of confidence; withdrawing if someone challenges your ideas.

- Dogmatic, inflexible behavior; closing your mind and being afraid of change.

- Unwillingness to make the effort to think critically; taking the easy way out.

GATHERING INFORMATION

One skill essential to critical thinking is the ability to organize ideas.[17] The first step to organizing your ideas is to assess the information you already have, identify gaps in that information, and then establish and implement a plan for plugging those gaps. In the information gathering stage, you cannot tell what is important and what is not, so you should use "sponge style" thinking—like a sponge, you want to absorb as much information as you can about your topic or issue.[18] You'll evaluate it later.

Assessing Information Needs.   Before group members begin their research, they first need to take stock of the information they possess (see Table 5.6). The quality of an output, such as a plan or policy, cannot be better than the information members have or the way they share and process it. The first step is to make an outline or list of the information you have to help you assess what you need. For example, a university committee was charged with revising the curriculum for communication majors. Members first pooled all the information they had, such as what the current major requirements were, the problems and issues they had observed, and information about what nearby colleges and universities required of communication majors. Committee members soon realized they needed to fill several important information gaps before they could begin any adequate discussion of the problem. For instance, the committee members hadn't assessed the perceptions of current students and alumni about the strengths and weaknesses of the existing program—a major oversight! In addition, prospective employers could provide information about the skills and deficiencies of recent graduates and current student interns. Finally, committee members knew they must have information about current practices in the field of communication, including what communication professionals were saying about the direction of the field.

TABLE 5.6	**Gathering Information in the Critical Thinking Process: Assessing Information**

1. Take stock of existing information.

2. Identify holes and weaknesses.

3. Make a master list of what information is needed and where it can be found.

4. Collect needed resources.

5. Assign members specific responsibilities for finding needed information from the master list.

6. Use all appropriate information gathering techniques:
   - Direct observation.

   - Reading.

   - Interviews (individual or group).

   - Other sources (radio, television, casual conversation).

Information lists help determine not only what information is missing but also where it can be found. The next step in the critical thinking process is the careful gathering of information to fill the gaps.

Collecting Needed Resources.　Group members should organize their information gathering procedures before proceeding. First, from their master list, members should list all the information they still need. Then they should assign themselves research responsibilities on the basis of their preferences, strengths, and time schedules. Finally, as members proceed with their research, they will discover additional information they need that should be added to the list and assigned to the appropriate group members.

As was illustrated by the example of the faculty curriculum committee, the information a group needs is rarely found in one location. Usually, a variety of information is needed and will have to be gathered in various ways. Some of these are described briefly.

Direct Observation.　Sometimes information you need will come from firsthand observation. For example, if your group is assessing the parking problem at your university, observing the parking lots to count the number of spaces available at different times of day and the number of cars "creating" spaces where there are none is an example of direct observation.

Reading.　A wealth of information can be found in many kinds of printed sources. Published material often can save you considerable time and effort needed to gather information yourself. Useful information may be found in newspapers, books, magazines, scholarly and professional journals, technical and trade publications, government documents, and so forth. The sheer number of sources available can be intimidating. A reference librarian can help save hours of wasted effort by pointing you in helpful directions and steering you away from likely dead ends.

In addition, a number of publications can save you time and effort in locating printed information. Annotated bibliographies and abstracts provide a preview of the type of information in a publication so that you can decide whether it will be worth the search. Encyclopedias summarize vast amounts of information. Specialized indexes and abstracts frequently can help you save time in locating relevant information. For example, the *Business Periodicals Index* summarizes articles from numerous business and trade journals.

The Internet.　An easy and convenient way to access information is through the Internet. Use a browser, such as Netscape or Explorer, to connect to your favorite search engine. (You may want to try more than one search engine, since no one search engine covers the entire Internet.) Use keywords for your search, following the rules of the particular search engine you're using. Although you may have thousands of hits, most search engines give you the most likely hits first, so search those carefully. You may have to try various keyword combinations. For example, if you are seeking information about the effect of riverboat gambling on state economies, you may have to try "riverboat gambling," "gambling," "gaming," and so forth.

Be particularly careful to evaluate information you derive from the Internet. Know that *anyone* can put up *anything* on the Internet; no review procedure evaluates the information for accuracy or truth. Any claim—no matter how outrageous—can be made on the Internet, and websites have been created that contain lies and misinformation. Make sure you use your best critical thinking skills to evaluate information you receive from the Internet.

Electronic Databases.   A highly efficient way of finding printed information is to use one or more of the many electronic databases available at most academic and public libraries. With the Internet access many people have, this is becoming easier all the time. Many sources formerly available only to those who had physical access to a library can now be accessed at home via the Internet. Electronic databases contain titles, abstracts, and sometimes the full text of magazine and journal articles, newspaper articles, and books on thousands of topics. Commonly used databases include InfoTrac, a general-purpose database that accesses nearly 1,000 business and trade journals; ERIC, which holds education-related materials gathered by the U.S. Department of Education; LexisNexis, which accesses legal and business resources; ComAbstracts, which contains information from all communication-related journals; and EBSCOhost, another general-purpose database of nearly 3,000 periodicals, with full text for nearly 1,500. In addition, many newspapers, such as the *The New York Times,* can be accessed electronically. As with Internet search engines, electronic databases typically operate using keywords or author names.

Go to **www. mhhe.com/ adamsgalanes** for additional weblink activities.

5.1   Critical Thinking about Internet Sources

MEDIA AND TECHNOLOGY

This chapter has stressed the importance of critical thinking. When using the Internet for information, group members have an ethical responsilibity to ensure that evidence and information are accurate and effective. Bourhis, Adams, Titsworth, and Harter recommend using the following criteria to critically evaluate Web sources:

1. *Is the supporting material clear?* Sources should help you add clarity to your ideas rather than confusing the issue with jargon and overly technical explanations.

2. *Is the supporting material verifiable?* You should be able to independently verify facts and details contained on a Web page.

3. *Is the source of supporting material competent?* You should determine the source of the Web material and determine whether or not the source is qualified.

4. *Is the source objectice?* All sources—even news reports—have some bias. Your responsiblity is to ensure that your sources minimize bias.

5. *Is the supporting material relevant?* Using irrelevant research may make your ideas appear well supported; however, critical listeners will see through this tactic. Only utilize sources that directly address the key points you want to make.

You should also consult the following sources to find more information on evaluating the quality of Web information:

http://www.virtualsalt.com/evalu8it.htm
http://www.ithaca.edu/library/Training/hott.html

SOURCE: J. Bourhis, C. Adams, S. Titsworth, and L. Harter, *Style Manual for Communication Studies* (New York: McGraw-Hill, 2002).

Interviews.   Members of your group may need to conduct several interviews. These may be face-to-face individual interviews, group interviews, or those conducted over the phone or via electronic mail. For example, the curriculum committee members interviewed their colleagues in person, phoned or e-mailed colleagues at other schools, and called a sample of alumni to ask for their perceptions and opinions. Examples of the kinds of closed-ended and open-ended questions typically used in interviews are shown in Table 5.7.

Other Sources.   Useful information may come when you least expect it. Radio, television, casual conversation with family or friends, browsing through electronic bulletin boards, stumbling onto relevant information in a magazine while waiting to get your hair cut—all are potential sources. Be prepared to take advantage of these sources by recording the information as soon as possible so you don't forget it. Once you have gathered the information you need, you must decide how useful it is to you.

EVALUATING INFORMATION

The next step in the critical thinking process is to evaluate the information after you have gathered it. As a sponge, you've absorbed all the information you think you'll need. Now you must "pan for gold" by trying to find the nuggets of information that are valuable to you.[19] If a group bases its decision on inaccurate or outdated information, its decision will be flawed, no matter how systematic the process of gathering it has been. For example, the curriculum committee described earlier recommended that communication majors take several writing courses offered by the English department. However,

TABLE 5.7	**Open- and Closed-Ended Questions**
Open-ended questions	**Closed-ended questions**
What do you think about the proposal to raise taxes?	Do you agree or disagree that taxes should be raised?
What is your opinion of the performance of the committee chair?	Has the committee chair done a good job?
How might we enhance our presentation audiovisually?	Should we use a skit or a videotape in our presentation?
How can we solve the parking problem on campus?	Where should we put the new parking garage?
How effective are your group's critical thinking skills?	Are your group's critical thinking skills: _____ Very effective? _____ Somewhat effective? _____ Average? _____ Somewhat ineffective? _____ Very ineffective

even though the recommended courses were listed in the school's current catalog, the English department had revised its curriculum, eliminating several courses and changing several others. This mistake was not a disaster, but it would not have occurred if curriculum committee members had double-checked with the English department to determine whether any course changes were anticipated.

How can you tell whether a piece of data is accurate and up-to-date, and whether a source is credible? Evaluation of available information is perhaps the most crucial step in the critical thinking process. Several factors play a role in evaluating information: determining what someone means, distinguishing fact from opinion, clarifying ambiguous terms, assessing the source's credibility, and assessing the information's accuracy and worth. Browne and Keeley's fifth edition of *Asking the Right Questions: A Guide to Critical Thinking* is an excellent summary of how you can assess the value of information.

Determining the Meaning of What Is Being Said.   The first thing you must do is decide exactly what the speaker or writer means. This is not as easy as it may sound. Frequently, people bury the meaning of what they are saying among a jumble of opinions and irrelevant statements. You should identify the author's conclusion, reasons for the conclusion, and evidence to support the reasons. First, ask yourself what conclusion the author is drawing. What does he or she want us to do, think, or believe? Is there an action (such as voting for a particular candidate, writing letters to a television producer, or buying a particular product) that the author wants us to take? Next, determine what main arguments the author provides to support the conclusion or recommended action. For instance, look at the sample letter provided in Apply Now 5.3. What conclusion does the author want you to reach, and why?

Often, keeping track of the arguments and evidence that supports them is easier if you outline the argument on paper. Write the main conclusion at the top; then list each argument beneath it with space after each one. In this space, list every piece of evidence the author or speaker offers in support of the claims. This will simplify your later task of evaluating how good the author's evidence and reasoning are and how valid the conclusions are.

Distinguishing Fact from Opinion and Inference.   You must be able to recognize the difference between a statement of fact and statements of opinion or inference based on that fact. **Facts** are descriptions that can be verified by observations and are not arguable. For example, we can verify that the population of Greene County, Missouri, in 2000 was 240,391 by looking in any of several government publications that record population data. Be careful, though—some statements presented as facts are not facts at all but false statements. For example, the statement "Greene County, Missouri, has 500,000 residents" is not true; therefore, it is not a fact. You will need to determine whether statements presented as facts are actually true and up-to-date.

Opinions and inferences go beyond what was observed directly and imply some degree of probability or uncertainty. **Opinions,** unlike facts, are not all equal, although everyone has an equal right to express an opinion. Some opinions are more valid than others. Einstein's opinion about the way the universe operates should carry more weight than the opinions of the authors of this book because we are not theoretical physicists. The value of an opinion depends on the evidence supporting the opinion and the quality of the reasoning that ties the evidence and opinion together. Determining an opinion's value is part of your job as a critical thinker. For example, someone might say,

---

GLOSSARY

Facts

Something that can be verified by observation and is not arguable

Opinions

Inferences that go beyond facts and contain some degree of probability

Assume you have received the following letter in the mail from the Parents' Excellence in Schools Committee. Use this as an example to practice evaluating the information you receive.

Dear Parent-Teacher Organization Member,

As you know, the vote to elect a new member to the school board will occur on April 6. We want you to know that the Parents' Excellence in Schools Committee supports candidate Mary Alice Beasley for our school board.

Mary Alice Beasley is the best candidate we have running for the Central City school board. We need people like her who care about our kids. She has lived in Central City all her life and now has three children of her own in the school system. She has been an active member of the P.T.O. for the past six years and was chair of the fund-raising committee for Westwood School. Her experience will be invaluable.

In her second term as city councilwoman, she was the chief author of the plan to desegregate the city schools; as we all know, other cities have used this plan as the model for their own desegregation efforts. Mary Alice can represent the entire community well—she taught for nine years before she ran for city council, and she has a master's degree in education. Hers is exactly the kind of caring, experienced leadership we need on the school board. Mary Beasley deserves your endorsement. Remember to vote on April 6.

Either individually or in groups of four to six, answer the following questions and then discuss them as a class:

1. What conclusion are you being asked to reach? Is there an action you are being asked to take in this letter?

2. Like most letters of this type, this letter interchanges fact and inference, or opinion. Make a list of all the facts presented in the letter and a list of all the inferences presented.

3. Ambiguous terms are sometimes difficult to spot because we each think we know what words such as *experienced* mean. Make a list of all the ambiguous terms (terms that can reasonably be understood in more than one way) presented in the letter. Before you assess how the letter's writer interprets each of these terms, what do you mean by each of them? For instance, what does *experienced* mean to you?

4. For each of these terms, what evidence is presented in the letter that supports the author's opinion about Mary Alice Beasley? For example, what facts are presented to support the author's view that Ms. Beasley is "experienced"?

5. Would you vote for Mary Alice Beasley on the basis of this letter? Why or why not? What other information about this candidate would you like to have to help you make your decision? Where would you go for the information you need?

GLOSSARY

Ambiguous

A term that has more than one possible meaning

"Greene County, Missouri, is growing rapidly." That is not a fact; that is an opinion. It is your responsibility to determine the validity of the opinion by asking questions such as the following: What was Greene County's population 10 years ago? What is the average annual rate of growth in the United States? In Missouri? How does Greene County's rate compare with other cities in Missouri? If you learn that Greene County's rate of growth for the last 10 years has been 15.6 percent, compared to Missouri's 9.3 percent, you can reasonably conclude that "Greene County is growing quickly." Thus, opinions are arguable and should be evaluated systematically during a group's deliberations. Groups that make poor decisions do so in part because inferential errors impair their critical thinking.[20]

Identifying and Clarifying Ambiguous Terms.   Authors or speakers often make the job of evaluating information hard by using terminology that is **ambiguous,** or unclear. For example, candidate Beasley in Apply Now 5.3 is termed "experienced." What does that mean? What kinds of experiences has she had? Is she experienced as a teacher, a parent, or an administrator? Is she experienced at working in a small group? Each of these experiences is different and paints a slightly different picture of the candidate. Clarification of vague terms is very important in evaluating the worth of your group's information.

Earlier in the chapter, we examined the decision made by NASA officials to launch the *Challenger.* In their analysis of the decision-making process, Gouran and his associates discovered that failure to clarify ambiguous terms contributed to that terrible decision. They explain:

> *No one went so far as to say, "We recommend that you do not launch." Instead, they claimed making such statements as, "We do not have the data base from which to draw any conclusions for this particular situation"; "We did not have a sufficient data base to absolutely assure that nothing would strike the vehicle."*[21]

What do those statements mean? This kind of doublespeak confuses issues because it leaves room for a variety of interpretations by permitting others to read their own favorite interpretations into the message. At NASA, no one asked explicitly for clarification of the ambiguous terms.

Evaluating Opinions by Determining the Credibility of the Source.   We noted earlier that not all opinions are equal. How can you tell whether an author or a speaker is someone whose opinions are worth your attention? Ask yourself several key questions to help you decide how much trust to place in an opinion.

1. Is there any reason to suspect the person(s) supplying the opinion of bias? For example, if you find a source that debunks the idea that smoking causes lung cancer, you should treat that information with suspicion if it comes from a publication of the American Tobacco Institute. On the other hand, if that statement appears in the scientifically respected *New England Journal of Medicine,* you would have greater reason to expect objectivity.

2. Is the individual, or other source, a recognized expert on the subject? Is this someone whom other experts respect? Would you feel proud or silly quoting this person? We may feel comfortable citing Michael Jordan's opinions about basketball but very uncomfortable citing Aunt Tilly's.

3. Is the opinion consistent with other opinions expressed by the same source? Media sometimes misquote people. Are you reasonably sure the opinion stated is accurate? Is there a later interview or quote that reverses the inconsistent opinion? Sometimes people do change their minds for good reasons. What is the reason given for the change of opinion? Does the evidence offered to explain the change seem reasonable to you? If not, suspect inaccuracy or some unknown bias.

Assessing the Accuracy and Worth of the Information.   Now that you have established a context for evaluating the information by determining exactly what is being said and how credible the source is, you are in a position to evaluate how good that information is (see Table 5.8). After all, it could be misinformation. You should ask yourself a number of questions about the information before using it during group decision making.

1. What types of evidence are offered to support the argument? Is it a personal experience? Statistical support? The combined opinions of a number of recognized experts? Although many people do so, it is unsafe to accept personal experience as the sole basis for supporting an opinion. For example, assume you were once in a group with a dominant leader who decided what everyone should do and delegated these tasks to other members. Perhaps your group produced a high quantity and quality of work, and you were satisfied with the experience. Thus, your personal experience may lead you to believe that groups work best under strong, controlling leaders. Someone else's experience might have been different. Assume a fellow group member worked in a democratic group, where there was no one leader but all members contributed to leadership based on their areas of expertise. This member thinks that the only good group is a democratic one. Which of you is right? Each of you is right, for the particular circumstances of your experience, but neither of you is right to try to apply your experience to everyone else.

2. Is the information based on the testimony of a number of experts or authorities in the field? If so, you can place greater trust in it, especially if these experts are widely recognized and accepted by their peers. Be sure to determine if other experts disagree and why. Be especially careful about accepting information from an expert in one field about another field. For example, movie stars frequently express strong opinions about the American political scene. While some may be well informed, others are not.

3. Is the information based on valid scientific or statistical reasoning? You should ask how the information was gathered, how the questions were worded, whether the data came from a properly designed survey, and so forth. Information must follow strict guidelines before it can legitimately be termed scientific. First, such information must be verifiable by others. Thus, although an experience that happens to someone may be true, it is not scientific unless the event is observed or can be recreated by other people. Second, scientific information must be obtained under controlled conditions by controlled observations. Having an informal conversation with your classmates about the death penalty and concluding that "American college students have the following attitudes toward capital punishment . . ." may be interesting but it is not scientific. But if you surveyed a representative

	Evaluating Information in the Critical Thinking Process
TABLE 5.8	

DETERMINE WHAT THE SPEAKER OR WRITER IS SAYING

1. What is the conclusion?

2. What does the author want us to do?

3. What are the main arguments in support of the conclusion?

DISTINGUISH FACT FROM OPINION AND INFERENCE

1. What are the facts?

2. What are the opinions?

IDENTIFY AND CLARIFY AMBIGUOUS TERMS

1. What are the ambiguous terms?

2. What do you think the author means by each term?

3. If you can't decide with confidence, what problems does this create?

DETERMINE THE CREDIBILITY OF THE SOURCE

1. Who is the author or speaker? What are his or her credentials on this issue?

2. Is this a recognized expert?

3. Is this a biased source or one with something to gain by expressing this opinion?

4. Is the information consistent with other credible sources?

ASSESS THE ACCURACY AND WORTH OF THE INFORMATION

1. What type of evidence (e.g., personal experience, statistical support, opinions of experts) is being offered in support of the author's arguments?

2. Is the evidence supported by other experts or authorities, or just this author?

3. Is the information based on the scientific method?

4. If the information is based on interviews or questionnaires, was the sample large enough and representative enough? Were the questions clear and not biased or loaded?

sample of students, asked each of them the same questions, and systematically analyzed their answers, you could reasonably conclude: "Students at my college believe the following about capital punishment . . ." Finally, scientific information must be expressed precisely. Another researcher, after reading an account of a scientifically controlled research study, should be able to carry out a study in exactly the same way, using the same procedures, equipment, and statistical tests.

Information gathered by questionnaires or interviews poses additional questions regarding the individuals who were queried. Were there enough of them, and were they representative of a larger population? In most cases, random sampling is most likely to

5.1   What Would You Do?

ETHICAL DILEMMA

You and your group have been working on your panel presentation about the death penalty for several weeks, with one week to go before you are responsible for conducting the panel discussion in your class. This project represents a major portion of your grade in the small group class, and you are required to conclude your presentation by taking a position—your group must come out either in favor of or against the death penalty. After hashing this out for weeks, you have sorted through all your evidence and have almost reached consensus that you will come out in favor of the death penalty. This week, while doing library research for another class, you happen upon a new study, based on systematic examination of states with the death penalty, that it *does not* seem to deter crime. The study seems well done; you don't think you can dismiss it as a piece of biased or poorly done research. But you know if you present it to your group, you'll push your emerging consensus farther away, and you hate to do that! You are so close now to agreement, and you know this study will set you back. What do you do?

1. For what reasons would you *present* the article to your group?

2. For what reasons would you *withhold* the article?

3. What would you actually do?

ensure a representative response. For example, assume your committee is charged with making recommendations regarding parking on your campus and you decide to poll students who drive to campus. If you survey only students who park in one particular lot between 7 and 8 A.M., your results are not likely to reflect the views of the entire student population. Making parking recommendations that will affect thousands of students on the basis of responses from a few students is irresponsible. On the other hand, if you systematically survey students from all campus lots at varying times during the day and evening, your responses are more representative and your conclusions are likely to be more valid.

CHECKING FOR ERRORS IN REASONING

The final element in the critical thinking process is assessing the quality of the reasoning people provide for their opinions or for supporting one conclusion over another. Unfortunately, most speakers and writers often make a variety of common reasoning errors, called **fallacies,** that makes assessing reasoning challenging. Fallacies tend to divert a listener's attention from the issue or sidetrack the discussion so that members of a group begin to debate something other than evidence and claims. However, critical thinkers working together in a small group should be able to spot each other's fallacies (see Table 5.9). The differing but complementary bases of information that individual members bring to a group discussion help them compensate for each other's weaknesses to produce, on the whole, a superior group result.[22]

GLOSSARY

Fallacies

Mistakes in reasoning and faulty reasoning

TABLE 5.9	**Checking for Errors in Reasoning**

- Does the author overgeneralize?

- Does the author attack a person instead of the issue?

- Does the author argue that because two events are related, one caused the other?

- Does the author present you with an either–or choice when other alternatives are possible?

- Does the author present you with a comparison that is incomplete or invalid?

Overgeneralizing. Generalizations are made when information about one or more instances is said to apply to many or all instances of the same type. In other words, if something is true about a few instances or people, it is assumed to be true about most instances or people in the same category. For example, someone may read in the newspaper that a certain number of college students have defaulted on their government-guaranteed student loans. If that person concludes from this that "college students are irresponsible borrowers," he or she has made a generalization. Even though it isn't stated that way, this implies that all college students are irresponsible borrowers, and this is an overgeneralization. An **overgeneralization,** like the loan default example, is a conclusion that is not supported by enough data. Generalizations by themselves are not automatically wrong. Conclusions based on carefully gathered data that were analyzed with appropriate statistical procedures are often very accurate. Usually such generalizations are qualified and not stated as applying to all cases. Remember, for a generalization to be factual for all cases, someone would have to observe all of these cases.

To decide whether a generalization is a valid conclusion or an overgeneralization, ask yourself a few questions:

- How many cases is the conclusion based on?
- Are there any exceptions to the conclusion?
- What form of evidence is the source asking us to accept: personal or other forms?
- Is the generalization expressed as probability or in "allness" terms?

Attacking a Person Instead of the Argument. Attacking a person instead of the argument, even if subtly done, is a form of name-calling used to direct attention away from someone's evidence and logic (or lack thereof). Sometimes called *ad hominem* attacks, such arguments take this form: "Because So-and-So is a _____ (woman, Catholic, foreigner, intellectual snob, hillbilly, liberal, and so on), you can't believe his/her opinions about the topic." Such an argument sidetracks the discussion of the opinion into a discussion of the merits of So-and-So. So-and-So may indeed be a crackpot about some things, but his or her views about the topic might be quite accurate. More information is needed before a critical thinker would make that judgment.

GLOSSARY

Overgeneralization

A conclusion not supported by enough data

Confusing Causal Relationships.   Another common reasoning error occurs when the speaker or writer mistakenly states what caused an event. Two forms of this error are observed frequently. Sometimes people oversimplify by implying or stating that only one cause exists for an event. In other instances, they imply that, because two events are related by subject matter or in sequence, one causes the other. For example, we have heard students say that if a manager implements quality control circles in a company, the company's profits will increase. Such a statement implies that quality circles cause higher profits. In actuality, a variety of factors is likely to contribute to, or cause, increased profits. For example, better employee training, lower costs of raw materials, increased prices for a company's products, improvements in technology, and improved upward communication and morale produced by the quality circle—all of these factors may contribute to the increased profits. It is oversimplifying to assume that quality circles alone are the cause.

Neither can we assume that, just because one event preceded another in time, the first caused the other. It may be that both are caused by a third event or condition. For example, one of us recently overheard someone mention recent statistics indicating that female graduates of women's colleges are more likely to become members of the U.S. Congress and serve on the boards of Fortune 500 companies than are graduates of coed schools. The person speaking was arguing that attendance at women's colleges caused this type of career achievement. However, many women's colleges are academically selective as well as expensive. Women attending such schools are often both exceptionally bright and from families who own or are connected to Fortune 500 companies. It is plausible that these additional factors—ability and family connections—"cause" both the attendance at women's colleges and the career achievement. The relationship between college attendance and later achievement is likely to be a complex one that does not lend itself well to simple causal descriptions.

Either-Or Thinking.   **Either–or thinking** (sometimes called a false dilemma) says that you must choose one thing or another, and no other choices are possible. Seldom is this the case. For example, assume your group is preparing a panel discussion about sex education in the schools and you encounter the following statement: "Sex education is an important element of a young person's education. It is the parents' responsibility and privilege to teach their children about sex, and it should not be left up to the schools." Most people would readily agree with the first sentence. The second, however, reveals either–or thinking. The author is forcing the reader to accept the premise that either the parent will teach the child about sex or the school will. In fact, other alternatives are possible. Perhaps churches, synagogues, or Camp Fire USA leaders could take on the job; or parents and school officials together could design a cooperative program. Just because a writer does not mention other alternatives should not blind you to their existence.

Incomplete Comparisons.   Comparisons, especially **analogies,** help us understand issues more vividly. However, there are limitations to such comparisons. Because one thing bears a resemblance to another does not mean they are identical. At some point the resemblance will break down because no two situations are identical in all characteristics. An incomplete analogy (sometimes called a faulty analogy) asks us to stretch a similarity too far. For example, assume you and other students are discussing how well the public relations major at your school prepares students to be public

GLOSSARY

Either–Or Thinking

Asking members to choose between only two options as if no other choices existed

Analogies

Comparisons that help clarify ideas and issues

relations professionals. One student says, "You really can't learn much about public relations from school anyway. It's like trying to ride a bicycle by reading books about it but never getting on an actual bicycle."

At first glance, this remark hits home with many of us who complain that school can't prepare us for the "real world." However, let's look more closely. Yes, there are public relations experiences that cannot be duplicated in school. But there are many activities that do prepare students for professional practice. Designing flyers and brochures, writing news releases, taking photographs, planning a mock public relations campaign, and

5.4   Gun Control

Shortly after the school shooting in Springfield, Oregon, many news programs featured point–counterpoint "debates" between people who favored particular solutions to the problem of children killing children. On one morning news show, the first panelist proposed that legislation be passed requiring handguns and semiautomatic weapons to be fitted with lockable triggers. He explained that parents could lock these guards and keep the keys hidden. This would prevent children from accidentally shooting the guns. It would also mean that children who were enraged would not be able to pick up a gun to discharge their rage; they might start a fistfight, but the guns would be out of bounds. The opposing panelist said that requiring locking triggers would simply make it more difficult for homeowners to defend themselves; he favored stiffer penalties and zero tolerance for children violating rules pertaining to weapons. Each panelist argued strongly for his solution and identified all the possible flaws he could with the opposing panelist's solution.

In small groups or as a whole class, discuss the following questions. To get a more vivid idea of the types of arguments made, you may want to simulate the point–counterpoint discussion and ask two class members to role-play each panelist.

1. First, see how many arguments you can create to support each position and put them on the board for all to see.

2. What are the fallacies you are able to identify in the arguments presented?

3. What are the characteristics of that particular television format that encourage these kinds of fallacies to be presented?

4. Assume the two "debaters" are members of a small discussion group charged with identifying a policy to prevent school shootings. What would you say and do if you heard the kinds of fallacies being expressed during the discussion?

designing a survey are all examples of typical activities that public relations students perform in school and that are also necessary on the job. Thus, whenever you see or hear someone make a comparison, first determine in what ways the two things being compared are similar, but especially look for ways they are different. Ask yourself if the analogy breaks down at any point. If so, where? How does this affect the reasoning you are being asked to accept?

The fallacies previously described are some of the most common ones, but there are many others. Be alert for them by asking the right probing questions about the ideas, opinions, interpretations, and conclusions someone is asking you to accept. Then you need to pay careful attention to the answers you receive (or don't receive).

ASKING PROBING QUESTIONS

We noted earlier that group members with the right "critical thinking" attitude are willing to challenge information and opinions by asking probing questions. This is probably the most important thing you can do if you want to be a critical thinker; it is so important that we are mentioning it again. Do not accept information just because it sounds good, it is presented in an entertaining way, it comes from someone of high status, it supports what you already believe, or the majority of group members accept the information. Avoid an unwillingness to confront and question the accuracy of the information and the appropriateness of the reasoning you are being asked to accept.

According to Gouran et al., failures to ask probing questions at several steps during the decision-making process and groupthink (discussed in Chapter 9) were prime contributors to the *Challenger* disaster. The problem with the O-ring seals in cold temperatures had been observed for years before the launch, but no one asked the tough questions about what was being done to correct the flaw. The problem just kept being ignored. One engineer who opposed the launch assumed that his objection was passed to superiors, but he did not ask specifically whether this was so. When representatives of North American Rockwell, the manufacturer of the shuttle, relayed their concerns about the launch in vague terms, no one asked specifically whether or not they were recommending postponement. All these isolated incidents, in which no one asked the right questions, together contributed to the *Challenger* disaster. The single most important thing you can do to prevent this kind of disaster is to ask probing questions, even though this is not always easy or pleasant to do. If other group members call such questioning argumentative or quibbling, reassure them that the purpose of your questioning is not to argue or put anyone down, but to help the group by clearing up any possible misunderstandings, oversights, or fallacies.

A number of group systems support (GSS) tools can help members probe and evaluate information (see next chapter). GSS tools include electronic brainstorming, electronic outliners, idea organizers, and topic commentators. Working with neutral facilitators, groups can lessen the influence of biased information and can be guided in their attempts to track arguments, confront each other's claims, and develop their own lines of reasoning.[23]

■ To be effective problem solvers, group members must do a good job with both creative and critical thinking. Creative individuals are willing to communicate, to be unconventional, and to play in the group. Creative groups are willing to examine their norms and change those that interfere with creativity.

■ Creativity requires freedom from judgment and can be enhanced through the use of two techniques: brainstorming and synectics. Brainstorming explicitly suspends criticism and synectics works by attempting to make the familiar unfamiliar.

■ Critical thinking involves a concentrated effort to assess the value of ideas and conclusions by gathering relevant information, assessing that information carefully, and judging the reasoning that supports the conclusions and decisions. Critical thinking in small groups involves knowing when to use critical thinking and requires certain attitudes of group members, a methodical search for information, thorough evaluation of the information, and

careful assessment of the reasoning behind opinions and beliefs based on that information.

■ In gathering information, group members first should pool their knowledge and identify any gaps that are apparent. Then, they should fill those gaps by using appropriate research methods, including direct observation; reading; using electronic databases; interviewing individuals or groups; and consulting other sources such as television, the Internet, and radio.

■ When members evaluate information, they first should determine what is being said, which statements are facts and which are inferences or opinions, what terms are ambiguous, how believable the source is, and how accurate and valuable the information is.

■ When they check for errors in reasoning, group members should be especially alert to the common fallacies. Critical thinking consists primarily of asking the right probing questions, which can prevent harmful throughput processes such as groupthink.

1. Form groups of four to six students. Each of you should be given some ordinary, tangible object, such as a clothespin, an alarm clock, or a ballpoint pen. Find a new use for the item that has nothing to do with the item's ordinary use. To do this, you must perceive the item in entirely new ways. To help you do this, your teacher can lead you in a guided meditation. For instance, imagine that the clothespins are alive and are sending you messages about what they would like to be used for. After you have discussed the problem in your groups for 15 or 20 minutes, present your favorite solution to the class. Then all of you should vote to select the most creative idea. (Perhaps your teacher will award prizes to the winning group.)

2. The following exercise helps clarify the difference between statements of fact and statements of inference. Place a familiar item (such as a coffee cup, a chair, or a ballpoint pen) in

front of the class so everyone can see it easily. Make statements of fact about it. Each statement should be written on the board. After about 15 statements, identify as a class those statements that go beyond what was actually observed. Discuss why these statements are inferences rather than facts.

3. Videotape one of the many television programs that feature panel interviews with public figures (such as "Meet the Press" or "This Week"). Look for errors in reasoning, places where the interviewee seemed to camouflage what she or he was saying, or places where the interviewee was evasive. Discuss the program in class. It will be particularly helpful if you can show your tape in class.

 Go to **www.mhhe.com/adamsgalanes** and **www.mhhe.com/groups** for Self-Quizzes and weblinks.

KEY TERMS and CONCEPTS

ambiguous	critical thinking	open-minded
analogies	either–or thinking	opinions
arguments	evidence	overgeneralization
brainstorming	facts	probing questions
creative thinking	fallacies	synectics

www.mhhe.com/adamsgalanes
Use the flashcards and crossword puzzles on the Online Learning Center to further your knowledge of these key terms.

OLC

Group Problem-Solving Procedures

CHAPTER OBJECTIVES

After reading this chapter you should be able to:

1. Explain why using a systematic procedure for group problem solving usually produces better solutions than random or haphazard problem solving.

2. Define key terms such as *problem solving, decision making,* and *area of freedom* with examples.

3. Describe five characteristics of problems.

4. Explain why and how you would adjust the problem-solving process to accommodate any of the characteristics of problems.

5. Describe each step of the P-MOPS procedure.

6. Explain how you could use techniques such as the *problem census, focus groups, group support systems, RISK,* and *PERT* to help at various stages of the P-MOPS procedure.

7. Apply the P-MOPS procedure to fit a simple or complex problem.

The Merger

In 2000, a crisis loomed for Ozarks Public Television. OPT had operated in Springfield and Joplin, Missouri, for nearly 25 years with a community-owned broadcasting license, using studios rented from a small, private college in Springfield. But in the 1990s, the U.S. government mandated that all public TV stations had to switch to digital broadcasting equipment by 2003, a very expensive proposition for OPT. After assessing all their options with the help of a consultant, OPT board members decided to seek an educational partner. Eventually the board approached Southwest Missouri State University with a proposal for SMSU to take over the broadcasting license and allow OPT to merge with the university. The SMSU board accepted the proposal at its December meeting, and work toward the merger began immediately.

Ideally, the physical move would occur in the summer, when fewer students and faculty would be on campus, but before that could happen, a number of legal items and physical changes had to occur. Most importantly, the Federal Communications Commission (FCC) had to approve the license transfer. Space had to be found on campus to accommodate the OPT staff, equipment, and control room; the decision had to be made about how to finance and when to make the digital conversion; the merger and its benefits to SMSU had to be presented to the faculty, staff, and students; and program planning at a variety of levels had to occur.

Involving every OPT and university employee in each decision would have created chaos! Instead, several groups—each composed of different combinations of SMSU and OPT personnel—were established to bring about the merger. For example, a facilities subcommittee was charged with assessing SMSU space and determining how it needed to be modified. A public relations subcommittee handled the delicate process of explaining the merger to the university community and to the many volunteers who had worked for OPT over the years. Several similar groups were established, with their work overseen by the steering committee we introduced to you in Chapter 1. The steering committee established the timeline and kept track of the progress of each of the other groups to ensure that the merger would occur on time and with every detail accounted for.

The OPT–SMSU merger is a typical group problem-solving situation. In this case, two parent organizations—OPT and SMSU—appointed a number of groups to help the larger organizations manage information, make decisions, and complete tasks about a complex problem. A single individual trying to solve the merger problem would have become overwhelmed at the volume of information and the amount of work! Not only that, a single individual would have been unable to think of everything that needed to happen for this merger. Some important piece likely would have fallen through the cracks. On the other hand, involving the entire university community and OPT staff in participating equally to identify and evaluate solutions would have created a chaotic and unmanageable process. In this case, using several smaller groups, with the steering committee in charge, enabled the work to be done on behalf of the two larger organizations.

As we said in Chapter 1, groups can produce solutions to complex problems that are better than solutions produced by individuals; they also produce greater member understanding and more satisfaction.[1] The *assembly effect* is achieved when the group solution is superior both to the choice of the group's most expert member and to an averaging of opinions of all members. Verbal interaction among the members is the essential ingredient for this superior output.[2] The dark side, however, is that group problem solving is not always better (see Table 6.1). Groups can do a lot, though, to improve the quality of both problem-solving procedures and the solutions they generate. Systematic problem-solving procedures are a key factor in improving the overall quality of their activities. They usually produce better solutions and decisions than unsystematic discussion.[3] This chapter identifies the nature of problems and describes procedures for improving group problem-solving discussions.

TABLE 6.1	Advantages and Disadvantages of Solving Problems in Groups versus as Individuals

Advantages	Disadvantages
• Solutions for complex problems are usually superior.	• Groups take more time.
• Groups have more resources, including information and methods.	• Participation may be uneven; some members may dominate, others withdraw.
• Members accept the solutions more readily; satisfaction is higher.	• Interpersonal tension, disagreements about the task, and conformity pressures may interfere with critical thinking.
• Members understand the solution more completely.	

A Systematic Procedure as the Basis for Problem Solving

There are a number of ways to solve problems. Many people solve problems at an unconscious or preconscious level called *intuition*. This happens when you may be wondering what to do about an assignment and suddenly the answer occurs to you while you're taking a shower. Another way to solve problems is by turning to an expert or someone you consider to be an authority, the way many people turn to doctors for dealing with illnesses.

There's nothing wrong with these methods, particularly for problems that will affect only you. However, they can have serious limitations for group problem solving, especially if you use them alone without also using a systematic procedure for checking out the hunch or intuition. Careful, critical analysis of information is important as well. What would you say if you went to the doctor because of chest pains and, without doing any tests, she said, "My intuition tells me you need a shot of penicillin"? Ideas derived only through intuition must be examined critically before they are implemented because critical thinking can reveal flaws in the ideas that may not be apparent at first. It's possible the hunch is terrific and may only need to be tweaked to solve your problem, but it's also possible that the hunch may cause more problems than it solves. Systematic problem solving is a way for groups to assess ideas and to manage the mountain of information unearthed by the problem-solving process. For example, the OPT–SMSU merger involved keeping track of dozens of details—far more than any one person could have handled. If the steering committee hadn't met regularly and used a systematic process, some of the information would have been lost, and key options might not have been considered. Any less systematic procedure might have produced a successful merger, but chances are some important element would have been ignored.

Thus, no matter how a group discovers the possible solutions to a problem—through intuition, logic, or authority—the group must use a systematic process and the best critical thinking it can muster to check out how well the solutions will work. The rest of this chapter is designed to help you understand what problems are, how certain characteristics of problems affect the problem-solving process you use, and how you can organize group problem solving by using a systematic, yet flexible, procedure called P-MOPS. We also provide a number of specific techniques that help at different stages of the problem-solving process.

What Is a Problem?

Problem refers to the difference between what exists and what you expect or want. For example, you need your entire group to show up for a class presentation, but on the day of the presentation three members are no-shows. You have a problem!

Problem solving and decision making are related concepts and need to be distinguished before we go further. **Problem solving** involves all the things you have to do to move from the existing situation to the goal. It is a multistep process that includes

GLOSSARY

Problem

The difference between what exists presently and what you expect or want

Problem Solving

Everything you need to do to move from your present undesirable situation to what you want, including creating solutions and choosing among them

defining the problem, identifying or creating possible solutions, and choosing among the solutions. **Decision making** refers to the act of selecting one or more available options; it does *not* involve creating possible options. Problem solving is a more comprehensive procedure that includes decision making (choosing). The entire process of solving a problem often involves making many decisions, such as how to define the problem, what solutions to consider, which to suggest or act upon, and how to carry out the chosen solution. The steps you take and the order in which you do them can greatly influence the quality of your product. Can you imagine cutting out material for a coat without first having a pattern to guide your scissors?

Every problem situation has three major components. A group needs to understand and articulate these components completely to develop an appropriate solution for a particular problem.

1. **An undesirable existing situation.**

   If people believe that something is perfectly satisfactory as it is, there is no problem. For example, if a church's meeting place is accessible and affordable, the church board has no problem. But if the landlord suddenly triples the rent, the board will want to look for a new place to meet. The undesirable present situation in this case is an exorbitant rent the church can't afford.

2. **Desired situation or goal.**

   At the start, a goal may vary from a vague image of a better condition (safer neighborhood) to a very precise, detailed objective (starting a neighborhood watch program). Part of effective problem solving involves establishing a precise goal that is achievable, doesn't suggest a solution, and is understandable to all members. Outstanding groups have clear goals that all members support.[4]

3. **Obstacles to change.**

   These are conditions and forces that must be overcome by the chosen solution to achieve the goal. Typical obstacles include insufficient information, the competing interests of other people, lack of tools or skills, insufficient funds, or anything you must overcome in order to reach the goal. For example, the church whose rent tripled probably has no idea what other facilities are available, what similar facilities rent for, how soon another facility could be located, whether congregation members would be willing to move, what it can afford, and so forth.

AREA OF FREEDOM

The **area of freedom** is the amount of authority and the limitations given to a group charged with solving a problem. Group members must know, at the beginning, what they are and are not supposed to do. A fact-finding group, for instance, may be asked only to investigate a problem, not solve it. Another small group may have authority only to interpret information, as in the case of a jury that can decide guilt or innocence but not the penalty for guilt. Many advisory committees and conferences can recommend a solution but not make it binding. For example, the OPT–SMSU facilities subcommit-

For more information on the digital divide problem, go to the on-line learning center.

GLOSSARY

Decision Making

Choosing from available options

Area of Freedom

The amount of authority and limitations given to a group

6.1   **Improving Airport Security**

After September 11, 2001, it was clear that the United States had a problem with ensuring security on its airline flights, since terrorists had been able to hijack four different airplanes on the same day. Map this problem according to the problem components described above.

1. An undesirable existing situation: Describe the airplane boarding situation on 9–11 and explain what seems to be undesirable about that situation (e.g., rules permitted box cutter knives to be carried on planes).

2. Desired situation or goal: What would the desired situation look like? For instance, passengers would like to board quickly and efficiently, but they would also like to be protected from other passengers carrying weapons.

3. Obstacles to change: What are obstacles to our achieving these goals? For instance, do we lack information about how terrorists bypass safeguards in our system? Do we lack technology at airports to improve baggage screening?

tee charged with identifying available space for OPT was not empowered to start modifying that space until the steering committee had evaluated the options and given the go-ahead.

Committee members must understand the exact charge to the group before they proceed to work on any problem. Otherwise, they will waste time and may become frustrated or angry. A committee one of us observed was charged with making recommendations about the types of student activities on campus. Instead, this committee created a sweeping proposal to fire certain individuals and restructure the student activities department. Even though committee members worked long and conscientiously to develop the plan, it was not accepted because the committee went far beyond its area of freedom.

ADAPTING PROCEDURES TO FIT YOUR PROBLEM

Some problems are complex and others relatively simple. It makes intuitive sense that you would not use exactly the same process for all kinds of problems. Systematic processes for problem solving can and should be modified to fit the particular problem your group faces. To help you do this, you need to understand something about the characteristics of problems and how these can affect group problem solving in order to tailor your procedures to fit your problem. The components described earlier are common to all problems, but specific characteristics vary.

TABLE 6.2

Problem Characteristics and the Problem-Solving Process

TASK DIFFICULTY

How complicated (e.g., how can we merge OPT with SMSU) or simple (which color of pencils should we buy) is the problem? High task difficulty means a complicated problem; low task difficulty means a simple one. The more complex a problem is, the more information the group will need to understand the existing situation adequately.

Adaptation (for high difficulty)

- Detailed problem mapping among members.

- Many subquestions to the problem-solving procedure.

- Detailed implementation plan, in writing.

SOLUTION MULTIPLICITY

How many possible options are there? Low solution multiplicity has few; high solution multiplicity has many. The more possible options, the more time needs to be devoted to identifying them.

Adaptation (for high multiplicity)

- Use brainstorming or one of its variations in the idea-generation step.

- Use synectics or another creativity technique to help members relax and enjoy the process.

- Don't rush the process; leave plenty of time for idea generation.

INTRINSIC INTEREST

Are members interested and involved in solving this problem, or have they been "drafted" to work on it? High intrinsic interest means members are motivated and want to work; low intrinsic interest means they are uninterested or bored. The more interested members are, the less control they want from the discussion leader. Members want to vent and talk.

Adaptation (for high interest)

- Set aside a "ventilation" period early in the problem-solving process so members can express their feelings.

- Leave plenty of time for early ventilation.

- Don't overcontrol the ventilation process or introduce structured procedures too early.

MEMBER FAMILIARITY

How much do members know about the problem? Have they ever worked together on similar problems? High familiarity means members are used to working on similar problems; low familiarity means the problem is new to them. The less members know about a problem, the more they need to familiarize themselves with all aspects of the problem before they begin problem solving.

Adaptation (for low familiarity)
- Detailed problem mapping.

- Use consultants and outside experts for help.

Adaption (for high familiarity)
- Focus on evaluation of options.

- Focus on establishing criteria.

ACCEPTANCE LEVEL

How important is it that the solution be acceptable to people affected by it? With low acceptance, there is little risk if people don't like the solution; with high acceptance, it is critical that people affected accept it. Testing people's reactions is important if acceptance level needs to be high.

Adaptation (for high acceptance)
- Include representatives from groups that must accept the decision in the group.

- Use the RISK or similar "last chance" technique before finally deciding on a solution.

- Pretest solutions by partially implementing them and agreeing to pull back if they don't seem to work.

You should consider several important characteristics of problems when deciding on a problem-solving procedure. A great deal of research has gone into understanding these characteristics (see Table 6.2).

Sometimes problems are obvious—your group chair quits; your parent organization withdraws monetary support; you can't get anyone to come to meetings. However, most organizations don't want to wait for a problem to become a crisis before they consider what to do about it. The OPT board didn't wait until 2003—the deadline for converting to digital equipment—before investigating their options.

IDENTIFYING PROBLEMS WITH A PROBLEM CENSUS

The **problem census** is a posting technique for identifying important problems or issues. It can be used to establish agenda items for future meetings of a committee or identify problems on the horizon that a group should work on. Sometimes a group leader wants to encourage participation and make group processes more democratic but doesn't know exactly where to begin. The problem census is ideal for all

GLOSSARY

Problem Census

A posting technique to help a group identify important issues or problems

6.2   Characteristics of OPT's Problem

Assume you are members of the Ozarks Public Television governing board, and it is early 2000. You know that you have a 2003 deadline for converting to digital equipment, a very expensive proposition. You are currently bringing in enough money for OPT to operate both stations in Springfield and Joplin, Missouri, but you aren't making the kind of extra money you'd need—well over $1 million—to make the digital conversion. You have a problem!

1. Identify the elements of this problem: the undesirable existing situation, the goal, and the obstacles to change.

2. Look at the characteristics of the problem-solving process presented in Table 6.2. Evaluate OPT's problem in terms of these characteristics, explaining your evaluation:

   Task difficulty: high or low? Why?

   Solution multiplicity: high or low? Why?

   Intrinsic interest: high or low? Why?

   Member familiarity: high or low? Why?

   Acceptance level: high or low? Why?

these purposes because it requires all the members of a group to take responsibility for creating the group's work agenda. Members often become more committed to the group's task because they are enthused about working on items they perceive as important to them. For example, a university department conducts a problem census at the beginning of each semester, generating agenda items for future meetings. As various departmental problems are listed, different faculty members volunteer to investigate the problems and prepare an outline for discussing each problem as it comes up. The following are detailed steps (summarized in Figure 6.1) for conducting a problem census in a face-to-face meeting. Several of these steps are easily handled electronically.

1. **Seat the group in a semicircle facing a chart or board.**

   If you have access to a large computer screen and specialized hardware and software (discussed later), you may also position members at computer terminals facing a large computer screen.

2. **Explain the purpose of the technique, which is to bring out any problems, concerns, questions, or difficulties any member wants to discuss.**

3. **Ask each participant to present one problem or concern in** round-robin **fashion.**

   After the first person presents one problem, the second presents one, and so forth. Anyone who does not have a problem to list may pass. This continues until all problems are identified. One electronic alternative to this is to ask members to brainstorm problems individually and then send them to the centralized computer

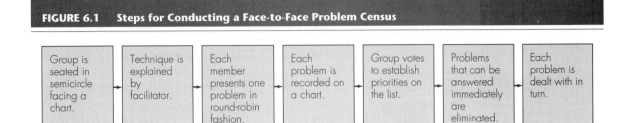

FIGURE 6.1   Steps for Conducting a Face-to-Face Problem Census

screen. That way all problems are posted for everyone to see. Another electronic alternative is to ask people to e-mail their list to the group's leader in advance of the meeting; these are easily compiled into a master list that members can be given ahead of time.

4. **Post each problem on a board or chart as it is presented.**

   As each page of the chart is filled, it is taped to the wall so that all problems are visible at all times. The group's recorder must never challenge or disagree but may ask for clarification or elaboration and may rephrase long problems. The recorder should always ask the speaker whether the rephrasing accurately reflects the speaker's intent.

5. **The group votes to establish priorities on the list.**

   Usually, each member votes individually for three or four top choices. The items are then ranked from most to least votes received. All items remain on the list; voting just prioritizes the agenda. With certain software, this ranking process can be handled electronically as well. Members rank the items individually; the computer automatically tallies and prioritizes the overall list based on member rankings.

6. **Problems that can be answered immediately are eliminated.**

   Sometimes group members can answer questions or solve problems to the satisfaction of the person who initially presented the problem. Such questions or issues are removed from the list.

7. **Each problem is dealt with in turn.**

   Some issues may call for an investigation and report, a lecture, or another informational presentation such as a brochure. Some require the services of outside consultants. However, major problems should be handled by the entire group or a subcommittee, following an appropriate problem-solving procedure.

Once an organization has identified problems to address, it will likely appoint a task force or study group to begin identifying solutions to the problem. Confronting the problem systematically is the best way to ensure that no important information is ignored or overlooked and that group members' time is used wisely. The procedure described below is easily modified so you can take advantage of its flexibility and adapt it to the particular problem your group faces.

The Procedural Model of Problem Solving (P-MOPS)

In the early 1900s, American philosopher John Dewey asked his students to think about a problem they had faced and solved, then to recall the sequence they used to solve the problem. From their reports, he created a general sequence of mental steps he called *reflective thinking*, which implied that the students' process was systematic rather than intuitive or haphazard behavior. According to Dewey, the individual problem-solving sequence usually goes like this: first we become aware of a difficulty, then define and describe it, think of some possible solutions, evaluate these potential solutions, evaluate these potential solutions, and make a decision about what to do. If possible, when we implement the solution, we monitor it to see how it's working, then keep it, adjust it, or replace it after testing it.[5] Various versions of this set of steps have been recommended in small group communication texts.

Numerous advantages of using a planned organization for problem-solving discussions in such small groups as task forces, committees, and quality circles have been documented. These procedures can minimize the bad habits typical of task groups, including getting off track, being pressured by domineering members, prematurely rejecting ideas, and focusing on solutions too early in the process. They help balance participation, improve a group's reflectiveness, coordinate members' thinking, and establish important ground rules for proceeding.[6]

Step-by-step procedures improve the quality of solutions because they give you logical priorities and steps that must be taken; they remind members of things they might otherwise forget to do.[7] Recent evidence suggests that much of the increase in the quality of solutions results from thorough analysis of the problem, generation of a variety of solutions, and detailed assessment of both positive and negative aspects of the alternative solutions being considered by the group.[8] In addition, focusing less on the positive aspects of a solution and more on the potential problems is more effective.[9] Several researchers have concluded that using *any* systematic procedure or outline produces better decisions than using no procedure.[10]

Group members themselves have said that one of their most urgent needs is receiving guidance about methods and procedures to use during group work.[11] One of the most troublesome barriers to effective problem solving that group participants have mentioned is the lack of strong procedural guidelines for decision making, particularly methods that help groups generate and organize their ideas about complex problems. One such guideline, the Procedural Model of Problem Solving (P-MOPS for short), has been used with good success.

The **Procedural Model of Problem Solving** is a flexible framework that can guide each phase of problem solving; it applies all the principles we have learned about effective problem solving by individuals and groups. The model provides a sequence to guide each phase of the problem-solving process and is flexible enough for you to adjust it to suit the special needs of your group. Also, it reminds the group to investigate and analyze the problem thoroughly before trying to solve it and to think critically about the positive and negative outcomes likely to occur with each alternative solution. We have shortened its name to P-MOPS to remind you that it will help you "mop up" the details needed for good problem solving. The five steps in this general problem-solving procedure are: (1) describing and analyzing the problem, (2) generating and explaining possible solutions, (3) evaluating all solutions, (4) choosing the best solution, and (5) implementing the chosen solution.

1. DESCRIBING AND ANALYZING THE PROBLEM

During the first stage of problem solving, the group concentrates on thoroughly understanding the problem. Members should consider all three major elements of the problem: what is unsatisfactory, what is desired, and what obstacles exist. This phase of problem solving may require nothing more than sharing the knowledge members now have, illustrated by the mapping procedure depicted in Figure 6.2. That's easier said than done, though. Group members have a tendency to share freely that information that they already hold in common.[12] Apparently, shared information is more credible and creates common ground among members, who have a tendency to withhold unique information, but this defeats the purpose. For group problem solving to be most effective, *all* information must be shared.[13] Members have to overcome their natural reluctance to share certain kinds of information and be willing to make whatever they know about a problem the property of the group. The description and analysis of a problem should never be rushed—it is crucial to effective problem solving.

FIGURE 6.2   Maps of a Problem Before and After Members Discuss It

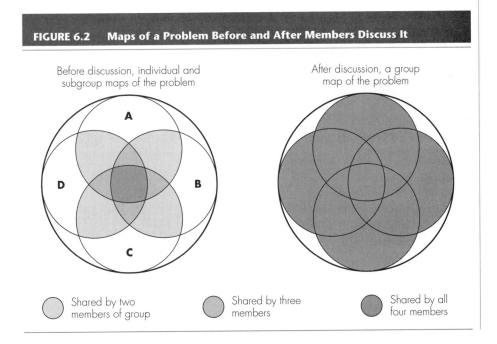

Before discussion, individual and subgroup maps of the problem

After discussion, a group map of the problem

○ Shared by two members of group

○ Shared by three members

● Shared by all four members

Following are several principles to guide your thinking and discussion in step 1 of problem solving.

a. *Be sure you understand the charge precisely.* The **charge** is your assignment of both responsibility and limitations, given by the organization or person who created the group. Getting the charge straight is what you do when you make sure you understand an assignment exactly as intended. Get the charge in writing if possible. A committee should ask for clarification of any unclear terms from the person presenting the charge. For instance, you need to know what form your final product is to take: a recommendation, a research report, a blueprint with perspective drawings, or any other tangible object. You will certainly need to know what limitations are placed on your freedom, such as what information you can obtain from company records, legal restraints, spending limits, and so on. You will want to know when your work must be done; deadlines are part of most charges to groups. Thus, be sure the charge is clear to all members and that it is understood alike by the small group and the parent organization.

b. *State the problem as a single, clear problem question.* A question that suggests the solution biases the group and limits its effectiveness. "How can we convince the administration to put in a new parking lot?" is a *solution question* that assumes the solution to the parking problem is to create a new parking lot. This *problem question* is better: "How can we improve the parking situation on campus?"

c. *Focus on the problem before discussing how to solve it.* One common source of poor solutions is getting solution-centered before the problem has been thoroughly investigated, described, and analyzed. If a group member suggests a solution too early, the discussion leader or another member should then suggest that the group refrain from any talk about what to do until after the group has completed its analysis of the problem.

d. *Describe the problem thoroughly.* Be sure to answer all questions about what is going on, what you hope to accomplish, and possible obstacles to that goal—the way a successful investigative reporter or detective does. A good way to describe the problem is to think of it as an uncharted map with only vague boundaries. Your first job as a group is to make a complete, detailed map of the problem. As we mentioned earlier, this process of information sharing is critical—don't be tempted to shortchange it! Table 6.3 outlines questions you will need to answer.

e. *Make an outline and a schedule based on the Procedural Model of Problem Solving,* especially if it is a major problem requiring extended work over several meetings. This outline and schedule can be modified later, if needed, but at least now the group will reap the benefits of a plan before getting too deeply into the problem analysis.

f. *Summarize the problem as a group.* This ensures that everyone understands it in the same way. In the case of a large problem, this summary may be done in writing by one member and edited by the entire group until all members are satisfied with it.

Sometimes the problem you are addressing will affect a number of people and you may need information about what is important to them. For instance, merging with SMSU was a scary prospect for the OPT employees; they had many concerns about whether their jobs would be retained or changed in major ways. Or a particular prob-

TABLE 6.3	**Questions to Ask as You Analyze the Problem**

WHAT ARE ALL THE RELEVANT FACTS?
- Who is involved? When? Where? How?
- What complaints have been made?
- What is the difference between what is expected and what is actually happening?
- What harm has occurred?
- What exceptions have there been?
- What changes have occurred?
- What other information do we need?

WHAT MAY HAVE PRODUCED OR CAUSED THE UNSATISFACTORY CONDITION?
- What events precipitated the problem?
- What other factors may have contributed to the problem?

WHAT DO WE HOPE TO ACHIEVE?
- What form will our solution take?
- What would be a minimum acceptable solution for each person concerned?

lem may have several aspects, and you may need to know which ones are the main issues or concerns. As an example, work on the license transfer to SMSU was a critical step that had to be undertaken first; if the FCC hadn't approved the transfer, nothing else mattered. One technique you can use to find out what is important to others is the focus group.

Spotlighting Key Issues with Focus Groups.   The **focus group** technique, which encourages unstructured discussion about a given topic, is often used to analyze people's interests and values. It is a great way for a group or an organization to find out what the important issues are regarding a problem facing the group; however, it is such a flexible procedure that it can be used at several steps in the problem-solving process.

In a focus group discussion, the facilitator introduces a topic to the group and instructs group members to discuss the topic any way they choose. The facilitator gives no further direction to the group but may probe or ask questions. Usually, the group discussion is tape-recorded for later analysis. After the group is finished, the facilitator or representatives of the parent organization listen to the tape for usable ideas.

Although focus groups were created within the advertising industry, they have been used in a variety of creative ways by many other types of organizations. For example, a public relations officer at a small campus used a focus group to discover more effective ways of scheduling and promoting evening classes. A group of evening students was instructed simply to talk about what it was like to be an evening student. From the discussion it was clear that evening students were often trying to juggle full-time jobs, families, and other responsibilities in addition to school. The school's schedule was forcing them to come to the campus for four nights a week to complete two courses. But the focus group discussion

GLOSSARY

Focus Group

An unstructured technique in which members freely explore thoughts and feelings about a topic

indicated the students would be happy to stay later in the evening if they could take the same two courses by coming to the campus only two nights a week. Campus officials found a way to "stack" the evening classes to allow this. In addition, the student comments spurred many imaginative ideas for advertising and promoting the evening offerings.

2. GENERATING AND EXPLAINING POSSIBLE SOLUTIONS

The quality of the solution to a problem will not be better than the quality of the pool of ideas the group considers. Studies of problem solving have shown that the ideas discovered later are more likely to be innovative and of higher quality than the ideas first mentioned.[14] Thus, the major issue of step 2 is not "What *should* be done to solve the problem?" but "What *might* be done to solve the problem?" This subtle change in wording is important.

During step 2, the group should focus on creatively finding and listing possible solutions, not on critically determining their relative merits or on trying to decide what to do. Creative thinking is crucial to this step and was discussed in detail in Chapter 5. The leader may need to remind the group not to argue (yet) the relative merits of proposed solutions.

No criticism should be allowed during step 2, but ideas may be explained and clarified. Someone may ask, "What do you mean?" or "Could you please explain how that would work?" Descriptive explanations help everyone understand the idea and may even stimulate further ideas.

Sometimes, while generating ideas, a member will recognize details of the problem that ought to be explored more fully. The group may then cycle back to the P-MOPS step 1 for further exploration about that issue. For example, faculty on a committee charged with revising the communication major realized, in the middle of evaluating options for the revision, that they had forgotten to solicit feedback from an important group—their alumni. The members conducted a quick telephone survey of selected alumni, thus temporarily setting aside their evaluation to return to analysis of the problem. When they are finished, members go back to listing alternatives.

Once a group has completed its list of alternatives, it is ready to proceed with evaluating them.

6.3   What Could OPT Do?

APPLY NOW

Assume you are on the OPT governing board and you have to decide what to do about continuing to operate *and* converting to digital equipment. Obviously, "business as usual" isn't going to work. What are your possible options for dealing with this problem? List as many as you can think of, and don't worry right now whether they are realistic or not.

3. EVALUATING ALL POSSIBLE SOLUTIONS

During the third stage of problem solving, *all* proposed solutions should be evaluated. Critical thinking, as discussed in Chapter 5, is especially crucial during this stage. The options must be tested against the criteria the group has established, and members must be sure the solution is consistent with the facts brought out during discussion, the goals of the group, and the restrictions imposed by the group's area of freedom. It is especially important to consider all possible negative consequences of each solution, or new problems it might create for the group or other people.

Criteria for Evaluating Solutions.   **Criteria** are statements that set standards and limits for comparing and evaluating ideas. For example, search committee members assessing applicants for a library dean's position streamlined their evaluation process by using criteria sheets the members developed. Committee members made a list of the essential qualifications (for example, academic degrees required, years of experience required) and the other desirable characteristics (for example, fund-raising experience, team approach to managing). Then they decided which of the criteria were most important and placed them in a priority listing. This gave each member a set of very specific guidelines to use as he or she read each application.

Serious secondary tension (see Chapter 7) may arise as people argue and disagree while they discuss the pros and cons of proposed solutions. Having agreed-upon criteria helps make arguments as constructive as possible and keeps personal defensiveness to a minimum. Establishing criteria is very important—groups that spend time discussing and establishing criteria are more effective than groups that don't.[15] Thus, group members should discuss, agree upon, and possibly rank (from most to least important) the criteria for judging their ideas and solutions.

Some criteria are absolute, which means they *must* be met (e.g., "The library dean must have at least a master's degree in library science from an American Library Association-accredited school" is an absolute criterion—the group has no leeway). Other criteria are important but give the group some flexibility (e.g., "A Ph.D. is a preferred qualification for the library dean").

There are criteria that are virtually universal in judging among solutions, such as Will the proposed solution actually solve the problem? Can the proposed solution be done? Will the benefits outweigh the costs? Is this solution within our area of freedom? and How acceptable is this idea to the people most likely to be affected by it? Such criteria encourage the group to consider whether or not the ideas proposed are legal, moral, workable, within the competence of the group or organization, within the control of the parent organization, and so on.

These are general, abstract criteria. You will need to express criteria as specifically and clearly as possible to avoid misunderstandings about their meaning. "We must have the OPT staff and equipment moved to SMSU by August 1" is more precise than "We have to move OPT sometime this summer."

GLOSSARY

Criteria

Standards and guidelines used to evaluate ideas and solutions

TABLE 6.4	**Charting the Pros and Cons of Two Proposed Solutions**

How to reduce passenger injuries in automobile accidents

Pass federal law to require the use of seat belts	Require new cars to be equipped with airbags
PROS	**PROS**
• Would reduce or elminate many injuries.	• Would be extremely effective.
• Would be inexpensive.	• Technology currently exists.
• Precedent exists in many states.	**CONS**
CONS	• Would increase the cost of cars.
• Infringes on individual rights; expect a heated legal fight.	• Infringes on individual rights; expect a heated legal battle.
• Difficult to enforce.	• Airbags might inflate incorrectly and cause an accident.
• Some injuries could be worse with seatbelts.	

Narrowing a Long List of Proposed Solutions.   When a list of ideas has been generated by brainstorming or any other technique, the group will need to reduce this list to a manageable size before it discusses the merits of the ideas. This can be done in a number of ways after the group has established its criteria. Here are three useful techniques:

1. Combine any ideas that are similar or overlapping. For example, "Hold a goodwill party" and "Have a get-acquainted cocktail party" could be combined into "Plan a social event."

2. Allow each member (including the leader) to vote for his or her top three choices. Tally the votes. Any proposed solutions that do not have at least two votes may be removed from the list.

3. Give each member five small cards on which to write the number or name of his or her five preferred solutions, one on each card. The cards are arranged from most to least preferred. A *5* is written on the top card, a *4* on the second, and so on down to the last card, which receives a *1*. The leader or recorder collects the cards and tallies ratings for each idea. The ratings are summed and divided by the number of members in the group to give an average rating to each idea. Any idea with no rating is crossed off the list. The group then discusses the pros and cons of only the proposed solutions with the highest ratings.

Charting the Pros and Cons.   During the evaluation discussion, a recorder can help greatly by creating a chart of the ideas being discussed, with the pros and cons mentioned for each idea, as shown in Table 6.4. Instead of *Pros* and *Cons,* the chart headings

6.4   What Is OPT's Best Choice?

Again assuming the role of the OPT governing board, look at the choices you established in Apply Now 6.2. Before you evaluate those options, what criteria would you use?

1. Develop the criteria against which you will evaluate your choices about how to handle OPT's problem.

2. Evaluate each choice according to the criteria you just developed. Which option or options seem most likely to succeed?

3. If you were OPT, what would you recommend for the organization?

might be *Advantages* and *Disadvantages, For* and *Against,* or even + and −. Using such a chart that everyone can see helps the group remember major arguments and think critically about the proposals under consideration. This, too, can be done electronically, either with specialized software or by ordinary e-mail, with someone compiling the comments.

Using Group Support Systems to Evaluate Solutions.   **Group support systems (GSS)** are computer-based systems designed to improve the quality and speed of group problem solving. Specifically, GSS exist to help groups with such tasks as idea generation, information organization, evaluation of options, and decision making. Many are designed to allow group members to work collaboratively on a problem even though they may be meeting in different locations at different times. Examples of GSS include e-mail, voice messaging, and computer conferencing. Two of the more well-known support systems for problem solving are GroupSystems and Software Assisted Meeting Management (SAMM). Both include modules created to help groups in every area of problem solving.[16] They are particularly helpful during the evaluation stage because they structure the procedure by which members can honestly react to each other's suggestions and ideas.

Such systems have rapidly increased in number, ease of use, and effectiveness, especially as more and more organizations use local area networks that allow several computers to be connected to each other. People can employ group support systems for either long-term use or for one problem-solving task. For example, workers in geographically dispersed areas can connect via computer to perform group work, even though they may be far apart. Often, however, people meet electronically in the same room, each at his or her own computer terminal. This allows several members to "talk" at once by entering their messages into the computer, which compiles them quickly. It also permits anonymity; who submitted a particular comment, idea, criticism, and so forth is not identified. Some group support systems are highly specialized. For example, several are designed to improve the idea-generation step of brainstorming. Others, such as SAMM, are more general and are designed to improve the entire problem-solving and decision-making process, in part by providing structure.

GLOSSARY

Group Support Systems (GSS)

Computer-based system designed to improve various aspects of group work

Group decision making using computer support systems seems to be at least as good as traditional group decision making.[17] Members are often more satisfied and like the fact that the computers permit simultaneous talk. Studies conducted in organizations using group support systems suggest that bigger groups are even more satisfied than smaller ones, that group support systems seem to help group members sustain their task

6.1   Using Chat Rooms for GSS

OLC

Go to **www. mhhe.com/ adamsgalanes** for additional weblink activities.

MEDIA AND TECHNOLOGY

Group support systems can be as simple as using e-mail to facilitate information exchange between group members or more complex when using specialized group meeting software programs. An important characteristic of effective GSS is anonymity. Group members can feel free to share ideas without fear of reprisal or ridicule if their statements are anonymous. Unfortunately, many e-mail systems make anonymity difficult, and specialized meeting software can be expensive.

One alternative for using GSS is to create a chat room and have group members "log on" using anonymous nicknames. Chat rooms are special websites that allow any number of users to interact in real time (synchronous communication). Thousands of chat rooms already exist on the Internet. Many online services allow users to create free private chatrooms that could be used for private discussions among friends or for anonymous group discussions. Here are directions for creating a free GSS resource for your group:

1. Got to www.lycos.com and click on the "clubs" tool at the left. This will display general categories of clubs available on Lycos.

2. Click the "register" button on the left. You should register using anonymous information. Remember to write down your anonymous user identification and password so you can access the club in the future.

3. One group member (or your teacher) can create a new club. As you will discover, clubs provide more resources than chat rooms. You should create a public club so that other group members can easily find it. Let other group members know the name of the club and what category (for example, Education—Resources) you placed the club in.

4. Each group member should log in using anonymous nicknames and then navigate to the newly created club. Members can chat, create discussion boards (discussion boards are saved whereas chats are not), and even take part in polls created by group members.

Using resources like the Lycos clubs is an easy way to create functional GSS for your group. Using Internet chat rooms (or Lycos clubs) is easy once you are familiar with their many features. Group members should familiarize themselves with the chat room or club interface before the group uses this technology to facilitate a group discussion.

focus better, and that less time seems to be spent in meetings. In addition, the anonymity such systems provide is important, more so for groups with individuals of widely varied status than for groups of peers. Group support systems also help improve organizational record-keeping and memory.

Group members should recognize that using GSS is not always beneficial. Problems include some group members' discomfort with using computers, GSS procedures that may structure group interaction too tightly, and managers who may not want group members under their supervision to have full access to information easily obtained via computers.[18]

Be careful with any conclusion drawn about GSS. They are changing daily. They seem to be especially beneficial for certain types of tasks, such as idea generation and decision making.[19] However, face-to-face groups seem to be superior for negotiation and complex, cognitive tasks. Whether or not group support systems improve performance depends on a variety of factors.[20] Groups using support systems generally make better decisions; such groups generate more alternatives; and participation among members is more even. On the other hand, groups take longer to reach decisions, experience less consensus, and are less satisfied than face-to-face groups. An important key to satisfaction appears to be user familiarity—users' reactions are usually negative at first. Several reviews of GSS have found that group members need to be given time to become familiar with the spirit or intention of GSS. As long as a GSS is used consistently with its intentions, it can be very effective; however, merely using a GSS program without considering its intent may fail. GSS do not do the work *for* the group, nor do they work if group members fail to use good communication skills. The same communication skills crucial to traditional face-to-face problem solving are still needed when groups use GSS as tools. The most we can say definitively is that GSS are generally good for groups, although they are not useful in every circumstance.[21]

After all proposals have been thoroughly evaluated, the group has set the stage for the emergence of a final decision on a solution or policy. A favored solution may already have begun to emerge during the discussion.

4. CHOOSING THE BEST SOLUTION

Just as groups experience predictable phases in their overall development, they also go through identifiable decision-making phases. Several well-respected researchers have contributed to our understanding of group decision-making phases.[22] For example, Fisher found that groups first enter an *orientation* phase, proceed to a *conflict* phase when they argue about their various options, and finally enter the phases of *decision emergence* and *reinforcement*.[23] Decision emergence may begin during step 3, as members gradually move toward a consensus and coalesce around one proposal. The members will usually know when this has happened. Often a discussion leader can hasten this by asking something like, "I think we may have decided on a solution. Is that right?" If members agree aloud or nod their heads, a straw vote by show of hands or simply asking, "Does everyone agree?" or "Does anyone disagree?" can confirm this consensus.

Reinforcement refers to the complimenting and back patting that members give each other after a job well done. They will say things like, "That took a long time, but we really came up with a workable solution," "I really think we did a fine job with that," or "We done good, folks!" Such back patting expresses and reinforces the positive feelings members have toward each other.

The School Board Breaks a Deadlock

The school board in a city near where one of us lives had been stymied for several meetings over an issue related to a tax increase for schools and what arguments the members should make in the local media to support the tax increase. Most of the members wanted to stress that the tax increase would mean higher salaries for teachers, more teachers in the system, and smaller class sizes. One very vocal member wanted to emphasize the deterioration of the buildings and the necessity for basic facility maintenance. The board was stuck over this and other issues. Members didn't want to alienate the "buildings" member, so, wanting to be polite, they worked hard to find positive things to say about his arguments. However, this just fueled his enthusiasm. The school board president decided to use the university's "Decision Room," a room that had 20 terminals with capacity for full GSS.

Two faculty members assisted the school board; one served as "chauffeur" to run the software while the other served as a neutral facilitator. The school board members typed their ideas into a terminal, where they appeared on a large, overhead screen that all could see. They were able to make anonymous comments about each idea. Finally, they rated each idea on a scale of 1 to 5 and rank-ordered each one as well. The ratings and rankings were instantly tallied and a bar chart was produced that visually reproduced their numerical assessments. It was clear from the ratings and rankings that the "buildings" member was an outlier in the group. His ideas were not supported at all, which became obvious to everyone in the group, including him. This visual representation on the computer screen got through to him when the members' gentle oral comments had not. He dropped his insistence on the building maintenance platform for the tax levy.

1. What do you think are the advantages and disadvantages of using GSS?

2. Why do you think members were direct and clear using GSS where they had not been in face-to-face discussion?

3. What was persuasive about the visual representation that was not persuasive about the oral discussion?

4. For what other kinds of decisions do you think GSS would be helpful?

5. Are there situations where you would not want to use GSS?

Not all groups experience exactly the same phases during decision making. That would be too simplistic. Poole, for example, found that many factors influence the types of phases groups experience and the order in which they occur.[24] We present the idea of group phases to help you analyze what may be occurring in groups you belong to, but remember that the subject is more complex than we have described here (see Chapter 7).

Methods of Making Decisions.   A group can make decisions in many different ways, but some methods are likely to produce worse results than others. In some groups, the leader has authority to make decisions and may do so frequently for the group. One person may be perceived as the most expert member on the problem the group is discussing; that person may be asked to make the decision for the group. As a way of avoiding conflict, the group can use a method of chance, such as flipping a coin, drawing straws, or rolling dice. Sometimes numbers can be averaged to produce a decision, such as averaging individual applicant rankings to decide who should be offered a job. Often groups decide by voting, which is mandatory in committees governed by Robert's Rules for Committees.

Three common ways of making group decisions are for the leader or another designated member to decide without consulting the group, for the group leader to consult with other members but then make the final decision, and for the group to make the decision by consensus. A **consensus** decision is one that all members agree is the best one they can make that is acceptable to all; it doesn't necessarily mean that the final choice is anyone's first choice! The first method, decision by leader or designated member, is appropriate for minor decisions, such as where to meet, what refreshments to serve, what color notepads to put in the conference room, or even whom to ask to type the report. It is also appropriate for those decisions for which the leader (or designated decision maker) has all the information needed to make the decision, and support from the group members is guaranteed in advance. The second method, the consultative method, is appropriate when the leader does not have all the needed information, when group members are likely to accept the decision, or when time is short. The consensus method is appropriate for major decisions, such as what policy to recommend or how to solve a complex problem, where acceptance is important and the group has the time to deliberate.

Voting, in which a majority decides for the group, merely weighs the power of numbers, not the relative merits of ideas. A majority can be wrong, and a minority of one member may have the best idea. Further, voting may leave a group split, with some losers who may resent the decision and try to sabotage it. A vote may be required to confirm that a decision has been reached, but whenever possible all members should agree that they have reached the best decision they all can support—a true consensus decision. Even with a large majority, such as five to two, a split vote does not establish such agreement. Scientific research and experience both confirm that you should make a major decision with a majority vote *only* when the group must make a decision without enough time to reach consensus, or the group has exhausted every possible way of achieving consensus. Chapter 9, on conflict, provides suggestions for achieving consensus.

GLOSSARY

RISK Technique

A technique to help a group assess potential problems or risks with a potential solution

We noted earlier that once a solution has been tentatively adopted, it is a good idea to test that decision among the people who will most be affected. It is especially useful to identify any negative consequences that may occur to others but that the committee has overlooked. The RISK technique helps accomplish this.

Testing a Tentative Solution with the RISK Technique. The **RISK technique** is designed to help an organization assess how a proposed change or new policy will negatively affect the individuals and groups most involved. Suppose you are responsible for implementing a new employee benefits program at your company. Before you start putting the plan into effect, you want to make sure all problems that could come up have been identified and, if possible, dealt with in advance. RISK will help you do this. The steps for a face-to-face RISK meeting follow and are summarized in Figure 6.3. Like other group techniques, RISK can also be conducted electronically.

A group may have selected an alternative and discovered, with RISK or some other technique, that the solution is acceptable to all concerned. However, its job still isn't finished! Most groups are then responsible for seeing to it that the solution is implemented. Sometimes, that task is given to another group. Nevertheless, the problem-solving process is not complete until the solution has been put into effect.

5. IMPLEMENTING THE CHOSEN SOLUTION

The final step in group problem solving is implementing the solution. Sometimes groups break off their discussion as soon as they have decided on a solution without working out a plan to put their decision into effect. They may feel finished, but they truly are not. Good leaders see that the group works out the details of implementation. During this stage of problem solving, the group answers questions such as the following:

Who will do what, when, and how so that our decision is enacted?

How will we write and present our report?

How will we word our motion to the membership meeting, and who will speak in support of it?

What follow-up should we make to monitor how well this solution is working?

FIGURE 6.3   Steps for Conducting the RISK Technique in a Face-to-Face Meeting

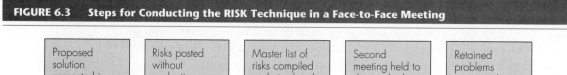

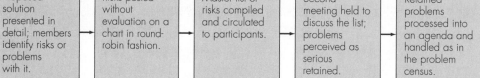

Proposed solution presented in detail; members identify risks or problems with it. → Risks posted without evaluation on a chart in round-robin fashion. → Master list of risks compiled and circulated to participants. → Second meeting held to discuss the list; problems perceived as serious retained. → Retained problems processed into an agenda and handled as in the problem census.

"You mean no one remembered to bring a rock?"

Implementation requires careful planning to succeed. (© The New Yorker Collection; 1985 Charles Addams from cartoonbank.com. All Rights Reserved.)

Some implementation plans are simple, but others are complicated and detailed, especially if the solution involves many people and numerous assignments. PERT is a procedure designed to help group members track the implementation of a complex solution; however, it is useful for implementing simple solutions as well.

Using PERT to Implement a Solution.   PERT (Program Evaluation and Review Technique) is a set of concrete suggestions to help a group keep track of who will do what by when. It can be difficult to follow a complicated implementation plan that involves many people, groups, and tasks. PERT helps do this by asking those responsible for implementation to make a chart showing deadline dates for completion of various tasks and the names of individuals or groups responsible.

Following are the main points:

1. Determine the final step by describing how the solution should appear when it is fully implemented.

2. List all the events that must occur before the final goal is realized.

3. Order these steps chronologically.

4. For complicated solutions, develop a flow diagram of the procedure and all the steps in it.

5. Generate a list of all the activities, materials, and people needed to accomplish each step.

6. Estimate the time needed to accomplish each step; then add all the estimates to find the total time needed for implementation of the plan.

7. Compare the total time estimate with deadlines or expectations and correct as necessary by assigning more or less time and people to complete a given step.

8. Determine which members will be responsible for each step.[25]

Another way to construct a PERT chart is to work backward from a target date. For instance, the students who created the chart in Figure 6.4 worked gradually backward from the due date for their presentation by taking into account how long each major step of the process would take. By doing that, they had a clearer picture of when they'd have to start working on the project to get it completed without undue haste. We recommend PERT to our students whenever they have complex group assignments to complete.

Although groups rarely stick exactly to the P-MOPS (or to any problem-solving guidelines), if you attempt to follow this sequence in the form of an outline of questions written about the problem, you will help guarantee that no important question, issue, or step is overlooked, and thereby create a good solution. The flexibility of the procedure allows you to tailor it to the characteristics of any problem. So that you can understand better how such adaptations are made, we next present examples of outlines written, adapted, and followed by problem-solving groups.

FIGURE 6.4   Sample PERT Chart for a Student Group Project

Date	Aretha	Barney	Candy	Denzil	Entire Group
Tues Apr. 1	Report on prelim observ.		Report on prelim observ.		Decide group to observe; decide variables
Thu Apr. 3		Prelim report, conflict	Prelim report, ldship	Prelim report, roles	Discuss prelim reports; decide methods of analysis
Tues Apr. 8		Complete lib research, Conflict	Complete lib research, Leadership	Complete lib research, Roles	
Thu Apr. 10		Observe group, 8 PM	Observe group, 8 PM	Have observ materials ready: survey, SYMLOG	
Tues Apr. 15		Complete SYMLOG of group	Complete SYMLOG of group		Meet after class, discuss preliminary findings
Thu Apr. 17			Observe group, 8 PM	Observe group, 8 PM Have tape recorder ready	
Tues Apr.22					Discuss overall observations; listen to tape
Thu Apr. 24		Complete first draft, Conflict	Complete first draft, Leadership	Complete first draft, Roles	
Mon Apr. 28	Begin overall editing and typing	Final draft, Conflict; Intro done	Final draft, Leadership; Conclusion done	Final draft, Roles	Look at each other's sections to improve style
Tues Apr. 29					
Wed Apr. 30					
Thu May 1					
Fri May 2	Editing and typing done	Tables and charts to Aretha (conflict)	Tables/Charts to Aretha (leadership)	Tables/Charts to Aretha (roles)	
Sat May 3	Proof: make copies			Proof; make copies	
Sun May 4	Distribute copies to all by 8 PM	Assemble full report by 5 PM	Assemble full report by 5 PM	Make large charts for class presentation	
Mon May 5		Read full paper	Read full paper	Read full paper	Rehearsal at Aretha's, 7 PM
Tues May 6					Final presentation to class

6.5   Moving to New Facilities

APPLY NOW

Assume you're a member of the committee responsible for moving OPT to SMS facilities. You're working within a four-month time frame, April through July. OPT will need to decide what is staying, what is coming, and what new digital equipment needs to be ordered. Office equipment will be moved, along with 14 staff people. A room on the SMS campus needs to be emptied and rewired for the new equipment, among other things.

Draw up a PERT chart for the move, covering four months:

1. What activities would have to be done and in what order? (For instance, you would want the wiring in the new room ready before you installed the new equipment.)

2. How long do you estimate each activity would take? (For instance, assume it takes two months from the time you order new equipment until the time you receive it.)

3. How many "supervisors" would you put in charge of each activity?

4. Where would you put your PERT chart?

Applications of P-MOPS

Use the information about problem characteristics in Table 6.2 to help you determine how to modify the P-MOPS to suit your particular problem.

The first example of a procedural outline, shown in Table 6.5, was created by a self-appointed advisory committee of students concerned about pedestrian safety on a street just east of campus. The group of students first decided on the general problem they wanted to tackle, then created an outline to guide their investigation over an eight-week span. They devised possible solutions, decided on what to recommend, and finally presented their report to both the city council and the president of the university. You will notice that it closely follows P-MOPS. The students' work was tragically timely—shortly after their presentation, a student was killed crossing that very street.

The outline in Table 6.6 is much shorter and simpler; it is designed to be used for a brief discussion in class

TABLE 6.5	**Sample Outline Using P-MOPS for a Complicated Problem**

Problem question: What shall we recommend that city council and university administration do to reduce pedestrian injuries on National Avenue east of campus?

I. What is the nature of our problem involving vehicle–pedestrian accidents on National Avenue east of campus?

    A. How do we understand our charge?

        1. What freedom do we have in this matter?

        2. What limits do we have (such as cost, structure of report, etc)

        3. To what does the general problem question refer?

    B. How do we feel about this problem?

    C. What do we find unsatisfactory about the way traffic and pedestrians currently affect each other on National Avenue?

        1. Diagram of present street, buildings, crossing, medians, lights, and so on.

        2. How serious is the problem of injuries to pedestrians?

            a. What kinds of accidents and injuries have occurred?

            b. When do these accidents happen?

            c. Do they tend to occur at any specific times?

            d. What kinds of persons are involved?

            e. How does this compare to accidents and injuries elsewhere?

            f. Are there any other facts we need to learn?

    D. What seems to be causing these accidents:

        1. Characteristics of the location?

        2. Human behavior?

        3. Other factors?

    E. What do we hope to see accomplished:

        1. In reducing the number of accidents and injuries?

        2. In practices of city council and administration?

        3. Any other features of our goal?

(continued)

TABLE 6.5	*Continued*

    F. What obstacles exist to prevent achieving our goal:

        1. Financial?

        2. Priorities of council or administration?

        3. Vested interests, such as businesses?

        4. Other?

II. What might be done to improve the safety of pedestrians crossing National Avenue east of campus?

    A. Brainstorm for ideas.

    B. Do we need explanations or descriptions of any of these proposed solutions?

III. What are the relative merits of our possible solutions to accidents and injuries on National Avenue?

    A. What criteria shall we use to evaluate our list of possible solutions:

        1. Costs?

        2. Acceptability to involved persons?

        3. Probable effectiveness in solving the problem?

        4. Appearance?

        5. Other?

    B. Shall we eliminate or combine any ideas?

    C. How well does each remaining potential solution measure up to our criteria and the facts of the problem?

IV. What recommendation can we all support?

    A. Has a decision emerged?

    B. What can we all support?

V. How shall we prepare and submit our proposal?

    A. In what form shall we communicate with council and administration?

    B. How will we prepare the recommendation?

        1. Who will prepare the recommendation?

        2. How will we edit and approve this report?

    C. How will we make the actual presentation?

    D. Do we want to arrange for any follow-up on responses to our recommended solution?

TABLE 6.6	**Sample Outline Using P-MOPS for a Simple Classroom Discussion**

I. What sort of final exam would we like for Communication 315?

   A. What is our area of freedom concerning the exam?

   B. What facts and feelings should we consider as we discuss what sort of exam to request?

II. What are our criteria in deciding on the type of exam to recommend:

   A. Learning objectives?

   B. Grades?

   C. Preparation and study required?

   D. Fairness?

   E. Other?

III. What types of exams are possible?

IV. What are the advantages and disadvantages of each type?

V. What will we recommend as the type of final exam?

SUMMARY

- Effective group problem solving uses guidelines to help members think critically rather than relying on their intuition, overrelying on expert authority, or overrelying on personal experience.

- A problem consists of a situation perceived to be unsatisfactory, a desired situation or goal, and obstacles to reaching that goal.

- The Procedural Model of Problem Solving (P-MOPS) provides a sequence of major steps and substeps for problem solving based on extensive research into how groups make high-quality decisions. Before using P-MOPS, the group may want to use a procedure such as the problem census to identify the most important problems facing the group or organization.

- P-MOPS steps are the thorough description and analysis of the problem, listing a variety of proposed solutions before evaluating them, thorough and critical thinking about the possible positive and negative outcomes of every proposed solution before a selection is made, and plan of action needed to implement the decision.

- Several specific techniques can help at each step. For instance, focus groups can help identify key issues pertaining to the problem; group support systems can help, especially with evaluation; the RISK technique can identify problems with a proposed solution the group is seriously considering; and PERT helps a group implement its solution.

- Group decisions can be made by the leader, by voting, or by consensus.

E X E R C I S E S

1. Think of a current or recent problem you have encountered. Analyze your problem by identifying its component parts (present situation, obstacles, and goal). Pay particular attention to the obstacles you identify. Form into groups of four to six and discuss each of the problems. Ask your team members to help you brainstorm ways of overcoming the obstacles you have identified.

2. As a class, choose two problems, one that is relatively simple and has few options and one that is relatively complex with high solution multiplicity (such as how the university should spend its contingency reserve money of $500,000). Write a leader's outline for structuring a discussion of each of these two issues by adapting P-MOPS to fit the discussion topic.

   After everyone has created an outline, select two leaders, one to guide each of the discussions using his or her outline. After the discussion, talk about what worked and what did not in the outline. How would you modify each outline to improve it?

3. View Part 3 ("An Ineffective Problem-Solving Discussion") of the videotape *Communicating Effectively in Small Groups* that was designed to accompany this text. This segment depicts a group doing a terrible job of problem solving. After viewing the tape, explain what you would do to correct the deficiencies. The following can guide your critique:

   a. Give specific examples of either poor or excellent problem-solving skills demonstrated by the group members.

   b. Examine the behavior of the leader, Alyce. What could she have done to improve the discussion process?

   c. What specific behaviors helped the problem-solving process and what behaviors hurt it? Why did they have such an effect?

 Go to **www.mhhe.com/adamsgalanes** and **www.mhhe.com/groups** for Self-Quizzes and weblinks.

KEY TERMS and CONCEPTS

area of freedom	focus group	problem census
charge	Group Support Systems (GSS)	problem solving
consensus		Procedural Model of Problem Solving
criteria	PERT	
decision making	problem	RISK technique

 www.mhhe.com/adamsgalanes
Use the flashcards and crossword puzzles on the Online Learning Center to further your knowledge of these key terms.

PART THREE

Understanding and Improving Group Throughput Processes

The interaction that occurs among group members is the heart of small group communication. Part 3 focuses on this interaction and describes in detail several important group throughput processes. Chapter 7 looks at how a group develops from an initial collection of individuals into a team, with a leadership structure, roles, norms, and a unique group climate. Chapter 8 explores some of the challenges that occur when members with diverse skills, backgrounds, and approaches to the task must work together. Chapter 9 describes why conflict occurs in a group and how it can be managed to benefit a group. Finally, Chapter 10 highlights important leadership principles and provides suggestions for applying them.

Becoming a Group

After reading this chapter you should be able to:

1. Define primary, secondary, and tertiary tension; give examples of each.
2. Describe the two main phases groups experience and give examples of the kinds of tasks members must handle during each phase.
3. Describe the communicative dynamics of each phase of group socialization.
4. Differentiate between the terms *leader* and *leadership* and between the terms *designated* and *emergent* leader.
5. Describe each of the five sources of influence and give an example of each.
6. Describe the process of leadership emergence and explain why it is important to understand leadership emergence.
7. Describe each of the three main categories of roles in groups.
8. Differentiate between formal and behavioral roles and describe how behavioral roles emerge during group interaction.
9. Differentiate between rules and norms and describe the four methods by which norms develop.
10. Explain what you would say and do if you wanted to change a group norm.
11. Describe each of the three main components that contribute to a group's climate.

The *Man of La Mancha* Cast and Crew

Noel, his church's choir director, broke his back in an airplane crash. To make his hospital time pass more quickly, he imagined the choir performing one of his favorite plays, *Man of La Mancha*. When he got out of the hospital, Noel decided to realize his dream by directing the play; he cast all the roles with choir members and performed the lead role of Don Quixote himself. Geoff, an experienced actor, was sidekick Sancho. Geoff couldn't carry a tune, but his acting experience and his unfailing good humor helped the cast mesh into a cohesive team. Gena, in the role of Aldonza, was also an experienced actress but had never before sung solo; however, she had a good sense of rhythm and was able to coach the dancers. Very few of the choir members could sing well, but they had an amazing array of other talents. Davida, who was both shy and clumsy, nevertheless was an outstanding artist and created two fabulous horse heads out of papier-mâché. Her talent created a minimal but effective set that could be positioned and removed quickly from the sanctuary. There were not enough men for all the roles, so Noel cast women in several parts, including the Barber and the horses. Delores had no sense of rhythm and could sing only whatever part the person next to her was singing, but she was a whiz at creating costumes out of Salvation Army thrift shop treasures.

The cast had only three weeks to rehearse, from the play's first read-through to opening night. Given the lack of singing and acting talent, lack of experience, lack of money for costumes and set materials, and time constraints, this play should have been a disaster. Instead, it was a great success. Several experienced theatergoers said that, although they had seen more professionally mounted productions of *Man of La Mancha*, this performance had touched them emotionally more than other performances.

The cast and crew had grown into a cohesive team whose output far exceeded reasonable expectations. Members contributed all their talents (singing and otherwise) to make the performance a success. Why did this small group work, when all "objective" assessments suggested that it would fail?

This chapter explores what groups such as the *Man of La Mancha* cast and crew have to do to become effective. Groups whose individual members merge into a productive team somehow figure out how to manage their tensions, develop a stable leadership structure, establish roles and norms that let everyone contribute productively, and create a supportive climate.

Primary, Secondary, and Tertiary Tensions

One of the first things group members must do is to handle the tensions that always arise when individuals come together, especially for the first time. During **primary tension,** which occurs when a group first begins to form, members are overly polite, stiff, and often experience long, uncomfortable pauses in the conversation.[1] Recall how you feel the first time you meet with a new group. Like most people, you probably worry about whether the others will like you and whether you will belong. You want to be valued by the group, and so does everyone else. This makes members careful not to say or do something that might alienate the others. Thus, early in the group's life, most members avoid behavior that might offend other members. This stiff, cautious behavior contributes to that overly formal, excessively polite atmosphere often observed in newly formed groups.

Secondary tension usually occurs later in the group's life; it is work-related tension stemming from differing opinions about substantive issues. For example, Sallie favors Candidate A to fill a vacant position, but Sarida prefers Candidate B. The disagreements may be mild or intense; members may be soft-spoken or loud as they disagree. Nevertheless, the group must somehow resolve these secondary tensions that are a normal part of a group's development. While primary tension manifests as uneasiness, fidgeting, or perhaps even boredom, secondary tension shows up as open, sometimes vehement, disagreement.

Much of the tension we have observed in groups is not strictly primary or secondary. Instead, groups often become bogged down in arguments that seem to recycle over and over. This inability to manage issues often represents a power or status struggle over who fits where in the system. These status or power struggles produce **tertiary tension.** Members disagree about who will decide the rules and procedures for the group. Conflict may occur over how to decide, how to resolve conflicts, who has the authority to determine what will happen in the group, who can make assignments and how, who is expert at what, what the rights and privileges of membership are, and so forth.

One of us observed a classroom group experiencing such a struggle. The group's class assignment was to observe a task group and gather data about it, either through observation or by talking to the members. Mike insisted that the group use his questionnaire as one method of gathering data. Michelle demanded instead that the group use her questionnaire. This endless argument was a thinly masked power struggle. If this really had been only secondary tension, Mike and Michelle could easily have combined their questionnaires. Instead, each demanded to be in charge of deciding the group's procedures while the others frustrated themselves trying to come up with a compromise that neither would accept. This potentially destructive tension—neither primary nor really secondary—is an example of tertiary tension.

Although it's usually easy to distinguish between primary and secondary tension, differentiating between secondary and tertiary tension is trickier. For example, you may observe an argument between two group members over which of two proposals the group should accept and conclude that you are observing secondary tension over ideas and opinions. However, it's possible that you are really observing a power struggle that uses ideas and opinions as the battleground. If so, you have experienced tertiary tension. How can you tell the difference? If the same argument is repeated over and over again without resolution, as with the earlier example of Mike and Michelle, or if two members always argue, no matter what the issue, you are probably seeing the symptoms of tertiary tension.

For a group to perform at its best, all three types of tension must be managed appropriately. Table 7.1 summarizes suggestions for managing tensions in a group. First, group members can move through the primary tension stage more quickly if they know each other. The choir described in the opening case study had an advantage in that members already knew each other fairly well when they began play rehearsals. A get-acquainted period helps members do this—even when members do know each other. Don't hesitate to suggest this, even if your group's designated leader doesn't. The members will be able to accomplish their task much more effectively and quickly if they know the backgrounds of the other members, what they do on the job, and even what hobbies and outside interests they have. Joking, laughing, and having fun together before getting down to work help as well.

Second, members can reduce both primary and secondary tension by sharing what they know about the problem at hand. For instance, if a committee is charged with recommending

---

TABLE 7.1   **Suggestions to Manage Tensions in a Group**

Make sure members know each other as individuals.

Include a get-acquainted period.

Schedule an informal chat period before each meeting.

Engage in group social activities.

Have members share information and feelings about the group's task so members arrive at a common understanding.

Make sure members display tolerance for disagreement.

Use sensitivity in expressing disagreement; disagree without putting down the other person.

Remind the group that disagreement can help achieve a better outcome.

Confront inappropriate behavior by describing its effect on the group.

Use humor, joking, and shared laughter to lighten the mood.

solutions to a campus parking problem, each member's perception of the scope and seriousness of the problem can be shared so that all will have some common understanding of the problem. This mapping process was described in the previous chapter.

Third, secondary and tertiary tensions can be managed if group members demonstrate tolerance for disagreement. When group members believe that their opinions and ideas are appreciated, even if these opinions are contrary to the ideas of others, then they feel valued by the group. They also are less likely to demand high status if they already believe the group appreciates them. Showing that you appreciate someone else's thoughtful analysis, even if you don't fully agree, can help: "I see what you mean about the hidden costs of that option, Tom, and that's something I hadn't considered" shows Tom that

7.1   Managing Tertiary Tensions

APPLY NOW

A situation arising between Gena and Geoff on the set of *Man of La Mancha* illustrates the type of situation that often leads to tertiary tension. Gena had been in several plays and had studied acting informally. She loved the process of uncovering a character from the inside out and discovering the meaning of a scene or a line through the rehearsal period. Geoff was a more experienced actor with some directing experience as well. He had strong ideas about how certain lines should be read and certain scenes played. When he took it upon himself to advise Gena about how to read certain lines, she felt herself becoming both irritated and confused. She liked Geoff and respected his experience, but she had her own preferred way of developing a character. She knew she had several choices about what to do, and some choices were likely to be more effective than others for the entire enterprise. Consider Gena's situation:

1. What are several options Gena has for handling this situation? For example, she could do nothing or she could quit the cast. (List at least five in addition to these two.)
2. How is Geoff likely to react to each of these choices?
3. What are the likely outcomes to the group as a whole of each of these choices?
4. If you were faced with this choice, what would be more important to you, keeping control of "your" character or keeping harmony among the cast? Are there other things that would be more important to you in this situation than harmony or control? What would those be?
5. What choice would you be likely to make, and why? How effective do you think this choice would be?

Ask two class members to select one of Gena's options and to role-play this situation. After discussion about what worked and what didn't, ask two different class members to role-play a different option. Which communication strategies seem to be more effective? Why?

you were listening and that you appreciate the careful thought he gave to the issue. Statements that acknowledge confidence in the group (e.g., "We'll be able to find an answer—we've done a good job so far") help develop solidarity in the group system.

Humor is also an effective way to handle secondary and tertiary tension in a group. A well-timed, lighthearted comment can move a group past an obstacle that seems insurmountable. Joking and laughing together increase the members' good feelings toward each other. This in turn helps members become more open toward each other, which can lead to resolution of their substantive and status differences. However, NEVER joke to change the topic or to put someone in his or her place because this can destroy the cohesiveness the group has developed.

Tertiary tension is always tricky to handle; indirect methods often don't work. Group members will probably have to address the problem directly by saying something to the offending members. Either a group's designated leader or one of the other members can politely but firmly confront the members involved in the status struggle by pointing out the negative effects the power struggle is having on the rest of the group.

Phases in the Development of a Group

Groups go through predictable phases, just as people do, on their way to maturity. A group usually does not function smoothly as a system at its first meeting. When group members are dealing with primary tension, they are expending emotional and mental energy that is unavailable for productive work. Thus, before a group can concentrate fully on its assignment, members need to manage several interpersonal issues. On the other hand, when group members concentrate on their work, they pay less attention to each other's human needs. Robert F. Bales calls this the equilibrium problem. A group's attention must shift between concentrating on the task and concentrating on the relationships among members.[2] Attention to both is necessary for a group to function well. First, the group must develop dependable, harmonious interpersonal relationships that will give it stability. Bales called this the group's socioemotional concern. Second, the group must focus on its assignment. This attention to the work of the group is called the task concern, from which come secondary tensions. Neither task nor socioemotional concerns can be ignored if the group is to succeed. Both need to be attended to, in some degree, throughout the life of the group.

Task and socioemotional concerns predominate at predictable periods in the group's development. The first overall phase of the development from a collection of individuals into a group is the **formation phase,** in which socioemotional or interpersonal concerns predominate. In this phase, members work out their relationships with each other. During this structuration process, rules, roles, and a leadership structure emerge. For example, perhaps Lee is an excellent organizer but is not skilled at coming up with creative alternatives. Pat, on the other hand, is a great idea person but is unreliable on follow-through. As the group progresses through the formation stage, members of effective groups begin to mesh themselves into a coordinated unit that includes all needed behaviors. The *Man of La Mancha* cast and crew did a particularly good job of working out their relationships effectively and finding a valuable place for everyone.

Production Phase

Second stage of a group's development, during which a group can concentrate more fully on its task

Group Socialization

Process by which new and/or established members learn to fit together through communication

The group moves gradually into the **production phase,** the stage in which the group is able to concentrate on its assigned task. Most groups do not have the luxury of getting to know each other well before they have to start working. Instead, members begin resolving their primary tensions at the same time they have to deal with the task-oriented business of the group. Thus, instead of being separate and sequential, the phases partially overlap and parallel each other. The *Man of La Mancha* cast and crew had to start rehearsing and putting together a show before they had all their interpersonal relationships fully worked out. As the socioemotional concerns become resolved, the group can expend more of its energy on task-related concerns, so the formation phase gradually gives way to the production phase, although the formation phase never completely disappears. The better job the group does of resolving primary and tertiary tensions and developing a stable leadership structure in the formation phase, the better job it can do of completing its assignment efficiently in the production phase.

The process of managing the task and socioemotional demands can be further complicated if a group uses electronic technology as a tool. Many people believe that computer-mediated technology increases a group's task communication while it decreases its socioemotional communication. This occurs because electronic tools keep groups focused on such task-related processes as record-keeping, listing ideas, and structuring the problem-solving process. In addition, GSS tools such as e-mail, which provide limited ways to express nonverbal cues, may encourage members not to think of each other as individual people. However, researchers examining groups using computer-mediated communication have discovered that members find ways to communicate socioemotional information that is the same as the information exchanged in face-to-face groups,[3] as we discussed in earlier chapters.

As you can see from our brief discussion of group phases, any group's communication evolves into distinguishable patterns, which change over the life of the group. Phase or stage models such as the one above attempt to describe the most salient characteristics of each phase in the development of a group. However, such simple descriptions fail to reveal that many groups do not proceed cleanly through the phases. Missing from the above discussion of phases is the impact new members have on group development, both in newly formed groups and in existing groups. We now turn our attention to exactly how both individuals and groups deal with socialization of members.

Group Socialization of Members

When we hear the word *socialization* we generally think about someone who is learning to become part of a group or even society at large. Just as children are socialized into families and society, group members are also socialized into newly formed and established groups. Carolyn Anderson, Bruce Riddle, and Matthew Martin provide a definition of group socialization that supports our belief in the central role of communication in group processes including the socialization of members.[4] **Group socialization** is a

> *reciprocal process of social influence and change in which both newcomers and/or established members and the group adjust and adapt to one another through verbal and nonverbal communication as they create and re-create a unique culture and group structures, engage in relevant processes and activities, and pursue individual and group goals.*[5]

This definition is lengthy so let's take it apart and examine what it implies about the process of group socialization. First, the adapting and adjusting that happens when a new group forms or when new members enter an established group occurs through *communication* among group members. Anderson, Riddle, and Martin point out that communication is instrumental in reducing the uncertainty that is often felt during this time.[6] For group socialization to be effective, everyone involved must practice open communication, be accepting of the new member, and exhibit a desire to facilitate the positive change new members can bring. For instance, if the community theater cast members do not talk to each other about Ted (see Apply Now 7.2), welcome him into the troupe, and see his presence as a way to move in new directions, then his willingness to replace Richard will have been a waste.

Second, the definition above highlights the importance of recognizing that effective socialization requires a balance between individual member and group goals as well as comparable positive satisfaction levels between the member and the group. Ted, the community theater director, and the other cast members must have similar goals and levels of comfort if Ted's stepping in for Richard is to be a positive experience.

Finally, the definition rightly focuses on the realization that socialization is an ongoing process that is not only about the new member but also about the group. Our questions about how the community theater group might handle Ted's entry into the group involve thinking about what Ted, the director (or leader), *and* the cast (the group) can do to manage this kind of group change. Understanding the phases of group socialization may help you to further consider how this community theater group and Ted can best manage his entrance into the cast.

7.2   Integrating a New Member

APPLY NOW

One week before a community theater's opening night of *Hotel Paradiso*, his doctor told leading man Richard, who had been complaining of shortness of breath, that he needed heart bypass surgery—immediately! The cast was devastated. Members were concerned about Richard, of course, but they also were concerned about watching their six weeks of rehearsals go down the drain. The cast and crew had become a tight, cohesive group. Rehearsals had been going well, with the play promising to be the season's top moneymaker. The director debated canceling the run, but prevailed on his talented friend Ted to assume Richard's part. Opening night was delayed for a week to give Ted time to learn the lines and the cast time to integrate a new cast member.

1. If you're the director, what would you do to help the reformulated cast get through its formation phase so members can focus on the play? Is there anything that can speed up the cast's formation phase?

2. If you're Ted, what would you do to help the other cast members feel comfortable with you?

3. If you were the cast members, how would you help Ted feel at ease?

7.1 Socialization in Online Groups

Go to **www.
mhhe.com/
adamsgalanes** for
additional weblink
activities.

MEDIA AND TECHNOLOGY

Previous chapters have introduced you to the Internet as a tool for communication among small group members. Because of the Internet, groups can now be formed and sustained entirely through electronic communication channels such as chatrooms, instant messaging, and e-mail.

Many online groups have "frequently asked question" or FAQ documents that explain norms and expectations for group members. For instance, you might belong to a discussion group devoted to your favorite sports team. One norm for that group might be that members not post commercial messages (e.g., advertisements) or that members avoid using swear words.

Assume that you are assigned to coordinate the communication among group members in an online group. What do you think should be in your group's FAQ document? More specifically, what norms and expectations do you think should guide your group? Use the following website to get started thinking about your FAQ document:

http://jade.wabash.edu/wabnet/info/netiquet.htm

After jotting down some ideas for your FAQ document, consider how the process of socialization in online groups is both similar to and different from face-to-face groups. Are FAQ documents useful for online groups? Would FAQ documents be useful for face-to-face groups? If you have participated in online groups, how did socialization occur in that group?

For more
information on
antecedent
socialization in
online groups,
go to the online
learning center.

GLOSSARY

Antecedent Phase

*Phase in group
socialization during
which members bring
previous group
experiences, attitudes,
beliefs, motives, and
communication traits
to the process*

PHASES OF GROUP SOCIALIZATION

Anderson, Riddle, and Martin explain group socialization processes as an intricate interplay between five phases: antecedent, anticipatory, encounter, assimilation, and exit.[7] When you study the unique communication demands of each phase, remember several things. This model of group socialization assumes that group members are typically also members of other groups, that socialization involves either newly forming groups or established groups dealing with new members, that groups may move through these phases at different speeds and may revisit one or more of these phases in their acceptance or rejection of new members, and, finally, that behaviors in one phase have a ripple effect through the other phases.

In Chapter 2 we discussed group inputs such as member characteristics and their potential impact on group throughput and outputs. In Chapter 3 we talked about the influence of different listening styles on group interaction and outcomes. In Chapter 8 we will talk about cultural differences and group processes. These individual characteristics play a key role in the **antecedent phase** of group socialization. All members, including Ted in our above example, bring to a group their own attitudes, motives, and communication behaviors, which can profoundly affect how ready and able they are to engage in the socialization process and how willingly they approach group work and building relationships. Let's take, for instance, the attitude commonly referred to as *grouphate*.[8] Many of the ideas and attitudes people bring to new or existing groups are based on previous experiences in groups. If someone has been a member of groups that have struggled to get anything done, she or he may internalize this experience and, in future groups, show a negative bias toward groups and group work. Your authors, Gloria and Kathy, hear students in their small group classes repeatedly verbalize their dislike for anything resembling group work because of horrific experiences in the past. This kind of pessimism would make joining a group difficult. It is very difficult for someone with bad group experiences to join a new group and equally difficult for other group members to welcome such a person to the group.

Another antecedent factor that affects group socialization is our disposition or motive for communication. Recall our discussion of listening styles in Chapter 3. Some of us listen in order to sustain the relationships in the group and others to make sure the work gets done. Others focus their listening on meeting a time schedule and others on information only from trusted sources. These listening preferences are also tied to our motives for communicating and influence effective socialization of members. For instance, those members who communicate in order to build relationships rather than control others or distance themselves from others report more satisfaction with groups. Those who communicate to facilitate the work talk more in the group. Members highly motivated for both reasons are generally more willing to engage in the socialization process.[9]

Communication apprehension and verbal aggressiveness are two other antecedent factors influencing group socialization. Individuals or group members who are not comfortable talking in groups—that is, who experience communication apprehension—find it hard to participate actively in socialization. If socialization in groups is to be effective, members have to communicate with each other to reduce the uncertainty inherent in the socialization experience. On the other hand, individuals or group members may be quite comfortable talking and may even be verbally aggressive—they attack others when expressing disagreement. This kind of communication typically alienates others and does not promote positive socialization experiences.[10]

The **anticipatory phase** of group socialization involves all the initial expectations members have of each other and the group. These expectations are an aspect of socialization because they are the basis for what the individual and the group anticipate will happen over the life of the group. Have you ever expected to really like someone and to have a successful meeting with them, only to have your expectations crushed? Suppose the director had really talked Ted up to the cast, who were led to anticipate a master actor and great opening night. In turn, suppose Ted had been told about the great cast he was joining. Both parties would anticipate a successful experience. However, if their expectations were not accurate, socialization could be a disaster. In both examples, the more the group members' expectations differ from their actual experience, the more chance there is for anxiety and even anger between members.

Socialization involves both individual expectations (Ted) and group expectations (cast). Individuals enter new or existing groups with all sorts of expectations, including estimating how well they will be received and how much they will be respected as individuals. Ted may predict that he will be well received and, although he is stepping in for Richard, the cast will understand that he brings his own interpretation to the role. If his predictions are not met, he will have a stressful entry into the group and both he and the

GLOSSARY

Anticipatory Phase

Phase in group socialization describing individual and group initial expectations of each other

group may have a negative experience—even perhaps an unsuccessful adjustment. For the cast members (in this case comprising an existing group), their anticipatory phase begins when Ted agrees to take over for Richard. If cast members are open to the adjustment ahead of them, they are more likely to promote Ted's integration into the group.

We asked you to think about what each party could do to help welcome Ted (see Apply Now 7.2). Group socialization is enhanced when groups systematically have in place ways to welcome new members.[11] In the case of the community theater cast, this could include a meeting with Ted in which members introduce each other and talk about their expectations, an informal dinner with Ted, and a tour of the theater, stage, and dressing rooms. Stewart Sigman calls these kinds of activities *audition practices* and they help both the new member and the group draw more realistic expectations and experience less primary tension during socialization.[12]

The third phase of group socialization is the **encounter phase.** The learning that occurs in all forms of socialization begins in earnest during this phase. It begins when the expectations of the anticipatory phase meet the realities of the group and lasts for an indefinite period.[13] During the encounter phase, the individual and the group are adjusting the group's norms, culture, climate, goals, roles, and leadership structure—topics we discuss later in this chapter.

As we mentioned earlier in our discussion of group socialization, it is important to negotiate a balance between individual and group goals. During this phase, members also negotiate their roles in the group. The roles established in a newly forming group can be disrupted later with the addition of a new member. Communication about individual role expectations and careful assessment of what the group needs are necessary if socialization is to be a positive experience. For instance, newcomers who proactively seek information about role expectations are socialized more effectively than those who do not seek this kind of information.[14] We talk more about roles and norms later in the chapter.

The **assimilation phase** is characterized by full integration into the group and its structures.[15] In full integration, new members have become comfortable with the group culture and show an active interest in the group's task and relationships. In turn the existing members demonstrate acceptance of the new member. Members show a productive and supportive blending, enacting communication necessary to sustain the group's culture. If this integration does not occur smoothly, as is often the case, secondary tension could throw the group back into the anticipatory and encounter phases. Do not be surprised if these regressions occur because, over a group's life span, members will often have to negotiate a good fit between themselves and the rest of the group.

The fifth phase of group socialization is the **exit phase.** Earlier we remarked that group socialization is a process that continues over the course of a group's life. This process is experienced at both the individual and the group level and actually ends when the new member leaves or when the group ceases to exist. Exiting a group, whether because an individual leaves or a group breaks up, can be a difficult transition and is one that group members often minimize.[16] If a member leaves, such as Richard in the community theater example, the group must deal with why he left, how he left, how his departure changes their communication, and what comes next. When an entire group disbands, members deal with variations of the same issues.

When an individual leaves a group, the leaving is often complicated because the member may have left psychologically earlier than she or he left physically. Kathy, one of your authors, watched as a colleague and good friend retired. Almost a year before he actually left the department, he mentally pulled out. Kathy watched his interest in department issues fade, which affected what issues he fought for and the votes he cast in faculty meetings. Should you or anyone else leave a group voluntarily, it is a good idea to let others know you are leaving, help the group adjust to your leaving, and try to remain in some sort of contact after you leave. This can help to avert such things as grouphate.

Group turnover is common. How many times have you watched as a member left, and then found yourself dealing with the loss and the adjustment to a new member? This process can be filled with uncertainty and resentment or it can be managed quite well. A group can effectively manage turnover by developing a positive group attitude toward turnover—see it as a way to redefine who you are. When an entire group ends, do not treat it lightly—how you disband affects the kind of experiences you take into the next group. Joann Keyton recommends that groups give themselves an opportunity to say good-bye and to process their experience.[17]

Group socialization is a complex process spanning the entire life of a group. Recognizing its characteristics adds depth to our understanding of group phases and acknowledges that groups usually do not mature with the same members but does so adapting and adjusting to members coming and going. The encounter phase of group socialization involves several components of group life including leadership, roles, rules and norms, and group climate. We turn now to a discussion of group leadership and its importance in a group's overall effectiveness.

Leadership and Leaders

Leadership is an essential element in the success of effective groups. Leadership refers to behaviors or functions performed by any individual in a group that help the group achieve its goals. This includes, but is not limited to, the person who is appointed or elected the group's leader. We explained in Chapter 1 that effective groups capitalize on the leadership behaviors of all members to reveal distributed leadership. We will now look more closely at how members actually provide leadership to the group.

LEADERSHIP AND SOURCES OF POWER IN THE SMALL GROUP

All groups need leadership to succeed, but what is leadership? Hackman and Johnson define **leadership** as "human (symbolic) communication which modifies the attitudes and behaviors of others in order to meet group goals and needs."[18] This definition recognizes that communication is the central essential activity of leading, and it implies three things. First, leadership is accomplished through communication. The focus is not on an individual's traits or personality but on what that individual actually says and does within the group. Leadership involves persuasion and discussion, not psychological coercion or physical force. One person influences the attitudes and actions of others by a give-and-take process of person-to-person communication. Second, the definition states that group leadership consists of those behaviors directed toward helping the group attain its goals. Thus, a group rebel, even a popular one whom others admire and follow, would not be considered a leader of the group if the rebellious actions interfere with the

---

GLOSSARY

Leadership

The use of communication to modify attitudes and behaviors of members to meet group goals and needs

GLOSSARY

Influence

The use of interpersonal power to modify the actions and attitudes of members

Legitimate Power

Influence based on a member's title or position in the group

Reward Power

Influence derived from someone's ability to give members what they want and need

Punishment Power

Influence derived from someone's ability to take away what members want and value

Coercion

Using threats or force to make a member comply

Expert Power

Interpersonal influence that stems from someone's perceived knowledge or skill

group's accomplishment of its goals. Finally, the term *modify* in the definition suggests that the individual demonstrating leadership must be adaptable to the changing conditions of the group. Leadership is a dynamic process of exchange, not a fixed quality or set of behaviors. If you want to modify other members' attitudes and actions, you must be aware of their beliefs, attitudes, and needs so you will communicate in ways likely to shape their behavior toward achievement of the group's goals.

Leadership implies **influence,** which is the exercise of interpersonal power to modify the attitudes and actions of other members to help a group achieve its goals. For example, notice that Noel, the play director, did not manipulate, bully, or coerce his cast members into performing the work necessary to mount the play. He used his interpersonal skills to guide, teach, and help the other members perform for the benefit of the group as well as himself. In the process, the group's tasks got accomplished and the members developed their own leadership skills. Geoff developed his directing skills; Gena, her performing skills; and Davida, her artistic skills. Noel's power came from his efforts to support the others as they learned their new roles and contributed the talents they already had to the overall effort.

Where does the power to influence others come from? Why do some people seem to have an easy time getting others to work with them, but others do not? Raven and French have identified five sources of interpersonal power, which gives people the ability to influence others: legitimate, reward, punishment, expert, and referent power.[19]

A group member who has a special title or position has **legitimate power,** which stems from someone's title or position in the group. Other members assume their president or chair has the right to exert influence in the group, and they expect the leader to call meetings, establish an agenda, and coordinate tasks. The group leader may have been elected by the members themselves, appointed by someone from the group's parent organization, or have a title (such as Dr. or President) that confers power.

Reward power comes from the ability of an individual to give others what they want and value, and **punishment power** comes from someone's ability to take away what members want and value. Both rewards and punishments can consist of tangible or intangible items. For instance, Sandra rewards her fellow members with praise and encouragement. These intangible items, along with others such as attention and smiling, have great power to influence others. Similarly, frowning, ignoring someone, asking someone to redo an assignment, and so forth are intangible ways of punishing group members. Tangible rewards can also be such things as special privileges, monetary bonuses, and promotions. Tangible punishments may include taking away special privileges or firing someone.

A form of punishment power that we think is inappropriate in a small group is **coercion,** or the use of threats or force to make a member comply with what someone wants. These tactics can breed resentment, sabotage, and rebellion.

Another source of power is expertise. An individual with **expert power** is perceived by the other members to have knowledge or skill valuable to the group. Geoff possessed expert power as an experienced actor in the *La Mancha* cast because the others knew he had been in many plays. When they had questions about how they might read a line or create a "bit of business" on stage, they often went to him for informal advice if Noel, the director, was busy.

Finally, a person whom others admire and want to be like has **referent power.** Most of us want the people we like and admire to like us, too. That desire gives those we admire a tremendous amount of power over us because we will often do what we think they want us to do so that they will like us, too. In high school, one of us belonged to a social group that had an informal leader with considerable referent power because she was "cool." The rest of the group accepted Sue's opinions on a variety of issues such as how to dress, whom to date, and what school activities to join.

A group leader's influence usually stems from more than one of these power sources (see Table 7.2). For example, as choir director, Noel was the legitimate leader of the *La Mancha* cast, but he also had expert power and referent power—people really liked him a lot! In addition to referent power, President Ronald Reagan possessed legitimate power as well as the power to reward and punish. As you can guess, the more sources of power an individual has, the greater that person's influence in the group.

The perceptions of the members determine a member's influence within a group. For example, one classroom group had a member who convinced the other people in her group that she was proficient in using the school's computer to analyze data. The other members believed Sonya and deferred to her judgment on this and a variety of other matters. Unfortunately, Sonya was not proficient at using the computer. By the time the group realized this, it was too late to turn in a good project report. Nevertheless, for a long time Sonya was quite influential in her group because other members perceived her to be an expert. Thus, your ability to influence others comes not just from your actual skills and legitimate authority but also from the amount of power other members attribute to you.

Thus far, we have equated group leadership with the ability to influence others, and we have examined the source from which that influence may stem. Now we turn our attention to the specific people who exercise influence—the leaders of a group.

TABLE 7.2   **Sources of Power and Influence**

LEGITIMATE POWER
Leader is elected or appointed; has a title (chair, coordinator, etc.).

REWARD OR PUNISHMENT
Leader can give or take away items of value; may be tangible (money, promotion, titles) or intangible (praise, acceptance).

EXPERT POWER
Leader has information, knowledge, or skills needed and valued by the group.

REFERENT POWER
Leader is admired and respected; other group members try to copy his or her behavior.

GLOSSARY

Leader

Any person in the group who uses interpersonal influence to help the group achieve its goals

Designated Leader

An appointed or elected leader whose title (chair, president) identifies him or her as leader

Emergent Leader

A person who starts out with the same status as other members but gradually emerges as informal leader in the eyes of the other members

LEADERS

Any person who exercises interpersonal influence to help the group attain its goals can properly be termed a **leader;** it is this fact that makes distributed leadership, discussed in Chapter 1, possible. There are several important implications to this statement. First, this definition of *leader* implies that all individuals in a group can (and should) supply some of the needed leadership services. Second, it does not require that a leader hold a particular title or office. Any member of the group, with or without a title, can at times function as the group's leader. Third, communication is the process through which a person actually leads others. Rather than assuming that leaders are born or must have particular titles, the definition suggests that leaders perform behaviors to help a group achieve its goals.

Designated Leader.   The **designated leader** is the group's legitimate leader, an individual who holds a title, such as chair, coordinator, moderator, facilitator, or president, that identifies him or her as having a specific leadership role to play within the group. Usually group members expect the designated leader to perform a variety of coordination functions for the group, which we will describe in detail in Chapter 10. The designated leader may be elected to the position by the other members of the group or may be appointed by the individual or parent organization that established the group.

Emergent Leader.   An **emergent leader** is a person who starts with the same status as any other member in a group of peers, but who gradually emerges as an informal leader in the perceptions of the other members by providing leadership services the others value. Most of the groups to which you belong have a designated leader, but understanding how informal leaders emerge will give you insight into what constitutes effective group leadership.

Much of what is known about the emergence of a leader in an initially leaderless peer group comes from a series of studies conducted by associates of Ernest Bormann at the University of Minnesota.[20] These researchers observed groups of college students placed in leaderless task groups and found that, at first, all members of an initially leaderless group have the potential to be recognized by others as the leader of the group. However, members who don't speak up or are uninformed are quickly eliminated as a possible leader. Next to be eliminated are members who, compared to the rest of the group, are overly bossy or dogmatic. Those who remain as potential leaders speak frequently; are well-informed on the issues facing the group; and are open-minded, democratic, sensitive, and skilled in expressing ideas for the group. The individual who ultimately emerges as a group's leader is the member who seems able to provide the best balance of task and people skills for that particular group. Especially important is the ability to coordinate the work of other members by communicating effectively with them. The only significant predictor of leadership emergence appears to be communication relevant to the group's task.[21]

Although early small group research suggested that men usually emerge as leaders, biological sex now seems irrelevant. Task-oriented women emerge as group leaders just as often as task-oriented men. But although biological sex is irrelevant, psychological gender may not be. One recent study found that, regardless of sex, masculine and androgynous individuals emerged as leaders more often than feminine and undifferentiated individuals.[22] Groups appear to choose leaders based on performance. Research into gender and leadership shows that men and women lead equally well and that group members are equally satisfied with both male and female leaders.[23]

Most groups have a designated leader, but the process of leadership emergence is essential for you to know. Two important points learned from studies of emergent leaders have a direct bearing on groups with designated leaders. First, emergent leaders influence people primarily with referent, expert, and reward power. They do not have a title with a job description or a set of duties to fall back on, so they must rely on their communication skills to lead the group. Emergent leaders, by definition, have the support of the other members of the group. This is something to which designated leaders should pay attention. Even though you may hold a title in your group (coordinator, president, and so forth), you should strive to be the person who would also emerge as the acknowledged leader.

Second, a person who emerges as a leader in one group will not necessarily emerge as a leader in another. Because each group's situation is different, each group requires a unique blend of leader skills. The type of task the group has to complete and the personalities

7.3   Informal Leadership in the Group

APPLY NOW

The *Man of La Mancha* cast had two principal leaders, both of whom contributed greatly to making the performance a great success. Noel was the designated leader and Geoff the emergent, informal leader. Cast members liked both of them, and each had strong ideas about what would work for the play. Each found a way to work effectively with the other and to acknowledge the other's expertise and talent. However, this is a tricky situation. Many groups have self-destructed because neither leader would make room for the other. Imagine yourself in Noel's and Geoff's situation:

1. From what sources of power does each person's ability to influence come? Give a specific example of how both Noel and Geoff can use their power to influence the cast members and each other.

2. As Noel, what would be your main concern about having a strong informal leader in your cast? What are the negative aspects of this? What are the positive aspects?

3. As Noel, what are the choices you have about dealing with Geoff? (List at least five.)

4. As Noel, what would you most want to have happen in this situation? What is most likely to produce that?

5. As Geoff, what would be your main motivation in exerting interpersonal influence in this situation? What would be your biggest hope? Your biggest fear?

6. As Geoff, what are the choices you have for dealing with Noel? (List at least five.)

7. As Geoff, what would you most want to have happen? What is most likely to produce that?

and preferences of the members help determine what style of leadership that group prefers. For example, members who are highly task-oriented tend to be impatient with relationship-oriented leaders. Such a group would prefer a task leader who is all business and helps the members complete their tasks without wasting time on chitchat. But another group composed of extremely sociable members may perceive a highly task-centered coordinator as hostile and uncaring This suggests that, when you are serving as designated leader, you pay careful attention to the group's situation and its members' needs so there is a good fit between the group's needs and your behavior as a leader. More information about leadership, along with guidelines for performing as a group-centered democratic leader, is presented in Chapter 10.

Leaders, formal and informal, fulfill special roles essential to creating effective teams, but many other kinds of roles are important to effective groups. We now examine several of those roles and discuss how they develop.

Group Roles

Your **role** is the part you play in a group. The role you perform in any particular group is a function of your personality, your behavior, your expectations, the expectations of other members, and any formal titles or instructions you may have been given regarding that group. Just as an actor has a role in a play, so do we all have a part to play in each group we belong to. And just as an actor has different parts in different plays, so do we have a unique position in each group we join.

TYPES OF ROLES

Two main types of member roles are formal and informal. Formal roles are assigned on the basis of a member's formal position or title. Formal roles are sometimes called positional roles. For example, one member may hold the title of secretary for the group. Secretary is a formal role that carries with it certain requirements and expectations, which the group's rules will state: "The secretary shall write and distribute to all members minutes of all meetings held by the group. At the end of each year the secretary shall provide a written summary of the group's work during that year to the president of the student senate."

Informal roles, sometimes called behavioral roles, are the parts people play that reflect their personality traits, habits, and behaviors in the group. Through trial and error, every member of a group begins to specialize in certain behaviors within the group. For example, one work group included a member who knew how to use databases to find pertinent research reports. She became the group's bibliographer, as well as its prodder by constantly encouraging everyone to finish assignments when promised. Specific roles result from an interplay between the individual's characteristics and other members of the group and emerge from group interaction.

ROLE FUNCTIONS IN A SMALL GROUP

Members' roles in small groups are categorized according to what they do for the group: How does this behavior help or hinder the group in achieving its goal? Small group roles are typically classified into three main behavior categories: task, maintenance, and individual. The first two are helpful to the group; the third is not.

Task Roles.   A task-oriented behavior is one that contributes directly to the accomplishment of the group's task. You probably can think of many task-related behaviors you have seen performed in groups. Recently, one of us served on a church building committee trying to find a new place to meet. One member said, "Let's make a list of all the possibilities in our price range." After the committee completed the list, the member said, "Now, let's split up the list and each visit one or two before our next meeting. Who will volunteer to look at the two buildings on Glenstone Avenue?" These remarks, which suggested procedure and also helped coordinate the work of the group, are examples of task behavior (see Table 7.3).

Maintenance Roles.   Maintenance behaviors are those that help the group maintain harmonious relationships and a cohesive interpersonal climate. One member of the church building committee welcomed another member back from a three-week trip by saying, "It's great to have you back! Here's a summary of everything we did while you were gone. We held off making a decision until you got back because we really wanted to know what you thought." These remarks demonstrate a gatekeeping function by allowing the absent member to contribute to the discussion, and they show solidarity and support. Table 7.4 lists maintenance roles.

Individual Roles.   Individual roles consist of self-centered behaviors (see Table 7.5). A self-centered member places his or her needs ahead of the group's. These roles do not help the group in any way and may be extremely harmful. Self-centered members may end up reducing their ability to influence other members because they generally are less well-liked. Members prefer colleagues whose communication is other- rather than self-centered.[24]

THE EMERGENCE OF ROLES IN A GROUP

Through communication with each other, members gradually structure their unique contributions and roles. Think for a moment about the groups you belong to. Do you act exactly the same way in each one of them? Probably not. There are variations in your behavior because each group brings out different combinations of your skills, abilities, and personality characteristics. Normal people want to contribute their unique talents and abilities so they will be valued by the group. When the other group members appreciate and reward those behaviors, they perform them more often. In that way, roles and a division of labor develop in the group.

Let's look at an example of how this occurs. Jan had a gift for storytelling. Because Jan felt uncomfortable whenever there was a lull in her seminar's discussion, she generally filled the silences with a story. Stories about her extensive travels easily captured the other members' attention and relieved the uneasiness that silence sometimes caused. The rest of the group encouraged her to relate her stories. Because of both Jan's ability to entertain and the other members' desire to listen, she carved out an informal (behavioral) role as the group's storyteller.

The other members of the group must reinforce a member's behavior if a role is to become stable and strong. If the other members had not been eager to set aside their work momentarily to listen to Jan, they would not have encouraged the development of her storyteller role. Instead, they would have discouraged her by paying little attention or reminding her that she was deflecting the group from its task. In that case, Jan would have downplayed her storytelling and searched for another way to contribute. For example, she also was an active listener who clarified and summarized what others said. If she had

TABLE 7.3	**Task-Related Behaviors and Statements**
Initiating and orienting	Proposing goals, activities, or plans of action; defining the group's position in relation to the goal. "Let's get started by assigning ourselves tasks to complete before the next meeting."
Information giving	Offering facts, information, evidence, or personal experience relevant to the group's task. "Last year, the library spent $50,000 replacing lost materials."
Information seeking	Asking for facts, information, evidence, or relevant personal experience. "John, how many campus burglaries were reported last year?"
Opinion giving	Stating beliefs, values, interpretations, judgments; drawing conclusions from evidence. "I don't think theft of materials is the worst problem facing the library."
Clarifying	Making ambiguous statements clearer; interpreting issues. "I could support that as long as the cost isn't outrageous, meaning that it is less than $10,000."
Elaborating	Developing an idea previously expressed by giving examples, illustrations, and explanations. "Another thing that Toby's proposal would let us do is . . . "
Evaluating	Expressing judgments about the relative worth of information or ideas; proposing or applying criteria. "Here are three problems I see with that proposal."
Summarizing	Reviewing what has been said previously; reminding the group of items previously mentioned or discussed. "So, by next week, Angie will have the library research finished and Carl will have entered the data on computer."
Coordinating	Organizing the group's work. "If Carol videotapes the mayor's interview by Monday, Jim and I can arrange to videotape his opponent's response by Tuesday's meeting."
Consensus testing	Asking if the group has reached a decision acceptable to all; suggesting that agreement has been reached. "We seem to be agreed that we'll accept the counteroffer."
Recording	Keeping group records, preparing reports and minutes; serving as group memory. "I think we decided that two meetings ago. Let me check the minutes."
Suggesting procedure	Suggesting a method or procedure to follow. "Why don't we try brainstorming to help us come up with something new and different?"

TABLE 7.4	**Maintenance Behaviors and Statements**
Establishing norms	Suggesting ways to behave; challenging unproductive ways of behaving; calling attention to violations of norms. "It's not productive to call each other names. Let's stick to the issues."
Gatekeeping	Helping another member get the floor; suggesting or controlling speaking order; asking if someone has a different opinion. "Pat's been trying to say something for the past couple of minutes. I'd like to hear what he has to say."
Supporting	Agreeing; expressing support for another's idea or belief; following another's lead. "I think Tara's right. We should examine this more closely."
Harmonizing	Reducing tension by reconciling disagreement; suggesting a compromise or new alternative acceptable to all; combining proposals into a compromise alternative; conciliating or calming an angry member. "Jared and Sally, I think there are areas where you are in agreement. I'd like to suggest a compromise that might work for you both."
Tension relieving	Joking and otherwise relieving tension; making strangers feel at ease; reducing status differences; encouraging informality. "We're getting tired and cranky. Let's take a 10-minute break."
Dramatizing	Storytelling and fantasizing in a vivid way; evoking fantasies about other people and places. "You just reminded me about the time when . . . "
Showing solidarity	Indicating positive feelings toward the other group members; reinforcing a sense of group unity and cohesiveness; promoting teamwork. "We've done a great job on this" or "We're all in this together."

TABLE 7.5	Individual (Self-Centered) Behaviors and Statements
Withdrawing	Giving no response to others; avoiding important differences; refusing to cope with conflicts; refusing to take a stand. "Do whatever you want; I don't care" or not speaking at all.
Blocking	Preventing progress toward group goals by constantly raising objections, repeatedly bringing up the same topic or issue after the group has considered and rejected it. "I know we already voted, but I want to talk about it some more!" (However, it is not blocking to keep raising an idea or issue the group has not really listened to or considered.)
Status and recognition seeking	Stage hogging, boasting, and calling attention to one's expertise or experience when that isn't really necessary; game playing to elicit sympathy; switching the subject to one's own area of expertise. "I think we should do it the way I did it last year. I won the Committee Chair of the Year award, you know."
Playing	Refusing to help the group with the task; excessive joking, dramatizing, and horsing around; making fun of members who are serious about the task; interfering with the group's work. "Don't be such a stick-in-the-mud; we've still got lots of time to finish. Let me tell you this great joke I heard."
Acting helpless	Trying to elicit sympathy by constantly needing help to complete assigned tasks; showing inability for independent thought or action; forcing other members to complete or redo work turned in. "I don't know what you want me to do here, and I've never used the InfoTrac in the library. I don't think I can do it."

7.4   Creating a Space for Yourself in the Group

Everyone needs to feel valued and appreciated by his or her fellow group members. Sometimes, it isn't clear what your contribution—your role—should be. It was especially hard for members of the *Man of La Mancha* extras to know what their contributions should be. Most of them were not actors or dancers; quite a few were not even very good singers! Assume you are Davida, one of the people cast as extras, with limited performing talent. However, you really like the idea of the project, you like your fellow cast members, and you really want the project to succeed. What can you personally do to make this project your own?

1. As Davida, do a brainwriting assignment: list your assets and talents. (In addition to the artistic talent we know you have, list at least five other assets.)
2. How could those assets and talents be used for this project?
3. Of the talents/assets listed in step 1, which one or ones would you prefer to use to help this project?
4. What strategies could you use to help ensure that you get to contribute in this way?

not won esteem as the group's storyteller, she might have become the group's recorder, or historian. From this example, you can see how a member's role in a group depends not only on that member's characteristics, but also on how the other members respond.

In addition to developing roles, group members also develop rules and norms within a group. We turn now to a discussion of how rules and norms form and how they can affect a group.

Rules and Norms

Rules and **norms** are the standards of behavior and procedures by which group members operate. Norms (informal standards) are not written down. In contrast, rules are more formal and usually are written in minutes or bylaws. Norms and rules tell members what they are allowed to do (e.g., "Members may call for a soda break after an hour"), what they are not allowed to do (e.g., "The seat at the head of the table is reserved for the group's chair and no one else may occupy it"), and what they should do (e.g., "The designated leader is responsible for reserving the meeting place"). Both rules and norms belong to the group as a system rather than to any individual and differ from each other only in their degree of formality. Rules are formally stated, but norms are informal. Norms are enforced by peer pressures, whereas rules are usually enforced by the designated leader. Rules must be changed by voting, but members may agree to change norms after an informal discussion.

GLOSSARY

Rules

Formal, explicit standards of behavior and procedures by which a group operates

Norms

Informal, implicit standards of behavior and procedures by which members operate

Rules and norms serve several functions for the group. By letting group members know what is and is not acceptable behavior, rules and norms reduce the uncertainty members feel about how to act. They establish procedures for working as a coordinated team. In the long run, productive rules and norms help the group achieve a high level of efficiency and quality control so that it can accomplish its assigned task well. Can you imagine how hard it would be if, every time you had a meeting, you had to negotiate the procedures by which the group should operate? You would be wasting all your valuable time deciding how you should work instead of getting your job done.

Formal rules are constructed in a couple of ways. Sometimes committees and other small groups establish their own formal rules for how they want to operate. At other times, the parent organization that created the group also gives it rules by which to operate. For example, many large organizations use the committee procedures in *Robert's Rules of Order Revised* to govern meetings.

Norms usually are not discussed openly, but they still have a strong effect on the behavior of the group members. A friend of ours serves on the city council of a small town. The council had developed a norm of meeting until all old business had been cleared, which meant that they sometimes met until midnight. Carla, a new member appointed to fill a vacancy for a council member who had been transferred, started to pack up her materials to leave at 9 o'clock. She explained that she assumed the group would end the meeting by 9 whether members had finished or not, and she had not made child care arrangements past that time. The other members looked at her in surprise. Some were sympathetic, but all continued to meet after she had left. At subsequent meetings Carla, who realized her mistaken assumption about meeting norms, changed her child care arrangements so she could stay until the meeting's end.

DEVELOPMENT OF GROUP NORMS

How do you suppose the council members established their norm of working until the old business was cleared business? There are a number of ways norms are set in a small group (see Table 7.6).[25]

TABLE 7.6	**How Group Norms Form**
Primacy	Behaviors and events occurring early in the group's history.
Explicit statements	Statements made by members (including the group's leader) about what is and is not expected behavior.
Critical events	Important happenings that indicate what is or is not acceptable behavior.
Carryover behaviors	Patterns of behavior that are part of the general culture, or environment, of the group.

Behaviors that occur early in the group's history often establish norms through primacy. When group members first meet, they feel uncertain and uncomfortable. Anything that reduces the uncertainty is welcomed. Thus, what first occurs in a group can easily become habit because it helps reduce the feeling of uncertainty. For example, you serve on a committee that includes faculty and students. Initially you aren't sure whether to address the faculty members by their first names; if you hear a fellow student member addressing them by titles, chances are you will follow that lead.

Sometimes norms are established by explicit statements that a leader or another member makes. For example, one member might tell a new member, "The boss likes to have proposals in writing. If you want to make a suggestion about work procedures at the staff meeting, you should bring a handout for everyone to use." This statement relays information about the group leader's preferences and also subtly lets the new member know that suggestions are supposed to be well thought out before being presented to the group.

Some norms are established through critical events that occur in a group. For example, one of us once taught a graduate seminar of nine people who came to trust each other, often revealing personal information in the class. Two of the students told nonmembers some of what occurred in the class. When the other members discovered this, they felt angry. At the next class meeting, members expressed their feelings of betrayal. Before the critical incident, some members thought it was all right to reveal in-class information to selected outsiders, but after the meeting it was clear to all members that such behavior was a serious violation of a group confidentiality norm.

Finally, many norms are taken from the general culture in which the group members live. For example, you know a lot about how to behave as a student, no matter what the class. True, some professors are more formal than others, but certain standards of behavior (such as raising your hand when you have a question or a comment and not calling the professor or other students rude names) carry over from one class to another. Thus, many carryover behaviors in a group are ones we have learned as members of a particular culture.

This particular origin of small group norms may become troublesome when we interact with members from different cultures. For example, we have observed students from Asian cultures behave very submissively in groups of American students. These international students are following the norms of their native cultures, just as are the American students. Likewise, African Americans and Hispanics tend to use the vocal backchannel (saying things like mm-hmm and OK while another is speaking) more frequently than European Americans. Lack of understanding of another's cultural norms can cause problems in a group.

ENFORCEMENT OF GROUP NORMS

If norms are not written down, how do group members learn them? Observant group members pay attention to how other members act. From this information, norms can be inferred. In particular, you should pay attention to two types of behaviors: those that occur regularly and those that incur disapproval.

Behaviors that occur consistently from one meeting to the next probably reflect a group norm. For example, if at every meeting each group member sits in the same seat and waits for the leader to start the discussion, you are seeing evidence of two norms.

GLOSSARY

Deviants

Members who consistently violate group norms

Behaviors that are punished by peer pressure also indicate norms. The strongest evidence of a group norm is members' negative reaction to a particular behavior. Most peer pressure comes in the form of nonverbal signals, as group members roll their eyes at each other, glare, shake their heads, or turn away from the violator. Sometimes they pointedly ignore the offending member's contributions. Carla, the new council member who left early, received only mild expressions of surprise and even some verbal expressions of sympathy, but there was no doubt that she had violated a norm, and she quickly came into compliance with that norm at the next meeting.

Members who consistently violate important group norms are called **deviants,** and they make the other group members very uncomfortable—even angry. To conscientious group members, deviants seem to thumb their noses at the group by implying that their own needs and wishes are more important than the needs of the group. The other members try to force the deviants to fall in line by applying increasing pressure to conform (see Table 7.7).[26] This is what the rest of the city council might have done had the new member not corrected her behavior right away.

Just because groups usually pressure a deviant to conform does not mean the deviant should automatically cave in to such pressure. Sometimes groups consider people deviant if they disagree or won't go along with a group's plans. However, such people can

TABLE 7.7	**How Groups Deal with Deviant Members**

First, members try to persuade the deviant member to conform to the group norms:

- They try reasoning with the deviant: "When you aren't here, Carla, we miss your important input."

- They try to persuade the deviant, first with teasing and then more insistently: "Your husband can survive one evening without you, can't he, Carla?" and "Look, Carla, it really messes up the rest of our schedules when you leave early. Why don't you get a babysitter for one night a week—that wouldn't be so bad, would it?"

- They may attempt to punish or even coerce the deviant: "If you really want to be a part of this council, Carla, you're going to have to put in the same amount of effort as the rest of us. Otherwise, we can't support that ordinance you've been promoting."

Second, solidarity builds among the other members against the deviant:

- "I don't see why we should go out of our way to help Carla pass that ordinance—she doesn't seem to care about any of our schedules!"

Third, members ignore and will eventually isolate the deviant:

- "Carla, we've all agreed that it would be better if you resigned from the council. We need a full-time member."

actually be helpful to a group if they cause the other members to examine information and ideas more carefully. Even so, the other members may not recognize that such disagreement, or idea deviance, can be helpful, so they try to force agreement. This pressure can be hard to resist, even when the deviant has a good case. We present more information about the effect of idea-deviant disagreement in Chapter 9.

CHANGING A GROUP NORM

We noted earlier that behaviors occurring at the first few meetings may become norms that can cause problems later on. For example, recall that when members first meet, they experience primary tension, which makes them so polite and stiff that they do not confront or disagree with each other. This can easily develop into a norm of "no conflict," which stops members from expressing disagreements or doubts. As you have seen from the previous chapter on critical thinking, this "no conflict" norm can be detrimental to the group's later decision-making abilities.

Although it isn't always easy, groups can change unproductive norms. One effective approach is to focus the group's attention on the norm and the harm it is creating rather

7.1   When Is It OK to Be Deviant?

In the 1980s, Beechnut, the second-largest producer of baby food in the United States, was found knowingly to have sold adulterated apple juice.[27] The company had been losing money, and using concentrate with artificial ingredients saved millions of dollars. Beechnut officials argued that other companies were also selling fake juice, that it was perfectly safe, and that their own research and development laboratories couldn't prove that their suppliers were providing fake concentrate.

Assume you are a Beechnut executive who strongly disagrees with the action the rest of the Beechnut officials seem determined to take. You've mentioned your disagreement a couple of times and have been getting both subtle and not-so-subtle pressure to keep quiet. Members have said things to you like, "We've been over this and over this. You keep bringing this up after we've decided." You're marketing the juice as "100 percent pure," which isn't accurate. But on the other hand, no one is claiming that the impure juice is unsafe. Is that really so bad, when it's saving money and jobs for the company?

Groups can be vicious to members who are deviant, and you are definitely a deviant in this group.

1. What do you say to the other members?
2. How can you withstand the pressure the others are placing on you? Should you withstand it?
3. For what reasons would you go along with the other members?
4. For what reasons would you resist?
5. What would you do?

than on the person violating the norm. In addition, do not try to force other members to accept your suggestions for changing the norm. They are likely to become defensive, refuse to change, and resent your attempt to control them. Instead, you want the group to think of ways to change the norm so that all the members participate in establishing a more productive group norm, for only the group can make a lasting change in a norm. The guidelines in Table 7.8 will help you.

The elements we have discussed thus far—the way group members manage their tensions; how they work through important tasks in their development and formation; and the leadership structure, roles, rules, and norms they establish—all help create the group's climate. We now examine how the group's climate contributes to the formation of an effective team.

TABLE 7.8	**Changing a Group Norm**

PREPARE

1. Make sure you are seen as a responsible, loyal member of the group; others won't appreciate your comments if you have been unreliable or act "holier than thou."

2. Ask yourself, "What harm is the norm causing?" Observe the effects of the group norm on the members and the group as a whole; count the offending behaviors and make notes of your observations.

CONFRONT CONSTRUCTIVELY

1. Select an appropriate time to share your information with other members.

2. Share your observations about the effects of the unproductive norm on the group; explain what you have observed the norm to be and the problems it causes.

3. Ask whether others also have observed these effects or share your concerns.

4. Express yourself supportively, not defensively:

   a. Defensive comment: "I'm sick and tired of always being on time while the rest of you wander in any time you please!"

   b. Supportive comment: "For the past four meetings we have started between 15 and 25 minutes late. We seem to have developed a norm that scheduled starting times do not need to be observed. Two of us have had to leave these meetings before they were finished in order to go to class. As a result we have missed several key decisions, and the rest of you have had to bring us up to date on what happened. Does anyone else see this as a problem?"

7.5 Changing a Norm You Believe Is Harmful

Carla, our city councilwoman, chose to accept the group norm of meeting as long as it took to complete the group's work. However, there are pros and cons to that norm. Yes, the work is not permitted to pile up and the group achieves closure at each meeting. But members are visibly fatigued at midnight and there is a noticeable loss of concentration and productivity after 10 P.M. Assume Carla's position for a moment and address the following questions:

As Carla, you genuinely believe the group would be more productive and make better decisions if they had more, but shorter, meetings. List at least three choices you have for dealing with this norm.

1. What are the consequences, both to you and to the group, of each choice?
2. What strategy do you think would be most likely to succeed? Why?
3. If you decide to try to change this group norm, how would you go about trying to change it? In your answer, include any planning you might do for bringing this up to the group. Also, describe exactly what you would say to bring this up.

Select five people, including one to play Carla, to role-play a city council meeting where Carla brings up the question of the meeting length norm. After the role-play, discuss as a class what worked and what did not. Make sure to let the participants in the "meeting" express any feelings they might have experienced during the role-play.

Development of a Group's Climate

Group climate refers to the psychological atmosphere or environment within the group and is another key element in forging a team from a collection of individuals. As we mentioned in Chapter 1, maintaining a pleasant interpersonal climate was the most frequently mentioned element by a group of managers.[28] Members who could disagree without being disagreeable, who could admit mistakes, and who could keep emotions on an even keel were particularly valued. You probably have attended group meetings where you felt the warmth and affection of the members for each other. Conversely, you probably also have observed meetings where you felt tension and distrust. These are but two examples of different types of group climates. There are many dimensions of a group's climate. We explain three we consider most important—trust, cohesiveness, and supportiveness.

TRUST

Trust refers to the general belief that members can rely on each other. When group members trust each other, they do not have to worry that others might be lying to them or may have secret reasons for their behavior. Instead of being suspicious and secretive, members who trust one another are more likely to create an open climate where people share freely. Two kinds of trust are particularly important to groups: task related and interpersonal.

A member who is trustworthy regarding the task can be counted on to complete assignments and produce top-notch work for the group. The higher the quality of the individual work that members do for the group, the higher will be the quality of the group's outputs. One behavior that can destroy trust quickly is failure to complete assignments for the group. A member who does not come through for the group forces the other members to pick up the slack. This is one of the most common sources of conflict and can poison a group's climate.

Interpersonal trust refers to the belief that the members of the group are operating in the group's best interests and that they value their fellow members. Assume that a member you trust says to you, "I think there are lots of problems with your idea." You are likely to ask that member for reasons and to pay careful attention to the reasons given. On the other hand, if the same statement comes from someone you don't trust, you may wonder what's behind the statement, ignore it, get into a shouting match, or try to

7.2   Can You Be Trusted?

ETHICAL DILEMMA

This is a particularly busy semester for you and you feel as if you barely have time to breathe. You will graduate at the end of the semester, and you don't know how you'll manage all your coursework, to say nothing of job hunting. One of your courses entails a group project; you have just met with your team members for the first time in class. The others are enthused about the project and have already started to make a schedule of meeting times for the semester. You think they are planning far too many meetings—many more than the project will need. Privately, you think you can get your own work on the project finished and attend perhaps half of the meetings the others have scheduled. But if you say that to your fellow group members, you're afraid that they'll think you don't care about the project. If you just skip meetings without saying anything now, you're afraid they'll think you're a slacker. But then again, you'll probably never see these people again. Either way, though, it seems like you can't win.

1. What other choices do you think you have besides saying no to the meetings now and just not showing up later?
2. Do you stay silent and make a private decision to make the meetings you can and not worry about the rest?
3. Do you say something to the group? If so, what?
4. For each of the options you came up with, what are the consequences to the group of that action?
5. What action is least likely to undermine the group's trust in you?

find subtle ways of sabotaging that member's suggestions. Members who appear to operate from **hidden agenda** motives, or personal and private motives, are seen as untrustworthy by others. So are "politicians" who always seem to have a personal angle for their behavior that has nothing to do with the group. In fact, politicians can be so destructive to a group that Larson and LaFasto, who studied excellent groups, recommended that the group leader get rid of them as soon as possible.[29]

COHESIVENESS

Cohesiveness refers to the attachment members feel toward each other, the group, and the task—the bonds that hold the group together. In a highly cohesive group, members feel a strong sense of belonging, speak favorably about the group and the other members, and conform to the norms of the group. In a group that is not cohesive, members do not feel much sense of belonging. They may not attend faithfully or may even leave the group because they find other groups more rewarding.

As with trust, there are two types of cohesiveness, task cohesiveness and social (or interpersonal) cohesiveness.[30] In a group that has high task cohesiveness, members understand and accept the task, are committed to completing it, may be excited about working on it, and experience what has been called group drive, or motivation to accomplish the task.[31] This describes the *La Mancha* cast very well. Interpersonal, or social, cohesiveness means that members like and are attracted to each other as people. They like to spend time together and enjoy each other's company. These two forms of cohesiveness affect group productivity and decision-making quality in different ways.[32] When a group's cohesiveness is due to interpersonal attraction, the task may take a back seat, which can lower the quality of a group's decisions. In particular, members have to be particularly careful to guard against groupthink (see Chapter 9), the tendency to accept information without thinking critically about it. In addition, sometimes groups high in interpersonal cohesiveness develop norms that keep productivity low, or may find themselves getting off track easily. A friend of ours sorted letters for the postal service. His coworkers let him know that he was working too fast and that if he wanted to stay in their good graces, he would not exceed the informal production norm they had developed. In contrast, groups with high task cohesiveness generally are more productive and decision making is enhanced. Thus, the presence of task-focused norms in a group moderates the effect of cohesiveness—groups with strong task norms and high cohesiveness outperform cohesive groups without strong task norms.[33]

Highly cohesive groups are more satisfying to their members. You have no doubt belonged to a cohesive group where you felt the warmth and closeness among the members. Terry, one of our former students, decided to campaign for office in a campus organization because she had so envied the obvious cohesiveness expressed by the previous year's officers—she wanted the experience of being part of such a group. Table 7.9 provides suggestions you can use to increase the cohesiveness of a group.

SUPPORTIVENESS

In a supportive climate, members encourage each other, care about each other, and treat each other with respect. Supportive members uphold ethical principles about how to treat each other. In a supportive climate, members believe their opinions are valued by the group, even when other members disagree with their opinions. Because members feel safe

TABLE 7.9	Increasing Cohesiveness in a Group

- Develop a strong group identity.

- Encourage group traditions, such as annual parties, special greetings and handshakes, and rituals.

- Develop in-group insignia, such as T-shirts and sweatshirts, pins, or hats.

- Refer to the group members as *we* and *us*.

- Give credit to the group as a whole when representing the group to outsiders or other groups.

- Give credit to individuals within the group for contributions they make toward the group's goal achievement.

- Support both disagreement and agreement by encouraging openness and freedom of expression.

- Create a climate of supportiveness in which every individual feels appreciated and believes his or her ideas are valued.

- Set clear and attainable goals for the group.

  —Goals should be difficult enough to provide a challenge and produce group pride when they are met.

  —Goals should not be so hard that they are nearly impossible to attain because failure will lower cohesiveness.

from psychological assault, they are free to direct most of their energy toward helping the group accomplish its task. On the other hand, a defensive climate emerges when members try to control, manipulate, and criticize each other.[34] If members are afraid they will be attacked by other members, they will hesitate to offer their opinions. They will spend so much time defending themselves or being on the alert for psychological assault that they will not pay much attention to the task of the group. Table 7.10 provides a list of supportive and contrasting defensive behaviors with sample statements for each.

All the defensive behaviors include an element of negative evaluation. These are judgmental behaviors that hurt interpersonal relationships within a group. Instead of critically evaluating ideas, members are critical of each other as persons. Notice, also, the relationship between cohesiveness and supportiveness. It is hard to feel strongly attached to a group if you don't know from one moment to the next when you are going to be attacked. Perhaps you also can see the relationship to open-mindedness—a supportive group consists of members who are willing to listen actively to each other and who are

| **TABLE 7.10** | **Defensive and Supportive Communication Behaviors and Statements** |

Defensive behaviors	**Supportive behaviors**
Evaluation Judging the other person; indicating by words or tone of voice that you disapprove of a person. "That's a pretty dumb idea!"	**Description** Desiring to understand the other's point of view without making the other person wrong. "Tell me more about how your idea would work."
Control Trying to dominate or change the other person; insisting on having things your way. "I want to do it this way, so that's what we're going to do."	**Problem orientation** Trying to search honestly for the best solution without having a predetermined idea of what the solution should be. "What ideas do you all have about how we might solve this?"
Strategy Trying to manipulate the other person; using deceit to achieve your own goals. "Don't you really think that it would be better if we did it this way?"	**Spontaneity** Reacting honestly, openly, and freely. "I really like that, and here's something else we could do. . . ."
Neutrality Not caring about how the other group members feel. "We don't have time to hear about your car accident right now; we have work to do."	**Empathy** Showing by your words and actions that you care about the other group members. "You had a car accident on the way here? Are you OK? Is there anything we can do to help?"
Superiority Maximizing status differences; pulling rank on other members with title, wealth, expertise, and so on. "Well, I'm chair of the committee, and I believe I make the final decision about how we do this."	**Equality** Minimizing status differences; treating every member of the group as an equally valued contributor. "I know I'm the chair, but the solution belongs to the whole committee, so don't give my ideas any more weight than anyone else's."
Certainty Being a know-it-all; acting positive that your way or belief is the only correct one. "I know exactly what we ought to do here, so I'll take care of it."	**Provisionalism** Being tentative in expressing your opinions; being open to considering others' suggestions fairly. "I have an idea I think might work. . . ."

egalitarian in their approach to others. Openminded members will not demand that the group perform in a particular way, the one and only right way. Can you begin to see how each element of the group system is related to all the other elements?

All the factors we have discussed in this chapter contribute to the structure that creates a team out of individual members. The way members manage their tensions, the leadership that emerges, the roles and norms that develop, and the climate members create all work together to make each team a unique entity.

SUMMARY

■ Groups normally experience two major phases in their development. During the formation phase they find ways of managing primary tension and the interpersonal relationships among members. In the production phase, they cope with secondary tension by directing most of their attention toward the accomplishment of their goals.

■ Group socialization of new and/or established members and the group is a complex process of learning how to fit together. Effective communication between all parties is crucial to successful and positive socialization, which in turn influences other group processes such as leadership, roles, norms, and climate. The process can be described in five phases: antecedent, anticipatory, encounter, assimilation, and exit. Group socialization continues throughout the life of the group until the new member leaves or the entire group disbands.

■ One of the most important processes in creating an effective team is the development of a group's leadership or the goal-directed interpersonal influence in a group that any member may exercise. A leader is any individual in the group who exercises interpersonal influence.

■ Five common sources of a leader's power include legitimate authority, the ability to reward or punish members, expertise, and referent power.

■ Task, maintenance, and individualistic roles are functions members perform in the group.

■ Rules and norms, the standards of behavior for members of the group, differ only in their degree of formality. Group norms, or informal rules, are established through primacy, explicit statements members make, critical events in the group's history, and carryover behaviors from the culture at large.

■ The group's climate is the psychological atmosphere in which members work. Three important aspects of a group's climate include trust, cohesiveness, and supportiveness.

EXERCISES

1. Watch a film that shows group formation (good examples include *The Breakfast Club, The Commitments,* or *Lord of the Flies*) and discuss the following questions:

    a. How did the group manage important issues in its formation phase? Were there any unresolved issues that later hurt the group?

    b. What instances of primary, secondary, or tertiary tensions did you observe?

    c. Who became the emergent leader of the group? Why did this person emerge? What were the sources of this person's power as a leader?

2. Observe an actual group or watch a video of a task-oriented group. (Two videos produced especially for this textbook contain suitable segments for this exercise.) Make a chart based on the task, maintenance, and individual behaviors described in the chapter and in Tables 7.3, 7.4, and 7.5. List the people's names at the top and the task, maintenance, and individual behaviors along the left side. Whenever each person speaks, categorize his or her remarks by making a note in the appropriate category. For each person in the group you observe:

    a. What sort of role profile would you draw for that person?

    b. How would you label that person's informal role?

    c. Do you think the person's behaviors were helpful or not? Why?

d. How would you change the category system to be more useful for you?

3. Think of the most (or least) cohesive group you have ever belonged to and explain why this group was so cohesive (or uncohesive). Which supportive (or defensive) behaviors were most prevalent in the group? What forms of trust did you observe (or not observe) that made the biggest difference in the group's climate?

 Go to **www.mhhe.com/adamsgalanes** and **www.mhhe.com/groups** for Self-Quizzes and weblinks.

KEY TERMS and CONCEPTS

antecedent phase	expert power	primary tension
anticipatory phase	formation phase	production phase
assimilation phase	group climate	punishment
coercion	group socialization	referent power
cohesiveness	hidden agenda	reward power
designated leader	influence	role
deviants	leader	rules
emergent leader	leadership	secondary tension
encounter phase	legitimate power	tertiary tension
exit phase	norms	trust

 www.mhhe.com/adamsgalanes
Use the flashcards and crossword puzzles on the Online Learning Center to further your knowledge of these key terms.

Celebrating Diversity in the Small Group

After reading this chapter you should be able to:

1. Define *diversity* and give several examples of diversity within a group.

2. Explain how diversity benefits a group.

3. Describe the four learning styles identified by Kolb and explain how each can benefit a group.

4. Describe the four dimensions of the Myers-Briggs Type Indicator® personality inventory.

5. Define *culture,* describe three dimensions on which cultures differ, and explain how each can affect group interaction.

6. Explain how gender, generational, race, or ethnic differences are cultural.

7. Explain why symbolic convergence and fantasy can help group members bridge differences by contributing to a group identity.

8. Explain how SYMLOG methodology can be used to help a group identify and overcome differences.

The Misfit

Judy, a gregarious and sociable class member, had the gift of making everyone laugh. When the class formed task groups that would stay together for the entire semester to complete a major project, several groups wanted Judy to join them. She chose to join a group with two other women and two men who, from their participation in class discussions, were bright and conscientious students. This group had a good mix of talent—members who could organize a task, members who could write well, members who had many contacts throughout the university to help them find the resources they needed, and members, like Judy, who could make the task enjoyable. The group appeared to be headed for success. All the elements existed to make this a productive and fun experience.

Several weeks later, the group members were ready to kill each other. Three of them wanted to fire Judy from the group. The fourth member, Misty, liked Judy well enough, but was also frustrated by her behaviors that pulled the group off task. Her constant joking, socializing, and attempts to ensure that everyone was having a good time had backfired. Instead, the others concluded that Judy was an airhead and they were frustrated by her inability to stay on task and what they perceived as her lack of seriousness. The members wanted an A+ for this major project. They had decided to give the finished project to their instructor a week early for feedback about how to revise and polish it. Judy's constant socializing had slowed them down. The others blamed her for missing their original, self-imposed deadline. By the end of the semester, Misty was the only member who would speak directly to Judy and thus served as the only link between Judy and the others, who ignored Judy whenever they could. The project was turned in on time but not early enough to receive instructor feedback; it received a B, for which everyone (but Judy) blamed Judy.

These students' journals revealed that none of them had much insight into their own or other members' behavior during the semester. Misty and the others held Judy responsible for everything that went wrong. But Judy was the most puzzled and frustrated member of all. She never understood why the others were so "cold." She had looked forward to making some new friends during the project, but her group members didn't seem to be interested in her. The harder she tried to take an interest in them, the more she felt rebuffed.

One of us had the chance to observe a meeting of this group. Judy's sociability and humor could have added quite a bit to the process—if she had only recognized that the others' priorities were not social. But the others, with their extreme task-orientation, were unable to see how Judy's personality could potentially have benefited their group. Instead, group members were locked into a struggle for control over their priorities, and no one won the struggle.

This situation is all too typical. Many groups self-destruct because they misman-
age members' diverse perspectives and personalities. Most of us think others
should share our goals, priorities, communication patterns, and working styles.
When they don't, we often blame them for being wrong. Few of us appreciate others
who are quite different from us. Ironically, it is our very differences that contribute to
making a group potentially more effective than an individual. After all, if you and I
think alike, act alike, and process information alike, one of us is unnecessary to the
process! Diversity is the heart of effective group problem solving; it is not the cause of
difficulty! Rather, ineffective management of diversity produces the difficulties so
many groups experience.

This chapter hopes to show you how you can celebrate and capitalize on diversity to
produce a better group outcome. We discuss several types of diversity, including differences in motives for joining a group, in learning styles and personality, and in cultural backgrounds. We conclude by discussing symbolic convergence and fantasy as a
way members can naturally bridge their differences and we present a methodology,
SYMLOG (system for the multiple-level observation of groups), designed to help
groups identify their differences and develop strategies for capitalizing on them.

What Is Diversity?

Diversity in a group refers to differences among members. There is a nearly endless variety of ways in which members are unlike each other, ranging from differences in how
members learn, to personality differences, to differences of opinion. For example, Roger
may remember everything someone tells him, but Tia remembers only what she has read
or seen. Suzanna may want to get right to business and complete a task; for her, chitchat
is a waste of time. Jamal, however, is able to focus on the task better after he's had a
chance to connect informally with the other members; when he can't connect via
chitchat, he feels at loose ends.

The best teams have a balance of member abilities, with member approaches and skills
complementing one another.[1] However, differences among members make communication more challenging because less can be taken for granted. Even so, it's not enough to
be satisfied just coping with diversity—instead, we want to celebrate it as the essence of
small group problem solving. Taking the extra time to make diversity work for rather
than against the group is a worthwhile goal.

Don't expect your fellow group members to change their basic needs, learning styles,
personality styles, or cultural backgrounds! Too often, we assume that we are doing
things right and someone else needs to conform to our preferences. One reason we, as
teachers, think it is necessary to talk about group diversity is that we want our students
to know some of the explanations behind others' behaviors. Members who act differently
from you aren't setting out to make your life difficult; they are simply behaving consistently with their own needs, styles, and cultures. Understanding, sensitivity, and appreciation of the differences are more likely to produce a willingness on everyone's part to adjust behavior so the differences have a chance to help rather than harm your group.

GLOSSARY

Diversity

*Differences among
group members,
from personality
and learning style
differences to
differences of opinion*

DIFFERENCES IN MOTIVES FOR JOINING A GROUP

One of the first differences to face group members is that they haven't all joined a group for the same reasons. People join groups in large part to satisfy psychological needs, among which are the needs for inclusion, affection, and control mentioned in Chapter 1. However, members who join for reasons of affection and inclusion are likely to be looking for something very different in a group than members joining to meet control and achievement needs.

Robert Bales, the small group pioneer mentioned in Chapter 7, notes that our behavior stems from our values and our psychological needs.[2] Members who join primarily to meet control or achievement needs will be task-oriented, whereas members whose needs for affection and belonging predominate will be socioemotional, focusing on the interpersonal relationships in the group. These two sets of needs, and their corresponding approaches to the group's work, can often compete with each other in a group, as you saw in the opening story.

Task-oriented individuals, with their focus on control and achievement needs, believe the group's task is the reason for the group's existence. They perceive any digression from the task as a waste of members' time, so they keep chitchat to a minimum. They feel highly frustrated when the group digresses and may give dirty looks to those who pull the group off task; they are likely to be the ones who bring the group back to task when the group has digressed. Task-oriented members value accomplishment and feel a tremendous sense of achievement and relief when the group's task is completed.

Relationally oriented individuals, on the other hand, value human relationships more than they do task accomplishment. These individuals want to get to know the others in the group and want to experience each member as a friend. Their needs for affection and inclusion take precedence over their needs for control. Thus, if a member is having a personal problem, socioemotional individuals will usually perceive that member's needs as being more important then the group's task and will willingly sacrifice the group's task accomplishment to help the member.

Both kinds of members are valuable to the group.[3] The most effective and rewarding teams are often those that combine secondary (task-oriented) and primary (relationship-oriented) elements, as we noted in Chapter 1. In addition, most of us participate in groups for several reasons, of which accomplishing the task is only one. We want to experience the pleasure of each other's company and the fun of interaction.[4] Judy's group fell down on one count—understanding the members' social realities. Judy expected the others to change their task orientation, but that's like asking a tiger to change his stripes. Likewise, the others wanted Judy not to have strong needs for inclusion and affection—another impossible wish. Appreciation for and open discussion of their differences could have helped members overcome what turned out to be an insurmountable obstacle to group success.

DIVERSITY OF LEARNING STYLES

Group members also differ in their learning styles. Our learning preferences affect how and what we talk about, whether we understand one another, and what aspects of a group's task we feel most comfortable taking on. Our learning style differences can set us up for misunderstandings if we aren't careful. For example, Gloria is a visual learner.

8.1   Handling Different Motives and Orientations toward Work

Judy and her fellow group members were highly frustrated by each other, in part because their needs and corresponding orientations toward the group's work were so different. However, instead of recognizing this as a potential plus, they responded by blaming each other for not doing things "right."

Assume you are Judy, and you're having a hard time understanding why your group members seem constantly to be rebuffing your attempts at friendship.

1. What is your perception of the group's situation? If you were to describe the situation to a friend, what would you say about it?
2. What effect is your perception of the situation having on your behavior in (and outside) the group?
3. What could you do to make the situation better, from your perspective? List at least five possible things you could do.
4. Which of those actions do you think is most likely to improve the situation, and why?

Assume you are one of the other members of the group and you don't understand why Judy isn't getting the message.

5. What is your perception of the group's situation? If you were telling a friend about it, what would you say the problem was?
6. What effect is your perception of the situation having on your behavior in (and outside) the group?
7. What could you do to make the situation better, from your perspective? List at least five possible things you could do.
8. Which of those actions do you think is most likely to improve the situation, and why?

In one group meeting, John, another member, tried to explain something to her in several different ways, none of which seemed to be getting through. Then a third group member drew a simple diagram and Gloria instantly "saw" what they were talking about. Had the third member not observed that a different way of explaining the information was needed and been flexible enough to provide it, both Gloria and the rest of the group would have stayed stuck on one point.

Other group members may be kinesthetic or touch learners, who process information best if they can physically do something with the information. Group members often reveal these preferences in their talk. For instance, Gloria often says, I see what you mean," when she understands someone. John says, "I hear you," to indicate understanding, while a third member may say, "I've got it!" Each of these metaphors for "I understand" reveals a clue as to the dominant sensory learning style of the speaker. In cohesive groups, members tend to converge on a single dominant sensory metaphor without even

FIGURE 8.1   The Kolb Learning Cycle

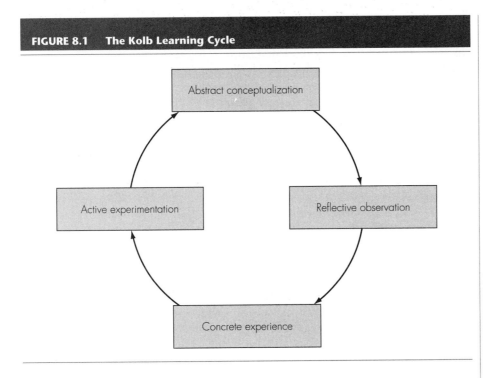

knowing it.[5] For instance, after a while group members will all start to say things like "It fits," "I grasp what you're saying," or "There's a hole big enough to walk through in that argument" if the kinesthetic or touch metaphor has been "chosen."

There are strengths to having all three preferences included in a group. For example, in a proposal created by the group, Gloria will contribute diagrams and visual displays that communicate well to other visual learners. John may be the member best suited for presenting the proposal orally to the parent organization. Sometimes just talking about these preferences is enough to help members appreciate them and work a little harder to communicate well with members whose preferences are different.

David Kolb has developed another learning style model that demonstrates several key differences in learning styles that can affect how group members work together.[6] He suggests that people have one of four basic preferences for learning new information and they enter the learning cycle by way of their preferred style (see Figure 8.1). We present this information to you as a way to heighten your awareness of the learning style differences among group members. Each of the styles has strengths to lend a group, which is best served with an overall balance of the styles.

The **concrete experience learning style** describes those individuals who learn well from events they actually observe or activities in which they actually participate. They are concerned with unique, particular experiences rather than theories and generalizations. They trust their feelings and are intuitive. As group members, they are do-ers and may become impatient with theoretical discussions or researching background information. For example, if your group is charged with investigating a parking problem on campus, a concrete experience learner may volunteer to count cars illegally parked or observe how many cars leave a lot without finding a parking place. Such a person may be uncomfortable if asked to synthesize three theoretical articles about traffic flow and facility usage.

The **reflective observation learning style** describes individuals who prefer to gain perspective on their direct experience by standing back from it, gaining psychological distance from it, and thinking about it reflectively. They emphasize understanding rather than practical application; they are the group "thinkers." They mull information over in their minds, may talk to others about it, and learn particularly well by writing about the experience. As group members, they are likely to benefit from group discussion about issues. They may help the group think through a group project or show how theoretical concepts are applied, but they may be less comfortable jumping in to help implement a group project.

The **abstract conceptualization learning style** describes learners who process a considerable amount of information by reading and solitary study. They are comfortable working alone, can perceive broad patterns, readily understand theoretical material, and can pull together information from a variety of sources in a way that makes sense. They are logical and emphasize thinking as opposed to feeling. In a group, they are the "synthesizers" and would enjoy pulling together available research for the group's project; however, they may be less enthused about conducting observations or implementing the project.

The **active experimentation learning style** describes individuals who learn by trying out different things until they find one that works. Such people are comfortable trying something new. They can apply information in a variety of ways. They like to actively influence others and prefer to do rather than observe. As group members, they will be effective in a crisis because they can think and problem-solve on their feet. Such a member might like to be given responsibility for conducting a pilot test of your group's recommended solution to the parking problem but is likely to have less patience for solitary thinking and writing about the problem.

Generally, our preferences usually lead us to develop strengths in some styles more than others. In a balanced group, though, all styles are represented; the group has members who can research a problem, extract the important information from the research, develop a plan, test the plan and modify what doesn't work, then finally implement the plan. For example, a member who can conceptualize abstractly may be a big asset in step 1 of P-MOPS, when careful analysis of a problem is necessary. On the other hand, a member comfortable with active experimentation may be an asset at step 5, when the group needs to adjust the way a solution is implemented. Members who discover that one or more of the styles is not represented can be conscious of that deficiency, can make an effort to expand their own abilities, or can invite consultants or trusted outsiders to supply the perspectives they lack.

PERSONALITY DIFFERENCES

Mishandled personality differences create as much havoc in groups as any other factor. As mentioned earlier, it isn't the fact that members have different personal styles that causes the problem—it's the fact that many members don't know how to work with others whose personalities are markedly different. They waste their energy trying to get those with dissimilar personalities to change or are simply unwilling to work with people different from themselves.

Hundreds of personality characteristics have been investigated by social scientists. Instead of making an inventory of characteristics that affect group interaction, we have chosen to look in depth at one classification system, the **Myers-Briggs Type Indicator® (MBTI).**

The MBTI, based on the work of psychologist Carl Jung, is a personality measure developed by Isabel Briggs Myers and Katherine Briggs.[7] The system looks at four dimensions that relate to how individuals interact with the world. Each dimension is a continuum with opposite characteristics at either pole. Each of us leans, a little or a lot, toward one or the other of the poles. The MBTI classifies us into 16 basic personality types based on the particular combination of dimensions toward which we lean. Thus, MBTI assesses our preferences and, for each type, describes the characteristics we display and the behaviors with which we are most comfortable. However, all of us display some characteristics of all the personality types—no one is a "pure" type. In this next section, we will describe the four dimensions (see Table 8.1).

The **extraversion/introversion dimension** bears on whether your energy is directed toward the outer, observable world or your inner, mental landscape. Extraverts are tuned in to the outer world. They are outgoing, sociable, like variety in their activities, and love being with other people. They may be impatient with slow tasks and don't mind being interrupted. Do you recognize Judy, from our opening story? Introverts, in contrast, like to work alone and dislike being interrupted. They can be patient with details, may be socially reserved, and make decisions relatively independently of what others such as family and friends want. As group members, extraverts usually like and get along well with the other members and are open to others' ideas. Introverts may be uncomfortable working in groups; however, they enjoy working with ideas and can contribute effectively to group problem solving. They may prefer to work independently and bring their work to the group rather than working together with others. Unless extraverts and introverts each know something about the personality characteristics and work styles of the other, their approaches are so different that misunderstandings can easily occur.

The **sensing/intuiting dimension** refers to the type of information you naturally tune in to. Do you prefer to focus on facts in the here and now or are you more likely to dream of possibilities and imagine new connections? Sensing types prefer to deal with facts and information and mistrust intuitive leaps. They are impatient with abstract theories and are comfortable dealing with details (but they may miss the big picture). Intuitive types become bored easily, especially with details, and relish change. They can see possibilities and like to deal in theories. Imagination and invention are important to them and their conversation may leap from idea to idea (but skip concrete facts). As group members, sensing types are careful and factual and will be able to provide specific and concrete examples for reports and papers. Intuitive types are creative and imaginative; they may come up with an innovative plan or a novel way to present a project.

The **thinking/feeling dimension** concerns how individuals make decisions, whether by analysis and objective evidence or through empathy for others and subjective feelings. Thinkers use evidence, logic, and careful analysis to arrive at verifiable conclusions and to make decisions. They may forget to take others' feelings into account. They are comfortable setting up a single standard and holding everyone to it, regardless of individual circumstances. Feelers, on the other hand, use empathy for others as the standard by which they make decisions. They are comfortable adjusting standards to meet individual

TABLE 8.1	**Strengths and Weaknesses of the Myers-Briggs® Dimensions**

	Introvert	**Extravert**
STRENGTHS	• Can work independently	• Interacts well with others
	• Likes working with ideas	• Is open
	• Is careful before acting	• An active do-er
WEAKNESSES	• Dislikes being interrupted	• Is impulsive and impatient
	• Misses opportunities to act	• Needs change and variety
	• Can be secretive or appear unsociable	• Needs others to work best
	Sensor	**Intuitor**
STRENGTHS	• Pays attention to details and facts	• Sees possibilities
	• Is patient and systematic	• Likes complicated issues/problems
	• Is practical	• Likes working on novel problems
WEAKNESSES	• Can't see the forest for the trees	• Impatient with tedious work
	• Cannot see possibilities or imagine the future	• Inattentive to detail or practical considerations
	• Is frustrated by complexity	• Jumps to conclusions
	Thinker	**Feeler**
STRENGTHS	• Logical, analytical, organized	• Considerate of others' feelings
	• Good critical ability	• Understands others' needs/feelings
	• Fair but firm	• Interested in maintaining harmony
WEAKNESSES	• Doesn't notice others' feelings	• Can be disorganized
	• Uninterested in harmony; shows less mercy	• Is overly accepting (of others, of information)
	• Misunderstands others' values	• Not logical or objective
	Perceiver	**Judger**
STRENGTHS	• Sees all sides of an issue	• Decisive
	• Flexible, spontaneous	• Persistent in staying with a task
	• Is nonjudgmental, accepting	• Makes plans and sticks to them
WEAKNESSES	• Indecisive	• Stubborn and inflexible
	• Easily distracted; does not finish tasks	• Controlled by the plan/tasks rather than in charge of the plan
	• Does not plan	• Decides with insufficient data

SOURCE: Adapted from John N. Gardner and A. Jerome Jewler, *Your College Experience: Strategies for Success*, 2nd ed. (Belmont, CA: Wadsworth, 1995), pp. 83–89

circumstances and are more interested in group harmony and interpersonal relationships than on achieving group task goals. As group members, thinkers will be able to evaluate information critically, to spot flaws in arguments, and to produce a logical plan. Feelers will make sure that the group takes people's feelings into account and will help ensure that a decision is acceptable to those who will be affected.

The **perceiving/judging dimension** refers to the way people organize the world around them, whether they are spontaneous and flexible or planned and orderly. Perceivers are like sponges. They tend to gather as much information as they can and to postpone making decisions. They are open and nonjudgmental, welcoming new perspectives and approaches. They are able to see all sides of an issue, but they also have a hard time deciding and reaching closure. When they finish a task, they are constantly second-guessing themselves to see if there was a different or better way they could have done it. Judgers, on the other hand, are decisive and firm in their convictions. They set plans and stick to them. They finish tasks and are ready to go on to the next project. However, they also don't like to have their plans changed and may appear rigid and inflexible. In a group, judgers will help ensure that the group's work gets done. They will

GLOSSARY

Perceiving/ Judging Dimension

The Myers-Briggs® dimension that describes whether someone is spontaneous and flexible or planned and orderly

8.2   Balancing the Church Board

APPLY NOW

A friend of ours served on the board of directors of a Unity church. The board and congregation were having problems getting things done. The board made decisions and set policies, but no action took place. For example, the board noticed that, although many new members had joined the church, they often drifted away after a few months. Board members decided to create a program that would help new members integrate themselves quickly into the church community so that they would feel a part of the congregation and so that they would be motivated to stay. They instituted a volunteer program to help members, especially new ones, identify their talents and find places where they could make their talents available to the church. However, this program never got off the ground, and although new members continued to join, they also continued to leave.

At about this time, a representative from the Association of Unity Churches came to conduct a board/congregation seminar based on the Myers-Briggs® classifications. Of the seven board members, six were identified as intuitive feelers and one as an intuitive thinker.

1. What relationship do you see between the classification of board members and the kinds of problems the church was experiencing?

2. What classifications do you think would be most helpful in supplying balance to this board?

3. If you were the board president, what would you do with this information? For instance, would you ask potential board members to construct their profile before endorsing them to run for the board? What ethical problems might this create?

help the group establish a work plan and encourage fellow members to follow it. They aren't truly comfortable until the group's work is complete. Perceivers, however, can roll with the punches and aren't thrown when circumstances upset the plan. Their flexibility helps members think of options B and C when A falls through. However, they are not so concerned with finishing a plan and are more excited when they start a new project. Judgers and perceivers can drive each other crazy in a group!

The Myers-Briggs® personality types are related to Kolb's learning styles. For example, introversion and reflective observation exhibit similar preferences, as do extraversion and active experimentation. Concrete experience preferences are related both to sensing and feeling; abstract conceptualization preferences are related both to intuiting and thinking.

CULTURAL DIVERSITY

Cultural differences represent a major form of diversity in a group. Groups of the future will continue to be increasingly more diverse, so information about how cultures differ can help you be a more effective group member. **Culture** is the system of beliefs, values, symbols, and rules that underlie communication patterns within a discernible grouping of people. It doesn't necessarily refer to people from another country. A subculture is a smaller identifiable group contained within a larger cultural grouping. It is important to note that the *sub* in subculture does not mean "less important" or "less valuable." It simply means that the subculture in question is smaller in numbers—although perhaps highly influential—than the larger culture of which it is a part. In this text, we use the word *culture* to refer also to race, gender, and generational differences, which we'll discuss later.

Unless someone calls our attention to a feature of our culture, we don't think too much about the significant role it plays in shaping our behavior. In addition, we tend to assume that individuals from other cultures share our values, behaviors, and communication patterns, but they don't! Cultures differ along a number of dimensions that affect communication rules and preferences (see Table 8.2).[8] Knowing something about them will help you communicate better in groups made up of individuals from diverse cultures so that you can capitalize on the strengths of these cultures.

The first important dimension along which cultures vary is the individualist–collectivist dimension. An **individualistic culture,** such as the predominant culture of the United States, values individual goals more than collective, or group, goals. In a **collectivist culture,** the needs of the group take precedence over the needs of the individual, and conformity to the group is valued. So, for example, a group member from a collectivist culture will willingly abandon personal plans to attend a group meeting, but a member from an individualistic culture will say something like, "I've already got plans, so you'll either have to meet without me or reschedule the meeting at a time that I can make." The underlying value—what's most important—differs. It is easy for group members who value collectivism to become frustrated with a highly individualistic member, whom they will perceive as selfish and uncaring. However, it is also easy for individualistic members to perceive collectivist ones as caring too much about what others think.

Individuals from collectivist and individualistic cultures have developed different communication preferences. For instance, individualistic members value clear and direct communication that is unambiguous.[9] In contrast, members from collectivist cultures,

**MHHE.com/
groups**
For more
information on
exploring cultural
diversity, go to
the on-line
learning center.

GLOSSARY

Culture

*The system of beliefs,
values, and symbols
shared by an
identifiable group
of people*

**Individualistic
Culture**

*A culture that values
individual needs
and goals more than
group needs
and goals*

**Collectivist
Culture**

*A culture that values
group needs and
goals more than
individual needs
and goals*

TABLE 8.2	Three Important Dimensions of Culture

Individualism/Collectivism

HIGH INDIVIDUALISM — Values independence, autonomy, and privacy; encourages dissent; encourages people to "do their own thing."

- "I won't be at the meeting tomorrow. I've got a chance to go skiing with a friend and I really need some time off from school."
- "I know you all agree, but I don't, and I won't support that decision."

HIGH COLLECTIVISM — Values harmony, conformity, and loyalty to the group; discourages dissent.

- "I'm taking my mother to the hospital for surgery in the morning, but I'll be at our meeting for sure at noon. I can call from there to see how she's doing."
- "I'll go along with whatever you all want to do."

Power Distance

HIGH POWER DISTANCE — Maximizes status differences between members; values hierarchical structure and strong authoritarian leadership.

- Leader says, "I've decided that we're going to do it this way."

LOW POWER DISTANCE — Minimizes status differences between members; values sharing power, participatory decision making, democratic leadership.

- Leader says, "We've all got to live with the decision we make, so we should all have a say in it. Tell me what you think?"

Context

LOW CONTEXT — The words themselves carry most of the meaning; values direct, unambiguous communication.

- "Your idea is intriguing. Maybe we should explore it in more detail" (said with a smile) means, "I'm interested and I want to explore it in more detail."
- "I love that idea" means "I love that idea."

HIGH CONTEXT — The situation, or context, carries most of the meaning; communication is indirect; nonverbal signals are crucial to understanding a message.

- "Your idea is intriguing. Maybe we should explore it in more detail" (said with a smile) may mean, "I hate it" or "I really like it" or "It might have some possibilities but I can't commit yet."

GLOSSARY

Power-Distance

Whether a culture maximizes or minimizes status and power differences

Low-Context Culture

A culture where the words used convey more meaning than the situation or context

High-Context Culture

A culture where features of the situation or context convey more meaning than the words people use

which value harmony, prefer ambiguous communication that is more subtle and tentative. For example, assume both Nguyen and Sam disagree with something contained in a group report being prepared. Nguyen, the collectivist member, says, "I wonder if we should look more closely at Part 2 of the report? Was anyone else confused in that section?" But Sam, the individualist member, says, "I think Part 2 sucks and has to be done over." Nguyen likely thinks Sam is selfish and rude, whereas Sam sees Nguyen as wishy-washy and spineless.

Each way of stating the same opinion has advantages and disadvantages. Nguyen's way is polite and allows the writer of Part 2 to save face; however, we can't tell how strongly Nguyen feels about it, so Part 2's writer can easily misinterpret Nguyen. In contrast, there's no mistaking how Sam feels, but his statement may make the author so angry that nothing in Part 2 gets changed.

The second dimension of culture we discuss is **power-distance,** or the extent to which a culture maximizes or minimizes status and power differences among individuals. In a low power-distance culture (the United States has relatively low power-distance), status and power differences among individuals are downplayed. Individuals believe that power should be distributed evenly, that just because someone has a title or money does not entitle them to privileges under the law that others don't have, and so forth. In a group, members from a low power-distance culture believe that they have as much right to speak up and participate in decisions as the group's leader. In high power-distance cultures such as Mexico and the Philippines, status differences are magnified and a rigid hierarchy exists. Members of such cultures believe that each person has a preassigned place in the society and should not seek to step out of that niche. In a group, members from high power-distance cultures expect the leader to control and direct the group and may become frustrated with participatory leadership.

Members from low power-distance cultures prefer to participate in decision making, prefer a democratic leadership style, and assume that everyone else wants to speak up and participate in decision making as well. For instance, group leader Sarah says to her group, "What ideas do you all have for solving the parking problem?" Members from high power-distance cultures value authoritarian leadership and may see a democratic leader as weak and incompetent. They expect low-status members to conform to high-status members. They assume others will accept the leader's control and direction. For example, group leader José says to his group, "I believe the parking problem is due to bad class scheduling. Here's what I want you to do. . . ." You can see the possibility for misunderstanding and hurt feelings here!

The third dimension is that of context. In a **low-context culture,** such as that of the United States, the verbal part of the message carries the meaning—what you say is exactly what you mean. If you say that you like my proposal, I can trust the fact that you really do like it. In a **high-context culture,** such as most Asian and Native American cultures, features of a situation or context are more important than the words themselves. So if you tell me you like my proposal, I'd have to be able to take into account the setting, the people, the purpose of our conversation, and other factors to know for sure whether you really liked it or you were just being polite to avoid hurting my feelings. High-context cultures tend to be collectivist, with group harmony an important value. Ambiguity and indirectness may help preserve this harmony by allowing disagreement to happen gently in a way that doesn't upset the balance of the group.

Group members from low-context cultures, which tend to be individualistic, prefer direct and unambiguous communication because they want to be able to tell exactly what someone means from what that person says. Such members will try to force others to be direct and clear. They may perceive members who are not straightforward as manipulative or insincere. On the other hand, members from high-context cultures perceive members who are verbally blunt as rude and aggressive. As the earlier example demonstrates, the advantage of being clear, like Sam, is that your meaning is unmistakable. However, the advantage of being tentative, like Nguyen, is that you allow discussion to occur without polarizing members' opinions or making them lose face.

Appreciation of cultural differences in a group is very important. The United States is a pluralistic culture, to which many different cultures have contributed. This means little can be assumed or taken for granted. It is common now—and will become even more common in years to come—for groups in the United States to be composed of

8.3 Euro-Disney Stumbles

APPLY NOW

According to Carl Hiaasen's book, *Team Rodent: How Disney Devours the World,** Disney's venture in France, Euro-Disney, got off to a slow start when it opened in 1992. Disney executives decided to import the Disney concept intact when they created their European theme park. The Disney parks in the United States have a clean-cut image—at least, as Americans define *clean-cut.* Those who work in the park, mostly young people, abide by strict rules of dress and demeanor. For example, they must not wear bright nail polish, heavy makeup, or facial hair. In addition, the parks do not serve wine or other alcoholic beverages, which contributes to the clean-cut image in the United States.

However, these rules seemed offensive and ridiculous to Europeans, particularly the French. Not serve wine in France? Unthinkable! These factors contributed to Euro-Disney's dismal early performance. Recently, however, Disney rethought its rules and relaxed several, in particular the makeup, facial hair, and wine rules. And, Euro-Disney is beginning to catch on in Europe, the way it has in the United States.

1. Are there any other "rules" or communication patterns observed by North Americans that Europeans might consider silly?

2. Are there any "rules" or communication patterns observed by Europeans that North Americans might consider silly?

3. What does the above story suggest to you about cultural practices, particularly applying in one culture practices that are normal in another?

4. Disney executives are intelligent and experienced. What factors do you think might have contributed to this not-well-thought-out decision by Disney in the first place?

*Carl Hiaasen, *Team Rodent: How Disney Devours the World* (New York: Ballantine Publishing Group, 1998).

GLOSSARY

Gender

Learned characteristics of masculinity and femininity

Sex

The inherent biological characteristics of male and female with which people are born

members from different ethnic or racial groups, different generations, and different sexes. Often, open discussion of cultural differences is all that's needed to clear up communication misunderstandings that may occur. Patience helps. So does goodwill and kindness toward others whose communication preferences and practices are different from your own.

Gender Differences as Cultural Differences.   You will never be able to escape one of the most important influences of culture: the effect of gender roles in a group. **Gender** refers to the learned characteristics of masculinity and femininity; **sex** refers to the inherent biological characteristics with which men and women are born. At this point, we don't know which characteristics are inherent and which are learned. However, we do know that the communicative rules we all use have been taught to us by our culture, and that men and women are taught different communicative rules.[10] Gender roles continue to change rapidly, so any discussion about gender roles in communication is likely both to be an overgeneralization and to be out of date in coming years.

One difference researchers have observed in the United States is that men and women seem to have different goals when they communicate. Men in general perceive conversation as a way to build or maintain status, whereas women perceive it as a way to connect to others. Thus, men have been observed to play one-up games in conversation and to compete. Men's talk tends to be direct, task-oriented, and uses "I" quite a bit. In contrast, women's talk is more relationally oriented, cooperative, and indirect. Women will work hard to ensure that everyone has the chance to get the conversational floor, while men expect others to take the floor if they want it. Men display more signs of power (e.g., claiming more space and interrupting) and women more signs of liking (e.g., smiling and nodding). Women seem to work harder to keep a conversation going. They initiate more topics, partly because men often respond minimally ("Uh-huh" or "Mm-hmm" without elaboration) and often don't follow up on the topics women initiate.

Men and women tend to use questions differently. Men use questions to acquire information, whereas women use questions to keep the conversation going. Thus, "Do you think we should accept the first or the second option?" from Allen is probably asking for a short answer, perhaps with some reasoning to support the answer. The same question from Lorraine is probably intended more as an invitation to discuss the topic than a request for information. The problem comes when Allen and Lorraine misinterpret each other. For instance, Allen answering, "The first option," to Lorraine's question, and stopping at that, will wonder why she is frustrated with him, and she will wonder why Allen's giving such curt, unfriendly answers.

Generalizing about the differences between the communication rules for men and women is difficult, in part because the social rules are changing so quickly and because gender differences capture our attention more than similarities. What is considered appropriate behavior now has changed from 30 or even 10 years ago. Despite the evidence that females and males are more similar than different, we insist on emphasizing the differences, in part because they seem to make sense to us intuitively. However, behaviors typically attributed to women and those attributed to men are both valuable in groups. Gender balance seems like a good idea.

Race and Ethnic Differences as Cultural Differences.   When we talk about diversity, the first thing that comes to most people's minds is ethnic or racial diversity. In the United States, we often don't deal well with ethnic and racial differences. We

8.1   Different Voices for Making Ethical Decisions

Assume you are on a student judicial committee charged with deciding the punishment of students who have violated your institution's rules and policies. Sam, the student before you, is charged with plagiarism. He submitted a paper very similar to one that another student had turned in the previous semester to another teacher for the same course. Sections of Sam's paper are identical with the earlier paper, but some parts of the paper contain new research and appear to be Sam's own work. Sam has admitted that he plagiarized portions of the paper, but pleads extenuating circumstances and is asking for your committee's mercy. Soon after he started his research for the paper, he learned that his younger sister, still in high school, was diagnosed with leukemia. She is being treated, so far successfully, but for the last few weeks Sam has driven home on weekends to be with her. He and his sister are close; she relies on him for emotional support, which he has been happy to provide. But helping her has drained him of the ability to concentrate and consumed all his time. He took the easy way out, but made sure that he incorporated his original research into the paper he "borrowed." Sam asks you to let him drop the course with no penalty so he can take it again the next semester. However, your institution has an honor code all students sign as freshmen; the code specifies a *minimum* of one semester's suspension for all honor violations, including plagiarism. In practice, though, the student judicial committee's recommendations are accepted. Here are your choices:

- Let him drop the course with no penalty.
- Give him an F in the course.
- Give him an F in the course with a notation that the F is due to plagiarism; this remains on his permanent record.
- Give him an F in the course and suspend him for one semester.
- Give him an F in the course and expel him from school permanently.

1. Before you form groups of five or six, what would you personally recommend for Sam? What is your reasoning for your recommendation?

2. Get together in groups, as if you were the student judicial committee, and come to consensus about what you would recommend. Then discuss what your reasons were for your ultimate recommendation. What considerations were most important to you?

3. How did you balance being fair to Sam, being fair to other students, and upholding your honor code?

(continued)

8.1   *Continued*

This example allows for a number of individual differences in ethical reasoning to emerge. Educator Carol Gilligan, in her book *In a Different Voice,** suggests that men and women use different ethical logic systems when making decisions like this. Men are believed to make ethical decisions from so-called objective positions that focus on abstract concepts such as justice, freedom, and truth. Women, Gilligan believes, make ethical decisions based on concerns for people, taking compassion, desire to alleviate suffering, and loyalty into account.

4. Did you observe either of these ethical systems during your discussion? Did any other ethical systems emerge during your discussion?

5. To what extent do you agree with Gilligan's assessment of men's and women's reasoning during ethical dilemmas like this?

6. What implications might the conflict of different ethical systems have for small groups?

*Carol Gilligan, *In a Different Voice: Psychological Theory and Women's Development* (Cambridge, MA: Harvard University Press, 1982).

seem to shout at each other, producing more heat than light. However, if we don't quickly find a way to celebrate one another's ethnic and racial differences while at the same time finding a way to cooperate in solving common problems, our culture—a grand experiment in democracy—will not succeed. In the 21st century, multiracial and multiethnic groups will be the norm, so we have to do better than we've done in the past.

Major ethnic and racial groups in our country include African Americans, Asian Americans, European Americans, and Hispanic Americans. We know quite a bit about the communication within many cultures, but we don't know very much about interaction between individuals from a variety of cultures. In the next section, we provide information about some of the major differences in communication styles and patterns in these groups, but we focus on differences between African Americans and European Americans because relationships between these two groups are among the most problematic. We offer a very important caution, however. We discuss each culture as if members from that culture display a single consistent pattern of communication, but this is not the case. There are as many communication style differences within the African-American community as there are between African Americans and Asian Americans. The same can be said about gender. Although we know we are overgeneralizing, if you aren't aware of differing cultural practices, your lack of knowledge may interfere with effective group discussion. If you find yourself uncomfortable in an encounter with someone whose race or ethnicity is different from your own, and your impulse is to blame the other person for your discomfort, stop! Your discomfort may be due to unexamined differences between two cultures; the other person may be just as uncomfortable as you are.

Earlier we presented information about collective and high-context cultures. Asian cultures tend to be both. Asian Americans who are close to their original family cultures may communicate indirectly. Group harmony takes priority, so conflict will be expressed indirectly and ambiguously. Non-Asian Americans may have to pay careful attention to know they've been disagreed with. Words themselves are not as trusted as actions and context.

Most Hispanic cultures are collective and have a high power distance. This means that individuals are expected to subordinate their wishes to the group and that strong, authoritarian leadership is expected. These expectations and values may clash with the individualism and relatively low power distance in the predominant European American culture in the United States.

The relationship between African Americans and European Americans can be particularly touchy. These two cultural groups have traditionally misunderstood each other, often with serious consequences to both. We hope the information we provide about communication differences between these groups will prevent you from saying or doing something insensitive that contributes to group self-destruction.

The African-American culture values sharing, emotionality, verbal expression, and interactivity.[11] These values express themselves in a variety of ways. African Americans appreciate verbal inventiveness and expression. Verbal play as a type of performance is particularly valued. However, what African Americans intend as a playful display is often interpreted by European Americans as bragging or strutting. African Americans are generally more expressive and interactive. Open expression of feelings is encouraged and seen as an important way to share and connect. However, this too can be misinterpreted. African Americans think European Americans are cold and underreactive because they don't share feelings as readily and are not as expressive. Similarly, European Americans think African Americans are overly emotional and overreactive.

Each group perceives the other negatively.[12] A number of communication patterns may contribute to this. For instance, African Americans stand closer to each other than European Americans, who may interpret that nonverbal behavior as threatening. European Americans make more direct eye contact when they listen than when they talk. For African Americans, the pattern is reversed; they make more direct eye contact when they talk than when they listen. This can seriously affect perceptions of trust, interest, and acceptance.

The African-American communication style is much more interactive than the typical European-American style. For instance, traditional African-American church services often display the call-response style, where congregation members shout "Amen!" and "Tell it like it is, brother!" while the preacher is talking. They also use the backchannel more than European Americans. This means that they say things like "Uh-huh" and "Mm-hmm" in everyday conversation to signify interest and attention. However, European Americans can easily interpret someone talking during another's talk as rudeness. On the other hand, African Americans, who are used to getting such verbal signs of attention, may interpret that lack of backchannel responses from European Americans as lack of interest. African-American conversational style is a narrative, storytelling style. European Americans may interpret it as disorganized, rambling, or off-task. To European-American teachers, a paper written in traditional African-American narrative style can appear disorganized and sloppy.

Most African Americans have had more practice in understanding European-American culture than vice versa because they have been forced to.[13] Many African Americans consider themselves bicultural because they can negotiate "typical" African-American conversational contexts as well as the European-American contexts that currently predominate in the business and education arenas. However, it is difficult for minority group members to express themselves fully in groups composed primarily of individuals from other cultures.[14] Unfortunately, this suggests that multicultural groups are not realizing their full potential as groups because they aren't incorporating fully the ideas of the minority group members.

Generational Differences as Cultural Differences.   A few years ago, Gloria served on the board of directors at her church. Gloria is a baby boomer and was the youngest member of the board. As a boomer, she believes all people—women included—have the right to express opinions; she also values frank and open discussion in the course of making decisions. It simply never would occur to her that she *shouldn't* say what she thought. Most of the other members of the seven-member board were a generation older. During their board meetings, they signaled—primarily through their nonverbal behavior—that they were uncomfortable with her high level of participation. It seemed to her that she was violating an unspoken rule of "be seen and not heard until you've paid your dues." Her values and beliefs seemed to clash with the others' values, and she interpreted the clash as stemming from generational differences.

Think, for a moment, about your parents' and their friends' generation. Do you have the same values? Do you live your life in the same way as your parents? What differences do you observe? If you are old enough to have children, what differences do you observe between your own beliefs, behaviors, and values and those of your children?

A number of writers have characterized major generational differences that appear in the U.S. workplace today. Much of this information has been synthesized by Rick and Kathy Hicks, whose work provides the basis for this section.[15] Although the Hickses do not use the term *subculture,* that is in fact what they describe. Their key assumption is that each generation forms a particular subculture, with similar values, goals, and outlook on life. The members of each generational subculture are highly influenced by the major events, people, and activities prominent during their formative years, particularly during the time when they were about 10 years old. At 10 years old, forces outside the family—friends, teachers, the media—begin to assume increased and lasting importance in our lives. To really understand the core values of a particular generational subculture, it is necessary to take a look at those deciding events.

The Hickses describe four broad generations that are found in today's workplace: builders, boomers, generation X, and the net generation. Table 8.3 summarizes this information. As we describe these generations, we recognize that we are again overgeneralizing and oversimplifying. However, you are bound to experience generational clashes in every arena of life—including in small groups you join. Appreciating some of the differences—and perhaps the reasons for them—will help you draw from the strengths of these generational differences instead of being mired in resentment.

The **builders** are a large group of individuals, born from 1901 to 1945, that include many subgenerations. However, there are characteristics that many in this large generational subculture share. These individuals were influenced by the expansiveness following World War I, the bust of the Great Depression, and the horrors of World War II. They learned to work hard, to save their money, and to postpone gratification. Many people who lived through the Depression are uncomfortable about buying goods on credit and prefer to save their money first for things they need. They may be uneasy about spending their money, even when they have enough. Although many builders have retired from the work force, they still are active participants in American governmental and civic life. These people believe in hard work, are patriotic, trust government

TABLE 8.3	Characteristics, Strengths, and Weaknesses of Four Dominant Generations		
	Characteristics	**Strengths**	**Weaknesses**
Generation BUILDERS (1901–1945)	• Major influences: Depression and WWII • Cautious about spending money • Will work hard at a single task until completed • Put own interests aside for common good	• Careful with resources (e.g., money) • Plan ahead • Reliable, dependable • Disciplined	• Too cautious with resources • May lack spontaneity and flexibility
BOOMERS (1946–1964)	• Major influences: TV, Vietnam War, the Pill, assassinations, civil rights movement, size of generation • Major consumers; value "good life" • Self-absorbed; believe they're special • Work as an end in itself; expect to be fulfilled at work • Value education	• Confident • Willing to put in whatever time a task takes • Willing to challenge "old ways" of doing things • Willing to take on big causes	• Think they're right all the time • Expect others to hold similar beliefs/values • May break rules of ethics if they think it's best for them
X-ERS (1965–1976)	• Major influences: rising divorce rate, Watergate, Pentagon Papers, MTV • Distrust institutions, particularly government • Comfortable with diversity • Work is means to an end • Value family (broadly defined) • Comfortable with technology • Endure education	• Independent thinkers • Sensitive to people; value relationships • Tolerant; accept competing points of view • Comfortable with change • Highly computer literate	• Appear pessimistic and negative • Unwilling to put personal life/concerns aside to complete task • May seem alienated and unmotivated

(continued)

TABLE 8.3	*Continued*		
Generation	**Characteristics**	**Strengths**	**Weaknesses**
N-GENERS (1977–1997)	• Major influences: AIDS, technology and the Internet, death of Princess Diana	• Open minded and tolerant; welcome different viewpoints	• Seem to lack initiative; seem unmotivated
	• Still young and in process of being formed	• Completely technology and media savvy	• Unlikely to conform to bureaucracy, hierarchy, organizational "rules"
	• Value diversity; highly tolerant	• Optimistic	
	• Major consumers	• Innovative	
	• Nonlinear thinkers	• Comfortable with and like collaborative work, networking	
	• Value family		

and other institutions (such as religious institutions), and trust authority. They are comfortable with hierarchy, willingly climbed the corporate ladder, understand responsibility, and are willing to put their own personal interests aside to complete a task. They have learned to postpone gratification and believe strongly in personal discipline and self-sacrifice. They value education, even though many of them were not able to obtain it for themselves. Builders are team players; they do not challenge authority and they will work very hard toward a goal. These values seem old-fashioned and out-of-date to later generations. Because of their own experiences in the Depression and World War II, the builders wanted things to be easier for their own children, the boomers.

The **boomers,** born from 1946 to 1964, were the largest generation for many years. Because of their sheer size, they were the focus of much marketing activity after World War II. Many companies (to say nothing of indulgent parents) paid lots of attention to the needs and wants of the boomers. Consequently, they have a strong belief in their own importance! Boomers were the first television generation, which has helped make them impatient for answers and immediate solutions. They lived through the decade of assassinations, civil rights marches, and general social upheaval. They also were the first generation to have the birth control pill, which dramatically changed the boomers' view of traditional morality. The boomers questioned everything having to do with tradition, although as they age they seem to be moving back to many of the traditions important to their parents. This was an idealistic generation that sought education as a way of addressing societal ills. Although they have a strong belief in hard work, they also believe that work itself should be fulfilling. Many have willingly neglected family life in favor of work. This is also the generation that experienced a massive increase in the divorce rate. The boomers, the first generation able to consume to a great extent, want the good life *now* and believe they should have it. Others'–and their own–attention was so focused on their wants and needs that the boomers have an ingrained belief that they are right, that whatever they want is good for them and others. Many believe that as long as what they

GLOSSARY

Boomers

Individuals born from 1946 to 1964; influenced by TV and social upheaval of 1960s

"Take a load off, Leonard—we're watching Generation X and Y duke it out."

are doing isn't directly harming anyone else, they have the right to do what they want as individuals. The boomers are currently in many leadership positions in industry, education, and government–holding places that gen-Xers would like to have!

Gen-Xers were born between 1965 and 1976. Xers, as they are sometimes called, were the first latchkey generation, often emotionally neglected by their boomer parents. They grew up during Watergate, Nixon's resignation, and the Pentagon Papers, all of which heralded a growing mistrust of institutions, particularly government. Because they are small in numbers, they have not received the attention of the boomers and feel somewhat neglected. They would like to prove themselves, but the boomers are hanging onto the jobs Xers believe they are entitled to. This is ironic in that the Xers have been described as having relatively fewer job skills and a lower sense of self-confidence than the generations that come before and after. They want the good life and don't want to wait. They value relationships and are not willing to sacrifice them for career, as the boomers were. Work is a means to an end for them, and they don't see themselves climbing the corporate ladder, like the builders. They tend to be cynical and pessimistic, with the highest suicide rate of any of the four generations. They are comfortable with computers, particularly as a mode of entertainment–this was the first generation to experience Atari as children. Xers do not respond well to or respect authority. They don't appear to be team players or want to make long-term commitments. Builders and boomers perceive them as unreliable, ungrateful, and difficult to manage. On the other hand, they have grown up with more diversity than builders and boomers and value it. They have a broad concept of family, which encompasses people they feel emotionally connected to, related or not.

The **net generation** (or N-gen) individuals were born between 1977 and 1997. This group is larger than the boomers and sometimes has been called the echo boom. Because

GLOSSARY

Gen-Xers

Individuals born from 1965 to 1976; influenced by Watergate and general mistrust

Net Generation

Individuals born from 1977 to 1997; influenced by computers and information/digital revolution

these individuals are still young, they have not had the opportunity to make their influence felt, but like the boomers, this group promises to be a major influence, in part because of its size. N-geners are the first truly wired generation—they have grown up with computers in the home and are completely comfortable using the 'net. Whereas the Xers grew up with computer-based entertainment programs, N-geners use the net for everything—information, shopping, and keeping in touch with friends and acquaintances around the world, in addition to entertainment. More hopeful than the Xers, N-geners are even more comfortable with diversity, confident of their skills (particularly their computer skills), and have better relationships with their parents. They are accustomed to collaborative work in school and via the 'net, which makes them value peer relationships and networking, but not hierarchical relationships. They can be good critical thinkers because they have the tools at their disposal to question, seek information, and challenge anything. They tend to judge people by their contributions and don't see any point in "waiting their turn" before they contribute. They are also the most stressed generation—from a young age they have had to keep track of play dates, school activities, lessons, and so forth on their day planners. Personal relationships are more important to this group than insitutions, and they have developed a strong live-and-let-live philosophy. They thrive on innovation, but like the Xers, can be seen by boomers and builders as lazy, unmotivated, and rude. Nevertheless, all levels of business, industry, education, and government will have to adjust to this very large and eventually influential group.

The builders are gradually fading from the scene as the boomers assume and hang onto power. The Xers, small in numbers and impaired in terms of job skills and self-esteem, are not a powerful force in the workplace. The N-geners, however, because of their complete mastery of technology and their size, will be a huge force in the workplace and some foresee a major values clash between them and the boomers. In many ways, because the N-geners have used collaborative learning in schools and are used to interacting with people from all over the world, they are well-suited to small group collaboration. But they

8.1   The Net Generation and You

Go to
**www.mhhe.com/
adamsgalanes** for
additional weblink
activities.

MEDIA AND TECHNOLOGY

The net generation is a wired generation. This group has grown up with the Internet as a consistent source of entertainment, education, and connection with others. The net generation, like generations of the past, does not espouse a monolithic view of the world. However, members of the net generation do share relatively uniform characteristics.

Don Tapscott's website, Growing Up Digital, describes in detail the characteristics of the net generation. The address for that website is http://www.growingupdigital.com/. Look through the website and lean about Tapscott's description of the net generation. How well does that description characterize your own attitudes and behaviors? What characteristics do you think the *next* generation will have? Is there a way you can characterize the next generation with a label? Do you think the next generation will embrace diversity and group interaction to the same extent as the net generation?

won't sit quietly and wait to be called on. They want to be respected for their competence and contributions, regardless of their age or position in the company. If you're a boomer, with the expectation that you will command and lead, expect to be challenged!

The previous discussion, as we mentioned earlier, represents overgeneralization and oversimplification. We all can see characteristics of each generation in ourselves. We also know people who display few or none of the characteristics that are supposed to exemplify their generation. However, the point to remember is this: Our early influences from family, friends, and institutions such as the media affect the way we perceive the world around us and the way we communicate, which in turn affects our behavior in small groups. Understanding something about members of generations different from yours—what their hopes and fears are, what pressures operate on them, what the formative events were in their lives—will help you make the most of your differences in small groups instead of bogging you down.

It is easy for a group to get off track or make negative attributions about others whose communication styles and practices differ from ours. We have to learn not to interpret others' actions through the lens of our own culture but to learn to appreciate what other cultures have to offer. If we take the time to do that, our groups and their outputs will

8.4   Moms's in My Group!

APPLY NOW

In the early 1990s, one of us observed a classroom group of five members who included two men and two women in their early 20s and one woman in her mid-40s. This group had made some progress on its assignment, but tensions were beginning to build between one of the young women, Mindy, and the older woman, Sarah. Sarah, a single mother with teenagers at home, had a very full schedule. She tried hard to keep the group task-focused so the project could be completed early, in time for feedback from the instructor. The more she made suggestions about the content of the project, about meeting more often, or about establishing deadlines for the members' individual assignments, the more Mindy resisted: "I can't meet then, I've paid for tickets to a concert and I'm not going to give them up," and "Chill, Sarah, it'll get done" were typical remarks. Mindy, exasperated with Sarah's task focus, complained to one of the other members that Sarah reminded her of her mom—"Always hassling me about something!" This conflict threatened to derail the group's progress.

1. What generations do Mindy and Sarah represent?
2. In what ways does each seem typical of her generation? What communication behaviors seem rooted in generational differences?
3. With whom do you personally have more sympathy? Why?
4. Assume that you are one of the other students in the group. How might you use what you know about generational differences to help the group resolve this problem?

benefit. Evidence suggests that, although groups composed of culturally diverse individuals experience more process problems and perhaps lower cohesion initially, over time they can overcome these problems to experience improved performance in certain areas.[16] Groups composed of members from the same nationality and ethnic background demonstrated more effective decision-making processes at first, but over time, the culturally diverse groups caught up. At the conclusion of this study, the diverse groups were outperforming the homogeneous groups in the range of perspectives considered and the number of alternatives generated. Clearly, working in a culturally diverse group is more challenging and requires members to pay greater attention to their communication behaviors, but the payoff can be significant!

We have not intended to teach you everything there is to know about cultural differences. Rather, we have tried to alert you to some common causes of misinterpretations in the listening process. Remember that cultural rules are not automatic; they are taught and constantly evolving. Remember also that cultural differences are not a matter of right or wrong, and that you have absorbed the rules of your culture so completely that they are invisible to you until you start to examine them or to interact with people from a very different culture.

Celebrating Diversity/Bridging Differences

So far in this chapter, we have stressed the value of diversity and provided information and examples to illustrate how diversity can make small group communication more complex. Our ultimate goal, however, is to help group members blend into a well-functioning team that capitalizes on member diversity. How does a group merge into a cohesive, productive team when members are diverse? Naturally occurring fantasy chains can promote a common team identity, and SYMLOG can be used to help groups talk about, and eventually bridge, their differences.

CREATING A GROUP IDENTITY THROUGH FANTASY

Diversity is potentially useful, but somehow group members must find common ground if they are to transcend their diverse styles, talents, and perspectives and operate as a team. Developing a symbolic life meaningful to all members can help accomplish this.

Even in the most hardworking, task-oriented groups, members do not stick to business all the time. They often get sidetracked, as if they have made a tacit agreement to "take a work break." Whenever a group is not talking about the here and now of the group, it is engaged in **fantasy.** This technical definition of fantasy does not mean unreal or untrue. It simply means that group members are not discussing the present task of the group but are discussing an apparently unrelated topic.

The study of fantasy stems from the theory of **symbolic convergence.**[17] This theory recognizes that human beings create and share meaning through their talk. For a group to exist, there has to be some shared meaning among the members; otherwise, there would be no group. "Convergence" signifies that members have "come together" on what certain events, ideas, words, and so forth, will mean. Members have developed similar feelings and beliefs about certain things (e.g., "We hate the boss's pep talks because she has no clue whatsoever about our work"). They may have in-jokes, a shared identity, or special meanings for words that only they understand (e.g., "We use 'fish face' as a term of affection because everybody in our group loves to go trout fishing"). They may also have developed rituals that are meaningful to them (e.g., "We always go out for a pizza on Friday afternoon before everybody goes separate ways on the weekends"). These shared symbols help establish common ground and common bonds that can overcome differences among members.

Fantasy helps such shared symbols come into being. The process works like this. One member introduces a fantasy and other members pick up on it and add to it. This group storytelling, called a fantasy chain, is similar to a party game most of us played as children. One person starts a story, the person to the left adds something, and this continues around the room until each person has contributed to the final story. Group fantasy chains are created in a similar way, and like the party game they have a central idea, or fantasy theme, that suggests what the fantasy is about.

The following is an example of a fantasy theme that occurred at a student government association executive committee meeting, where members were bemoaning the lack of a day care facility at the campus and were trying to figure out what to do about it. This group includes three men and two women, one of whom (Nan) is a nontraditional student with children.

Char: I'm not surprised that we don't have a center! We have such a retro-administration. [Char introduces the fantasy, which contains the retro idea.]

Rob: I know; they're stuck in the 1970s. Next they'll probably let their sideburns grow! [Rob picks up the fantasy and starts the chain.]

Bill: Can't you just see President Kramer coming to school in a tie-dyed suit? [Bill adds his part in a vivid, colorful way.]

Nan: Better yet—a tie-dyed leisure suit! That would be about his speed.

Joel: I can just see a big, tie-dyed sunspot on his chest and peace-sign earrings in his ears! And they ought to change the sign on the administration building to Retro-administration Building! [Joel joins in, embellishing Nan's and Bill's comments.]

Rob: I feel like we're trying to drag all of them into the 21st century. [Rob's comment hints at what this fantasy might mean to this group.]

Char: I know they're really behind the times, but we really need to get back to the day care center. How can we get our retro-administration to listen to our ideas about that? [Char ends the fantasy and gets the group back on track.]

What do you think this fantasy is about? Fantasies actually have two themes—the manifest, or obvious, theme and the latent, or underlying, theme. The manifest theme is what the fantasy chain is about at the surface level. The student government committee members were imagining the 70s attire of their retro-administration. The manifest theme is "Wouldn't that kind of clothing be funny?" The underlying meaning, which is actually not very far from the surface, was hinted at by Rob: "I feel like we're trying to drag all of them into the 21st century." In other words, "We, the students, are very forward thinking, but our retro-administration has to be forced to move forward, and we're the ones who have to drag them forward." It's an "Aren't we wonderful, but aren't they a mess" type of self-identity. The operative word here is we—these students, different though they may be, have defined themselves as "we" and the retro-administration as "they."

Fantasies—digressions unrelated to the group's task—are introduced by members all the time, but not all fantasies are picked up on by the rest of the members or are meaningful to the group. When a fantasy captures the group's imagination, it usually means that it has some deeper relevance to the members. Thus, although it may appear during a fantasy chain that a group is goofing off, the group may be accomplishing something quite important. First, fantasies can help the group define itself by creating symbols that are meaningful and that help determine its values.[18] For example, the student government committee members who sidetracked into a discussion of tie-dyed clothing were actually using fantasy to help define themselves as forward-thinking representatives of the student body.

Second, fantasies enable a group to discuss indirectly matters that might be too painful, emotionally "heavy," or difficult to bring out into the open.[19] For example, Cassie, one of our students, managed a social service agency. A particular client had become adept at getting what she wanted by manipulating the social workers against one another. The social workers were pointing fingers at each other for the client's problems. Cassie, as the person in charge, dreaded chairing the meeting where the social workers had to come to a decision about what to do with the client. Before the meeting started, one social worker started to talk about the movie *Erin Brockovich* (clearly an off-the-topic fantasy). In particular, she thought the main character exhibited "borderline personality disorder." Others picked up on this idea and added examples from the movie to support the "diagnosis." Soon, one social worker mentioned how Erin Brockovich reminded her of the client they were gathered to discuss. The rest of the social workers started laughing. They had an "aha" reaction when they realized how the client had been able to jerk them around. Cassie reported that they were able to come to a quick, cordial consensus about what to do. Their shared fantasy had allowed them to talk about this potentially difficult topic.

USING SYMLOG TO "PICTURE" DIVERSITY

We have said that diversity in a group is a desirable feature, but we also know that diversity makes group discussion more challenging. Sometimes the very diversity that enhances group problem solving may become difficult or impossible to manage. Something is needed to help members diagnose where their differences are and to know where to start to make a plan for reconciling those differences so that the group's diversity can help rather than hurt it. SYMLOG provides a methodology that can "show" a group where its most acute differences are and in what directions members should move to get the group on track.

SYMLOG is an acronym that stands for System for the Multiple-Level Observation of Groups; it is both a comprehensive theory and a methodology that produces a diagram, like a three-dimensional snapshot, of relationships among group members.[20] We present a simplified explanation here so you can understand how SYMLOG can be used to describe and help a group. (Detailed instructions for completing a SYMLOG diagram may be found in *SYMLOG Case Study Kit*, a workbook that explains SYMLOG theory and provides special forms for constructing a diagram.)

SYMLOG theory assumes that behaviors in a group can be classified along three dimensions: dominant versus submissive, friendly versus unfriendly, and task-oriented versus emotionally expressive. An observer uses a 26-item rating scale to categorize each member's behavior; the rating scale is then tallied in a special way so that each member can be placed on the SYMLOG diagram. An example of a SYMLOG diagram, or map, is shown in Figure 8.2. The more a member is task-oriented, the closer he or she is to the top of the diagram; the more emotionally expressive, the closer to the bottom. (The F stands for forward, or task-oriented behavior, and the B stands for backward, or emotionally expressive behavior.) The friendlier a member is toward the other members of the group, the closer he or she is to the right; the more unfriendly, the closer to the

FIGURE 8.2   *SYMLOG* Diagram of a Noncohesive Group

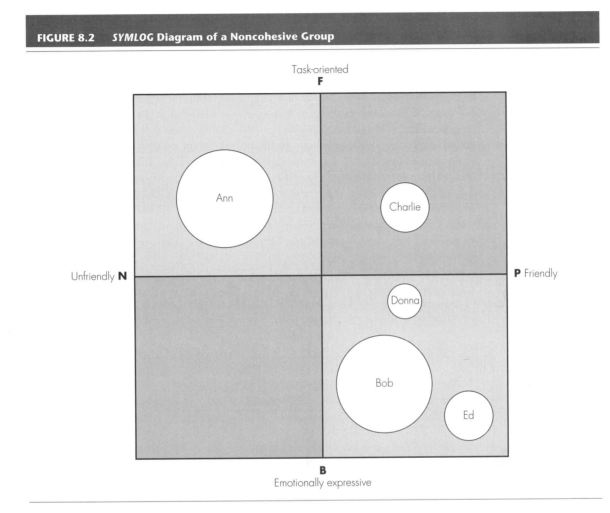

left. (The P stands for positive or friendly behavior, the N for negative or unfriendly behavior.) The third dimension, dominance or submissiveness, is shown by the size of the circle; a dominant member has a large circle, while a submissive one has a small circle.

In the SYMLOG diagram in Figure 8.2, Ann is very dominant, task-oriented, and negative toward other members of the group. In contrast, Bob is friendly and emotionally expressive, although he also is dominant. A group with two such strong, but opposite, individuals is likely to experience conflict during meetings. Charlie is moderately dominant, positive, and task-oriented. (This is how democratic leaders and members of productive, democratic groups often appear on SYMLOG diagrams.) If you were asked to describe this group, you would probably say it is unproductive, it lacks cohesiveness, and members appear to waste a lot of time during meetings because there's a struggle between the most task-oriented and most emotionally expressive members of the group.

The SYMLOG diagram in Figure 8.3 shows a unified, cohesive group. All the members are in or near the upper right-hand quadrant (decision-making quadrant), which shows that they are task-oriented enough to make progress toward the group's goal but friendly enough toward each other that interpersonel relationships are probably harmonious. This group is likely to be productive and efficient.

Thinking in SYMLOG terminology helps you manage the complexity of group interaction as you create a snapshot capturing the essence of a group. Because SYMLOG gives you that visual representation, it is easy to grasp several complex relationships at once. That makes this tool particularly effective in helping you and your fellow group members analyze and diagnose yourselves. It also gives you an idea of what you might do if problems are revealed. A SYMLOG diagram represents the perceptions of the person who constructed it; this provides potentially valuable information to help group members begin discussing their perceptions and preferences. For instance, those members whose SYMLOG diagrams show they perceive Ann as unfriendly may be asked to share specific examples that led them to that conclusion. Likewise, those whose diagrams place Bob in the emotionally expressive area can explain why they see him that way and what they feel about it.

If it is too threatening or frightening for group members to conduct such discussions on their own, a trusted facilitator can help manage the discussion. Consultants who use

---

FIGURE 8.3   *SYMLOG* **Diagram of a Cohesive Group**

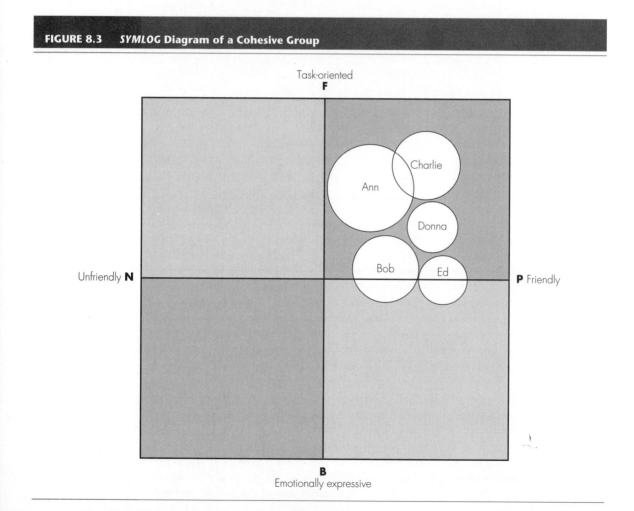

SYMLOG often ask members of the group being observed to complete the SYMLOG forms in advance. From these, they create SYMLOG diagrams to distribute to the group. Having the SYMLOG "pictures" prompts members to talk about themselves and their relationships with each other in a relatively nonthreatening way. This can set the stage for tremendous growth and development of the group.

There are a variety of ways to use SYMLOG, and several computer programs have been created to make its use easier.[21] However, it is possible to construct a SYMLOG diagram by hand. If this analysis appeals to you, we recommend that you purchase the *SYMLOG Case Study Kit*, which contains all the instructions and forms you need to produce a diagram by hand.

8.5 Using SYMLOG to Help a Group

APPLY NOW

Assume you are a consultant who has been brought in to help Judy and her group, described in the opening case. In preparation for meeting with the group, you have asked all the members to rate their own and the others' behaviors with the SYMLOG rating scales and you've constructed five SYMLOG diagrams, one for each member of the group. Judy's diagram is shown on the left below. The other four members' diagrams are almost identical; the diagram on the right is an average of those four diagrams.

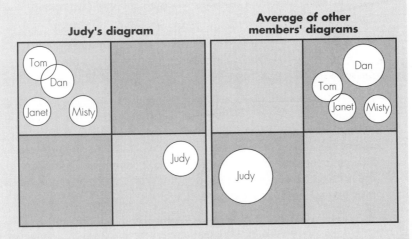

Judy's diagram

Average of other members' diagrams

1. Interpret the group from Judy's perspective.
2. Interpret the group from the other members' perspectives.
3. As a consultant, how would you use this information to help the group? What would be the focus of your work with this group?
4. In what ways do you perceive SYMLOG to be helpful to groups such as this?

We have presented two ways in which group members can bridge their differences. However, the most important thing members can do to triumph over and transcend their differences is to want to overcome them. Assuming members want to work together productively to celebrate whatever differences they may have, the suggestions in Table 8.4 provide several tips for doing just that.

TABLE 8.4   Tips for Diversity and Bridging Differences

- Decide that you want to appreciate the differences among you. Making understanding and appreciation of your diverse talents, approaches, and styles a priority for your group is the single best thing you can do.

- Schedule plenty of "get to know you" time. This can be a purely social gathering with no business conducted or you can set aside a brief "check-in" time before you get started on your business. However, don't rush this process. You will need time to learn about each other.

- Be willing to talk about and praise the differences among you. When people believe their unique approaches or contributions are valued, they relax and are willing to contribute more to the group process.

- Be open to new ways of doing things. Nothing dampens the positive potential of diversity more than rigid adherence to doing things the same way as they've always been done. Be willing to listen and to try out new ideas.

- Find ways you can create common experiences for group members. For instance, you may want to schedule a retreat, an outdoor experience, a social outing to a baseball game—anything that gets all members participating in the same activity.

- Create rituals for the group. Meaningful rituals can go a long way toward reminding members that their purpose in coming together is greater than any individual differences they may possess. For example, one church board always begins its routine meetings with a prayer and its annual retreat with a communion service. However, rituals don't have to be serious. Some work groups pass out cookies and bagels at the beginning of the meeting, with members taking turns bringing the bagels.

- Encourage members to create symbols that represent the group. Many groups have T-shirts with a meaningful saying or symbol. Sometimes, members participate in creating symbols or logos for the group.

- Use methods, such as SYMLOG, that provide a vehicle for members to talk about their differences and how they can surmount them. SYMLOG and other methods provide a relatively safe way and a nonjudgmental vocabulary for members to depict and discuss their perceptions of their own and others' behaviors. SYMLOG also gives members a handle on how to establish direction for the future to help the group capitalize on its diversity.

- Diversity is the essence of group problem solving. The differences by themselves are not a problem, but members often don't know how or don't want to manage their diversity so the group can benefit.

- Diversity comes in many forms. Members may have different motives for joining a group; they may differ in their learning and personality styles.

- Another major way group members differ is in their culture or subculture. Three main dimensions along which cultures differ were presented: collectivist/individualistic dimension, power-distance, and context dimension.

- Gender and race or ethnic differences are, at heart, cultural differences. Men and women have been taught different rules for communicating; similarly, African-, Asian-, European-, and Hispanic-American cultures have developed different communication patterns that can be misunderstood by outsiders.

- Diversity is valuable, and group members can bridge their differences through fantasy and using the SYMLOG methodology.

- Several suggestions were provided for helping group members bridge their differences.

1. Look at the descriptions of four different work styles below:

   - Task-oriented people, who believe a group's main job is to get down to business as soon as possible.

   - Relational people, who believe group work can be fun and that getting to know each other is part of the fun.

   - Systematic decision makers, who believe in gathering all the facts and weighing them before deciding.

   - Intuitive decision makers, who assess a situation instantly and leap to a conclusion quickly.

     a. Each of the four work styles should be assigned to a different corner of the room. Then, without thinking about it too long or too hard, go to the corner of the room that represents the work style most like yours.

     b. Elect a reporter to record your group's responses and report to the class at the end of the session.

     c. In five to six minutes, write down all the advantages people like you have to offer a group.

     d. In five to six minutes, write down all the disadvantages people like you bring to a group.

     e. Reconvene the class as a whole and ask each group to report, first the advantages and then the disadvantages, while a class member or your teacher writes each one on the board for all to see.

     f. After each group has presented its list, the other groups may add advantages or disadvantages to the list.

     g. Talk as a class about what you learned from this exercise and what you perceive can be the advantages such diversity of approach represented in the group.

2. Your family represents one example of a subcultural grouping. Form into groups of four to six and ask each person to assume that he or she has invited the rest of your group members home for Thanksgiving dinner with the

family. Each person should describe what the "rules" are for Thanksgiving dinner. For example, where does everyone sit? When do you know you may start to eat? Does the food get passed around or does someone put food on each person's plate and pass the plate down? What are acceptable topics of conversation? Is conversation lively or muted? How did the "rules" become established in the family, and so forth?

When everyone has finished, discuss the differences you discovered among each other's "cultures." What dimensions of culture seem to be most important in each family grouping? Were there any surprises? What does each family do when it encounters a violation of the rules? Are the rules ever discussed openly among family members? Are there rules that prohibit what you can talk about?

3. Class members should divide themselves into groups of four to six along gender, race/

ethnicity, or age lines. For example, the class might form several single-sex groups. Each group should first appoint a recorder/spokesperson to take notes. Then each group should discuss the following two questions:

a. How do you see yourselves as group members? What characteristics do you believe you have?

b. How do you see the other group as group members? What characteristics do you believe they have?

Finally, when each group is finished, all should share their results with the class and the class should take this opportunity to talk about the stereotypes they hold and how accurate those stereotypes are (or are not).

 Go to **www.mhhe.com/adamsgalanes** and **www.mhhe.com/groups** for Self-Quizzes and weblinks.

KEY TERMS and CONCEPTS

abstract conceptualization learning style

active experimentation learning style

boomers

builders

collectivist culture

concrete experience learning style

culture

diversity

extraversion/introversion dimension

fantasy

gender

gen-Xers

high-context culture

individualistic culture

low-context culture

Myers-Briggs Type Indicator®

net generation

perceiving/judging dimension

power-distance

reflective observation learning style

sensing/intuiting dimension

sex

symbolic convergence

SYMLOG

thinking/feeling dimension

 www.mhhe.com/adamsgalanes
Use the flashcards and crossword puzzles on the Online Learning Center to further your knowledge of these key terms.

Managing Conflicts Productively

CHAPTER OBJECTIVES

After reading this chapter you should be able to:

1. Define conflict.

2. Discuss the three prevailing myths about conflict in small groups.

3. Define groupthink and explain its relevance to small group problem solving.

4. Explain the three symptoms of groupthink.

5. Discuss ways to prevent groupthink in small group interaction.

6. Compare and contrast the five major conflict styles.

7. Explain how group members can disagree productively.

8. Discuss how members can maximize their chances to influence the group.

9. List and explain the steps of the nominal group technique.

10. Describe the four steps in principled negotiation and explain how to use them to help resolve a conflict.

The Cask and Cleaver Work Crew

The Cask and Cleaver is a local restaurant in California's central valley. Its management requires all its servers (usually students) to meet semiannually and select their shifts. At these meetings, about eight servers take turns, in round-robin fashion, picking a shift. The server with the most seniority picks first, and so on, until all shifts are covered. The servers want to choose shifts that make the most money in the least time so that they can survive financially and still have enough time to study and play. The stakes are higher for those with greater financial needs because they must live with the schedule for six months.

One recent meeting has become legendary as the most contentious meeting in the restaurant's 18-year history. Mark, the senior server, took charge and chose first. At his fourth turn, he realized an earlier turn had been skipped and servers with less seniority had taken one more turn than he had. Mark suggested that they start over again. Some supported his idea, but Tom and Paul did not. They were pleased with their shifts after having lived with very poor schedules during the previous six months. After discussing it, the group decided to start over. During the second round it became apparent that the members were choosing differently; furthermore, the new schedule heavily favored Mark and Beth (Mark's wife), whereas Tom and Paul were not faring well at all. Opposition to starting over was voiced again with greater emphasis. Mark and Beth became defensive, arguing that it was not their fault Tom and Paul had two night classes. Tom and Paul perceived this reaction as callous and reminded Mark and Beth that they had no other options in class sections to choose from. Mark replied, "That's not my problem." Another server, Nathan, sided with Paul and Tom, forming a clique that characterized Mark and Beth as self-centered and unsympathetic to the financial needs of others. Mark, Beth, and another server, Maria, all believed that the others' school schedules were not their concern and shift scheduling was a hit and miss process anyway: Sometimes you do well and sometimes you don't. To them, Tom and Paul were "crybabies" who wanted special treatment because they were university students. Tracey and Jeremy, two other servers, remained neutral, moving between the two cliques, listening to both sides, and conferring between themselves without ever sharing their views of the conflict.

To make the best decision about something, group members must use their collective thinking skills. When group members think critically, disagreement almost always occurs. Conflict, expressed and managed appropriately, can help members sharpen their thinking and decide wisely. In contrast, unexpressed disagreement contributes to *groupthink,* the term popularized by Irving Janis in his classic 1972 analysis of the faulty decision-making process used by President Kennedy's advisers resulting in the Bay of Pigs disaster. We discuss groupthink in this chapter as well as the causes of conflict, how it affects a group, and how it can be managed so that it helps, rather than hurts, a group.

What Is Conflict?

Conflict can range from a simple disagreement to a war. You can observe conflict in a small group when two or more people express incompatible ideas. Marsha suggests that her group present a skit for its presentation, but Silvio believes skits are childish. That conflict must be effectively managed for the group to successfully complete its task of making a class presentation. Most conflicts you experience in a group will be disagreements like this one, and they can become heated, as it was in the Cask and Cleaver meeting. But conflict does not have to be expressed to be experienced.[1] Group members can be acutely uncomfortable without saying a word. Nevertheless, even unexpressed conflict can affect a group's interaction and ultimate decision.

Myths about Conflict

We would like to dispel a number of commonly believed myths about conflict. These are summarized in Table 9.1.

1. **Because conflict is harmful to a group, it should be avoided.**

   We all have seen examples of how conflict can hurt a group. Minor misunderstandings can lead to hurt feelings, and a group may dissolve over a conflict. Clearly, conflict can be harmful to a group. However, many students see only the harm and don't realize that conflict can be beneficial to the group *if it is expressed and managed properly.*

   Conflict can help members understand the issues surrounding a decision or problem more completely. One of us served on an advisory board for a nonprofit organization. The administrative officer of the organization wanted to fire an employee immediately, without issuing a warning or giving the employee a chance to correct the offending behavior. One member, experienced with personnel laws, disagreed strongly with what appeared to her to be a lack of due process in the proposed dismissal. When the other members understood the legal problems with discharging employees before giving them a chance to improve their performance, they agreed to give the employee a clear set of guidelines and expectations to be followed. One group member's willingness to disagree enabled the others to understand the issue more completely. This type of disagreement illustrates *idea deviance,* mentioned in Chapter 7.

TABLE 9.1	**Myths about Conflict**	
Myth 1 **Conflict is harmful** **and should be avoided** • Conflict can help members understand an issue more clearly. • Conflict can improve group decisions. • Conflict can increase member involvement. • Conflict can increase cohesiveness.	**Myth 2** **Conflict represents a** **misunderstanding or** **breakdown in communication** • Some conflicts occur over differences in values, goals, methods of achieving goals, limited resources.	**Myth 3** **Conflicts can be resolved** **if parties are willing to** **discuss the issues** • Conflicts over basic values and goals may not be resolvable. • Conflicts over limited resources and methods of achieving goals may be resolvable through communication if the basic values and goals of the parties are compatible.

Conflict also can improve a group's decision. A logical outcome of members' understanding an issue more clearly is improved decision making. In the previous example, the dismissed employee could have sued the organization and the board for arbitrarily firing him. Not only was the board's decision fairer than immediate dismissal would have been, but it also protected the organization against charges of capriciousness. Clarifying the employee's job duties and the board's expectations gave him the best possible chance to perform effectively. This produced a much better outcome than the original proposal to dismiss him.

Also, conflict tends to increase member involvement and participation. Group discussions can become boring, but when a controversy occurs, members perk up and voice their opinions. In the previous advisory board example, members who had begun to miss meetings started to come regularly again. Usually, members become more interested when they believe their opinions can make a difference in the group's outcomes.

Finally, conflict can increase cohesiveness. Have you ever had an argument with your dating partner, spouse, or friend, then observed how close you both felt after you had reconciled your differences? If so, you know how conflict can increase your positive feelings toward one another. During the advisory board's discussion about firing the employee, members expressed strong feelings on several sides of the issue. After all members aired their views, the group came to a consensus decision. As consensus emerged, members became closer than ever. Several members expressed their appreciation to the member who initially spoke up against the firing. They believed that her comments forced the group to anticipate possible problems and to create a better solution. Members realized that they could disagree, express themselves in forceful terms, and emerge more united than before the conflict; cohesiveness increased. After the Cask and Cleaver crew managed to constructively deal with their issues, lighthearted banter about this meeting being the "ugliest scheduling meeting of all time" followed, as well as a promise never to let such contention happen again.

So, although conflict can be harmful to a group, it doesn't have to be. Whether a conflict helps or harms a group depends on a number of other factors, including whether the conflict is resolvable in the first place.

2. **Conflicts stem from misunderstandings and breakdowns in communication.**

Certainly some conflicts occur due to misunderstandings and communication failures, but others do not. Often conflicts occur when individuals understand each other, but disagree on basic values or the distribution of rewards. For example, a classroom group trying to agree on whether to recommend the repeal of the *Roe v. Wade* court decision making abortions legal in the United States was unable to arrive at an answer acceptable to everyone. Several members believed that life begins at conception and that abortion is murder. Other members believed that a woman's life should take precedence over the fetus, at least until the fetus reaches a certain stage of development. Each subgroup understood accurately the position of the other subgroup. Misunderstanding and communication breakdown did not occur. However, the subgroups' differing values and assumptions made agreement difficult.

Other conflicts occur over what goals the group will set, how to achieve them, or how the group will distribute limited resources such as bonus money or access to computer time. Although misunderstandings may contribute to these conflicts, the underlying reason for them is much more basic than a communication breakdown. Such conflicts often reflect a struggle over power or wealth. The underlying resources at issue for our Cask and Cleaver crew were money and time.

3. **All conflicts can be resolved if parties are willing to discuss the issues.**

MHHE.com/ groups
For more information on conflict resolution, go to the online learning center.

As you can see from the previous example, not all conflicts are resolvable. Whether or not a conflict can be resolved depends in part on the underlying reason for the conflict. The conflict over basic values on the abortion question is not resolvable at the present time because it is based on differences in assumptions and values. The two assumptions represented—a fetus is a person from conception and has rights equal to those of the mother versus a fetus becomes a person sometime after conception, until which time the woman's rights take precedence—are not reconcilable. Both cannot be true simultaneously. A group experiencing such a conflict will not be able to come to consensus on a policy regarding abortion.

Conflicts over scarce resources are also difficult, if not impossible, to resolve. One of us serves on a library committee with representatives from many areas of the school. Meetings to distribute limited money fairly are usually full of acrimony. Full agreement is rarely possible. Even members who acknowledge that one area deserves more money for books may vote against that proposal if it means their areas will receive less money. The problem, recognized by everyone, is that funds to support the legitimate requests of all areas are very limited.

Conflicts over goals can sometimes be difficult to resolve as well. Assume that you want an A on your group project and someone else is satisfied with a C. If you can't convince the other person of the value of striving for excellence and the other person can't persuade you to lighten up, you can't resolve this conflict. If your goal of receiving an A is very important to you, you may end up having to do a lot of extra work on the project—yours and the other person's.

Conflicts over how to reach goals are sometimes easier to resolve than other types, especially if the basic values of the individuals are similar. In the project grade example, if you and the other member both want to get As, but you prefer to show a movie and the other member prefers a skit, you may be able to compromise or find a third alternative that satisfies you both. Because your basic values and goals are the same, you are more likely to see each other as allies, not enemies, which makes it easier to resolve the conflict.

Conflict itself is not the issue. Any social system, due to the interdependence of the system's components, will experience some kind of conflict. How parties manage the conflict is really the issue. Mishandling of disagreement can produce problematic group outcomes such as faulty decision making. Groupthink refers to a certain kind of mishandling of group disagreement, and we now turn our attention to how it emerges in a group and how a group can avoid its negative consequences.

The Bay of Pigs blunder was made by a group of intelligent, well-informed policy experts who should have seen the warning signs. Irving Janis's exhaustive study of this event concluded that these policy experts made several major miscalculations. For example, the American Joint Chiefs of Staff believed that, once the invasion was launched, Cuban citizens would rise up against Castro in support of the invasion. This support was necessary to the invasion's success. However, the Cuban people loved Castro and

Bay of Pigs Invasion

CASE 9.2

In April 1961, a group of Cuban exiles, supported by the U.S. Navy, Air Force, and CIA, invaded Cuba at the Bay of Pigs.[2] The invasion was a disaster for the Cuban exiles and the United States. Two of the four invading ships were sunk by Cuban Premier Fidel Castro's air force; the other two retreated. Twenty thousand well-equipped Cuban troops surrounded the invaders; 1,200 of the original 1,400 exiles were captured and imprisoned. Most of the rest were killed. The decision to invade Cuba is widely regarded as the worst decision of President John F. Kennedy's administration. The main problem was not just that the invasion failed. After all, any decision, no matter how well conceived, can turn out to be a mistake because of information not known to the decision makers. The problem with the Bay of Pigs decision was that President Kennedy and his advisers should have predicted, from information available at the time the decision was being made, that the invasion would fail.

supported him, not the invading troops, which the CIA predicted. This miscalculation was not a failure of American intelligence gathering but a failure of the decision makers to use *all* available information.

Unfortunately, the intelligence branch of the CIA had not been asked to supply evidence about the amount of support the invaders could expect. This important information went unreported. Janis concluded that, if Kennedy's policy advisers had shown any skepticism about the success of the invasion, the intelligence experts and others would have been happy to share their expertise.

Similar to the decision to launch the *Challenger,* described in Chapter 5, the decision to invade Cuba represents a failure by a decision-making group to think critically. As with the *Challenger* launch, the policy advisers were generally in favor of the invasion. They failed to look for information that might contradict their original biases. Some advisers had personal reservations they did not express. Historian Arthur Schlesinger, one of Kennedy's advisers, has said that, although he had doubts, he did not want to be thought of as a nuisance in committee meetings, so he chose to remain silent. So did others.

Fearing that one could be perceived as a nuisance in meetings is not peculiar to presidential cabinet meetings. Nineteen percent of members of upper management teams in a study of 26 American corporations said that they best went about company business by not making waves, and 9 percent reported a preference for fostering their relationships at the expense of getting the job done.[3] In other words, faulty decision making, like the Bay of Pigs decision, represents failure of a group's throughput processes in handling disagreement and managing conflict effectively. Let's take a closer look at how this kind of group dynamics can happen.

Groupthink

Conflict can help a group perform its best, but it is not easy for members to disagree with fellow group members, especially in highly cohesive groups where a disagreement can be seen as disloyalty or "making waves." **Groupthink** refers to the tendency of highly cohesive groups not to examine critically all aspects of a decision or problem the group is considering.[4] Groupthink represents a failure in the group's critical thinking process—the failure to express doubts, disagreements, and conflict within the group. As a result, the group's decision is flawed because it is made with partial information that has not been examined carefully; surprisingly, some group members believe they *have* made the best decision. Those members who may privately have their doubts about the group's decision keep their reservations to themselves, as with the Bay of Pigs advisory group. Thus, the group is deprived of the full benefit of members' opinions and reasoning.

SYMPTOMS OF GROUPTHINK

Groupthink is most likely to occur in highly cohesive groups under pressure to achieve consensus. In particular, cohesiveness based on interpersonal attraction is related to groupthink, but task-related cohesiveness is not.[5] Groups that exhibit high degrees of cohesiveness based on their interpersonal attraction to each other tend to be more psychologically connected to each other and so they resist challenging each other.[6] This is a problem because groups *in general* tend to favor discussing what they already know as opposed to discussing new information.[7] Under conditions of groupthink, this tendency

GLOSSARY

Groupthink

A negative relational outcome of group decision making characterized by a group's failure to think critically about its decisions

Groupthink. (© 1987 King Features Syndicate, Inc. World rights reserved. Reprinted with permission of King Features Syndicate.)

is even harder to monitor. In addition, groupthink is more likely to occur in groups with a long history, groups strongly embedded in their larger organizations, and groups that insulate themselves from their outside envirnoments.[8] Spotting groupthink thus becomes crucial if your decision-making groups are to be effective as they critically analyze problems and draw conclusions. Here are three important symptoms to help you spot groupthink, summarized in Table 9.2:

1. **The group overestimates its power and morality.**

   Group members believe their cause is so right that nothing can go wrong with their plans. President Kennedy's advisers believed that the Cuban people wanted liberation from Castro. Several of the invasion plans rested on this assumption, but the advisers neglected to determine whether or not it was true. In fact, this belief was wrong.

   Government policy groups are not the only groups that overestimate their power and the rightness of their causes. Many business, education, nonprofit, and student groups have fallen into this trap as well. Sometimes classroom groups become so excited about one creative aspect of their performance that they ignore the rest of the presentation. For example, the members put all their efforts into preparing a lively skit but leave out key information relevant to their topic. However, they convince themselves that the presentation will be well received by the teacher: "She'll love it. No one else has tried anything like it. I just *know* we'll get an A."

2. **The group becomes closed-minded.**

   Closed-minded people are biased when they evaluate information. Instead of looking open-mindedly at all relevant information, members consider only information that supports their beliefs. Group members may also have a preferred course of action and ignore any information that contradicts their preference. In the Bay of Pigs decision, group members (including President Kennedy) were

TABLE 9.2	**Symptoms of Groupthink**	
The group overestimates its power and morality	**The group becomes closed-minded**	**Group members experience pressure to conform**
• Group believes its cause is right. • Members convince themselves they cannot fail.	• Group is selective in gathering information; chooses only information that supports its predisposition. • Group is biased in evaluating information. • Group excludes or ignores members and outsiders who seem to hold opposing views.	• Members censor their own remarks. • Members who voice contradictory opinions receive pressure from other members to conform. • Members have the illusion that the group opinion is unanimous.

predisposed in favor of carrying out the invasion for a variety of political reasons. Information that should have served as a warning was ignored if it contradicted the invasion plans. For example, Kennedy's advisers ignored intelligence reports about the strength of the Cuban air force and ground troops and the efficiency of the Cuban government.

In a more ordinary example, one of us served on a faculty committee that recommended several major changes in the department's curriculum. The committee downplayed information about how upset some department members would be with the proposed changes: "Oh, it won't be a major problem." In fact, the proposed changes caused an uproar that could have been avoided if committee members had sought out disagreements to begin with instead of listening only to their own opinions, all of which supported the changes.

3. **Group members experience pressure to conform.**

Group members experience both internal and external pressures to go along with the group, which show up in several ways. First, members censor their own remarks without apparent pressure from other members. When all the other members of a group favor a certain action, most people are hesitant to express their doubts. This is natural—you want the people in your group to like and respect you, and you don't want to appear like someone "popping others' balloons." Thus, self-censorship often prevents conflicting opinions from reaching the group, to the detriment of the group's problem-solving process.

Second, a member who does voice a contradictory opinion can be seen as a deviant or "making waves" and receive overt pressure from the group. Groups are uncomfortable with deviants (even idea deviants) and pressure them to go along with the group. During the Bay of Pigs decision, Robert Kennedy, President Kennedy's brother and most trusted adviser, stopped Arthur Schlesinger from voicing his doubts about the invasion by telling Schlesinger that the president needed his support and loyalty, not his doubts and fears. This friendly warning, delivered at a party, effectively silenced Schlesinger. Typically, groups joke and tease other members to bring them into line with the rest of the group: "Why are you being such a worry wart, Pham? The rest of us think it's a great idea!" Pham usually gets the message and joins the bandwagon of support without expressing his reservations. Apparent "consensus" to avoid conflict comes at the cost of many poor decisions.

Finally, because self-censorship and group pressure suppress disagreement and doubt, the group experiences the illusion that members unanimously support the decision or proposal. Assuming that the whole group is in accord, the group carries out the decision without testing to see whether the consensus is genuine. What appears to be an agreement may have little support from some members.

PREVENTING GROUPTHINK

You can take a number of steps to prevent groupthink from occurring. Following are suggestions for both group leaders and members, also summarized in Table 9.3.

1. **Encourage members to "kick the problem around" before they start focusing on a solution.**

   One group behavior that fosters groupthink is arriving at premature consensus.[9] The group has shortchanged the recommended first step of most structured problem-solving procedures, which is exploring the problem before trying to solve it. In addition, encouraging conflict at this stage can help group members understand the problem better. Recall that one of the benefits of conflict is the increased knowledge and understanding group members receive. Active disagreement at an early stage of problem exploration promotes this benefit.

2. **Establish a norm of critical evaluation.**

   The most important thing a group leader and other members can do to prevent groupthink is to establish a group norm to evaluate carefully and critically all information and reasoning. Such a norm can offset the proven human tendency to ignore or reject information that contradicts one's existing beliefs and values.

   Especially helpful is a norm promoting members' expressions of all disagreements. If a group emphasizes getting along instead of critical thinking, members will hesitate to disagree. A norm supporting open expression of doubts and disagreements makes it OK for members to be in conflict with each other.

   Another way of encouraging honest disagreements is to assign the role of devil's advocate to one or more members of the group. A **devil's advocate** is a person who has been assigned the task of arguing against a popular proposal. Thus, this person serves as an "official" idea deviant because the devil's advocate helps spot potential flaws in a plan or holes in arguments. If Josie agrees to be the devil's advocate for a particular meeting, it is unlikely the other members will take her criticisms personally.

   Groups have also used group support systems and computer-mediated communication (CMC) to encourage honest opinions. As we have mentioned in previous chapters, computer use in group problem solving is valued for its anonymity. Users believe that this produces less pressure to conform and thus encourages more honesty. However, a member operating from behind a computer is still

GLOSSARY

Devil's advocate

A group member who formally is expected to challenge ideas to foster critical thinking

TABLE 9.3	**Preventing Groupthink**

ENCOURAGE MEMBERS TO "KICK THE PROBLEM AROUND"

- Be alert to prevent premature consensus.

- Explore the problem thoroughly before attempting to develop a solution.

- Encourage freewheeling argument before settling on a solution.

ESTABLISH A NORM OF CRITICAL EVALUATION

- Encourage members to express disagreement.

- Encourage critical thinking rather than the appearance of harmony.

- Assign a devil's advocate to argue against popular proposals.

- The leader must accept criticisms of his or her ideas open-mindedly.

LEADER SHOULD NOT STATE PREFERENCES AT THE BEGINNING OF A GROUP'S SESSION

- Let other members express opinions first.

- Offer an opinion only as another alternative (not the alternative) to be considered.

- Encourage the group to meet without the designated leader present.

PREVENT INSULATION OF THE GROUP

- Invite outside experts to present information.

- Discuss tentative solutions with trusted outsiders to get an unbiased reaction.

- Be alert to information that contradicts the prevailing opinion of the group.

aware of expectations from others. Thus, CMC can both enhance and limit the impact of individual members' influence and power.[10] Sometimes the effect of perceived status differences is actually stronger in CMC.

The norm of critical evaluation must be supported by the leader's behavior. One of us worked with a boss who asked staff members to identify any problems we saw with a plan he had devised to improve the working environment. Taking the boss at his word, a couple of staff members began to question various elements of the plan. As they spoke, the boss became defensive, minimized their concerns, defended his proposal, and appeared to view the questioning members as disloyal. Soon the rest of the members became silent without voicing their objections to the plan. The meeting concluded with the boss thinking the staff supported the plan, although it did not. In the future, whenever the boss asked for honest reactions to proposals he favored, no one was willing to go on the "hot seat" by expressing a criticism.

9.1   Terrorism, TV, and Groupthink

MEDIA AND TECHNOLOGY

On September 11, 2001, people from around the world watched images of violence on their televisions. In the wake of terrorist attacks on the World Trade Center and the Pentagon, TV news organizations such as CNN and MSNBC transitioned to 24-hour, nonstop coverage of the attacks and eventual war against terrorism.

Consider your own experiences watching TV reports of the terrorist actions, anthrax scares, and subsequent war on terrorism. You may also want to refresh your memory by exploring archived reports on CNN.com or MSNBC.com. To what extent do you think mediated reports of these events made the public susceptible to groupthink? In emergency situations like these, what are some potential negative consequences of mass groupthink?

In small groups, members can reduce the effects of groupthink by "kicking the problem around," establishing norms of critical evaluation, preventing insulation of the group. In larger groups of people, like the mass audiences watching TV reports of terrorism, how could these same principles be applied? Are there ways that our culture, like small groups, can reduce the effects of groupthink on the way we assign meaning to mediated messages?

Go to **www. mhhe.com/ adamsgalanes** for additional weblink activities.

3. **Leaders should not state their preferences at the beginning of a group's decision-making or problem-solving session.**

One important source of groupthink is a strong or charismatic leader's preference. In the Bay of Pigs decision, President Kennedy clearly favored the invasion and told his advisers so. The advisers, who all admired him and wanted his respect, hesitated to speak up against the invasion because they didn't want to appear disloyal. Thus, the presence of a strong, opinionated leader inhibited dissent and contributed to groupthink. Even if you don't have "Kennedy" charisma, as a group's leader you do have legitimate power that may make it difficult for other members to disagree with your stated preferences.

In addition to not stating your preferences early in a group's discussion, ask the group to meet without you, especially if you are the supervisor rather than an elected chair. If you suspect that your presence or personality inhibits the group members from saying what they really feel and think, schedule one or two meetings that you do not attend. This will make it easier for other members to express their opinions freely.

4. **Prevent insulation of the group.**

Groupthink often occurs when group members become so cohesive and so caught up in their own ideas that they become insulated from external opinion and expertise. In the Bay of Pigs decision, some Cuba experts with information relevant to the invasion plans were not consulted by the National Security Council. Even ordinary groups can become insulated. The faculty committee mentioned earlier worked for an entire year developing a sweeping proposal to alter the school's curriculum. Members' enthusiasm and shared vision carried them along. However, the group had insulated itself from relevant external opinion. As a result, members misjudged how the rest of the faculty would react to their proposals. In contrast, a faculty constitution committee to which one of us belonged did exactly the opposite. This committee sought out external opinions and conflicting views. Members then incorporated suggestions into the plan, which the faculty overwhelmingly adopted.

Leaders and members of the group can offset this tendency. They can encourage members to present tentative decisions to trusted associates outside the group, then report back to the group with the feedback. They can hold public hearings, at which any interested person can speak on the issues facing the group, as zoning commissions do regularly. They can also arrange for outside experts to talk to the group. Most important, they can be alert themselves for any relevant information from outside the group instead of protecting the group from outside influence.

9.1   Learning from Our Mistakes

APPLY NOW

Throughout this chapter you have learned quite a bit about the faulty decision making of John F. Kennedy's advisers. Their efforts led to the failed Bay of Pigs invasion and the death of Americans as well as Cubans. Groups that are prone to groupthink rush to agree, do not practice critical thinking, and fear confrontation. You have also read about ways that groupthink can be prevented.

As a class, divide into groups of five or six members and review the Bay of Pigs material. After you have revisited the story, pretend you are the group of Kennedy advisers. Given what you have learned from the Bay of Pigs decision and what you know about preventing groupthink, devise a set of guidelines for your next strategy session should you be asked to advise the president. Don't just repeat the four prevention steps but be very specific about how you, as a member of this group, would act differently next time.

Each group should report its guidelines to the class and, as a class, compile them into one master set. Then research the Cuban missile crisis. Look at Janis's work and find out for yourselves if Kennedy and his advisers, did, in fact, learn from the Bay of Pigs fiasco. Did Kennedy and his advisers follow any of the guidelines your class came up with?

Managing Conflict in the Group

Conflict is inevitable when people must reach decisions together. Trying to squash conflict does not eliminate it—it just sends it underground. If managed inappropriately, conflict can hurt a group. In this section we discuss how to manage conflict productively.

CONFLICT MANAGEMENT STYLES

There are many different ways of describing how people manage conflict. The five styles we discuss here were described by Kenneth Thomas.[11] Whatever style an individual chooses is based on the answers to two questions: (1) How important is it to satisfy your own needs? and (2) How important is it to satisfy the other person's needs? Figure 9.1 shows how these two dimensions intersect to produce the five common conflict management styles of avoidance, accommodation, competition, collaboration, and compromise. Table 9.4 gives examples of statements illustrating each style. *No one conflict style is best to use in all circumstances.* The most appropriate conflict style depends on the situation. Factors to consider include how important the issue is, how serious the consequences are if the group makes a mistake, whether the group is under any time pressure, and how important it is that the positive relationship between the conflicting parties be maintained. In most groups, preserving and enhancing relationships among the members are important. So conflict management styles incorporating the legitimate needs of all parties are preferable to those producing winners and losers.

The conflict style that group members use depends largely on how they perceive the situation.[12] The situation is more important, in fact, than what members believe "started" the conflict. Factors such as how often the members have been in conflict in the past and how many negative feelings they harbor against each other, how mutual

---

FIGURE 9.1 Conflict Management Styles

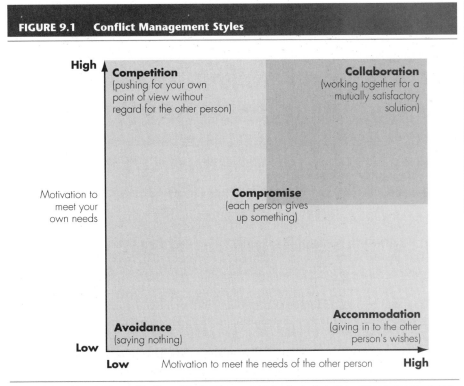

SOURCE: Adapted from K. Thomas, "Conflict and Conflict Management," *Handbook of Industrial and Organizational Psychology,* ed. by Marvin D. Dunnette, 1976. Used by permission of Marvin D. Dunnette.

| TABLE 9.4 | **Statements that Illustrate the Five Conflict Management Styles** |

Mary, the college financial director, wants the snack shop to close at 5 P.M. Roger, the evening student counselor, wants it to stay open until 8 P.M. Following are examples of how Roger might respond to Mary, using each of the conflict management styles discussed in the chapter:

Mary: We'll have to close the snack shop at 5. There isn't any money to keep it open later.

Avoidance	Accommodation	Competition	Compromise	Collaboration
Roger: [Says nothing; accepts Mary's statement]	**Roger:** I'd really like to keep it open, but, if there's no money, I guess there's nothing else we can do.	**Roger:** I won't accept that! We can't let the evening students down that way. Cut something else to get the money!	**Roger:** I would accept keeping it open just until 6:30 if you could cut some money from another program.	**Roger:** I understand that it's necessary to contain costs. Its also important to serve evening students. Is there some way we can provide them food service without increasing costs?

This was an actual problem faced by a student services committee. The solution? Provide vending machine service. This maintained constant labor costs but gave students food service after 5 P.M.

their goals are, and how ambiguous or structured the solution all affect how a member will approach handling the conflict. Ideally, members recognize that they have a mutual stake in the solution and are motivated to cooperate in resolving the conflict.

Avoidance.   **Avoidance** occurs when any group member chooses not to disagree or to bring up a conflicting point, thus downplaying her or his own needs and the needs of others. When group members fight about other people in the group, group members tend to avoid further conflict with each other. However, if the conflict is about the task, group members tend to be more willing to work together.[13] Avoidance is the basis of groupthink.

We have talked about the dangers of avoiding conflict, but the avoidance style is sometimes appropriate. If the issue is not very important and you are certain that the group's decision will not be hurt by your failure to speak up, avoiding a possible conflict is appropriate. One of us served on a committee that was planning a banquet. The rest of the members favored a different restaurant from the one your author preferred. Both restaurants were comparable in price, service, and atmosphere. Making an issue over this would have been silly because there was no risk of making a serious mistake. This was not an important enough issue to argue about.

GLOSSARY

Avoidance

Conflict style describing a person's unwillingness to confront or engage in conflict

Accommodation.   **Accommodation** (also called appeasement or giving in) occurs when one person or faction gives in to the other without arguing strongly for a different point of view. This style is similar to avoidance in that a person downplays her or his own needs, but it differs in that the person works harder to meet the needs of others. You should be honest with yourself if you choose to accommodate. Don't give in if the issue really is important to you. We realize this could be hard for those group members who fear talking in front of others.[14] However, if you give in but privately resent it, in the future you are likely to find yourself arguing with the other person for no apparent reason. On the other hand, if the issue is not crucial to you but you know it is important to the other person, then accommodation is appropriate. For example, a faculty/student committee was charged with redecorating a student lounge. The chemistry professor did not like the color scheme recommended by the art professor and said so. But, since the students liked it, the chemistry professor willingly accommodated their preferences. This is an appropriate use of accommodation to resolve conflict.

Competition.   **Competition,** sometimes called the *win–lose* style, occurs when you fight hard to win and you don't care whether the other person is satisfied with the solution or not. The 1994–95 baseball strike is an example of this. Most of the time, highly competitive ways of handling conflict are harmful to a group. If one person tries to impose his or her will on a group, the other members will probably fight back. Competitive tactics often escalate a conflict, especially when people stop listening to understand each other. Each side tries harder and harder to force the other side to go along. At an advisory board meeting, one member, Sherman, argued strongly for one solution to a particular problem. Two members disagreed with Sherman, who then began to use a variety of tactics to win the argument, starting with persuasion but moving quickly to attempted coercion and intimidation. Sherman's behavior indicated he was more concerned about winning the argument than preserving the group. The visible conflict ended when the rest of the group reacted negatively to the intimidation tactics by voting against Sherman's suggestion.

When a group is doing something you believe is harmful, wrong, or against your values and beliefs, then competition is appropriate. Don't accommodate or avoid conflict if you think your basic values are being compromised or if you think the group is about to make a major mistake (as in the *Challenger* or Bay of Pigs cases). Remember, though, that if a conflict is managed with one person winning and others losing, hurt feelings will almost certainly damage teamwork in the future. Search for an alternative everyone can accept, if that is possible.

Collaboration.   **Collaboration,** the *win–win* style of conflict management, occurs when the people in the conflict want to meet opposing parties' needs along with their own. Like competition, collaboration assumes individuals may argue strongly for their points of view. Unlike competitors, collaborators take care not to attack each other as people or to say or do anything that will harm the relationship. They behave ethically by treating each other as equals. They invest a great deal of energy in searching for a solution that will satisfy everyone. Group members whose communication is collaborative are more satisfied with their group outcomes than members who avoid conflict.[15]

The library committee mentioned in Chapter 4 experienced conflict over how to narrow the eight semifinalist candidates down to four finalists to be invited for campus interviews. Some members wanted to conduct telephone interviews. Others said it would

"And this is the loyal opposition."

The right way to view someone who disagrees with you. (© The New Yorker Collection; 1989 Robert Mankoff from cartoonbank.com. All Rights Reserved.)

be impossible for all members of this large committee to attend all phone interviews; they wanted the candidates to submit additional written materials. Still other members said that would take too long and wanted to decide based on the information supplied by the references. One member suggested that the committee conduct phone interviews that would be taped so that all members could hear the interviews, even if they couldn't actually be present.

You may think that collaborative solutions are ideal for groups because they attempt to preserve positive relationships among conflicting parties while members hammer out mutually acceptable solutions. However, collaborative solutions often require much time and energy, which groups don't always have. Not all decisions are important enough for the group to commit the time or energy to create a collaborative solution. If basic values differ or trust is lacking, collaboration may be impossible.

Compromise. **Compromise** represents a middle-ground conflict management style that can be called a *partial-win/partial-lose* solution for each party. Unlike collaboration, parties using compromise give up something to get something in return. This type of horse-trading is typical of labor–management and government bargaining: "I'll settle for a $1-per-hour raise if you give up the demand for mandatory overtime," or "I'll vote for your bill if you support my amendment." If you know you are going to have to compromise, you will be tempted to inflate your original demands. For instance, if you know you will have to settle for less money than you want, you'll ask at first for a higher figure than you really need.

Although there may be problems with compromising, it is appropriate for many conflicts. When collaboration is impossible due to time pressures or differences in values, compromise may represent the best option available. With compromise, each party does not completely receive what it wanted to begin with. However, if what each party had to give up seems balanced and the solution appears *fair* to all sides, then compromise can work quite well. *We cannot emphasize too strongly the importance of fairness.* A compromise can work only if all parties feel the solution is fair, and that no one has *won.* But parties cannot assume they know what "fair" means. Instead, both parties should explain honestly what they believe is fair, and these individual conceptions of fairness should be included as absolute criteria by which to evaluate the final decision.

EXPRESSING DISAGREEMENT

In Chapter 3 we emphasized that all messages have both content and relationship aspects. This distinction is important in the expression of conflict. *How* you express your disagreement with another group member has a major bearing on how the conflict will be resolved. An accurate and valid concern (content) can be expressed so insensitively (how) that even a rational group member becomes defensive rather than receptive to what you have to say. The following suggestions should help you express disagreements without damaging the relationships between you and other members (see Table 9.5).

1. **Express your disagreement.**

   A disagreement has no chance of helping a group if it is not expressed. An unexpressed disagreement does not disappear—it goes underground, to resurface in inappropriate ways. Avoiding a conflict is only a temporary "solution." Issues can pile up so that eventually a large blowup occurs when each issue could have been handled individually. Remember that disagreements can help a group arrive at the best possible decision or solution, and that failure to express disagreements can lead to groupthink.

TABLE 9.5	**How to Disagree Productively**

EXPRESS YOUR DISAGREEMENT
- Failure to express doubts and disagreements deprives the group of potentially valuable information and reasoning.

EXPRESS DISAGREEMENT IN A TIMELY WAY
- Don't wait until the deadline is near to speak.

EXPRESS DISAGREEMENTS WITH SENSITIVITY TOWARD OTHERS
- Disagree with the idea, but do not criticize the person.

- Use neutral, not emotionally charged, language.

REACT TO DISAGREEMENT WITH A SPIRIT OF INQUIRY, NOT DEFENSIVENESS
- Ask for criticism of your ideas and opinions.

- Show you are interested in the other's opinion by listening actively and sincerely.

- Clarify misunderstandings that may have occurred.

2. **Express your disagreement in a timely way.**

Research demonstrates that *when* you disagree may be just as important as what you say.[16] When group members approach a deadline, they are less tolerant of a member who introduces a dissenting opinion. This suggests you should express your doubts and disagreements early during the discussion. If you save them for later, when the rest of the members are ready to achieve closure, they will not thank you.

3. **Express your disagreements with rhetorical sensitivity toward the rest of the group.**

Disagree with the idea, or parts of the idea, without criticizing the person. Suppose you have just suggested that your campus shut down its snack bar at 5 P.M. to cut costs. Which response would you rather hear: "That's stupid! What are the evening students supposed to do, starve?" or "One problem I see is that your suggestion does not consider evening students' needs for food service." The first response implies that the speaker is stupid, arouses defensiveness, and cuts off further examination of the issue. The second response describes a major problem with the suggestion but leaves room for discussion regarding how to cut food service costs. The second response is helpful; the first is not.

Another way to show your sensitivity is to use neutral instead of emotionally charged language. Name-calling or otherwise pushing people's emotional buttons is never helpful. One of us recently attended a meeting where one member, John, who disagreed with another member, Janos, made a snide play on words using Janos' last name. Naturally, Janos was offended and the atmosphere remained tense until John apologized. Disagreeing by making fun of others does not improve the group's decision-making process. Steer clear of words that you think might be offensive; be rhetorically sensitive.

4. **React to disagreement with a spirit of inquiry, not defensiveness.**

Whether you are the group's leader or just a member, you have a lot of power to determine the atmosphere in your group. When someone disagrees with you, if you show that you are interested in what the other member is saying and his or her reasons for disagreeing, you send the right message to the rest of the group. Even if the disagreement was expressed poorly, you do not have to let someone else's insensitivity control your reaction. Listen actively to the person who disagrees, make sure that person has understood your position accurately, clarify any misunderstandings that may have occurred, and show that you are willing to work together to find the best possible solution.

Kareema's committee had worked for several months on a proposal to change the criteria for promotion in her department. A new member, appointed to the committee to replace someone who had left the department, questioned the committee's preliminary investigation, saying, "I don't see how that's going to work. Seems to me you'll have more problems than you had before." Although Kareema felt defensive, she reacted calmly and asked, "Derek, what problems do you see with the proposal?" Derek explained his concerns, several of which uncovered problems Kareema's committee had overlooked. The committee's revised proposal accommodated Derek's concerns. The final proposal was much stronger and was overwhelmingly approved by the rest of the department. Examples like this show how you can make disagreement and conflict work *for* your group rather than against it.

MAXIMIZING YOUR CHANCES TO INFLUENCE THE GROUP

Expressing your disagreement is the only way to make your ideas and reasoning available to the group. Even so, it is often difficult for people who are perceived as group deviants, even beneficial idea deviants, to influence the other members of the group. Whether you stand alone as an idea deviant or belong to a minority subgroup, the following suggestions will help you maximize your influence when you express your disagreement. Table 9.6 summarizes these suggestions.

1. **Make sure your arguments are of high quality.**

   This is the single most important thing that you can do. Garlick and Mongeau found that, although several factors—including the idea deviant's expertise, attractiveness, and job status—affect that person's status within the group, only the quality of the deviant's argument directly influences the other members' attitude change.[17] That means you must think the problem through carefully and be willing to listen to the objections others may have.

2. **Make sure your arguments are consistent.**

   Lisa Gebhart and Renee Meyers found that subgroups expressing minority opinions are more successful if they express their positions and arguments consistently and generally stick to a consistent message.[18] This is especially important during the latter part of a discussion. These authors recommend, however, that a minority subgroup not be so consistent that it appears rigid and unable to understand others' views.

3. **If you are a member of a subgroup, make sure all the subgroup members publicly agree with each other.**

   Subgroups, or coalitions, are a powerful way group members have of influencing each other in conflict.[19] They occur for a variety of reasons. Some form around popular members, some because members are not sure who has the power and who does not. Most commonly group members form coalitions when, in light of little resources or power, members feel a need to increase their influence through the popular philosophy that there is "power in numbers." However, coalitions containing members who disagree with each other are less influential

---

TABLE 9.6   Maximizing Your Chances to Influence the Group

- Make sure your arguments are of high quality.

- Make sure your arguments are consistent.

- If you are a member of a subgroup, make sure all the subgroup members publicly agree with each other.

GLOSSARY

Nominal Group Technique

This technique alternates between individual work and group work to help a group hear from every member when discussing a controversial issue

than coalitions presenting a united front.[20] The subgroup should meet privately and hash out any disagreements among themselves before they meet with the rest of the group so that they can agree on a consistent message.

NOMINAL GROUP TECHNIQUE

A major advantage of group over individual problem solving is that several heads can be better than one. But capitalizing on that advantage can be difficult. While the number of ideas increases with additional members, the opportunity for conflict also increases. One technique, the **nominal group technique,** can be used by a group to help members reach a decision on a controversial issue without bitterness from a win–lose conflict.

Nominal means "in name only." The nominal group technique capitalizes on the finding that sometimes people working individually while in the presence of others generate more ideas than while interacting as a group. In addition, sometimes dominant members inhibit the participation of quieter members. The nominal group technique gets around this potential problem by alternating between solitary work and group interaction. One organization used the nominal group technique as part of a detailed decision analysis procedure to decide what type of computer system to buy. This complex organization consisted of many different units and subunits that coordinated work with each other, but it also had unique needs that had to be satisfied. The nominal group technique helped all these individual units achieve consensus about the best computer system to buy. Participants were satisfied with both the process and the outcome.[21]

In the nominal group technique, members (usually six to nine) work individually in each other's presence by writing their ideas. Then members record the ideas on a chart, discuss them as a group, and finally evaluate them by a ranking procedure until members reach a decision. The following steps (summarized in Figure 9.2) comprise the process.

1. **The problem, situation, or question is stated clearly and concisely.**

   Elements of the problem or question are described, and discrepancies between what is desired and what currently exists are explained, often by a member of top management. Care must be taken not to mention possible solutions. Group members can ask questions to clarify or add information about the problem. If the group is large, it may be subdivided into smaller groups, each with its own facilitator.

2. **The coordinator asks participants to generate a list of the features or characteristics of the problem or question.**

   Steps 1 and 2 may be combined; the facilitator presents the problem and moves the group directly to step 3.

3. **The coordinator gives the group 5 to 15 minutes to work silently.**

   Each person brainwrites as many solutions or answers to the original question as possible.

4. **Each suggestion is listed and recorded in round-robin fashion on a chart visible to all members.**

   The first person gives one item from his or her list and the recorder lists it. Then the next person gives one item, and so forth, until the master list is complete. If any additional ideas or items occur to people while the list is being compiled, they should add them to the master list. During this step, no discussion of the merits of the suggestions is permitted.

FIGURE 9.2   Steps for Conducting the Nominal Group Technique

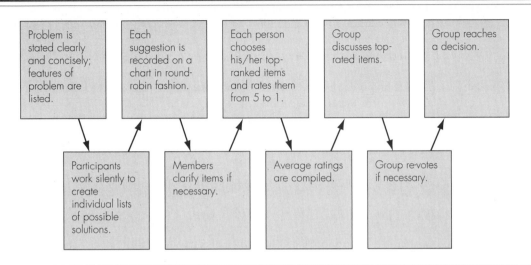

5. **Members clarify the items but do not yet evaluate them.**

    The group discusses each item on the list, but only to clarify or elaborate on it. Any member may ask what a particular item means, but arguing, criticizing, and disagreeing are not permitted during step 5.

6. **Each person chooses his or her top-ranked items.**

    Each person is given a set of note cards on which to write the five items he or she most prefers. These cards are rank-ordered. A rating of 5 is written on the top card, 4 on the next, and so on, and collected by the facilitator. The individual ratings are tallied for each item and divided by the number of participants. The five items with the highest average ratings become the agenda items for the group's discussion.

7. **The group engages in full discussion of the top-rated items.**

    This discussion should be a freewheeling and thorough evaluative discussion. Critical thinking, disagreement, and exhaustive analysis of the items are encouraged.

8. **A decision is reached.**

    Often, the discussion in step 7 will produce a consensus decision. If so, the group's work is completed. If not, group members can re-vote on the items and continue their discussion. Steps 6 and 7 may be repeated as often as necessary until support for one idea, or for a combination of ideas, emerges. The decision is then acted on by the group or the parent organization that established the group.

Thus, this technique minimizes the disadvantages of group discussion and maximizes the benefits. The solitary work neutralizes the stifling effect of domineering members and the tendency for lazy or shy members to let others carry the ball. The open discussion frequently produces well-thought-out group decisions. However, be careful not to overuse this technique when you wish to create a sense of teamwork. It doesn't always create cohesiveness and sometimes produces lower satisfaction ratings than normal discussion.

Both of us have used this technique, or modifications of it, with great success. One of us employed it to help a major manufacturer identify problems with package instructions for a product and to suggest possible solutions for these problems. Recently, we used a modification of the nominal group technique with students to help plan changes to the communication curriculum. In each example, it was not important for the group members providing the information to develop a sense of cohesiveness; thus, the nominal group technique was ideally suited for the situations.

In addition to knowing how to express disagreements, group members also need tools to help them arrive at fair solutions. One such technique for managing serious intragroup conflict is named *principled negotiation.*

STEPS IN PRINCIPLED NEGOTIATION

Each member of a group, along with the group's leader, is responsible for helping manage the conflicts that arise within the group. However, even though you may want to resolve a conflict effectively, you may not know how to proceed. The following helpful steps are suggested by Fisher and Ury in their book *Getting to Yes: Negotiating Agreement Without Giving In.*[22] Following these suggestions will help a group engage in **principled negotiation,** a conflict management procedure that encourages people to search for ways of meeting their own needs without damaging their relationships with others (see Table 9.7). Members can use this procedure collectively, or the designated leader can guide members through the process to a solution.

9.2   Helping the Cask and Cleaver Crew

APPLY NOW

The Cask and Cleaver work crew must come up with the next six-month shift schedule. They almost had their schedule until Mark discovered he had been skipped. Now they are taking sides, acting defensive, and calling each other names. Your job is to take the role of each crew member and use the nominal group technique to create a shift schedule that is satisfactory to all the crew. Mark and Beth are married, and Beth has major health problems. Mark is a full-time student, and Beth works full time. Maria is married and recently started her own business. Tom and Nathan are students at a local university working toward a teaching credential. Paul is a graduate student and single. Tracey is an undergraduate and recently divorced. Jeremy, an undergraduate, is single and lives at home with his parents.

Select a facilitator to help the "crew" go through the eight steps of the nominal group technique. After a solution is derived, the class can discuss the following:

1. What was difficult about the procedure?
2. Did the "crew" think that the technique helped in any way? If so, how? If not, why?
3. Read ahead and see if this crew's solution is anything like the one the real crew devised.

GLOSSARY

Principled Negotiation

One way of dealing with conflict that promotes finding ways to meet the needs of conflicting parties and respecting their relationship

1. **Separate the people from the problem.**

   Sometimes conflict produces such strong emotions that people cannot be objective. What may start as a disagreement about how to get something done becomes a personal declaration of war in which combatants try to hurt each other. Our Cask and Cleaver crew started out selecting shifts and ended up calling each other names. It is very important to separate the people from the issues. People believe and act in ways that make sense to them. Try not to take disagreement personally—usually, it is the result of strong beliefs that someone else holds. The administrative headquarters of a church recently experienced serious conflict among administrators. Members on both sides of the fence began to talk about the other side as *the enemy.* After several long sessions with a trained mediator, people on each side began to listen carefully to those on the other side. Each side learned that the other side cared deeply about the issues; they also realized that they shared many concerns. Eventually the conflict was resolved and the bad feelings healed. This occurred in part because both sides demonstrated that they cared about each other and because they focused on the issues that divided them rather than on personalities.

TABLE 9.7   **Steps to Principled Negotiation**

SEPARATE THE PEOPLE FROM THE PROBLEM
- Allow people to vent their emotions.
- Deal with the issue separately from the people.
- Do not personalize the issue.

FOCUS ON INTERESTS, NOT POSITIONS
- Look for the reasons behind the positions people adopt.
- Acknowledge people's interests as legitimate.
- Look for ways to reconcile opposing interests.

INVENT NEW OPTIONS FOR MUTUAL GAIN
- Do not accept the options the conflicting parties give you as the only possible options from which to choose.
- Look for creative solutions that combine the parties' interests.

USE OBJECTIVE CRITERIA
- Look for criteria that both parties accept as valid.
- Encourage parties to suggest criteria they believe are fair.
- Propose criteria if parties have not suggested them.

2. Focus on interests, not positions.

Group members are tempted to stake out positions from which they cannot be budged. If Roger says, "I insist that we keep the snack bar open in the evening," and Mary says, "We have to close the snack bar in the evening to save money," there is no way to reconcile those positions—they are incompatible. The harder individuals cling to them, the more difficult it will be to resolve the conflict. However, people stake out positions for reasons that seem good to them. It is the reasons for the positions (personal interests) that should be the focus of the negotiation. In our earlier example, Mary is interested in saving the campus money while Roger wants to make sure the evening students are provided with food service. Both are legitimate interests. One way to resolve them is to close the snack shop at 5 P.M. (thereby saving on labor and utility costs) but provide vending machines with a variety of sandwiches and snacks. In this way, the legitimate interests of each individual are served. The work crew of Cask and Cleaver all had reasons for their positions. Mark and Beth faced huge doctor bills because Beth has a congenital heart defect. Maria recently started a new business. Paul, Mark's former roommate, felt hurt by Mark's indifference to his schedule. All are legitimate feelings and interests and must be dealt with in the discussion if members are to manage their conflict productively.

3. Invent new options for mutual gain.

Group members should become creative at inventing alternatives. A number of techniques, such as brainstorming, are designed to help groups become more inventive. If Roger and Mary's committee had assumed there were only two available options—keeping the snack shop open past 5 P.M. or closing it—members could never have resolved the issue. The same committee later resolved a similar issue with the bookstore by inventing a solution that was not apparent when the committee first began to discuss the issue. You can probably remember other examples in which a group was able to invent a new option that met everyone's interests.

In our Cask and Cleaver case, the only options initially presented were to start all over again or keep going and ignore Mark's skipped turn. Another option, one that the crew did not consider, was to go back to the point where Mark was skipped, keep everything the same up until then, and start anew from Mark's skipped turn. In fact, Tracey's option effectively solved the problem. She pointed out that while it was not Mark and Beth's fault that Paul and Tom had night classes, it also was not Paul and Tom's fault that Beth needed surgery. She suggested that Mark give his night shift to Tom so he and Beth, who didn't work that night, could spend some time together. Mark saw the logic in Tracey's solution and gave his valued shift to Tom. All members apologized to those whom they had offended. The crew was able to come up with an option that gave them mutual gain given their reasons for their positions.

4. Insist on using objective criteria.

Much wasted time can be saved if members use criteria they agree are fair and appropriate for evaluating solutions. For example, the *Bluebook* establishes a price range that helps both used-car buyers and sellers determine the fair price for a car. You may want $10,000 for your 15-year-old Toyota Corolla, but both you and

9.3   **Should He Go Back to School?**

APPLY NOW

Sam and Tashie have been married for 12 years. Sam wants to quit his job because he is bored and believes they had an agreement that he would be able to complete his education after they had been married a few years. Tashie is the owner of her own company, which is finally getting off the ground, and she doesn't believe they have the money for Sam to leave his job. Select two students to role-play the discussion between Sam and Tashie in front of the class. After the role-play, use the principled negotiation procedure with the entire class to help Sam and Tashie manage the conflict.

People: Ask the role-players how they feel about the argument, themselves, and the other person. Emphasize the importance of recognizing feelings.

Interests: Distinguish between the irreconcilable positions and the interests behind each position. Have the class and the role-players participate in discovering what each person's interests may be.

Options: Ask the class and the role-players to brainstorm creative options for this couple. Emphasize the point that interests may be met in a variety of ways, one of which is bound to be acceptable to both.

Criteria: Explore whether any objective criteria might apply to this couple's dilemma.

potential buyers know that you won't get it! Using prices supplied by the *Kelley Blue Book* as criteria allows the negotiation to take place within narrower, more realistic limits.

The same use of objective criteria occurs in other situations too. One of us served on a church finance committee charged with reviewing salaries and recommending adjustments. The salaries for the organist and choir director had not been reviewed in several years. Not knowing whether these salaries were reasonable or not, the committee called the local Council of Churches director, who told members how much organists and choir directors with comparable responsibilities received at other churches of similar size. When the finance committee presented the recommendations to the full board of directors, the recommendations were easy to defend because of the objective criteria used.

Even with the best of intentions, sometimes a group becomes deadlocked when it tries to resolve a conflict. We recommend that groups try to resolve their own conflicts first, but if that isn't possible, a group can try mediation or arbitration. The principled negotiation procedure can be used by an outside facilitator. This may be necessary if the leader has been actively involved in the conflict. Finally, a group may bring in an outside arbitrator with power to settle the dispute. However, these are last resorts. It is far better if a group can resolve its own conflicts.

- Three common myths about conflict are that conflict is always harmful, it is due to misunderstandings, and it can be resolved by good communication.

- Groupthink is the tendency of highly cohesive groups not to examine critically all aspects of a decision; groups experiencing groupthink overestimate their power, evaluate information in a closed-minded and biased way, and experience pressures to conform to group opinions.

- The five common conflict management styles of avoidance, accommodation, competition, collaboration, and compromise are each ap-propriate in certain circumstances, but styles that encourage members to look for ways to satisfy all participants are usually preferable.

- Group members can use the nominal group technique, which balances solitary and group work, to help work through potentially contentious discussions.

- Group members can also use procedures such as principled negotiation, which focuses on people's interests rather than positions, finding creative options, and using objective criteria to resolve conflicts.

1. Rent either *The Commitments* or *Lord of the Flies.* Watch the movie and observe types of conflicts, how these conflicts were handled, the effects of the conflicts on the group, how decision making was affected by the various conflicts, and what the group could have done to improve its ability to manage conflict. You can do this yourself or you can discuss your observations with others in class who have also watched the video.

2. Think of a group you currently belong to. Recollect two recent conflicts in the group. Write an essay describing the conflict, labeling the type of conflict, and reporting how it was managed. Draw some conclusions about conflict in group interaction from these observations.

3. Divide yourselves into groups and come to a consensus regarding what you would do about each of the following group problems:

   a. Ann has missed the first three meetings of the group. For the first two she said she had to work, but she offered no reason for missing the last one. She also has completed none of the work she agreed to do for the group.

   b. Bob is a domineering individual who attempts to control the direction of the group. He evaluates each idea as soon as it is presented. As a result, the rest of the members have stopped volunteering suggestions and ideas.

   c. The members of the group have fallen into two subgroups, and competition has arisen between the subgroups. If you didn't have to work together, you would have split apart long ago.

 Go to **www.mhhe.com/adamsgalanes** and **www.mhhe.com/groups** for Self-Quizzes and weblinks.

KEY TERMS and CONCEPTS

accommodation	compromise	groupthink
avoidance	conflict	nominal group technique
collaboration	devil's advocate	principled negotiation
competition		

www.mhhe.com/adamsgalanes
Use the flashcards and crossword puzzles on the Online Learning Center to further your knowledge of these key terms.

Applying Leadership Principles

After reading this chapter you should be able to:

1. List and discuss the myths of leadership.

2. Discuss current thinking about leadership.

3. Describe the administrative duties leaders are expected to perform and explain how leaders can perform these effectively.

4. List and explain six tips for leading group discussions.

5. Explain how establishing a climate of trust, developing teamwork, and promoting cooperation can help develop the group.

6. Explain what is involved in managing the group's written communication.

7. Describe *distributed leadership* and discuss what it means to encourage it.

8. List and explain the ethical guidelines for group leaders.

The College Service Club

TerryAnn was so envious of the close, cohesive executive committee of her service club that she decided to run for office so she could be part of the team. When she was elected president as a junior, she was thrilled. She wanted the club and the executive committee to continue experiencing the same success she had witnessed as a member. Unfortunately, things wouldn't turn out that way. TerryAnn and the rest of the executive committee met soon after the spring election to make plans for the upcoming fall. Although many good ideas surfaced at this meeting, no one wrote them down. TerryAnn was somewhat intimidated by all the seniors on the executive committee, and she was reluctant to assign tasks or even ask the other members to do things. No one else picked up the ball either. Consequently, no one remembered what they had decided or knew who was supposed to do what. Committee members lost valuable summer planning time because they weren't organized. When fall came, they had to scramble to catch up.

TerryAnn's reluctance to take charge affected both the executive committee and the regular organizational meetings. She made no effort to start the meetings on time, so members got into the habit of coming late. Because there was no agenda, members did not know what they would be discussing or what materials they should bring to the meetings. Discussion was haphazard, jumping from one topic to the next without ever finishing a single subject. No meeting minutes were ever compiled or distributed, so members weren't sure what actions had been decided or who was assigned to what tasks. As a result of the disorganization in the executive committee, service club members became disenchanted with the organization. Membership decreased. As the frustrating year drew to a close, TerryAnn was increasingly depressed because her high hopes for the club had not come close to being realized.

This story could have had a different ending if TerryAnn had known what the other members expected of her. Because she was afraid to be seen as a dictator, she did the exact opposite. But the group members were practically begging for TerryAnn to give them structure and organization so that the club's jobs would get done. TerryAnn's "leadership" did not match what the group needed and wanted from her.

In this chapter we will discuss myths about leadership and current thinking about effective leadership, and explain the typical duties of designated small group leaders. In addition, we suggest guidelines to encourage distributed leadership and describe ethical leader behavior.

Myths about Leadership

Students usually say that leaders "control the actions of the other members," "give orders," and generally "tell people what to do." In this section we examine several other pervasive myths about leadership.

1. **Leadership is a personality trait that individuals possess in varying degrees.**

   From Plato to the 1950s, the study of leadership consisted of a search for the traits that make people leaders. These traits included intelligence, attractiveness, psychological dominance, and size. However, strict trait approaches to studying leadership are flawed in several ways. First, there is no trait or set of traits that leaders have but followers do not. There is no trait that differentiates leaders from members.

   A second flaw in the trait approach is the underlying assumption that all leadership situations call for the same trait or set of traits. Think about this for a moment. Does the leader of a classroom discussion group need the same traits as the leader of a military platoon? Do both situations require the same approach? No single set of traits will identify the best leader for any given group or situation.

   A third flaw in the trait approach relates directly to the concept of *trait* as something innate. In other words, "Leaders are born, not made." If you aren't born with the characteristics of a leader (whatever those may be), you will not become a leader. Instead, leadership consists of *behaving in ways that can be learned* (at least up to a point). Consider, for a moment, Candy Lightner, the woman who developed MADD, Mothers Against Drunk Drivers. Ms. Lightner was an ordinary single parent, not a recognized leader, before a drunken driver killed her daughter. Nothing in her previous background or experience could have predicted that she would become the leader of a national organization. But she cared enough to do the hard work of learning to lead. So can you.

2. **There is an ideal leadership style, no matter what the situation.**

   Since the 1950s, a number of researchers have examined the behaviors associated with leadership, including the styles displayed by various leaders. Several studies indicated that leaders perform both *task-oriented* and *relationship-oriented* behaviors.[1] Leaders rated high on either one, neither, or both of these dimensions. Many people believed that the ideal style of leadership was one rated high on both task and relationship dimensions, so many organizations instituted training programs to teach their employees how to be simultaneously task- and relationship-oriented.

   Other researchers have examined three general styles of people in leadership positions: autocratic (authoritarian), democratic (participatory), and laissez-faire (noninvolved). *Autocratic* leaders are primarily task-oriented people who personally make the decisions for the group and control the group's process. They say things like, "Here's what I've decided we'll do." They alone decide the group's

For more information on analyzing famous leaders, go to the online learning center.

agenda, select procedures the group will follow, and decide who will speak when. Highly authoritarian leaders can stifle group members who are expert, creative, and enthusiastic.

Democratic leaders want all the group members to participate in decision making, and so are more relationship-oriented than autocratic leaders. They say things like, "What ideas do you have for solving our problem?" Democratic leaders suggest but do not coerce. They try to discover the wishes of the group members and help them achieve their common goals. They encourage members to develop the group's agenda as well as to determine what procedures the group will use. Discussants can speak freely within the group. When members propose ideas, they are considered to be the property of the group as a whole. Democratic leaders see their function as helping the group accomplish what the members want, as long as it is part of the group's purpose or the charge given to the group by the parent organization. Members of groups with leaders who function democratically tend to be more satisfied, to participate more actively in meetings, to demonstrate more commitment to group decisions, and to be more innovative than members of groups with either autocratic or laissez-faire leaders.[2]

Laissez-faire "leaders," who consider themselves to be no different from the other members, display a hands-off style that really does not provide much leadership. They say things like, "Do what you want; it doesn't matter to me." They create a void that forces the other members to step in or flounder without coordination. This is the mistake TerryAnn made, but the others weren't able or willing to step into the void she created. Occasionally the other members of groups led by laissez-faire leaders blend their efforts to lead the group successfully, but more often such groups end up wasting a lot of time or following the structure provided by an autocratic leader who emerges and takes charge. Only groups of highly motivated experts tend to be more productive and satisfied with laissez-faire leaders than democratic leaders.[3]

Research looking for an ideal leadership style came up with inconsistent findings. While most group members prefer the democratic rather than the autocratic style, some groups composed of authoritarian members actually prefer the more authoritarian style. Plus, autocratic groups sometimes complete more work than democratic groups. About the only consistent finding was that groups prefer either the democratic or the autocratic style to the laissez-faire style.

A recent review of studies of democratic and autocratic leadership suggests that several factors in combination with leadership style influence a group's productivity.[4] Democratic leadership seems to be more productive when it occurs in natural, real-life settings and when the group's task is a complex one. In addition, member satisfaction with democratic leadership is not automatic.

The styles approach oversimplifies the complexities of groups as open systems. For example, consider the following two groups: (1) an advertising agency's creative group, in which the members have worked together successfully for two years, and (2) an outdoor survival group of young adolescent boys, strangers to each other, none of whom has ever been camping. Would you recommend the same style of leadership to the coordinator of the creative group and to the adult adviser of the survival group? Everything suggests a democratic approach with the creative group and a more controlling approach with the young boys. Most of us would agree that no one style is right for all situations.

The styles approach also assumes that a particular group will have the same needs over its lifetime. But just as different groups vary in their needs for different leadership services, a single group's needs will change greatly over time as well. Early in a group's history the more inexperienced members may appreciate a take-charge leader, but as group members become more experienced, they may prefer less control.

Most people today discredit the idea that there is an ideal leadership style no matter what the occasion. Rather, a number of factors such as the experience of the members, how long they have been together, how successful they have been in the past, how interesting the job is, and whether or not there is an impending deadline all contribute to determining the most appropriate style.

3. **Leaders get other people to do the work for them.**

When some students are elected or appointed to leadership positions, they assume that their job is to tell other people what to do and often seem surprised that it doesn't work. Recently, the president of a campus organization was disgusted that a colleague failed to complete an assignment for the organization. "I told her what to do, and I told her we needed the information for today's meeting," she said. She didn't understand that just telling someone to do something doesn't ensure that it will happen. If you think your position as leader makes your job easier, think again. As we saw with TerryAnn, her laid-back style may have prevented her from being perceived as a dictator, but expecting others to do the work without providing them any direction or guidance wasn't effective either. Effective leaders expect to provide service to the group rather than expecting the members to serve them.

Current Ideas about Leadership

Now that you know that small group leadership isn't a trait, a style, or bossing people around, let's discuss what it *does* involve. Several contemporary ideas about leadership will help you be more effective as a group leader. The ideas we discuss next complement each other.

THE FUNCTIONAL CONCEPT OF GROUP LEADERSHIP

The **functional concept** of leadership contains two premises. First, this concept assumes that certain important functions must be performed if the group is to be successful in reaching its goals. We pointed out in Chapter 7 that these functions are usually classified as task-related or people-related functions. Task-related functions, such as *initiating* discussion or action, *offering opinions, making suggestions,* and *elaborating* on other members' ideas, are behaviors directly related to getting the group's job done. People-related functions, such as *harmonizing, gatekeeping,* and *relieving tension,* help members work as a team.

Another important premise of functional concept is that performing the needed functions is the responsibility of all the group members, not just the individual who is designated as the group's leader. In addition to the group's leader, other members of a group

GLOSSARY

Functional Concept

Groups need to have certain functions performed, and all group members can and should perform needed functions

can and must provide leadership services needed by the group. One individual cannot perform all the services a group needs. We haven't seen anyone with all the knowledge and skills a group may need. Also, having only one person—the leader—supply everything a group needs deprives the other members of the chance to develop their skills and talents. Remember, people want to contribute and to be appreciated for their participation. Every member of a group needs to know that he or she is valued. When that occurs, members tend to be committed and loyal, and group cohesiveness is high.

The abilities of all members are needed in a group. In one committee, the chair summarized the discussion and kept the group's work organized. Another member was particularly good at devising compromises that all members could support. Yet another member's irreverent sense of humor helped the committee relieve tension when conflicts threatened to get personal or out of hand. The functional concept applied to group leadership encourages members to use their unique strengths in supplying needed leadership for the group, yet it puts a special responsibility on designated leaders to provide essential functions that aren't being provided by another member.

If all members are responsible for providing needed leadership functions, what is your job as a group's leader? As we stated in Chapter 1, the leader's job is *completing* the group by supplying any needed functions (services) that other members are not providing or at least seeing that someone supplies them.[5] This gives the designated leader a lot to do. The leader must constantly monitor the group's progress, identify what the group needs at any time, decide whether those functions are currently being performed adequately by other members, and, if not, provide them or encourage someone else to do so. For example, if the leader sees that one member has not offered an opinion about an important issue, the leader could gatekeep by asking that member's opinion. If the group seems confused, the leader should summarize, clarify, and reorient the group or ask that someone else do so. If secondary tensions are mounting, the leader should try to relieve them before they cause harm, perhaps by joking or suggesting a 10-minute break.

This approach requires the leader to figure out what functions are needed as well as to supply them. You have to be both smart and flexible! You must constantly be aware of what is happening in the group. The functional concept assumes that people can learn a variety of leader behaviors and that all of us should learn to function as leaders in certain circumstances.

THE CONTINGENCY CONCEPT OF GROUP LEADERSHIP

Related to the functions approach, the **contingency concept** holds that appropriate leadership behavior depends on the situation. As we noted earlier, it doesn't seem reasonable that the same leadership style should be used for a classroom discussion group as for a platoon during a firefight. TerryAnn's laid-back manner of leading did not work in her particular service club, but with a group of experienced pros, it may have proven quite effective. There are several contingency approaches; we will focus on those developed by Hersey and Blanchard.

Contingency approaches suggest that leaders should consider several factors before deciding the specific leadership services appropriate for the group. Among these factors are the type of task, how well the members work together, and how well members work with the leader.[6] A major factor that affects the way a leader should act is the maturity level, or readiness, of the followers.[7] Hersey and Blanchard have provided a model, shown in Figure 10.1, to help match appropriate leadership behaviors to the readiness level of the followers. In general, the more experienced, interested, and motivated the members are, the less direction is needed from the leader.

You should be able to adapt your behavior in a way that is appropriate for your group. Hersey and Blanchard's model, tempered with your common sense and knowledge of group leadership, helps you know how to adapt.

If group members are unable, are unwilling, or don't have enough information to complete the task on their own, they are low in readiness. *Telling* can be an effective leadership style. The leader needs to give them specific instructions and provide close supervision of their work: "Our goal is to increase sales by 15 percent, and here's what I want you to do . . ." The leader tells the members what, how, and when to do something, and the members have little say in the matter. Telling demonstrates high-task and low-relationship behavior.

With low to moderate readiness, group members are usually willing but do not have the skills or experience necessary to perform well. In this case, the leader takes a *selling* approach by providing much of the direction but seeking members' enthusiastic support

---

FIGURE 10.1   Model of Situational Leadership

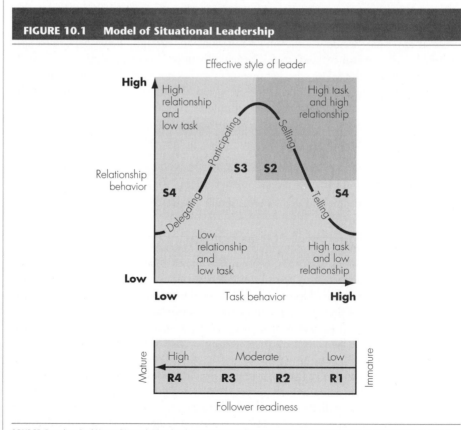

SOURCE: Based on Paul Hersey/Kenneth Blanchard, *Management of Organizational Behavior: Utilizing Human Resources,* 4th ed. (Englewood Cliffs, NJ: Prentice Hall). Reprinted by permission.

for this direction: "One of our goals is to increase sales by 15 percent, and I'd really like your input about how we can do that." Two-way communication occurs as the leader encourages members to ask for explanations and additional information. The leader's goal is to promote member enthusiasm while providing guidance needed to complete the task well. Selling is both high-task and high-relationship oriented.

With members of moderate to high readiness, the leader can pay less attention to the demands of the task and concentrate instead on the relationships among members: "How is the sales campaign going? What can I do to help you?" Here, followers have the skills to perform the job but may feel insecure about taking action or need coordination to work out a set of roles and division of labor. The leader's supportive, democratic style is called *participating* because decision making is shared and the leader's role is mostly one of facilitation and coordination. All members share in leading the group. When members reach this level of readiness, anyone in the group could probably serve as its designated leader.

In a fully ready group, members are both able and willing to perform. They need little task-related supervision or encouragement. In this situation, the *delegating* style is appropriate; the leader turns the responsibility for the group over to the group: "Let me know if you need anything." All members (including the leader) are equal in responsibility. This relatively low-task, low-relationship style is appropriate where a more active leadership style might be perceived as interference. However, even when the group is fully ready, the leader must still monitor the changing conditions of the group and be ready to step in to perform additional services the group may need. This was TerryAnn's style, but her followers were not at this level of readiness.

Most of us have styles of leading and small group services we prefer to perform. We are not infinitely capable of altering our behavior, and some of us are more flexible than others. Some leadership experts advise us to look for situations that need our preferred styles or to encourage supportive and capable members of the group to assist the leaders.

A theme unites the contingency and functional approaches to leadership: leadership is a property of the *group*, not of the individual who happens to have the title of "leader." This is called **distributed leadership**, which explicitly acknowledges that each group member should perform the communication behaviors needed to move the group toward its goal. The democratic values on which our society was founded suggest that participation by everyone is a healthy and desirable goal. Gastil, making a case for democratic leadership, argues that "democratic group leadership amounts to giving group members responsibility, improving the general abilities and leadership skills of the other members, and assisting the group in its decision-making process."[8] This is precisely what the functional approach to leadership suggests: All group members are capable of performing the variety of functions a group needs, even though no one person is capable of supplying the variety of functions needed. In addition, in a recent study, overall leadership activity was found to be more related to group productivity than activity of the designated leader alone.[9] Distributing the leadership functions may be good not only for the members themselves but for the group as well. We talk more about how to encourage distributed leadership later in this chapter.

We have discussed major myths surrounding group leadership, presented current thinking about leadership, and promoted the idea of distributed leadership. It is now time to investigate what behaviors members expect from their leaders.

GLOSSARY

Distributed Leadership

Each group member can and should provide leadership services to a group

10.1   Which Contingency Style Is Most Appropriate?

You have been asked to conduct a workshop on group leadership for a major corporation in your city. You have selected the contingency approach to leadership as the focus of your workshop. The corporation has asked that your workshop contain several activities to give the participants "hands-on" experience with current thinking about group leadership. You have decided that one of those activities will involve application of the contingency model to several different kinds of groups. Your task now is to construct the activity. To do so, you need the materials to set up the activity and the answers to the activity.

You first will ask the participants to create a matrix that lists the four Hersey and Blanchard leadership styles (participating, selling, delegating, and telling) across the top. Under each style, list the contingencies that make that style appropriate, along with how each contingency is likely to affect the style. Next, you will give participants a list of situations and ask them to determine what style is most appropriate using their matrix. The list of situations includes the following:

1. A group of college students studying together for a final exam.
2. A heart transplant team.
3. A task force of neighbors trying to rid the neighborhood of crack dealers.
4. A group of student senators planning the senate agenda for the following month.
5. A self-managed work group of employees assembling an automobile.
6. A group of four grown children planning their parents' 50th wedding anniversary party.

You will ask participants to use their matrix to determine the appropriate style for each of these. To be prepared to direct discussion after the participants have finished this part of the activity, you must first participate in the activity yourself.

1. Construct the matrix, as you will ask the participants to do.
2. Apply the matrix to the six situations listed.

What Groups Expect Leaders to Do

We emphasized in Chapters 1 and 7 and in this chapter that the leader has a lot of work to do, sometimes more than any other member of the group. In the United States, most groups expect their designated leaders to provide several specific services. Four major categories into which these services fall, described briefly in Table 10.1, are performing administrative duties, leading group discussions, developing the group, and managing

TABLE 10.1	**Major Duties Leaders Are Expected to Perform**
PERFORMING ADMINISTRATIVE DUTIES	Planning and preparing for meetings, keeping members informed, following up between meetings
LEADING GROUP DISCUSSION	Starting discussions and keeping them on track, encouraging participation, stimulating members' creative and critical thinking
DEVELOPING THE GROUP	Fostering a productive and supporting climate; developing teamwork, cooperation, and trust
MANAGING THE WRITTEN COMMUNICATION	Making sure the group keeps accurate records and copies of all written communication used and produced by the group

the group's written communication.[10] The following information can serve as your concise leader's manual whenever you find yourself elected or appointed leader of a group.

PERFORMING ADMINISTRATIVE DUTIES

Leaders should help a group run efficiently by performing administrative duties such as planning for meetings and following up on members' assignments. TerryAnn's performance was particularly weak in these areas.

Planning for Meetings.   As leader, you must plan meetings so you don't waste other members' time. Here is a set of guidelines you can follow:

1. **Define the purpose of the meeting and communicate it clearly to the members.**

   Don't have a meeting if there is no reason for it. If a meeting is needed, state the purpose clearly. "To talk about what we're going to do this year" is too vague; "to establish a list of priorities we want to accomplish within the next six months" is clear and specific. Tell the members exactly what outcomes should be produced at the meeting, such as a written report, an oral recommendation, plans for a party, a decision made, and so forth. Highly successful groups have clear goals that are understood and supported by every member.[11]

2. **Make sure members know the place, starting time, and closing time for the meeting.**

   Let members know this ahead of time. Make sure you stick to those starting and ending times. Consistently starting meetings late or running overtime kills enthusiasm and lowers attendance. In addition, state the meeting place exactly. "At the library" is vague and confusing. Some members may go to the lobby, while others to the student lounge. "In room 302 of the library" eliminates confusion.

"How about some little pads and pencils?"

It's the leader's responsibility to make sure members have all the supplies they need. (© The New Yorker Collection; 1985 Arnie Levin from cartoonbank.com. All Rights Reserved.)

The leader is responsible for communicating this information to members, though this task can be delegated to someone else (i.e., a secretary). Still, it is the leader's responsibility to be sure everyone knows when and where to meet.

3. **If special resource people are needed at the meeting, advise and prepare them.**

Groups often need information and advice from specialists. A personnel committee may need the advice of a psychologist or lawyer; a student group may need to consult with the parking services manager before recommending changes in parking policies. Make sure invited guests know what to prepare and what to expect at the meeting.

4. **Make all necessary physical arrangements.**

Reserve the room, arrange the seats properly, and bring needed materials (e.g., notepads, pencils, microphones, tape recorders).

Following up on Meetings.   Generally two kinds of follow-up are needed: reminding group members of assignments and serving as liaison with other groups.

1. **Keep track of member assignments.**

The leader must make sure that members know what their assignments are and when they are due. The group should keep written records of assignments, perhaps as part of the group's regular minutes. (Keeping written records is so important that it is dealt with separately later.) In addition, as leader you should keep in touch with members by telephone or e-mail to monitor their progress. Had

TerryAnn done these things throughout the summer following her initial planning meeting as president, her term might have been memorable for positive rather than negative reasons.

2. **Serve as liaison with other groups.**

   The leader is the group's spokesperson. Usually this means the leader represents the group to other groups, answers questions about the group and its work, and keeps the parent organization informed. For example, the chair of each subcommittee working on the Ozarks Public Television merger with the university, described in Chapter 6, was simultaneously a member of the steering committee overseeing the merger. This made liaison and coordination easy. The leader also makes all reports and motions for a committee at meetings of its parent organization and is sometimes interviewed by public media.

LEADING GROUP DISCUSSIONS

One of your most important duties as designated leader is to coordinate discussions so that they are productive. You should plan how you will initiate the meetings, keep the discussion organized, encourage all members to participate, and stimulate both creative and critical thinking. You also should monitor the group so that what is not accomplished at one meeting can be addressed at the next. This was TerryAnn's most crucial failing.

Initiating Discussions.   Opening remarks set the stage for the meeting and help members begin to focus on the group's task. Here are guidelines for you to follow:

1. **Help reduce primary tensions, especially with new groups.**

   Members may need to be introduced to each other. Name tags may be needed. An icebreaker or other social activity may be used to help members get to know one another.

2. **Briefly review the purpose of the meeting, the specific outcomes desired, and the area of freedom of the group.**

   Members should have been informed of these before the meeting, but some members may want clarification. Discussing them early helps prevent misunderstandings later. Food helps! It's amazing what coffee and snacks can do to relax people.

3. **Give members informational and organizational handouts.**

   These may include informational sheets, an agenda, outlines to guide the discussion, copies of things to be discussed, and so forth.

4. **See that special roles are established as needed.**

   Decide what roles are needed and how they will be handled. Most groups appoint a recorder to keep written records of meetings. Decide whether these positions will be rotated or handled by only one individual.

5. **Suggest procedures to follow.**

   Members should know whether decisions will be made by consensus or majority vote, and whether the group will follow the small group procedures recommended by *Robert's Rules of Order Revised* or another group technique. We recommend that you suggest procedures to the group, then ask the members to accept, modify, or suggest alternative procedures. (If bylaws or other laws impose specific procedures on the group, such as on a jury, you won't have this flexibility.)

6. **Ask a clear question to help members focus on the first substantive issue on the agenda.**

   This helps launch the group into the substantive portion of the meeting. You may want to review the examples of discussion questions in Table 4.2. A group leader might open the group's meeting this way: "At this meeting, we must decide which two of our five job applicants we should interview in person. You all received copies of the résumés prior to the meeting. Unless you'd rather proceed in a different way, I suggest we go in alphabetical order and assess each person's strengths and weaknesses against the criteria we adopted at our last meeting. After we've talked about each one, we can compare them to determine our top two. Does that seem OK? [Wait for feedback.] Fine, then let's look at James Adams's résumé first." Such a statement makes the meeting's goals, procedures, and desired outcomes clear from the beginning.

Structuring Discussions.   Once the group members are familiar with each other and oriented to the task, the leader should organize the discussion. Effective leaders help maintain productive relationships among the members, but their primary focus should be on the group's task. This is what most group members expect.[12] That includes constantly monitoring the group's process and making needed adjustments. Following are some suggestions:

1. **Keep the group goal-oriented; watch for digressions and topic changes.**

   Be sure the members understand and accept the goal. A certain amount of digression is normal and desirable because it can foster team spirit. You don't want to stifle every digression, but if a lengthy digression occurs, you should help bring it back on track: "We seem to be losing sight of our objective," or "We're getting off track. What we were talking about was . . ." Topic switches are common, so be on constant watch for them. When you notice one, point it out and suggest that the group finish one topic before going on to another: "We're jumping ahead. Let's finish our parking recommendation before we start talking about scholarships." When a change of issue, irrelevant topic, or premature solution crops up, ask if that person would mind waiting until the group has finished its analysis of the current issue.

2. **Put the discussion or problem-solving procedure on the board or in a handout.**

   If the group is using a procedure such as brainstorming, help the group remember the steps by summarizing them briefly in writing. This helps keep comments to the point.

3. **Summarize each major step or decision.**

   It is easy for members to lose track of what the group is doing. Before the group proceeds to the next issue or agenda item, help all members keep track by summarizing and asking members for feedback. In many cases, a secretary can help summarize. This also helps make a clear transition to the next step in the discussion.

4. **Structure the group's time.**

   Nothing is more frustrating than running out of time before you have a chance to discuss an issue important to you. Since members often get caught up in a discussion, it is up to the leader to keep track of time and remind the group of what still needs to be done and how much time is available.

THE FAR SIDE® BY GARY LARSON

"And so you just threw everything together?
Mathews, a posse is something
you have to *organize*."

The main thing a leader does is help the group get organized. (THE FAR SIDE ©
FARWORKS, INC. Dist. by UNIVERSAL PRESS SYNDICATE. Reprinted with permission.
All rights reserved.)

5. **Bring the discussion to a definite close.**

   Do this no later than the scheduled ending time for the meeting, unless all members agree to extend the time. In your conclusion, include a brief summary of progress the group has made, a review of assignments given, a statement of how reports of the meeting will be distributed to members and others, comments about preparation for the next meeting, commendations for a job well done, and, periodically, your evaluation of the meeting to improve the group's future interactions.

Equalizing Opportunity to Participate.   Along with keeping the group's discussion organized, the leader is responsible for seeing to it that everyone has an equal opportunity to speak. This is central to democratic participation discussed earlier in the chapter. You can do several things to produce such equality:

1. **Address your comments to the group rather than to individuals.**

   Unless you are asking someone for specific information or responding directly to what a member has said, speak to the group as a whole. Make eye contact with everyone, especially the less-talkative members. It is natural to pay the most attention to those who talk a lot, but this may further discourage quiet members.

2. **Control dominating or long-winded speakers.**

Occasionally a member monopolizes the discussion so much that others give up. This imbalance can destroy a group. The other members expect you to control domineering members and will thank you for it. You may have to try several techniques. First, avoid direct eye contact. Second, sit where you can overlook them naturally when you ask questions of the group. Third, cut in tactfully and say something like, "How do the *rest* of you feel about that point?" Fourth, help the group establish rules about how long someone may speak; then establish a timekeeper to keep track of members' remarks. Fifth, describe the problem openly to the group and ask the members to deal with it as a group. Sometimes even more drastic measures are needed, such as talking with the offending individual privately or even asking the person to leave the group. This is a last resort; use it only when other measures have failed.

3. **Encourage less-talkative members to participate.**

Quiet members may feel overwhelmed by talkative ones. Encourage less-talkative members: "Roger, finances are your area of expertise. Where do you think the budget could be cut?" or "Maria, you haven't said anything about the proposal. Would you like to share your opinion?" Make a visual survey of members continuously to look for nonverbal signs that a member wants to speak, seems upset, or disagrees with what someone else is saying. Give such members a chance to speak by asking a direct question such as, "Did you want to comment on Navida's suggestion?"

Other techniques for increasing the participation of quiet members include assigning them to investigate needed information and reporting back to the group or inviting them to contribute with their special areas of knowledge or skill. You might say, "Kim, you're a statistical whiz. Will you take charge of the data analysis for the project?" Listen with real interest to what an infrequent participant says and encourage others to do so as well. Nothing kills participation faster than the other members' apparent lack of interest.

4. **Avoid commenting after each member's remark.**

Some discussion leaders comment after each person has spoken. This produces a *wheel* network of verbal interaction. Eventually members start waiting for the leader to comment, and this inhibits the free flow of conversation. Listen, speak when you are really needed, but as a rule don't repeat or interpret what others say.

5. **Bounce questions of interpretation back to the group.**

Some groups follow the designated leader's opinions. Especially in a new group, hold back until others have had a chance to express their views. Then, offer yours only as another point of view to be considered. If a member asks, "What do you think we should do?" you can reply, "Let's see what everyone else thinks first. What do the rest of you think . . . ?"

6. **Remain neutral during arguments.**

If you are heavily involved in an argument, you will have a harder time being objective, encouraging others to participate, and seeing that each point of view is represented. If you stay neutral, you can legitimately serve as a mediator for resolving disputes. Of course, feel free to support decisions as they emerge and encourage critical thinking by all members.

Stimulating Creative Thinking. Many problem-solving groups create mediocre solutions. Sometimes inventive solutions are needed. Chapter 5 discussed the importance of creative thinking. Here we elaborate further on how to encourage group creativity:

1. **Suggest discussion techniques that are designed to tap a group's creativity.**

   Several techniques, such as brainstorming, are designed especially to help a group create inventive solutions. Many techniques employ deferred judgment—the group postpones evaluation until all possible solutions are presented. When people know their ideas will not be judged, they feel freer to suggest wild and crazy ideas, many of which may turn out to be useful.

2. **When the flow of ideas has dried up, encourage the group to search for a few more alternatives.**

   Often the best ideas appear late in a period of creative brainstorming. You might use these idea-spurring questions: "What else can we think of to . . . ?" or "I wonder if we can think of any more possible ways to . . . ?"

3. **Discuss the components of a problem one at a time.**

   For instance, ask, "Is there any way to improve the appearance of . . . ?" or ". . . the durability of . . . ?"

4. **Watch for suggestions that open up new areas of thinking and then pose a general question about them.**

   For example, if someone suggests putting up signs in the library that show the cost of losses to the users, you might capitalize on that idea by asking, "How else could we publicize the cost of losses to the library?"

Stimulating Critical Thinking. Chapter 5 also covered critical thinking in detail. We remind you here of your responsibility as leader for ensuring that group members carefully evaluate the decisions they make. Here are specific suggestions:

1. **Encourage group members to evaluate information and reasoning.**

   Ask questions to make sure the group evaluates the source of evidence ("Where did that information come from?" "How well respected is Dr. Gray in the field?"), the relevance of the evidence ("How does that apply to our problem?"), the accuracy of the information ("Is that information consistent with other information about the issue?" "Why does this information contradict what others have said?"), and the reasoning ("Are the conclusions logical and based on the information presented?"). Bring in outside experts to challenge the views of the group or to help evaluate information.

2. **See that all group members understand and accept the standards, criteria, or assumptions used in making judgments.**

   Fair, unbiased judgments are based on criteria that are clear to all members. You might ask, "Is that criterion clear to us all?" "Is this something we want to insist on?" or "Do we all accept this as an assumption?" Criteria were discussed in Chapter 6.

3. **See that all proposed solutions are tested thoroughly before they are accepted as final group decisions.**

   Make sure group members discuss tentative solutions with relevant outsiders, that pros and cons of each solution have been evaluated, and that members have had a chance to play devil's advocate in challenging proposals. For a major problem, propose holding a second-chance meeting, where all doubts, concerns, or untested assumptions can be explored.

10.2   Red Ribbon Committee and Sober Graduation

The Red Ribbon Committee is a community group in California's central valley. The committee develops, plans, and presents several community events each year that promote a sober and drug-free lifestyle. Each year the committee debates whether or not the sober graduation party should last all night or end at 2 or 3 A.M. Students, noting that their parents would not approve of an all-night event, have said they'd be willing to go even if it was not all night. Lupe (a 50-year-old Hispanic woman with strong community ties) and Tracy (a divorced Caucasian woman in her late 40s who is quite vocal about how things should be done) argue that it should end early because the students and chaperones get too tired. In addition, they note that the majority of problems usually happen after 2 A.M. They suggest that the main goal of sober graduation is to get as many students as possible to attend and that means guaranteeing their safety. The other four members of the group (a Caucasian female and former school board member; a wealthy female Portuguese dairy owner who is feared in the community; a Portuguese man who is very active in the community; and a young Caucasian man employed by the school district) argue that the goal is to ensure the kids are safe *all* night. Traditionally, they add, these events have been all-night affairs. Lupe and Tracy have become increasingly adamant; they want the others to try their idea at least once to see how it would work.

You are the leader of this group. At this point, how would you stimulate creative and critical thinking in this group?

1. Offer suggestions, relevant to this committee, about how members can stimulate creative thinking.

2. Offer ways the group can critically examine the suggestions generated by their creative thinking.

Fostering Meeting-to-Meeting Improvement.   Effective group leaders spend time evaluating each meeting to discover how it could have been improved. You might ask the group itself to participate in evaluation. Usually you will privately review your notes to determine whether the major meeting goals were met and how smoothly the meeting went. Then, establish your goals for improving future meetings and adjust your own behavior accordingly to meet the group's goals.

Several studies of effective leaders have shown that good leaders adjust their behavior from one meeting to the next, depending on the specific goals of the meeting. Good leaders monitor their own and the other members' behaviors so they can modify their actions to help the group.

1. **Review personal notes of the meeting.**

Keep personal notes of important happenings during the meeting. After the meeting, ask yourself, Did we accomplish our purpose? Did everyone have a chance to participate? Did anyone hog the floor? Was the group both creative and critical in its thinking? and, most important of all, What could I personally have done to ensure a better meeting?

2. **Decide how the meeting could have been improved.**

The answers to the previous questions will guide you. For example, if Sonya believes that the group jumped on an early solution without carefully assessing the problem just to get the meeting over with, then she might decide that the group needs to look at the problem again. If TerryAnn had evaluated her meetings, she would have discovered that the group needed more direction and guidance than she was providing.

3. **Establish specific improvements as goals for the next meeting.**

After determining where the meeting could have been improved, incorporate this information into planning for the next meeting. Sonya, for example, could place the problem back on the agenda, explain to the group that she perceived a lack of critical thinking, and invite the group to assess the problem again.

4. **Adjust behavior accordingly.**

Once you, as leader, have diagnosed areas of group communication where improvement could occur and have decided what needs to be done, then you should adjust their behavior to help ensure improvement. For example, TerryAnn needed to be more clear, direct, and concise in her communication. She also needed to keep the group on track instead of letting them digress. Notice that these are *communication* behaviors (not personality characteristics) that TerryAnn should change.

We now consider specific areas in which the designated small group leader can help group members develop, a topic we explored in detail in Chapter 7.

DEVELOPING THE GROUP

One of the most important functions of the leader is to assist in the development of the group from a collection of individuals to a productive unit. This involves such things as establishing a climate of trust, promoting teamwork and cooperation, and evaluating the group's progress.

Establishing a Climate of Trust.   Groups perform more effectively when members trust one another. The following suggestions help establish a climate of trust.

1. **Establish norms that build trust.**

Norms building trust encourage respectful active listening, cooperation, confidentiality, the timely completion of assignments, and the freedom to disagree without being considered deviant. Many leaders are far too slow to speak to members who are manipulative, do poor work, or act out of self-interest harmful to the group.[13]

2. **Function as a coordinator rather than a dictator.**

Foster a climate of trust by serving the needs of the group, not by ordering people around to serve your personal interests. That way, members feel free to express themselves and to develop skills needed by the group. Ask for volunteers to do jobs for the group rather than ordering: "Cal, get the . . ."

3. **Encourage members to get to know each other.**

Usually, members trust each other and feel safe in the group if they know one another as individuals. Sometimes an unstructured social period helps create a sense of teamwork. Graduate teaching assistants in one department have a tradition of planning a float trip at the beginning of each fall semester. Social gatherings like this help people get to know each other.

10.3   Marcos and His Fraternity

Marcos was appointed chair of the service committee of his college fraternity. He and Luis were the only experienced members on the committee; the other three members were new to the fraternity. His committee was responsible for organizing the fraternity's service projects and recruiting frat members to participate. The inexperienced members were excited about working on the committee, but they were not aware of all the fraternity's activities, procedures, and past efforts. Marcos faced a challenge. He did not want to stifle the enthusiasm, dominate the group, or do most of the work for the group. On the other hand, he did not want to lose valuable time while the new members felt their way along. He preferred working on a committee where all members could contribute equally, but he believed that, at least at first, these members weren't ready to contribute fully—they needed strong direction.

He and Luis worked together between the committee meetings to establish an agenda and select some of the early goals and service activities for the committee. During these meetings, Marcos kept close control over the agenda and the discussion. He assigned specific tasks, always making sure the tasks were acceptable to members. He also encouraged newer members to contribute to the group until they could speak on their own. As he recognized that the newer members were becoming capable of acting on their own, he began to encourage members to take over more planning and decision-making responsibilities. He eventually became less involved in the details of committee work, focusing more on the process of discussion and decision making during meetings. He moved from functioning as a director to functioning as a coordinator.

Marcos recently heard about TerryAnn's problems with her service club from a disgruntled committee member. Concerned that he may not be as effective as he thinks he is, he comes to you, a buddy, for advice. He knows you are taking a small group communication course.

1. What are his strengths and what may be his weaknesses?

2. Given the information Marcos has provided and the material you have read about performing administrative duties, leading group discussions, developing the group, and managing the group's written communication, devise a list of specific questions you think are important to ask if you want to get a good handle on Marcos's situation.

Developing Teamwork and Promoting Cooperation.   Although the leader's principal responsibility is to see that the group accomplishes its task, the development of teamwork can help group members work productively. Here are suggestions you can use:

1. **Speak of *us* and *we,* rather than *I* and *you.***

   Calling the group members *we* implies commitment to the group and its values. Ask what it means if another member speaks of the group as "you."

2. **Develop a name or another symbol of group identification.**

   Such items as T-shirts, logos, "inside" jokes, and slogans can display shared identification. For example, a successful advertising agency creative group called itself the "Can-Do Team."

3. **Watch for evidence of hidden agenda items that conflict with group goals.**

   If you suspect a hidden agenda item is interfering with the group's agenda, promptly bring it to the attention of the group. Avoiding such problems makes them worse, not better.

4. **Use appropriate conflict management approaches and procedures.**

   Conflict that is allowed to proceed too long or to become personal can cause lasting damage. Help prevent this by keeping arguments focused on facts and issues and by immediately stopping members who attack another's personality or character. Look for a larger issue that can bring together two or more competing subgroups. Find a superordinate goal—one that is more important to members than their individual subgroup goals and behind which they can rally.

   Sometimes, despite the best intentions of the leader, a group becomes deadlocked. If this happens, look for a basis on which to compromise. Maybe you can synthesize parts of one person's ideas with parts of another's to create a compromise or consensus solution. Perhaps you can serve as mediator. If you have been performing your job well as the group's leader, you have remained detached from the fray. This gives you a broader perspective from which to see a solution all parties can accept. It also helps your credibility—you'll be seen as more objective and fair. We discussed conflict in detail in Chapter 9.

5. **Share rewards with the group.**

   Leaders often receive praise from the group's parent organization, but wise leaders give credit to the group. Your comments about what *the group* has done, your pride in membership, and your acknowledgment of the service provided by members foster cohesiveness and team spirit.

6. **Lighten up; share a laugh or joke with the group.**

   Don't let the discussion get so serious that people can't enjoy themselves. Humor and fantasy help reduce tensions and make people feel good about each other. Most groups take mental "work breaks" in which they digress from the task. Wise leaders let the group develop fantasy chains that enrich the group's life and that help establish shared beliefs and values. The result can be more concerted work effort in the long run. Bring the group back to the task once the joke is over or the fantasy has chained out.

MANAGING THE GROUP'S WRITTEN COMMUNICATION

Although most communication among members of a small group is oral, the group needs written messages to provide continuity from meeting to meeting, to keep the parent organization informed about its activities, and to coordinate activities with other groups. As leader, you may not actually carry out these activities, but you are responsible to see that someone performs them. The four basic categories of a group's written messages are personal notes, group records, written notices and visuals, and group reports and resolutions.

Personal Notes.   During meetings, taking notes helps the leader (and other members) keep track of what is going on. Making brief notes helps you focus your listening so you won't forget what the group is discussing. Your notes may include important facts about a problem, proposed ideas, major interpretations the group has decided on, assignments you and others have accepted, and anything else that may be important to the discussion. Figure 10.2 is an example of personal notes made during such a problem-solving discussion.

FIGURE 10.2   Example of Personal Notes

November 12, 2002—Everyone present

DISCUSSION TOPIC

What topics should we include in our class presentation on group polarization?

MAIN CRITERIA

Judy & Bill—to get an "A", info must be accurate

Bart—has to have practical application

Bev—Dr. Adams wants innovative presentation

Everybody should have a part in presenting the topic to the class

TOPICS

- Definition of group polarization (all agreed)

  Risky shift (Hal says can become a cautious shift w/ cautious members—the term is outdated)

- Exercises to demonstrate when group takes risks & when it becomes cautious—Judy says there's a bunch of these in a book she has

- Need to show how this applies in real life

- Decision Made

  Assignments: Me (applications); Judy & Bill (library research); Hal & Bev (exercises—w/ Judy's book)

Next meeting—Mon, November 18, 2002

Group Records.   A committee chair should keep careful notes, or **minutes,** of what occurs during each meeting so that accurate information can be distributed to members. A secretary or volunteer is often designated to perform this duty. In some organizations, a professional secretary attends the group's meetings specifically to take notes and prepare minutes.

Written records of each meeting are essential for all continuing groups. Otherwise, as with TerryAnn's group, members find they are redoing work, forgetting important information, failing to consider some proposals, and not completing assigned work. Without written records, members will misremember what was reported and disagree about what they decided.

Minutes of small group meetings should contain a summary of pertinent information shared during the meeting, all ideas considered by the group, any criteria agreed upon, all decisions, all assignments, and any plans or procedures for future action. Minutes begin with a heading in memo form, the time and place of the meeting, and a report of attendance. The writer signs them and a copy is sent to each member as soon as possible after the meeting. Examples of two different minute formats are shown in Figure 10.3.

Because members need to express themselves freely, some things should not be included in minutes or reports. Confidentiality should be protected. Don't report sensitive information, who proposed a course of action, how anyone voted, or who provided what information. Do include all conclusions, decisions, and assignments.

Written Notices and Visuals.   Meeting notification should go to each member in plenty of time for each to prepare. Meeting notices include the following information (see Figure 10.4):

1. Name of group and person to whom the notice is being sent.
2. Name of person sending the notice or calling the meeting.
3. Place of meeting.
4. Time meeting will begin and end.
5. Purpose of meeting and specific outcomes that must be achieved.
6. Agenda, if more than one item will be discussed, and whether the agenda is open for additional topics or problems.
7. Any specific facts, reading sources, or other preparation members may need, and special techniques or procedures to be followed.
8. If this is a one-meeting conference, a list of all who will attend (if available).

When subcommittees or individual members conduct special research for a group, they give a copy of their major findings (including a list of all sources) to all members. This may include tables of statistics, graphs, duplicated copies of print material, lists, and drawings. All are easy to produce in this age of computers and fax machines. Such visual aids are best distributed in advance of a meeting or handed out during an oral summary at the meeting. These visual aids enhance any oral report. The reports themselves can be attached to the minutes.

Reports and Resolutions.   Frequently groups must prepare written reports of their work. A president's task force may investigate and make recommendations about

FIGURE 10.3   Examples of Group Minutes Using Two Different Methods

Minutes of November 13, 2002, Meeting of Committee A (Version 1)

Committee A held a special meeting at 1:30 P.M. on Wednesday, November 13, 2002, in room 14 of the Jones Library.

Attendance: Walter Bradley, Marlynn Jones, George Smith, Barbara Trekheld, Michael Williams

Absent: Jantha Calamus, Peter Shiuoka

1. The minutes of the November 6 meeting were approved as distributed.

2. Two nominations for membership in the graduate faculty were considered. A subcommittee of Bradley and Trekheld reported that their investigation indicates that Dr. Robert Jordan met all criteria for membership. It was moved that Professor Jordan be recommended to Dean Bryant for membership in the graduate faculty. The vote was unanimously in favor.

   The nomination of Professor Andrea Long was discussed; it was concluded that she met all criteria, and that the nomination had been processed properly. It was moved that Professor Long be recommended for appointment to the graduate faculty. The motion passed unanimously.

3. Encouragement of grant activity. Discussion next centered on the question of how to encourage more faculty members to submit proposals for funding grants. Several ideas were discussed. It was moved that we recommend to President Yardley that

   a. A policy be established to grant reduced teaching loads to all professional faculty who submit two or more grant proposals in a semester.

   b. Ten percent of all grant overhead be returned to the department that obtained the grant for use in any appropriate way.

This motion was approved unanimously.

Minutes of November 13, 2002, Meeting of Committee A (Version 2)

Attendance: Walter Bradley, Marlynn Jones, George Smith, Barbara Trekheld, Michael Williams (chair)

Members absent: Jantha Calamus, Peter Shiuoka

Topic	Discussion	Actions/ recommendations
Minutes of 11/4/99	None	Approved as distributed
Nominations for graduate faculty membership	Subcommittee of Bradley and Trekheld reported that both Dr. Robert Jordan and Dr. Andrea Long meet all criteria and should be recommended to Dean Bryant for membership.	Recommendation passed unanimously, for Drs. Jordan and Long
Grant activity	Discussion centered on how to encourage faculty members to submit proposals for funding grants. After discussion of several proposals, motion was made to recommend to President Yardley that	Motion to submit the two recommendations to Pres. Yardley passed unanimously

1. Professional faculty who submit two or more grant proposals in semester be given reduced teaching loads.

2. Ten percent of all grant overhead be returned to the department that obtained the grant, to use in any appropriate way.

Respectfully submitted,

George Smith, Secretary

FIGURE 10.4	Example of a Meeting Notice

Date: Thurs, October 24, 2002

To: Curriculum Committee (Drs. Berquist, Bourhis, Drale, Jackson, Persky, Shanker, Stovall, Spicer)

From: Dr. Galanes, Chair

Re: Curriculum Committee meeting

The next meeting of the Curriculum Committee will be on Thursday, November 7, at 11:00 A.M. in Craig 320.

Purpose of meeting: We need to (1) decide what our departmental assessment's focus will be (student outcomes, student perceptions, alumni perceptions, or something else), (2) decide what areas of the department will be assessed, and (3) establish subcommittees for each area.

Bring: The assessment guidelines provided by the Center for Instructional Assessment and any other material you think is relevant.

national problems such as health care, ocean pollution, and the quality of public schooling. The end product is usually a major written report accompanied by a brief oral report, often given to the CEO and a group of executives.

The designated leader is responsible for submitting the group's report by a certain deadline, but normally one or two group members actually write the report. A first draft is given to all members for suggestions and revisions, followed by discussion and agreement on the final version. Each committee member signs the final report.

Sometimes the final written product is a resolution or motion the committee's chair makes during a meeting of the parent organization. For example, a committee to study faculty morale develops recommendations; the committee's chair moves that the faculty senate accept the recommendations. Often, members of the committee accompany the chair to the meeting of the parent organization to answer questions, make supporting speeches, and counter objections. A common format for motions and resolutions can be found in any comprehensive parliamentary manual, such as *Robert's Rules of Order Revised,* or the organization may have its own manual for such reports.

As you can see, any group's designated leader is expected to perform a variety of duties associated with the title *leader.* Far from being the person who orders others around, the leader serves the group by making sure it has what it needs.

Encouraging Distributed Leadership

In Chapters 1, 7, and this one, we encouraged you to think about group leadership in a way that may be different from how you've thought about it in the past. We suggested that you as leader encourage other group members to assume responsibility for leading the group. Distributing the leadership in this way helps you, in the long run, by using all members' abilities and talents to the fullest. It helps the other members develop leadership skills and also helps the group by making a wider scope of abilities available to serve the group.

At first, our support of distributed leadership with a democratic focus may seem to contradict our earlier support of the contingency concept of leadership. We see distributed leadership as being an ideal to strive for, but it requires a certain maturity and self-confidence on the part of members. That takes time to develop, as Marcos recognized. You can't assume, as TerryAnn did, that members are fully ready to take over and run the group! Until they achieve this high level of skill and maturity, you'll need to be astute in supplying just the right amount of direction, particularly as members try to grapple with the initial ambiguity that typically faces a newly formed group. As you can see, to be an effective leader in a variety of situations, you must perceive what is happening with the individual members and the group as a whole, and adapt your behavior accordingly. Being perceptive requires listening ability, knowledge of group processes and procedures, and analytical ability. Adapting your behavior requires mastering a variety of leader skills.

10.4   The Great Leader

> **APPLY NOW**
>
> The following quote is attributed to Chinese philosopher Lao Tse:
>
> *The wicked leader is he whom the people despise.*
>
> *The good leader is he whom the people revere.*
>
> *The great leader is he about whom the people say, "We did it ourselves."*
>
> What do you understand this quote to mean? How can a leader lead, and still have people say, "We did it ourselves"?

Peter M. Serge, "The Leader's New Work: Building Learning Organizations," *Sloan Management Review Reprint Series* 32 (fall 1990) p. 22.

We think distributed leadership is the ideal. Most groups you belong to will have a designated leader, and we are not suggesting doing away with designated leaders. We are saying that, even if a group has a designated leader, the other members have capabilities that should be developed and used in service to the group. You may not be able to reach the ideal right away; you may never even see a group that has achieved that ideal. However, distributed leadership is the best way of ensuring that everybody's talents are used and that the group receives all the leadership functions it needs to perform well.

TABLE 10.2	**Guidelines for Encouraging Distributed Leadership**

- Be perceptive; analyze the needs of the group.
- Adapt behavior to fit the needs of the group; be a completer.
- Focus primarily on task needs rather than social relationships.
- Balance your active participation with good listening.
- Express yourself clearly and concisely.
- Be knowledgeable about group processes and group techniques.

This section contains several suggestions for leading effectively in a group where leadership is distributed (see Table 10.2). These suggestions do not ask you to change your personality. Instead, they ask you to focus on your *communication behavior* and adapt it appropriately.

1. **Be perceptive; analyze the needs of the group.**

   Effective leaders understand people. They know how to help others motivate themselves to contribute their best. In part they do this by listening carefully—actively—to what is going on in the group. For example, if group members appear confused, you know that the group should spend some time clarifying the discussion. Consider the following dialogue:

Jerry:	Yeah, we've got to finish everything Monday night, the charts and all, with the easel, and get the stuff to Maryann. Our presentation on Tuesday should be pretty good.
Maryann:	[Becoming agitated and visibly upset] That's not going to give me nearly enough time to type them! I have to have them by Friday at the latest! How can you expect me to type the charts, fix the table of contents, copy the paper, and have it ready to turn in by Tuesday if I don't get the stuff before Monday night?
Sheri:	[Trying to calm Maryann but also somewhat annoyed at her tone of voice] Lighten up, Maryann. It won't take that long—we've only got two charts to do, and I can help you.
Terrell:	[The group's coordinator, sensing this argument stems from a misunderstanding] Hold on, guys. I think we're talking about two different sets of charts. If I remember right, we promised we'd get the data tables that are supposed to go into our written report to Maryann by Friday so she can type them over the weekend. But I thought Sheri and I were supposed to make the two chart posters for our class presentation on Monday night. Isn't that what we decided?

In the preceding example, Terrell senses that the argument is over a misunderstanding and attempts to clarify it for the group. Notice that he states his clarification ("If I remember right" and "Isn't that what we decided?") provisionally, so others can disagree or improve on his understanding if he has been mistaken. Terrell can perform this function for the group only because he has been paying attention and listening actively.

2. **Adapt your behavior to fit the needs of the group; be a completer.**

   Groups need different things at different times. In addition to being able to analyze your group's needs, you must be able to adapt your behavior to perform a variety of functions, but it doesn't make sense to perform functions that others are already performing well. In the previous example, if Sheri had clarified Maryann's and Jerry's misunderstanding, there would have been no reason for Terrell to do so. Terrell jumped in because clarification was needed and no one else was providing it. He served as a completer by "plugging in the holes" for the others.

3. **Focus primarily on task needs rather than social relationships.**

   The person most likely to emerge as a leader is a task-oriented individual who clearly helps the group achieve its goal. This doesn't mean you should never tend to relationship issues, but it does mean that keeping one eye on the task should be your main focus as designated leader. This helps you make the best use of the members' time and provide the appropriate amount of coordination and structure for your group.

4. **Balance your active participation with good listening.**

   Emergent leaders are active group participants; your fellow members expect you to take an interest and contribute. However, balance your talking with good listening so you don't dominate the group. Don't feel you have to comment on everything. Let the discussion flow freely without overcontrolling it. Be a role model for effective group participation.

5. **Express yourself clearly and concisely.**

   When you do talk, get to the heart of the matter being discussed, clarify, and summarize what is being said. Don't ramble; be well organized, coherent, and relevant. The ability to verbalize the group's goals, procedures, ideas, values, and ideals is an important leadership skill.

6. **Be knowledgeable about group processes and group techniques.**

   This point may seem obvious, but many designated group leaders are clueless about how to lead a group. Too often, a committee head is appointed without ensuring that the individual has had adequate training to perform well. You may be willing to do the job but, if you don't know what you are doing, you, like TerryAnn, can make a shambles of what could have been a productive group. To be effective, know what to expect and what types of functions groups need to perform well.

   You also should be familiar with a variety of small group techniques, including computer-based group support systems, and suggest them when appropriate. Using GSS successfully depends on several factors, such as whether the group has good facilitative leadership with a leader sensitive to group dynamics.[14] Sometimes members can become caught up with the "bells and whistles" of GSS and lose sight of its purpose. Effective group leaders use these computer programs wisely and help members overcome their anxiety or lack of interest in computer technology.

Ethical Guidelines for Group Leaders

As a leader, your behavior should serve as a model for other members to follow. Hackman and Johnson suggest that leaders be held to the highest possible ethical standards.[15] We offer the following guidelines to help you maintain the highest ethical standards as a group leader (see Table 10.3).

1. **Do not lie or intentionally send deceptive or harmful messages.**

    Not only should leaders tell the members the truth, but they should hold truth to be the standard for the group's decision making. That means, for instance, that you should welcome all relevant information in the group, whether it supports your preference or not. It also means you must be willing to subject your ideas to the same standards of evaluation as the others' ideas.

2. **Place your concern for the group and for others ahead of your own personal gain.**

    In addition to willingly committing your time and energy to serving the group, never take advantage of your power as leader for personal gain or advantage. Leaders' hidden agendas are as counterproductive to the group as members' hidden agendas are.

3. **Be respectful of and sensitive to the other members.**

    Groups are effective problem solvers because several heads are better than one, but only if the members feel free to share their thoughts and ideas within the group. Never do anything intentionally to ridicule members or their ideas or to discourage their participation.

TABLE 10.3   **Ethical Guidelines for Group Leaders**

- Do not lie or intentionally send deceptive or harmful messages.

- Place your concern for the group and for others ahead of your own personal gain.

- Be respectful of and sensitive to the other members.

- Stand behind the other members when they carry out policies and actions approved by the leader and the group.

- Treat members with equal respect, regardless of sex, ethnicity, or social background.

- Establish clear policies that all group members are expected to follow.

- Follow the group rules, just as you expect the others to do.

4. **Stand behind the other members when they carry out policies and actions approved by the leader and the group.**

   Don't try to enhance your own position by betraying your fellow members. If something goes wrong with a decision the group has made, assume personal responsibility for the decision.

10.1   Your Needs or the Team's Needs?

In 1971, after the *Swann v. Charlotte-Mecklenburg Board of Education* decision that permitted busing to achieve racial integration, schools were required to become integrated immediately.* In Alexandria, Virginia, the previously all-white high school was closed and students were absorbed into the previously all-black school. Bob Yardley, who had been the winning, successful head football coach of the all-white school, expected to be named head football coach of the integrated school. However, Horace Bond, a young African-American coach new to the community, was offered the position. At first reluctant to accept the offer, Bond was encouraged by town leaders; he eventually accepted. Bond considered for a long time what he might do to bring his black and white players together—particularly when neither set of students wanted to be brought together! He offered an assistant coaching position to Bob Yardley.

If you were Bob Yardley, what would you do? You think you should have had the head coaching spot, and it's not fair that you didn't get the offer. But you also think that achieving racial integration is a positive step and you want to help the school achieve it. You have several choices.

- You could accept, refuse, accept and try to sabotage Coach Bond's efforts, and so forth. List at least 5 options in this situation.

- Assume you decided to accept Coach Bond's offer. What would be your communication behavior toward him? Respectful? Disdainful? How would you show your feelings through your communication behavior?

- You truly believe the top spot should have been yours, but assume that you've decided you want to make a positive contribution here. What would you do? How would you behave toward Bond and the players?

- How would you describe the ethical dilemma you face and on what basis would you make your ethical decision?

*This story is used with permission of Robin Swanson. Names of the schools and individuals have been changed. The actual outcome was positive—the coaches found a way to work together, the players were forced to operate as a team (although they initially resisted), and the team won the regional championship in an undefeated season.

5. **Treat members with equal respect, regardless of sex, ethnicity, or social background.**

   Respond to members without regard to their sex, ethnicity, social background, age, or other personal or social attributes. Members should be valued for their contributions to the group, not their sex or race. As an ethical leader, minimize status differences to encourage everyone's participation.

6. **Establish clear policies that all group members are expected to follow.**

   Group rules and procedures should be clearly understood. Group members should be encouraged to participate in establishing the group's procedures and policies.

7. **Follow the group rules, just as you expect the others to do.**

   Because of your status as the group leader, you may be given some leeway to violate rules others are expected to follow. Do not abuse this privilege. If others are expected to arrive on time, so should you. If you reprimand members for failing to complete assignments, make sure your own assignments are completed well and on time. As much as possible, be a model member for the group.

As Lao Tse said: "The great leader is he about whom the people say, 'We did it ourselves.' " Will you be that kind of leader?

10.1   Group Leaders and the Use of Technology

Go to **www.mhhe.com/ adamsgalanes** for additional weblink activities.

MEDIA AND TECHNOLOGY

This chapter has introduced a number of leadership functions. The leader must facilitate communication before, during, and after meetings; must ensure that appropriate materials are provided to group members; and must ensure that a historical record of the meeting, usually in the form of minutes, is kept.

A variety of forms of technology can help group leaders manage information. For example, e-mail can be used to disseminate agendas and other written material before meetings; Web pages can be used to display minutes of previous meetings; and computer networks can be used to store documents and other materials used by the group.

For groups with virtually unlimited access to technology, the leader or a knowledgeable group member must help coordinate how technology will be used. If you were designing a "wish list" of technology resources for a group you belong to (for example, a study group, a student group, a work team, etc.), what would you want? You group may already have access to e-mail, for example. How would you advise group members to use e-mail? What other technology resources would be useful for your group and how would you suggest using them?

- Three common myths about leadership are that leaders have special traits that followers don't, that there is an ideal leadership style, and that leaders get other people to do all the work for them.

- The functional approach to leadership encourages all group members to perform whatever functions a group needs and the contingency approach assumes that the type of leadership a group needs depends on the group's situation.

- Both approaches suggest that the leader serve as a completer, supplying whatever necessary functions the other members are not providing.

- Group members expect leaders to perform four broad types of tasks: providing administrative services for a group, structuring a group's discussions, helping a group develop as a team, and managing a group's written messages.

- Distributed leadership, in which each member takes responsibility for providing leadership services to a group, is an ideal worth striving for.

- Ethical leaders tell the truth, are sensitive to and respectful of others, support the other members, establish clear rules that they expect to follow themselves, and put group concerns ahead of their own personal gain.

1. View Part 1 (Leadership) of the videotape "Communicating Effectively in Small Groups" and discuss the following questions:

    a. What functions did the leader perform?

    b. How effective was each function? How appropriate?

    c. Were there any points during the discussion where the leader failed to supply needed leadership service? Did anyone else step in to provide it? Was the group hurt?

    d. On a scale of 1 to 10, how effective was the leader? Why do you say this?

2. Select five members from your class to act as a problem-solving group. Assign one of the members to be the leader of the group. Ask the group to tackle the following problem:

    The Teacher's Dilemma
    An English teacher in a consolidated, rural school has had extensive dramatic experience. She was chosen by the principal to direct the first play in the new school. The play will be the first major production for the school. Its success may determine whether there will be any future plays pro-duced at the school, and, if well done, it could bring prestige to both the teacher and the school. As a result, the teacher is exhausting every means available to her to make the play an artistic success. She has chosen all the cast except for the leading female part. The principal's daughter wants the part, and the principal told the teacher he really wants his daughter to have it. But she is a poor actress and would jeopardize the success of the show. Tentatively, the teacher has chosen someone who should do an excellent job in the role, but the principal has implied that if his daughter is not selected, he will appoint another director in the future. What should she do?

    Place the group of five in the middle of the class and surround it with the rest of the class members. They are to watch this group's discussion and to evaluate the leader on his or her ability to lead the group discussion. How well did he or she do? On what do you base your evaluation?

3. Form small groups of four to six members. Discuss the "ideal" group leader. Each group is to address not only the specific duties leaders should perform, but also the communicative

skills leaders should exhibit and the ethical principles they should both exhibit and uphold. Each group should create a "Guidelines for Group Leaders" manual that could be distributed to student leaders at your school. Discuss each group's guidelines to determine which ones tend to be common to all groups. Why do you think these tend to be the most common?

Go to **www.mhhe.com/adamsgalanes** and **www.mhhe.com/groups** for Self-Quizzes and weblinks.

KEY TERMS and CONCEPTS

contingency concept	functional concept	minutes
distributed leadership		

www.mhhe.com/adamsgalanes
Use the flashcards and crossword puzzles on the Online Learning Center to further your knowledge of these key terms.

PART FOUR

FOUR

Small Group Public Presentations

J ust as it is important to figure out the leadership roles and who will perform them, a group must also assess its strengths and difficulties when it comes to oral presentations. Up to now, we have discussed the complex nature of small group interactions as they occur within group meetings. The successful development of small group interaction helps ensure a more professional and successful oral presentation by individuals and group members. In Part 4, we discuss a three-step process to prepare your group's oral presentation, by focusing on the planning, organizing, and presenting stages of these presentations.

Planning, Organizing, and Presenting Small Group Oral Presentations

CHAPTER OBJECTIVES

After reading this chapter you should be able to:

1. Explain the different choices group members can make in the planning, organizing, and presenting stages.

2. Compare and contrast the three types of public discussions.

3. Discuss the role of the moderator in any type of public discussion.

4. Explain the essential parts of the introduction, the body, and the conclusion of an oral presentation.

5. Compare and contrast the four methods of presenting a speech.

6. Describe and apply relevant criteria to evaluate an oral presentation.

Food for the Homeless

CASE 11.1

Six students in a small group communication class spent more than half their semester discussing the problems faced by a local homeless shelter. One especially significant problem they noted was the great reduction in contributions, especially of food, during the summer. The shelter seemed to get more than enough donations during the fall and winter holiday seasons, when everyone seemed to be in a giving mood, but contributions dropped significantly during the summer. As part of the solution section of their report, the students recommended a way of getting more edible leftovers from local restaurants to the shelter, a program they had discovered already in operation in a few other communities across the nation.

The students' report earned them an A. Their instructor was so impressed that he showed the report to a close friend, the president of the local restaurant association. She, too, thought the students were on to something and invited them to make a 15-minute presentation about their project at the association's monthly meeting. The students were excited that their work might become something more than a classroom exercise and that they might be able to help the homeless shelter, but they did not know how they should respond to this invitation. Should they let their chair represent them? Should they all go and each say a few words? Should they let their most talkative member make the presentation or the one who seemed to be the best critical thinker? The meeting was coming quickly and they did not know what to do.

The Planning Stage

The moment your group is informed that a presentation will be needed you should immediately schedule a planning meeting to work through important details. Planning to speak to an audience requires advance assessment of the upcoming speaking situation. The most important areas of assessment include: your group's audience, occasion, purpose, topic, member strengths/difficulties, and supplemental logistics. This initial assessment as well as plenty of preparation is essential for a smooth production. In this section, we look at each area of assessment and describe different types of oral presentations that groups often deliver.

YOUR AUDIENCE

Assessing your audience is important for creating a comfortable speaking environment, not only for your audience, but also for your group. **Audience analysis** is a systematic approach to gathering as much information as possible about the audience. The more

GLOSSARY

Audience Analysis

Studying the unique character of who will receive a presentation in order to adapt how a speech will be delivered and what will be presented

information you know about your audience members, the more you can tailor the message to their needs. Once you are aware of *who* your audience is, you can determine the knowledge they may or may not have about the topic you are considering for discussion. As a group, you should answer specific questions about your audience. Will you be speaking only to your class or will your instructor be part of the audience? Will it be the entire membership of your fraternity or just the executive committee? Will it be people you know or will most of them be strangers? Will the audience members be there voluntarily or is someone forcing them to attend? The mood of your audience can depend on whether or not your audience feels required to be there.

A captive or required audience member is going to need a presentation with lots of enthusiasm and reasons why she or he should listen. What can you add to their knowledge or attitude about your topic? You do not want to bore an audience by repeating what they already know, nor do you want to talk over their heads about complex issues they don't quite understand. Don't hesitate to ask if you can observe, interview, or survey your audience before the speaking engagement. Remember, for more opportunities of audience inclusion find out as much as possible about the audience before you start writing your presentation.

YOUR OCCASION

Depending on who has invited your group to speak, you may be able to get much of your information about the audience and the occasion from this lead contact person. Ask if you may visit the facility and room you will be speaking in before the event occurs, check and recheck the time of the event as well as the major purpose and context of this occasion. How many people are expected? Where will you be placed in the speaking lineup and how much control do you have over your setting? Before your group begins serious purpose and topic planning, make sure you clarify why you have been asked to speak to this audience and whether or not there is a specific goal that needs to be met.

YOUR PURPOSE

Typically a speaker wants to have a general purpose of informing, persuading, or entertaining an audience. Knowing clearly what you are trying to accomplish is an essential step in any effective presentation. If your group is unaware of the purpose of your presentation, how can the audience members make sense of what they are supposed to do with the information you have presented? The **informative speech** is used when your group wants to educate, enlighten, or distribute information. For example, if your group is reporting on a new community service group that has just moved into the area and you are offering information that describes who they are, where they come from and what they offer, your purpose is to inform. If your group wanted the audience to donate time or money to this community service organization, your purpose would be to persuade.

A **persuasive speech** is defined by the call to action. Your purpose, as a group, is to get your audience to do something with the information you have given them. Another example of a persuasive purpose would be trying to influence your fraternity or sorority to try a new fund-raising technique. You want your audience members to agree with you and adopt your suggestion(s).

On occasion, you may be asked to give an **entertainment speech** such as if you are asked to wrap up the year's events or "roast" a colleague at the annual company picnic. You want the audience members to enjoy themselves, to laugh and have a good time.

GLOSSARY

Informative Speech

A speech given with the primary purpose of teaching something to an audience

Persuasive Speech

A type of speech containing a call to action

Entertainment Speech

A speech with the main purpose of amusing the audience

Sometimes it is hard to get an audience to warm up to jokes and different types of humor, so be prepared if you do not get the response you want. Also, be aware that most jokes are directed at or said at the expense of others, so be very careful that your humor is appropriate and tasteful, and does not turn off audience members. What is funny on an HBO comedy show may not be appropriate for your audience. You're speaking to make a connection with your audience, not to distance them.

Although your purpose may be to entertain, this speech could easily inform or persuade as well. We have heard speeches on many serious issues that were delivered in a thoughtful and entertaining manner.

YOUR SUBJECT OR TOPIC

As soon as you determine the general purpose, establish a specific subject or topic of your presentation. Your instructor or employer often will tell you what to talk about, but sometimes, the choice of a specific topic will be left up to you. This step is often one of the most difficult. Where do you start? The best topics come from your own experiences, beliefs, or skills. As a group, sit down and brainstorm different topic ideas from your own individual experiences. What are your interests, hobbies, and subjects you enjoy, read about, and find interesting? Often you are selected to speak because of some expertise you possess. You can also ask whoever asked you to speak which of several topics the audience would find most appealing.

Undoubtedly there will be a time limit for your presentation. You may have 5 minutes, 20 minutes, or you may be told simply to "be brief" or to "fill us in." Keep your time limit in mind when selecting what to say about your subject. Inexperienced speakers often make the mistake of coming to the podium with enough material for two or three speeches. As a result, the audience gets restless or your instructor tells you to stop so that others in the class may have time to speak. Don't try to cover everything you know about a subject; select those matters that are most important to you and of special interest to your audience.

MEMBER STRENGTHS AND DIFFICULTIES

Knowing the strengths and difficulties that your members may have with oral presentations will help in the organizing and presenting stages of presentation development. What information does each individual group member have about the topic that has been chosen for discussion? What contacts or research leads do you have as a group? What is the attitude or feeling of the group about the topic? After assessing the strengths of group members, deciding who will present different points will be easier. Also, if a question-and-answer period is established after your presentation, knowing member's strengths will help in determining who is best qualified to answer the specific questions that are asked.

In addition to looking at the strengths of the group's members, the group also should focus on member difficulties in making oral presentations. Member anxiety can prevent a confident and effective delivery. If your group does an early assessment of this communication apprehension, it will be easier to combat the problem. A group must not rely on the stereotype that "any leader can lead an effective oral presentation." Anxiety is normal and may be experienced in different ways. Just because your group leader or president has no problem speaking to *your* group as a whole doesn't mean she or he will be able to speak to a group that may be larger or unknown to the speaker. Knowing a member's difficulty with public speaking will allow your group to organize different presenting strategies that take the focus off of one person. This knowledge will also be a helpful reminder that your group should practice the delivery to ease tensions.

SUPPLEMENTAL LOGISTICS

Near the end of your planning stage your group should be more knowledgeable about what you need. Will you need supplies to set up your speaking environment? Are you using a visual aid? What will you need to run this visual aid properly (e.g., TV, VCR, laptop computer, projector, audio player, slide machine, etc.)? Speakers often forget a simple item, such as tape, and end up worrying about the poster that will not stand up straight instead of focusing on the words that are just as important as the visual aid. Do not expect a member of your audience, your teacher, or a contact person to provide you with these items. It is your responsibility to plan and remember these essential supplemental tools for your presentation. It never hurts to be overprepared.

Take for example the community service story earlier in the chapter. If your group hasn't gone the extra mile to find pamphlets, booklets, handouts, buttons, balloons, fact sheets, or other items that this homeless shelter has for distribution, then you may be missing out on updated information. Many organizations would be happy to have a volunteer group inform others about their needs and services, and your presentation would look that much more professional because you obtained original, from-the-source, information about your topic.

TYPES OF GROUP ORAL PRESENTATIONS

Once you have completed your presentation assessment, as a group, you must decide which presentation format best fits the purpose and occasion of your presentation. These formats allow for differing viewpoints to be expressed and are often followed by comments and questions from the audience. The three most common group presentation formats are the panel discussion, symposium, and forum (see Table 11.1).

A **panel dicussion** is a public interaction between a small number of people, often selected because of their competence and knowledge about a topic and usually holding conflicting viewpoints. The purpose of a panel is to make the audience more aware of a significant topic or to persuade them to act in a certain way (e.g., vote for a specific issue or candidate). For example, your group may be asked by your instructor to serve as a panel and explain your semester project and conclusions to the rest of your class.

The procedure to follow for a panel discussion includes the following:

1. Select a **moderator** to maintain order, see that all the major issues are covered, and ensure that everyone gets to speak. The moderator introduces the members of the panel and keeps the discussion moving by calling on speakers as necessary. The moderator acts as a conversational traffic cop, directing questions to the appropriate panelists and clarifying issues and statements as necessary. The moderator makes appropriate opening and closing remarks and directs any subsequent audience participation.

2. Before the discussion, make an outline of all the important points the group wants to cover and decide in what order to cover them. Follow this outline closely during the panel discussion.

GLOSSARY

Panel Discussion

One of three kinds of group public discussions in which panel members often bring different points of view to the discussion

Moderator

A participant in a public group presentation whose main responsibility is to regulate the discussion and guide any audience participation

TABLE 11.1	Types of Group Presentations	
Panel: Conversation among experts	**Symposium: Individual uninterrupted presentations**	**Forum: Questions and comments from audience**
Topics outlined in advance.	Panelists discuss different aspects of topic.	Different viewpoints encouraged.
Controversy encouraged.	No interaction among panelists.	Questions directed at individuals or at entire group
Moderator as traffic cop.	Moderator introduces topic and panelists.	Moderator selects audience participants

3. Make appropriate physical arrangements:
   a. Seat panelists so they can see each other and have eye contact with the audience; a semicircle is appropriate.
   b. Seat panelists at a table or desk so it is easy for them to write notes.
   c. Identify panelists with a name card on the table in front of them or their names on a blackboard behind them. The audience can then address questions to specific panelists easily.
   d. If the discussion is to be held in a large auditorium, place microphones on the table for the panelists to share. If audience participation will follow, strategically locate at least one standup microphone in the auditorium.
   e. Make provisions for panelists to present visual aids. Provide an easel or chalkboard that is easy to reach and will not block the view of the audience or panel.
4. The panelists should not hesitate to disagree with each other, but should do so politely. Even when they are not talking, the audience can see them, so they should refrain from inappropriate nonverbal communication.

A **symposium** is much more structured than a panel discussion. Instead of a relatively free interchange of ideas, the topic is divided into segments and each discussant presents an uninterrupted speech on a portion of the topic. The purpose of a symposium is similar to that of a panel: to enlighten an audience on a subject of importance. For example, on September 11, 2001, after the horrific attacks on the World Trade Center in New York City, Governor George Pataki and Mayor Rudolph Giuliani and other New York dignitaries presented a news conference to disseminate information to the public about the recent terrorist events. After these attacks, New York and the rest of the world wanted and needed information in a quick, controlled manner. This symposium allowed each presenter to deliver information in an uninterrupted format. Most symposiums are usually followed by a forum, which allows the audience to question the

GLOSSARY

Symposium

One of three kinds of group public discussions in which participants deliver uninterrupted speeches on a selected topic

panelists and permits the discussants to answer these questions and comment on each other's presentations. In the New York City press conference, reporters asked questions after the concluding remarks, leaving time for each member to comment from his or her own expertise. For example, Mayor Giuliani provided information from a city perspective, working hard to unite his community and disperse information, while Governor Pataki expressed what the state could be providing and how he was working with the President and other authorities to keep events running smoothly. Procedures for a symposium are as follows:

1. Select a moderator to introduce the speakers, introduce the topic, and make concluding remarks.

2. Select a small group of experts to present different aspects of the issue. Because each individual presentation is uninterrupted, make sure there will not be much repetition among the speakers.

3. As with the panel presentation, appropriate physical arrangements should be made.

A **forum discussion** allows members of an audience for a speech, symposium, panel discussion, debate, or other public presentation an opportunity to comment on what they have heard and to ask questions of the speakers. All sides of the question should be given an equal amount of presentation time, and no speaker should be allowed to monopolize the floor. The moderator's role is crucial. Some suggestions for the moderator are:

1. Let audience members know that a forum will follow the panel or symposium so they can prepare their questions or comments.

2. Make sure everyone understands any special rules of the forum segment. How will audience members be recognized? They might raise their hands or step forward to an audience microphone. Will speakers from the audience be allowed to ask a follow-up question? Will someone who has not spoken have preference over someone who has already spoken? If there is a time limit for questions, make sure it is announced and followed.

11.1   What Type of Group Presentation Should the Group Make to the Restaurant Association?

APPLY NOW

Form groups of about six people and discuss how you feel about making oral presentations. Next, pretend that you are the members of the discussion group described in Case 11.1 and decide how you would respond to the invitation from the restaurant association.

1. Would you prefer to work together and put on a panel or a symposium? If so, whom would you select to be the moderator? Why?

2. Would you prefer to send a single representative? If so, which of you would you send? Why?

3. Compare your group's answers to these questions with those of the other groups in your class. How do you account for differences and similarities?

3. Make sure everyone knows when the forum will end and do not accept questions once that time has been reached. Offer a warning before the last question or two.

4. Try to ensure that a diversity of views is offered. Ask for comments opposed to those that have just been expressed. On a very controversial issue, the moderator might deliberately alternate between a spokesperson from one side and then from the other.

5. Make sure everyone can hear a question or comment. If necessary, repeat it for the audience.

6. Following the last question or comment, offer a brief summary and thank everyone for their participation

The Organizing Stage

The success of the organizing stage depends on how well group members interact and listen to one another. If the group allows one person to take the lead, expecting that this person will plan and organize the presentation, many problems will arise. Not only will only one person know what is going to be discussed, but also resentment on both sides may arise. As with every stage, it is important to have every member present during the organizing stage. In this section on organization, we focus on the importance of delegating member duties, we explain different types of verbal and visual materials that the group can use, and we provide a speaker's blueprint for organizing these materials and the presentation.

DELEGATE DUTIES

Although the delegation of duties may sound like a function of the leader, this is not always the case. After assessing the strengths and difficulties of each member, it is important to determine where each member feels most comfortable and where his or her presentation strength has the best fit. If you don't speak up at this crucial time of organizing, you might be stuck with a job that you don't know how to perform or have no desire to do. When presenting on specific areas, examine the different backgrounds/experiences of your members and analyze where their strength lies. Think about the different majors in a college classroom. If these students had to build a presentation about the parking problem on their campus, which areas of the presentation would be best delegated to whom? For example, math majors could demonstrate, with the use of numbers, car/space ratios or problems with funding. History majors could give background to this ongoing problem. An art major would be our first choice when deciding on visual aids, and communication majors might have the duty of surveying students and administration on solutions to this problem.

Knowing each group member's responsibilities will help when you plan speaking duties and each member's order in the presentation. After you are aware of who is speaking when and about what, then you want to discuss who will obtain verbal and visual aid materials. Who will be required to set up the TV/VCR, turn the lights off during the slide show, set up a meeting with the American Red Cross? Each duty is extremely important to the success of the group and its presentation and should be planned before the day of the event.

GATHER VERBAL AND VISUAL MATERIALS

Verbal Materials.   Once your group is aware of each member's duties, you can now conduct much more focused research on each person's item for discussion. Often speakers will try to approach the audience with only the information they know, without obtaining supporting material. Listed are three of the most important types of verbal supporting materials: examples, statistics, and statements by authorities (testimony).

- **Examples:** Aristotle said that examples become "witnesses and a witness is everywhere persuasive."[1] Examples are used in inductive reasoning, where a generalization is drawn from looking at a number of specific instances. Examples can range from detailed factual ones (the story of a real victim of rape complete with dialogue, names, and dates) to undeveloped factual examples (a listing of the countries in the world where war is presently occurring) to hypothetical ones (how much a dollar will be worth in 10 years given a certain rate of inflation). You should choose typical examples and offer enough to make your point believable.

- **Statistics:** Statistics are the use of numbers or quantification to explain or support your position. Audience members can be easily confused by statistics, so make your statistics clear and meaningful. It is hard to imagine how large a country is if the speaker only tells us that it is 200,000 square miles in area. More helpful is a comparison: about the size of California and Oregon combined. To emphasize how large the state budget in California was in 2000 ($61.53 billion), point out that to spend that much, the state had to spend $168.5 million a day, $7 million per hour, or $19,511 per second.

- **Testimony:** Some people are recognized as authorities on certain issues. To support your position you may want to quote directly or paraphrase what these authorities have said or written about your topic. Obtain this from library research, interviews, or over the Internet. The group mentioned in Case 11.1 got useful materials from interviewing the director of the homeless shelter and from newspaper articles about similar shelters across the country.

Three common types of testimony are: lay, expert, and celebrity. *Lay testimony* is a statement taken from an ordinary individual. Information that is reported by a person who has special training or knowledge about the topic is *expert testimony*. A person who is famous would offer *celebrity testimony*. Let's imagine that your group has decided to give an informative presentation on tips for a long-lasting happy marriage. Who might you interview for lay, expert, and celebrity testimony? Think about the problems that might arise if you chose testimony from someone who is known too well by the audience. For example, picking Tom Cruise as your celebrity testimony might cause problems. Although Tom Cruise might offer interesting tips for your presentation, the public knowledge of his divorce might taint his message.

The bottom line when assessing verbal supporting material is to be aware of the attitudes that your audience might have around your research—who or what is seen as more credible?

Visual Materials.   Look also for visual materials to keep the audience's interest. Keep in mind what successful attorneys know: a visual aid helps your audience remember your main points. Most lawyers know that juries pay closer attention, understand technical points better, and remember more when oral testimony is coupled with a visual prop. Many will never forget the images of Johnnie Cochran slipping on the leather glove while repeating, "If it doesn't fit, you must acquit" in the courtroom while he was defending O.J. Simpon on trial for murder. If visual images were not important we would not have an obsession with televisions. Imagine listening to your news, sports, and favorite television programming only on the radio. Now that you have a better understanding of the importance of these images, here are a number of possibilities that can enhance your presentation.

- **Object:** If what you are speaking about is small enough, bring it with you. A small animal is a very effective prop if your talk is about birth control for pets or overcrowding at animal shelters. If your subject is too large or noisy to bring with you, use a model or picture instead.

- **Model:** A plastic model of the object can allow us to see what you are talking about when the real object is too large. The Concorde will be unable to land on your campus, but a model can easily be displayed on a small table in the front of the classroom.

- **Picture or video:** A photograph, slide, or videotape can focus the audience's attention on your topic. To show the problem of traffic congestion in your city, take a video of rush hour on a busy street, for instance. Slide shows need to be planned and rehearsed well in advance of the performance. Your group does not want to be known as the group with the upside-down slides.

- **Map:** Most Americans' knowledge of geography is weak. Don't assume just because you know where a city is, every one in your audience will, too. Give them a map of the place itself and show it in relation to other familiar points of interest.

- **Transparency:** Putting an outline of your presentation on an overhead projector allows the audience to see your main points and relieves you of having to use the chalkboard. Make sure the projector is centered with your screen and reveal only part of the outline at a time to keep the listeners focused on what you are saying and not looking ahead to what comes next. If too much information is given, in the form of an outline, audience members will wonder why you are reading to them and get quickly bored. Never add every detail of your speech on the outline; include only the main points so the audience has a map to follow along.

- **Chart:** Charts are especially useful for showing statistics. Numbers are sometimes hard to follow in a speech, especially when there are a lot of them. Make it easy for your listeners by putting the figures on a chart. If you are going to compare statistics, consider making a pie chart to demonstrate percentages, a bar graph to exhibit comparisons, and/or a line graph to illustrate increases.

- **Handout:** Many items mentioned earlier can be put on a handout and given to the audience before the presentation begins. If you give an outline, leave some blanks so the listeners can take notes and stay involved with your presentation. Don't forget to look into free handouts that might be provided by local organizations or businesses.

11.1   Using Presentation Technology

Go to **www.
mhhe.com/
adamsgalanes** for
additional weblink
activities.

MEDIA AND TECHNOLOGY

Presentation software is now becoming a standard tool for speakers while presenting information to audiences. You have likely had at least one if not several teachers use PowerPoint as a visual aid during lectures. The pervasiveness of this type of technology has led many public speaking professionals to question whether multimedia visual aids help or hinder speakers.

Based on your own experience, what are some effective and ineffective strategies used by speakers when integrating PowerPoint or other multimedia tools into presentations? Do some teachers use this technology better than others? Can there be "too much" multimedia in a presentation? In what ways do multimedia tools dramatically improve some presentations? What strategies should you and your group members use to maximize the benefits of multimedia presentation tools while at the same time minimizing the disadvantages?

If you would like to learn more about using Microsoft PowerPoint visit: *http://www.actden.com/pp/index.htm.*

- **Chalkboard:** Use the board only to illustrate something you are saying at the same time. For example, if you use an unfamiliar technical term, write it on the board. But audiences should not have to watch you make a chart on the board of the increase in automobile accidents over the past 30 years. Make a chart of this the night before and have it ready to go when you get to that part of your speech.

- **Multimedia:** Presentation software for your computer, such as Microsoft PowerPoint or Adobe Persuasion, can make your presentation polished and professional. You can program everything from charts and slides to video clips with sound for presentation in your speech. You can even create a link to the Internet that the audience can view on your screen. You will need access to a television monitor, a computer-projection table, or an LCD panel that can be placed on a regular overhead projector.

There are a number of do's and don'ts to keep in mind when using visual aids. First, personally make sure that any equipment you are using is in operating order before the presentation. Be prepared to give the speech even if your equipment fails. Second, make sure the visual is large enough for those in the back of the room to see easily. A Polaroid snapshot may picture exactly what you want to show, but unless it is blown up, even the front row may have difficulty seeing it. In addition, hold your visual up or tape it up long enough for everyone to see. Otherwise, someone looking away momentarily may miss the visual. Third, practice with the visual. Know exactly when you are going to use it in your speech. Students have been known to prepare visual aids and in their nervousness and excitement, they forget to show their hard work. Fourth, don't pass anything around during your presentation. Your audience's attention will be on the object itself or on the person handing the material to them rather than on you. Pass something out before you begin or tell your listeners that they will receive it after you have concluded. Fifth, use a visual aid only if it pertains to your speech. Although visual aids can make a great contribution to your presentation, this same visual aid will seem "thrown in" or "in the way" if it has no relationship to the topic.

ORGANIZE MATERIALS AND PRESENTATION

The verbal and visual information you have gathered will be a valuable asset as you plan the organization and writing of your presentation. Look at this step of organizing your materials as drawing a road map of how the audience should follow your speech. As with any road map, directions must be clear for the audience to understand how and why you are taking them through your chosen topic. Every speech should have an introduction, a body, and a conclusion (see Table 11.2). Plan to get the audience's attention, explain what you are going to be talking about, talk about it, and then summarize what you have said.

Introduction.   An **introduction** has three essential elements: an attention step, a need step, and a thesis statement. First, your goal is to motivate your audience to listen. This is called the *attention step,* and you can choose from a number of ways to capture an audience's attention.

1. **Use humor.**

   One way of getting an audience to listen to you is to make them laugh. However, be careful if you use this approach. First, what you say must be funny to others, not just to you. Preview the joke or story to other people before you use it in your presentation. If your friends enjoy it, chances are your audience will also. The humor must be in good taste. You do not want to offend anyone. You want favorable attention, with people wanting to listen to you. Don't risk alienating anyone by telling a story that is going to offend. Finally, your humor should be relevant to your topic or to the audience and occasion. Something that David Letterman said the night before may be humorous, but if it is not related to what you want to talk about, find something more appropriate and relevant.

2. **Ask a question.**

   A second way of getting attention is by asking the members of the audience a question. If you are going to talk about parking problems on your campus, ask, "How many of you have been late to a class because you could not find a close place to park?" or "How many of you have gotten a parking ticket from the campus Gestapo this semester?" If you want an answer, tell them how to respond: "Please raise your hand." However, don't make your question so personal that you won't get an accurate response. "How many of you use cocaine on a regular basis?" will probably get a laugh, but no hands will go up. Finally, use the information as a transition into the topic of your speech: "That's what I thought. Too many of us are spending too much money on parking tickets when the university should be building more parking structures." You must be able to use any answer as a transition. If no one raised a hand, say something like, "Well, you guys are lucky. In my research I've found too many of us spending . . ."

   A rhetorical question is a question that the speaker asks, but does not want the audience to answer aloud. The speaker will answer the question as part of the speech: "Is there any way to stop college students from binge drinking? I think

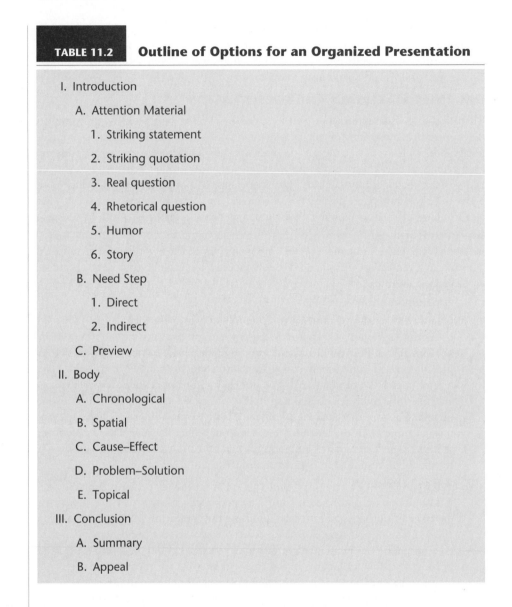

TABLE 11.2   **Outline of Options for an Organized Presentation**

I. Introduction

   A. Attention Material

      1. Striking statement

      2. Striking quotation

      3. Real question

      4. Rhetorical question

      5. Humor

      6. Story

   B. Need Step

      1. Direct

      2. Indirect

   C. Preview

II. Body

   A. Chronological

   B. Spatial

   C. Cause–Effect

   D. Problem–Solution

   E. Topical

III. Conclusion

   A. Summary

   B. Appeal

MHHE.com/ groups
Using the Net to find quotations.

there is and today I am going to offer you three practical solutions to what seems to be a growing problem at our school and at other colleges across the country." The audience will think about the question, but the speaker will provide the answer.

3. Make a striking statement.

Say something at the start of your speech to grab the audience's attention and make them want to listen. Saying, "I can guarantee you an A in this course and in every other course you take this semester" will probably gain the attention of every student in your class. Likewise, "Our division has been wasting at least $50,000 a year for the past three years" will gain the attention of your employer. You have to be able to carry out your promise in the rest of your speech, but you can be sure that for the first few minutes, at least, people will be listening to you. Another good example of a striking statement is the tag line used by news programs or talk shows to get you to stay tuned to an upcoming segment. This statement should make your audience feel like they want and need to listen to what your group has to say during the presentation.

4. **Offer a striking quotation.**

Giving a vivid quotation can attract attention. For example, if your group has been doing research on date rape, quoting a victim's own words about how she felt during the attack will attract attention to your topic. Reading a quotation from a song or a poem is another way of attracting favorable attention. Quoting someone familiar and well liked or someone saying something unexpected or out of character can gain attention. For example, a student giving a presentation on myths in student academic performance began, "I've heard it said that 'a theory is a thing of beauty, until it gets run over by a fact.' Nowhere is this more true than in the field of education." Although the quote does not directly relate to education, the speaker makes the connection for the audience while grabbing their attention with vivid word imagery.

5. **Tell a short story.**

People are interested in other people. Telling a story related to your topic is a great way to gain attention. The story can be true or fictional, but it must help you make your point. If a character in the story is someone audience members can relate to, so much the better.

The second essential part of an introduction is the *need step.* Follow your attention step with a short statement that shows audience members why they need or can benefit from the information you are about to give them. A direct purpose statement shows audience members how the presentation is relevant to their lives and how they can directly benefit by listening. If you are talking about a new medical discovery, tell the audience that your information could help save a life. If your topic is the outrageous prices at the college bookstore, tell them you can save them money. An indirect need step implies that, because the topic is so significant, everyone should know something about it: "What happens to social security will affect all of us no matter how young or old we are today."

The third element of a good introduction is the *thesis statement* and *preview.* Here you tell the audience what specifically you will be talking about. Like a road map, it shows your listeners where you are going, making it easier for them to understand your points. Use enumeration (i.e., words like "first, second, third") so listeners know how many main points you will cover. A completed introduction will gain the audience's attention, establish the need to listen, and demonstrate the purpose and main points of your speech.

Body. The **body** of the speech is the main portion of the presentation in which you actually talk about the ideas you want to cover. Present your ideas in an easily recognized

GLOSSARY

Body

The second of three components of a speech where the main ideas are introduced and developed

pattern so your audience sees the relationship among them. Remember to use transition statements that help move your speech smoothly from one point to the next. The following are some of the most common patterns of organization.

- **Problem–solution:** The problem-solution pattern is especially important if you are trying to persuade your audience to accept your recommendation. You talk about the problem, its causes and significance, and then present your proposal as a solution for the problem. This pattern is also easy to use if you want to inform, such as by showing how a problem has already been solved. "How New York City dealt with the devastating loss of the World Trade Center" could be discussed using this pattern.

- **Chronological:** A chronological order is a discussion of things as they happen in time. Talking about how something is made, explaining a historical event, or listing the steps one needs to follow when searching for a job naturally calls for a chronological order. The history of your sorority or the development of the motion picture calls for a chronological order.

- **Spatial:** A spatial order is used to describe things as they exist in space. A presentation describing the best areas to snow ski in California could go from north to south within the state or from east to west.

- **Cause and effect or effect to cause:** Explaining how a particular virus affects millions of people is an example of cause and effect organization. You describe how the virus was discovered and how it works and then discuss the suffering of the people who have contracted it. You can also reverse the process by first talking about the people who are suffering, then describing why this situation exists.

- **Topical:** A topical organization examines the inherent parts of a topic, its essential components. For instance, our American system of government is made up of the executive, legislative, and judicial branches. To cover the entire topic, you have to mention all three parts.

You may discover that pairing some of the organizational styles works more efficiently. No organization style is the best, but using some type of systematic approach is essential to the successful comprehension of your main purpose and ideas. A stream of consciousness is not considered a typical pattern. Members of the audience may not think along the same lines you do. Instead of presenting a topic in exactly the same way the ideas came to you, you are better off choosing a pattern with which audience members are likely to be familiar.

Conclusion.   If your purpose was to inform, your **conclusion** should be a summary of the main points you want the audience to remember. What do you hope listeners retain after they leave the room, even if they forget everything else? That should be in your conclusion. Your conclusion is similar to your introduction, but your final summary should be more concrete. Remind the audience of the specific items you covered and, while summarizing your position, explain what you want them to remember.

If your purpose is to persuade, this is your last chance to get the audience emotionally involved in your topic. Use this opportunity to reconnect with your audience, offer a challenge, or help them to see how things could change for better or worse if action is or is not taken.

GLOSSARY

Conclusion

The third of three components of a speech that summarizes the ideas a speaker wishes the audience to remember

The Presenting Stage

Surveys show that many Americans fear public speaking more than they fear spiders, snakes, or even death.[2] You may be in a group communication class because you were trying to avoid "the dreaded speech." However, as a group member, you may be faced with this feared endeavor. Many times in your career you may need to speak to a committee or larger audience, so it is wise to work through this fear of making an oral presentation now. We offer advice for checking your language, practicing your speech out loud, and, finally, evaluating your speech or the speeches of others.

CHECK YOUR LANGUAGE

In the English language, we have approximately half a million words to express our ideas. The average college student can recognize 60,000 words and actually uses about 20,000.[3] The more word choices speakers have, the better able they are to make language do their bidding and fulfill their purposes.[4] Speakers often forget that writing the speech is only half the battle; the delivery is just as important. Trying to make your audience feel compelled to listen, participate, and take action requires an effective use of language. Speak to your audience in a conversational style, just as if you are giving the speech to good friends, not in a dry monotone or reading manner. Generally, speakers should strive for a style that is clear, vivid, and appropriate.

Clarity requires language that is concrete rather than abstract. Note the difference between explaining that last night you saw Tom "coming down the street" and saying you saw Tom "staggering" or "crawling" or "stumbling" or "skipping down the street." Clarity also requires that you avoid jargon and use words that your audience will understand.

Vividness attracts our attention. Using figurative language, repetition, and amplification (supporting details that develop or reinforce an idea) will add vividness to your presentation and make it easier for your audience to pay attention. Try to imagine Martin Luther King's famous "I Have a Dream" speech without repetition or figurative language—part of what made his speech memorable.

Make sure your language choices are *appropriate* for the audience and the occasion. A formal classroom presentation probably should not be filled with expletives or street language unless they are being used to illustrate something in the speech.

PRACTICE ALOUD

There are four ways of delivering an oral presentation: manuscript, memorization, impromptu, and extemporaneous. Each method has advantages and disadvantages.

If you write out everything you want to say, word for word in a manuscript, you won't leave anything out when you present the speech. Everything you want to say is right there in front of you. Unfortunately, many speakers become so dependent on their manuscripts that they pay little attention to the audience. They have little eye contact with listeners and may not notice whether listeners understand the material presented. Listeners may feel that the speaker has little interest in them and may find the speech boring. News broadcasters and many political figures avoid this problem by using a TelePrompTer that makes it seem as if they are looking directly at their listener, but such equipment is probably not available to you. If you must use a manuscript, work diligently to make a connection with your audience through eye contact and body language while occasionally looking down to find your next point.

You could also memorize your speech. Thus, you make sure you don't leave anything out and at the same time maintain eye contact with your audience. However, this requires that you have a good memory and do not forget even minor points. No situation is more uncomfortable for a speaker than drawing a blank about what comes next. If you are going to attempt a memorized presentation, make sure it really is committed to memory and that it does not sound memorized. The delivery of a memorized speech often sounds robotic. Because the speaker spends many hours working on the memorization of the material, she or he doesn't have time to work on a natural conversational delivery. Even good eye contact will not fool an audience if you do not sound interested in the subject or in them.

An **impromptu speech** is one delivered off-the-cuff. There are no notes and no specific preparation; you speak from the knowledge that you have gained over a lifetime. Not having to prepare in advance is an advantage, but a disadvantage is that such speeches can sound disorganized or incoherent. The perfect example that might have easily explained your second point may not come to mind until you are well into your third point. The audience is left to put all the little pieces of information together. In a typical group meeting or interaction, the communication that occurs generally consists of members responding impromptu to each other.

An **extemporaneous speech** is a prepared speech, but instead of writing out a manuscript, you write an outline of what you want to cover, using as few or as many notes as you need to present your ideas. Don't prepare too many notes or you might as well read a manuscript. However, make sure that everything is in your note cards: ideas, statistics, quotations, or a final statement. The exact wording of the speech will be different every time you present it, but the main points will always be there. This method permits you to have much eye contact with the audience. It also allows you to react to your audience's feedback without fear of losing your place or forgetting something you want to say. If you realize that some of your listeners do not understand you, you can offer another example or repeat your point in a different way to make the point clear, then return to where you left off in your notes.

Once you have selected the method of delivery you plan to use, practice your speech aloud. Thinking the speech silently to yourself does not take as much time as saying it aloud does, but you may misjudge the length. You also need to hear what the speech sounds like because you may find that something said easily in your head is a real tongue twister when said aloud. A colleague of ours remembers his embarrassment when he wanted to say "needy student" but "nudey student" came out. After a second and then a third unsuccessful attempt at "needy" he was forced to switch to "impecunious." If possible, get someone to listen to your speech before you present it to an audience. That person will be able to tell you what you can do to improve the speech.

What Makes a Good Oral Presentation?

Since the time of the ancient Greeks and Romans, a number of criteria have been generally agreed upon as artistic standards to evaluate oral performances. These standards are called the *canons of rhetoric*. Karyn and Donald Rybacki write: "Because rhetorical the-

---

GLOSSARY

Impromptu Speech

A speech delivered without preparation or notes

Extemporaneous Speech

A speech that is prepared and delivered from notes and not read from a manuscript

11.2 Preparing an Individual Presentation

Congratulations. The group mentioned in Case 11.1 has selected you to make the oral presentation to the restaurant association. Although the other members will be present to help answer questions, the primary responsibility for the presentation rests with you.

1. Based on the information you already have, go through the planning stages of preparing an oral presentation. For example, decide whether you are going to try to persuade your listeners to act or to inform them of what your group has discovered. What do you think the audience will be like? How will audience members respond to you? What makes you think so?

2. List the verbal and visual materials you plan to use. Be specific. What types of visual aids would be effective? What kinds of statistics?

3. Assuming that all these materials are available, what pattern of organization would be most effective in presenting them? What type of introduction would best attract the audience's attention?

4. Compare your answers with those of the other members of your class.

ory was an outgrowth of observations of the practice of public speaking in classical cultures, the canons are particularly appropriate to the analysis of speeches."[5] The five classical canons were invention, arrangement, style, delivery, and memory. You can use these elements to render an overall evaluation of any presentation, to compare it to other presentations you have heard, or to offer suggestions for improvement. We will concentrate on the first four canons because memory, the use of codes and mnemonic devices the speaker relied on to recall lengthy speeches, has generally been replaced by written notes and the use of TelePrompTers (see Table 11.3).

The canon of **invention** deals with the raw materials of the speech and how they are adapted to a particular audience. Did the speaker choose an appropriate topic? Did the speaker select interesting examples and illustrations to explain an informative thesis? Did the speaker use significant and sufficient examples and statistics to support a thesis when attempting to persuade? Did the speaker relate the topic and show its significance to the audience? Did the speaker complete the presentation within any assigned time limits?

In a panel or symposium, did the speakers work together to present varied aspects of the issue? Did the moderator keep the discussion focused? Did the panel cover all the material that would be of interest to the audience?

The canon of **arrangement** is concerned with how the speech is put together or organized. Were the main points clear and easy to follow? Was there an interesting introduction that captured the audience's attention and previewed the body of the speech? Were there effective transitions? Did the conclusion summarize the main points and reinforce the central idea?

GLOSSARY

Invention

A canon of rhetoric identifying the raw materials of the speech and how they are adapted to a particular audience

Arrangement

One of the canons of rhetoric specifying how a speech is ordered or put together

---

TABLE 11.3	**Criteria for Evaluation (Canons)**

1. Invention: raw materials and adaptation to audience

2. Arrangement: organization

3. Style: choice of language

4. Delivery: oral presentation

In a symposium, did the moderator provide the audience with transitions between the individual presentations? Was there a clear introduction and a conclusion to the discussion? In a panel, did the participants stick to the topic and make clear when they were moving from one aspect to another?

The canon of **style** is concerned with the distinctive manner and appropriateness of the speech's language. Was the language clear and accurate? Was it appropriate to the audience and occasion? Was it free of grammatical errors that make it hard to understand? Was the language vivid and likely to hold the audience's attention?

The canon of **delivery** deals with how the presentation is offered to the audience. Did the speaker maintain eye contact with the audience? Did the speaker avoid any distracting movements and gestures? Did the speaker vary his or her pitch and rate? Was the speaker confident? Were appropriate movements and gestures used?

11.3   Using the Canons to Evaluate

APPLY NOW

Demosthenes, the great Greek orator of antiquity, is supposed to have claimed that the most important canon was delivery, the second most important was delivery, and the third most important was delivery.

1. Which canon do you think is the most important? How would you divide 100 points among the four canons to show their relative importance?

2. In a small group, discuss which of the canons you feel to be most important, rank them from 1 (most important) to 4 (least important), and figure out the average score for each based on the 100-point scale.

3. Can your group offer any examples of contemporary or historical public speakers that rate high on all the canons? Who rates poorly on all?

4. Compare your responses to those of the other groups in your class.

SUMMARY

■ Small groups are often called upon to make oral presentations of their work, so members need to understand how to be effective presenters.

■ Public presentation sessions include panels and symposiums, where speakers publicly discuss an issue before an audience; a forum often follows, where the audience can address or question the speakers.

■ In preparing a speech, the speaker must first determine whether the purpose is to inform, persuade, or entertain.

■ Speakers must analyze the audience to understand how to get their attention; find the most appropriate and interesting ideas, supporting materials, and visuals aids to present; and organize the material so that it is easy for the audience to follow the presentation.

■ An effective presentation includes an introduction, body, and conclusion.

■ Oral presentations can be evaluated using four criteria, based on the canons of rhetoric, which include invention, arrangement, style, and delivery.

EXERCISES

1. C-SPAN is a nonprofit cooperative of the cable industry. C-SPAN programming covers a variety of political events, including congressional hearings, press conferences, public policy conferences, and so forth. Watch C-SPAN for examples of panels, forums, or symposiums.

   a. Could you distinguish which kind of public presentation was taking place?

   b. Was there a moderator? How effective was the moderator? Why?

   c. What did you find interesting about how the public presentation was conducted? What did you see that was problematic?

   d. Did the public presentation meet with your expectations? Were you surprised? Why?

   e. Did you get any ideas about how you might or might not conduct your own public presentation?

2. Take some time to listen to the persuasive speech of a car salesperson and a minister. Compare and contrast the "sales pitch" of both. Both presentations are persuasive in nature, but they are delivered to different audiences. How are their oral presentations the same? How are their oral presentations different?

3. Various videos and CD-ROMs contain the text of famous speeches. You can rent these at your local or school library. Find one with excerpts or the entire speech of someone famous who interests you. Watch the speech and evaluate according to the four canons: invention, style, delivery, and arrangement.

Go to **www.mhhe.com/adamsgalanes** and **www.mhhe.com/groups** for Self-Quizzes and weblinks.

KEY TERMS and CONCEPTS

arrangement	extemporaneous speech	moderator
audience analysis	forum discussion	panel discussion
body	impromptu speech	persuasive speech
conclusion	informative speech	style
delivery	introduction	symposium
entertainment speech	invention	

www.mhhe.com/adamsgalanes
Use the flashcards and crossword puzzles on the Online Learning Center to further your knowledge of these key terms.

Techniques for Observing Problem-Solving Groups

Consulting to the Technical College Executive Committee

The technical college's executive committee meetings were boring. Members agreed that communication among the various departments was essential for the college to function effectively, but the weekly staff meetings somehow were not satisfying this need. Real communication about problems, solutions, and goals of the various departments was done outside the meetings. Members didn't complain much, but they showed little enthusiasm for the meetings. The chair of the committee, Basil, was concerned. He asked Gloria to observe the meetings, figure out what was wrong, make recommendations for improvement, and conduct training sessions to help members interact more effectively during the meetings.

For two months, Gloria systematically observed, analyzed, and evaluated the staff meetings. First, she attended meetings, took notes, and completed a content analysis that showed Basil doing most of the talking. He was almost the only member to initiate new ideas during the meetings. Other members contributed only when addressed directly by Basil. Thus, a *wheel* interaction pattern (with Basil at the hub and everyone else as an individual spoke) had become the group's norm. On a questionnaire asking about effectiveness, Basil indicated he believed the meetings were very effective, most other members thought they were moderately effective, and two members rated them completely ineffective. Gloria followed up the questionnaire by interviewing each staff member to determine how the meetings could be improved. She paid particular attention to the comments of the two dissatisfied members.

Gloria concluded that Basil dominated the meetings but that he was completely unaware he was dominating. Members felt stifled during the meetings but didn't know how to express those feelings to Basil or to change the pattern of their meetings. Members wanted to discuss freely the problems that had come up in their respective departments, and they hoped the staff meetings would provide an open forum for exchanging information and ideas. The two members who were most dissatisfied were quite knowledgeable about college operations and felt particularly ignored. Members were suppressing disagreements for fear of retribution by Basil; although Basil was not a tyrant, he made it clear from his behavior (rolling his eyes, interrupting people, speaking sarcastically) that he did not like it when others disagreed with his ideas. In short, this committee displayed some obvious and some hidden problems, all of which could be overcome with training and desire.

T his story highlights the value of having someone observe a group, describe its behavior, evaluate that behavior, and make recommendations to improve the functioning of the group. In this appendix we will present a variety of techniques to help you do that.

The Role of the Observer

The role of group observer can be valuable and helpful if the observer knows how to function. Most group members have not been trained to be effective group participants, so it's especially important for those who do know something about small group communication to monitor the group's discussions and help the group perform as well as possible. Knowledgeable observers function like athletic coaches, helping players improve their performance as a team.

In Chapter 1 we described the participant-observer, a group member who makes available his or her knowledge and skills to help a group perform more effectively. A second type of observer is the **consultant-observer,** an outsider brought in to observe, evaluate, and make recommendations to the group. The consultant-observer may be a member of the organization the group belongs to or an outside consultant trained in small group communication. When executives learn that someone within the organization has small group communication expertise, they often ask that person to apply his or her skills to help the group. That was Gloria's situation when she observed the technical college executive staff, and that may also be your position someday.

Participant- and consultant-observers have unique advantages and disadvantages. The consultant-observer may be able to maintain more objectivity regarding group members and group processes, but the participant-observer may have inside information that gives insight regarding what is happening in the group. A group that has been experiencing serious conflict may view the consultant-observer as a hatchet person for an executive. On the other hand, a participant-observer may be seen as biased rather than objective, thereby undermining his or her effectiveness as an adviser to the group.

GLOSSARY

Consultant-Observer

An outsider who observes and evaluates a group

In general, observers seek to answer two questions: How well is this group performing? and How can it improve? However, *many* elements contribute to a group's performance. Observers cannot look at everything at once or they will become overwhelmed. They plan their observation strategy in advance. Table A.1 contains a list of questions you can use as a general guide for observing. Don't try to answer all the questions; instead, use the list to screen out elements that seem to be working well so you can concentrate your observation on those that can be improved.

Both participant- and consultant-observers should follow several guidelines when they are giving feedback to a group:

1. *Stress the positive* and point out what the group or the leader is doing well.

2. *Do not overwhelm the group* by telling the members each and every thing you think should be improved. Instead, emphasize one or two things that most need improvement.

3. *Avoid arguing* when you present your observations and advice. Leave the group members free to decide whether and how your advice will be used.

4. *Do not interrupt the whole meeting* to give advice to the group's leader during a meeting. Instead, whisper or write your suggestions.

5. *Speak clearly and concisely* when you are giving feedback. Do not ramble or belabor your points. Consider the following remarks by Larry, who observed that group members were switching to new topics without completing the original one:

   One of the problems I see is that you are having trouble staying on track with your discussion! In the past five minutes, you have talked about a pedestrian overpass at Grand and National, why money was spent on artificial turf instead of library books, how you can handle a landlord who won't repair plumbing, and several other topics. Your discussion would be more efficient if you helped each other focus on the original question: How can pedestrian/car accidents be eliminated on National Avenue?

   In this example of giving feedback, Larry states the problem he has observed, gives a few (rather than 10 or 20) examples to clarify what he means, and provides a suggestion that makes the whole group responsible for solving the problem. He doesn't ramble endlessly about the problem or blame individual members.

6. *Prepare members to use special procedures* by explaining the procedure or giving them a handout that outlines the key steps. (Feel free to use the figures in this book, as long as you give credit to the source.)

7. *Make individual critical comments in private* to the appropriate person so that he or she will not feel attacked or publicly humiliated.

Now that you have an idea of what observers look for and how they present their findings, here are a variety of instruments to help you gather information about your group.

TABLE A.1   **Questions to Guide Your Observations**

GROUP GOALS

- Are there clear and accepted group goals?
- How well does the group understand its charge?
- Does the group know and accept limits on its area of freedom?
- Do members know what output they are supposed to produce?

SETTING

- Does the physical environment (seating arrangements, privacy, attractiveness) facilitate group discussions?

COMMUNICATION SKILLS AND INTERACTION PATTERNS

- How clearly do members express their ideas and opinions?
- Do members complete one topic before they switch to another?
- Is verbal participation balanced equally among all members?
- Is the pattern of interaction all-channel or unduly restricted?

COMMUNICATION CLIMATE AND NORMS

- Does the group climate seem supportive and cooperative or defensive and competitive?
- What attitudes do the members exhibit toward themselves and each other?
- Do any hidden agenda items seem to interfere with group progress?
- Do any norms seem to interfere with group progress or cohesiveness?

LEADERSHIP AND MEMBER ROLES

- What style of leadership is the designated leader providing?
- Is the leadership appropriate for the group's needs?
- Are the roles performed by members appropriate both for their skills and the needs of the group?
- Are there any needed functions not being provided by anyone?

DECISION-MAKING AND PROBLEM-SOLVING PROCEDURES

- Are members adequately prepared for meetings?
- Does the group use an agenda? How well is it followed? Does it serve the group?
- Is anyone providing periodic internal summaries so members can keep track of major points of discussion?
- Are decisions, assignments, and proposals being recorded?
- How are decisions being made?
- Has the group defined and analyzed the problem before developing solutions?
- Do members understand and agree on criteria in making decisions?
- How creative is the group in generating potential solutions?
- Do members defer judgment until all solutions have been listed and understood?
- Are information and ideas being evaluated critically or accepted at face value?
- Do you see any tendency toward groupthink?
- Has the group made adequate plans to implement decisions?
- Are special procedures (brainstorming, focus groups, etc.) being used as needed?
- Could procedural changes benefit the group?

Observation Instruments and Techniques

The following techniques and instruments may be used by group members as part of a self-evaluation of the group or by observers. They can be used as is or adapted to suit particular situations and groups.

VERBAL INTERACTION ANALYSIS

A verbal interaction analysis shows who talks to whom, how often each member speaks, and whether the group participation is balanced or dominated by one or more individuals. A model interaction diagram is shown in Figure A.1. The names of all participants are located around the circle in the same order in which they sit during the discussion. Whenever a person speaks, an arrow is drawn from that person's position toward the individual to whom the remark was addressed. Subsequent remarks in the same direction are indicated by the short cross marks on the base of the arrow. (For example, Gallo addressed three remarks to Brown in the model diagram.) The longer arrow pointing toward the center indicates remarks made to the group as a whole.

> **GLOSSARY**
>
> **Verbal Interaction Analysis**
>
> *A technique to discover who talks to whom*

FIGURE A.1   Verbal Interaction Diagram

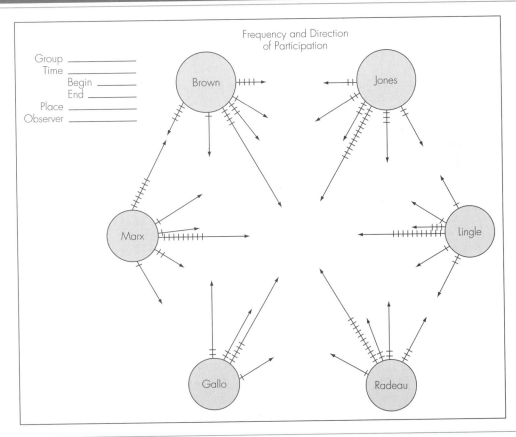

Frequency and Direction of Participation

Group _____
Time _____
Begin _____
End _____
Place _____
Observer _____

Brown • Jones • Marx • Lingle • Gallo • Radeau

FIGURE A.2 How to Display Data from a Verbal Interaction Diagram

Group *CURRICULUM COMMITTEE* Place *CRAIG HALL*

Observer *SMITH* Date *9-5-2002*

Beginning time *9:00 A.M.* Ending Time *10:30 A.M.*

FROM: \ TO:	Brown	Jones	Lingle	Radeau	Gallo	Marx	Group	Total
Brown	–	5	2	4	2	5	5	23 / 16.1
Jones	3	–	3	4	4	3	13	30 / 21
Lingle	2	2	–	3	2	4	12	25 / 17.5
Radeau	3	3	4	–	0	2	12	24 / 16.8
Gallo	3	3	2	0	–	0	6	14 / 9.8
Marx	8	2	2	3	2	–	10	27 / 18.9
Total number	19	15	13	14	10	14	58	143
Total percent	13.3	10.5	9.1	9.8	7	9.8	40.6	100

An interaction diagram can look messy or confusing. For easier interpretation, display the numbers and percentages in a chart (see Figure A.2). From the frequency of participation to the group as a whole and to specific members, who might you guess is the leader of this group? Do you consider the participation balanced or not? Does anyone appear to dominate the discussion?

CONTENT ANALYSIS PROCEDURES

Content analysis procedures examine the *type* of remarks being made by specific members. In Figure A.3, specific task, maintenance, and self-centered behaviors are listed along the left margin and the participants' names across the top. Each time a member speaks, the observer places a mark in the appropriate box according to the type of remark made. The tally marks are converted to percentages, as shown in Figure A.4. Who is probably the task leader of this group? Who is the maintenance leader? Are any individuals acting in self-centered ways?

GLOSSARY

Content Analysis Procedures

Techniques to help analyze the types of remarks being made

FIGURE A.3   Content Analysis of Task, Maintenance, and Self-Centered Behaviors

Group _____   Place _____   Observer _____

Date _____   Beginning time _____   Ending Time _____

Participants' Names

Behavioral Functions						
1. Initiating and orienting						
2. Information giving						
3. Information seeking						
4. Opinion giving						
5. Opinion seeking						
6. Clarifying and elaborating						
7. Evaluating						
8. Summarizing						
9. Coordinating						
10. Consensus testing						
11. Recording						
12. Suggesting procedure						
13. Gatekeeping						
14. Supporting						
15. Harmonizing						
16. Tension relieving						
17. Dramatizing						
18. Norming						
19. Withdrawing						
20. Blocking						
21. Status and recognition seeking						

Rows 1–12: Task-Oriented
Rows 13–18: Maintenance
Rows 19–21: Self-Centered

FIGURE A.4   How to Display Data from Content Analysis of Member Behaviors

Group _EXECUTIVE COMMITTEE_   Place _CU LOBBY_

Observer _ANDY_   Date _8-28-96_

Beginning time _4:30 P.M._   Ending Time _6:30 P.M._

		Participants' Names				
Behavioral Functions	Mary	John	Edna	Dave	Jodi	Total number percent
Task-Oriented						
1. Initiating and orienting	5	3				8 / 5.7
2. Information giving	6	5		2	3	16 / 11.4
3. Information seeking			3			3 / 2.1
4. Opinion giving	8	8	4	2	1	23 / 16.4
5. Opinion seeking			2			2 / 1.4
6. Clarifying and elaborating			3			3 / 2.1
7. Evaluating	2	4			1	7 / 5
8. Summarizing	2					2 / 1.4
9. Coordinating	8					8 / 5.7
10. Consensus testing				3		3 / 2.1
11. Recording			5			5 / 3.6
12. Suggesting procedure	3		6			9 / 6.4
Maintenance						
13. Gatekeeping			1	5		6 / 4.3
14. Supporting	2		2	6		10 / 7.1
15. Harmonizing				3	2	5 / 3.6
16. Tension relieving					6	6 / 4.3
17. Dramatizing		5			3	8 / 5.7
18. Norming				4		4 / 2.9
Self-Centered						
19. Withdrawing		1				1 / .7
20. Blocking	2	5				7 / 5
21. Status and recognition seeking		4				4 / 2.9
Total number / percent	38 / 27.1	35 / 25	26 / 18.6	25 / 17.9	16 / 11.4	140 / 100

FIGURE A.5   All-Purpose Discussion Rating Scale

Date _____   Group _____

Time _____   Observer _____

Group Characteristic	5 Excellent	4 Good	3 Average	2 Fair	1 Poor
Organization of discussion					
Equality of opportunity to speak					
Cooperative group orientation					
Listening to understand					
Evaluation of ideas					
Comments:					

Any category system can be used as the basis for a content analysis diagram. For example, you may want to focus on the defensive and supportive behaviors described in Chapter 7. In that case, you would record all the individual defensive and supportive communication categories (i.e., control, superiority, provisionalism, empathy, etc.) along the left side.

Other types of content analyses can be performed. For example, you might want to trace the development of any fantasy chains in the group, the progression of an idea from its original introduction by one member through all its modifications by the rest of the group, the types of conflicts, or the types of arguments members use to support their ideas. It is easier if you tape-record (with permission, of course) the group's interaction first.

RATING SCALES

Rating scales are questionnaires that ask members or observers to assess any aspect of a group, such as group climate, cohesiveness, efficiency, satisfaction, freedom to express disagreement, and organization of discussion. For example, the question "How well did the committee chair keep the discussion organized?" asks you to rate the leader's ability to conduct a systematic discussion. Scale questions may be closed-ended, in which the responses are already provided for you (such as *very well, adequately,* and *very poorly*), or open-ended, in which you are free to respond any way you choose. The following figures provide a number of examples of rating scales. Figure A.5

GLOSSARY

Rating Scales

Questions (scales) to help evaluate specific aspects of a group

| **FIGURE A.6** | **Problem-Solving Process Rating Scale** |

Instructions: Indicate the degree to which the group accomplished each identified behavior. Use the following scale for your evaluations:

	Poor	Fair	Average	Good	Excellent
	1	2	3	4	5

Circle the appropriate number in front of each item.

1   2   3   4   5   1. The concern of each member was identified regarding the problem the group attempted to solve.

1   2   3   4   5   2. This concern was identified *before* the problem was analyzed.

1   2   3   4   5   3. In problem analysis, the present condition was carefully compared with the specific condition desired.

1   2   3   4   5   4. The goal was carefully defined and agreed to by all members.

1   2   3   4   5   5. Valid (and relevant) information was secured when needed.

1   2   3   4   5   6. Possible solutions were listed and clarified before they were evaluated.

1   2   3   4   5   7. Criteria for evaluating proposed solutions were clearly identified and accepted by the group.

1   2   3   4   5   8. Predictions were made regarding the probable effectiveness of each proposed solution, using the available information and criteria.

1   2   3   4   5   9. Consensus was achieved on the most desirable solution.

1   2   3   4   5   10. A detailed plan to implement the solution was developed.

1   2   3   4   5   11. The problem-solving process was systematic and orderly.

is a general scale to evaluate any group discussion, and Figure A.6 is a scale adapted from one developed by Patton and Giffin to identify deficiencies in problem-solving procedures. Figure A.7 is the Seashore Index of Group Cohesiveness, which measures cohesiveness of a work group.[1] We encourage you to modify these scales or create your own.

FIGURE A.7   Seashore Index of Group Cohesiveness

Check one response for each question.

1. Do you feel that you are really a part of your work group?

_____ Really a part of my work group

_____ Included in most ways

_____ Included in some ways, but not in others

_____ Don't feel I really belong

_____ Don't work with any one group of people

_____ Not ascertained

2. If you had a chance to do the same kind of work for the same pay in another work group, how would you feel about moving?

_____ Would want very much to move

_____ Would rather move than stay where I am

_____ Would make no difference to me

_____ Would want very much to stay where I am

_____ Not ascertained

3. How does your group compare with other similar groups on each of the following points?

	Better than Most	About the Same as Most	Not as Good as Most	Not Ascertained
a. The way the members get along together	_____	_____	_____	_____
b. The way the members stick together	_____	_____	_____	_____
c. The way the members help each other on the job	_____	_____	_____	_____

SOURCE: From Stanley Seashore; *Group Cohesiveness in the Industrial Work Group* (Ann Arbor: Institute for Social Research, University of Michigan, 1954).

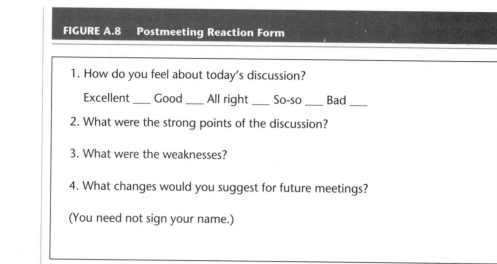

FIGURE A.8   Postmeeting Reaction Form

1. How do you feel about today's discussion?

   Excellent ___ Good ___ All right ___ So-so ___ Bad ___

2. What were the strong points of the discussion?

3. What were the weaknesses?

4. What changes would you suggest for future meetings?

(You need not sign your name.)

POSTMEETING REACTION FORMS

Postmeeting reaction (PMR) forms are questionnaires designed to get feedback from members about a particular meeting. PMR forms may focus on a particular aspect (such as leadership) or deal with several broad aspects (such as how effective members believe the meetings are). The leader, a member, or an observer distributes the PMR forms; members complete them anonymously, the results are tallied, and the findings are reported to the group as soon as possible. The findings provide a basis for the group to discuss how to improve its communication and effectiveness. Basil, the group leader in our introductory example, could have used PMR forms himself to get feedback from the other members about how the group's discussions could be improved.

PMR forms are tailored to fit the purposes and needs of the group. Questions may concern substantive items, interpersonal relationships, matters of procedure, or a mixture of all three. Two different examples of PMR forms are shown in Figures A.8 and A.9.

GLOSSARY

Postmeeting Reaction (PMR) Forms

Questionnaires members complete after a meeting to evaluate that particular meeting

Instruction: Circle the number that best indicates your reactions to the following questions about the discussion in which you participated:

1. *Adequacy of Communication.* To what extent do you feel members were understanding each others' statements and positions?

0	1	2	3	4	5	6	7	8	9	10

Talked past each other;   Communicated directly with
misunderstanding   each other; understanding well

2. *Opportunity to Speak.* To what extent did you feel free to speak?

0	1	2	3	4	5	6	7	8	9	10

Never had a chance to speak   Had all the opportunity to talk I wanted

3. *Climate of Acceptance.* How well did members support each other, show acceptance of individuals?

0	1	2	3	4	5	6	7	8	9	10

Highly critical and punishing   Supportive and receptive

4. *Interpersonal Relations.* How pleasant and concerned were members with interpersonal relations?

0	1	2	3	4	5	6	7	8	9	10

Quarrelsome, status differences emphasized   Pleasant, empathic, concerned with persons

5. *Leadership.* How adequate was the leader (or leadership) of the group?

0	1	2	3	4	5	6	7	8	9	10

Too weak ( ) or dominating ( )   Shared, group-centered, and sufficient

6. *Satisfaction with Role.* How satisfied are you with your personal participation in the discussion?

0	1	2	3	4	5	6	7	8	9	10

Very dissatisfied   Very satisfied

7. *Quality of Product.* How satisfied are you with the discussions, solutions, or learnings that came out of this discussion?

0	1	2	3	4	5	6	7	8	9	10

Very displeased   Very satisfied

8. *Overall.* How do you rate the discussion as a whole apart from any specific aspect of it?

0	1	2	3	4	5	6	7	8	9	10

Awful; waste of time   Superb; time well spent

FIGURE A.10   Participating Rating Scale

Date _____

Observer _____

_____
(Name of participant)

1. Contributions to the *content of the discussion?* (well prepared, supplied information, adequate reasoning, etc.)

   5   4   3   2   1
   ───
   Outstanding in quality   Fair share   Few or none
   and quantity

2. Contributions to *efficient group procedures?* (agenda planning, relevant comments, summaries, keeping on track)

   5   4   3   2   1
   ───
   Always relevant,   Relevant, no   Sidetracked,
   aided organization   aid in order   confused group

3. Degree of *cooperating?* (listening to understand, responsible, agreeable, group-centered, open-minded)

   5   4   3   2   1
   ───
   Very responsible   Self-centered
   and constructive

4. *Speaking?* (clear, to group, one point at a time, concise)

   5   4   3   2   1
   ───
   Brief, clear,   Vague, indirect,
   to group   wordy

5. *Value* to the group? (overall rating)

   5   4   3   2   1
   ───
   Most valuable   Least valuable

Suggestions:

Evaluating Individual Participants

In addition to evaluating general group processes, it is often useful to evaluate behaviors of individual participants. An observer or the members themselves may complete the following forms. Figure A.10 is a simple rating form that focuses on some of the most important aspects of participation. A more detailed form is shown in Figure A.11.

FIGURE A.11   Participating Rating Scale

Participant's name _____

Instructions: Circle the number that best reflects your evaluation of the discussant's participation on each scale.

Superior				Poor	
1	2	3	4	5	1. Was prepared and informed.
1	2	3	4	5	2. Contributions were brief and clear.
1	2	3	4	5	3. Comments relevant and well timed.
1	2	3	4	5	4. Spoke distinctly and audibly to all.
1	2	3	4	5	5. Contributions made readily and voluntarily.
1	2	3	4	5	6. Frequency of participation (if poor, too low [ ] or high [ ]).
1	2	3	4	5	7. Nonverbal responses were clear and constant.
1	2	3	4	5	8. Listened to understand and follow discussion.
1	2	3	4	5	9. Open-minded.
1	2	3	4	5	10. Cooperative and constructive.
1	2	3	4	5	11. Helped keep discussion organized, following outline.
1	2	3	4	5	12. Contributed to evaluation of information and ideas.
1	2	3	4	5	13. Respectful and tactful with others.
1	2	3	4	5	14. Encouraged others to participate.
1	2	3	4	5	15. Overall rating in relation to other discussants.

Comments   Evaluator _____

FIGURE A.12   Barnlund-Haiman Leadership Rating Scale

Instructions: This rating scale may be used to evaluate leadership in groups with or without official leaders. In the latter case (the leaderless group), use part A of each item only. When evaluating the actions of an official leader, use parts A and B of each item on the scale.

Influence in Procedure

Initiating Discussion

A.	3	2	1	0	1	2	3

Group needed more help in getting started   Group got right amount of help   Group needed less help in getting started

B. The quality of the introductory remarks was:

Excellent	Good	Adequate	Fair	Poor

Organizing Group Thinking

A.	3	2	1	0	1	2	3

Group needed more direction in thinking   Group got right amount of help   Group needed less direction in thinking

B. If and when attempts were made to organize group thinking, they were:

Excellent	Good	Adequate	Fair	Poor

Clarifying Communication

A.	3	2	1	0	1	2	3

Group needed more help in clarifying communication   Group got right amount of help   Group needed less help in clarifying communication

B. If and when attempts were made to clarify communication, they were:

Excellent	Good	Adequate	Fair	Poor

Summarizing and Verbalizing Agreements

A.	3	2	1	0	1	2	3

Group needed more help in summarizing and verbalizing agreements   Group got right amount of help   Group needed less help in summarizing and verbalizing agreements

B. If and when attempts were made to summarize and verbalize, they were:

Excellent	Good	Adequate	Fair	Poor

Resolving Conflict

A.	3	2	1	0	1	2	3

Group needed more help in resolving conflict   Group got right amount of help   Group needed less help in resolving conflict

B. If and when attempts were made to resolve conflict, they were:

Excellent	Good	Adequate	Fair	Poor

SOURCE: From D. C. Barnlund and F. S. Haiman, *The Dynamics of Discussion* (Houghton-Mifflin, 1960), pp. 401–4. Used by permission of Robert Goldsmith, M.D., executor of Barnlund estate.

Influence in Creative and Critical Thinking

Stimulating Critical Thinking

A. 3   2   1   0   1   2   3

Group needed more stimulation in creative thinking	Group got right amount of help	Group needed less stimulation in creative thinking

B. If and when attempts were made to stimulate ideas, they were:

Excellent	Good	Adequate	Fair	Poor

Encouraging Criticism

A. 3   2   1   0   1   2   3

Group needed more encouragement to be critical	Group got right amount of help	Group needed less encouragement to be critical

B. If and when attempts were made to encourage criticism, they were:

Excellent	Good	Adequate	Fair	Poor

Balancing Abstract and Concrete Thought

A. 3   2   1   0   1   2   3

Group need to be more concrete	Group achieved proper balance	Group needed to be more abstract

B. If and when attempts were made to balance abstract and concrete thought, they were:

Excellent	Good	Adequate	Fair	Poor

Influence in Interpersonal Relations

Climate-Making

A. 3   2   1   0   1   2   3

Group needed more help in securing a permissive atmosphere	Group got right amount of help	Group needed less help in securing a permissive atmosphere

B. If and when attempts were made to establish a permissive atmosphere, they were:

Excellent	Good	Adequate	Fair	Poor

Regulating Participation

A. 3   2   1   0   1   2   3

Group need more regulation of participation	Group got right amount of help	Group needed less regulation of participation

B. If and when attempts were made to regulate participation, they were:

Excellent	Good	Adequate	Fair	Poor

Overall Leadership

A. 3   2   1   0   1   2   3

Group needed more control	Group got right amount of control	Group needed less control

B. If and when attempts were made to control the group, they were:

Excellent	Good	Adequate	Fair	Poor

FIGURE A.13   Leader Self-Rating Scale

Instructions: Rate yourself on each item by putting a check mark in the "Yes" or "No" column. Your score is five times the number of items marked "Yes." Rating: *excellent,* 90 or higher; *good,* 80–85; *fair,* 70–75; *inadequate,* 65 or lower.

	Yes	No
1. I prepared all needed facilities.	___	___
2. I started the meeting promptly and ended on time.	___	___
3. I established an atmosphere of permissiveness and informality. I was open and responsive to all ideas.	___	___
4. I clearly oriented the group to its purpose and area of freedom.	___	___
5. I encouraged all members to participate and maintained equal opportunity for all to speak.	___	___
6. I used a plan for leading the group in an organized consideration of all major phases of the problem.	___	___
7. I listened actively and (if needed) encouraged all members to do so.	___	___
8. I saw to it that the problem was discussed thoroughly before solutions were considered.	___	___
9. I integrated related ideas or suggestions and urged the group to arrive at consensus on a solution.	___	___
10. My questions were clear and brief.	___	___
11. I saw to it that unclear statements were paraphrased or otherwise clarified.	___	___
12. I prompted open discussion of substantive conflicts.	___	___
13. I maintained order and organization, promptly pointing out tangents, making transitions, and keeping track of the passage of time.	___	___
14. I saw to it that the meeting produced definite assignments or plans for action, and that any subsequent meeting was arranged.	___	___
15. All important information, ideas, and decisions were promptly and accurately recorded.	___	___
16. I actively encouraged creative thinking.	___	___
17. I encouraged thorough evaluation of information and all ideas for solutions.	___	___
18. I was able to remain neutral during constructive arguments and otherwise encourage teamwork.	___	___
19. I suggested or urged establishment of needed norms and standards.	___	___
20. I encouraged members to discuss how they felt about the group process and resolve any blocks to progress.	___	___

SUMMARY

- A consultant-observer is an outsider brought in to observe a group; such observers may be more objective than participant-observers.

- Participant- and consultant-observers cannot look at everything at once, so they concentrate on those elements a group needs to improve most.

- When they give feedback, they focus on a few elements rather than risk overwhelming the group.

- Observers and group members themselves can use a variety of methods to gather information, including verbal interaction analyses, content analyses, and a variety of rating scales.

Chapter 1

1. Information for the following story about the El Cajon Book Club was taken from Marla Abramson, "The After-School Bunch," *Book,* May/June 2001, pp. 85–87.

2. Ellen Neuborne, "Companies Save, but Workers Pay," *USA Today,* February 25, 1997, pp. 1B–2B

3. Neuborne, "Companies Save," p. 1B.

4. Daniel McGinn, "Mired in Meetings," *Newsweek,* October 16, 2000, pp. 52–54.

5. Lawrence R. Frey, "The Call of the Field: Studying Communication in Natural Groups," in *Group Communication in Context,* ed. Lawrence R. Frey (Hillsdale, NJ: Lawrence Erlbaum Associates, 1994), pp ix–xiv.

6. Charles C. DuBois, "Portrait of the Ideal MBA," *The Penn Stater,* September/October 1992, p. 131.

7. Joann Keyton, "Relational Communication in Groups," in *Handbook of Group Communication Theory & Research,* ed. Lawrence R. Frey (Thousand Oaks, CA: Sage, 1999), p. 192.

8. Information about Saturn is compiled from the following articles: William B. Cook, "Ringing in Saturn," *U.S. News & World Report,* October 22, 1990, pp. 51–54; S.C. Gwynne, "The Right Stuff," *Time,* October 29, 1990, pp. 74–77; James B. Treece, "Here Comes GM's Saturn," *Business Week,* April 9, 1990, pp. 56–62; and Doublas Williams, "Shop Floor Democracy," *Automotive Industries,* June 1989, pp. 48–49.

9. This line of research began in 1928 and continues to the present. For a concise summary of the research up to 1980, see Marvin E. Shaw, *Group Dynamics,* 3rd ed. (New York: McGraw-Hill, 1981), pp. 57–64.

10. Herm W. Smith, "Group versus Individual Problem Solving and Type of Problem Solved," *Small Group Behavior* 20 (1989), pp. 357–74.

11. Dennis S. Gouran and Randy Y. Hirokawa, "Counteractive Functions of Communication in Effective Group Decision Making," in *Communication and Group Decision Making,* eds. Randy Y. Hirokawa and Marshall Scott Poole (Beverly Hills, CA: Sage, 1986), pp. 81–90.

12. Shaw, *Group Dynamics,* p. 8.

13. Paul V. Crosby, ed., *Interaction in Small Groups* (New York: Macmillan, 1975), p. 7.

14. Sandra Ketrow, "Nonverbal Aspects of Group Communication," in *Handbook of Group Communication Theory & Research,* ed. Lawrence R. Frey (Thousand Oaks, CA: Sage, 1999), pp. 251–87.

15. Dorwin Cartwright and Alvin Zander, *Group Dynamics: Research and Theory,* 3rd ed. (New York: Harper & Row, 1968), p. 7.

16. William C. Schutz, *FIRO: A Three-Dimensional Theory of Interpersonal Behavior* (New York: Rinehart, 1958).

17. Thomas J. Socha, "Communication in Family Units," in *Handbook of Group Communication Theory & Research,* ed. Lawrence R. Frey (Thousand Oaks, CA: Sage, 1999), pp. 475–92.

18. Carolyn M. Anderson and Matthew M. Martin, "The Effects of Communication Motives, Interaction Involvement, and Loneliness on Satisfaction: A Model of Small Groups," *Small Group Research* 26 (February 1995), pp. 118–37.

19. Kevin Wright, "Perceptions of On-Line Support Providers: An Examination of Perceived Homophily, Course Credibility, Communication and Social Support Within On-Line Support Groups," *Communication Quarterly* 48 (Winter 2000), pp. 44–59.

20. Susan A. Wheelan and Alan R. List, "Cohort Group Effectiveness and the Educational Achievement of Adult Undergraduate Students," *Small Group Research* 31 (December 2000), pp. 724–38.

21. Joseph M. Putti and Wong K. Choeng, "Singapore's Positive Experience with Quality Circles," *National Productivity Review* 9 (Spring 1990), pp. 193–200.

22. Henry P. Sims, Jr., and James W. Dean, Jr., "Beyond Quality Circles: Self-Managing Teams," *Personnel Journal* (1985), pp. 25–32.

23. Suggestions synthesized from Neil Clark, *Teambuilding: A Practical Guide for Trainers* (New York: McGraw-Hill, 1994); Glenn M. Parker, *Team Players and Teamwork* (San Francisco: Jossey-Bass, 1991); and Glenn H. Varney, *Building Productive Teams: An Action Guide and Resource Book* (San Francisco: Jossey-Bass, 1989).

24. Sharon L. Murrell, "The Impact of Communicating through Computers," unpublished doctoral dissertation, State University of New York at Stony Brook, 1983.

25. William C. Schutz, "Leader as Completer," in *Small Group Communication: A Reader,* 3rd ed., eds. Robert S. Cathcart and Larry A. Samovar (Dubuque, IA: Wm. C. Brown, 1979), pp. 454–60.

26. *The Random House Dictionary of the English Language,* 2nd ed. unabridged (New York: Random House, 1987), p. 665.

Chapter 2

1. Dawn Steel (Producer) and Jon Turtetaub (Director), *Cool Runnings* [Film]. Distributed by Walt Disney Pictures (1993) and available on video.

2. Daniel Katz and Robert Kahn, *The Social Psychology of Organizations,* 2nd ed. (New York: Wiley, 1978).

3. Benjamin J. Broome and Luann Fulbright, "A Multistage Influence Model of Barriers to Small Group Problem Solving: A Participant-Generated Agenda for Small Group Research," *Small Group Research* 26 (February 1995), pp. 25–55.

4. Linda Putnam and Cynthia Stohl, "Bona Fide Groups: An Alternative Perspective for Communication and Small Group Decision Making," in *Communication and Group Decision Making,* 2nd ed., eds. Randy Hirokawa and Marshall Poole (Thousand Oaks, CA: Sage, 1996), pp. 147–78.

5. Abran J. Salazar, "Understanding the Synergistic Effects of Communication in the Small Group: Making the Most of Group Member Abilities," *Small Group Research* 26 (May 1995), pp. 169–99.

6. Jeremy Rose, "Communication Challenges and Role Functions of Performing Groups," *Small Group Research* 25 (August 1994), pp. 411–32.

Chapter 3

1. Martin Fackler, "Homeward Bound: Carefully Worded Letter to China Earns Release of Crew Members," *San Francisco Chronicle,* April 12, 2001, pp. A1, A17.

2. Paul Watzlaweick, Janet H. Beavin, and Don D. Jackson, *The Pragmatics of Human Communication* (New York: Norton, 1967).

3. Kittie W. Watson, "Listener Preferences: The Paradox of Small-Group Interactions," in *Small Group Communication: Theory and Practice,* 7th ed., eds. Robert S. Cathcart, Larry A. Samovar, and Linda Henman (Madison, WI: Brown & Benchmark, 1996), pp. 268–82.

4. Dan B. Curtis, Jerry L. Windsor, and R. D. Stephens, "National Preferences in Business and Communication Education," *Communication Education* 38 (1989), pp. 6–14.

5. John Gastil, "Identifying Obstacles to Small Group Democracy," *Small Group Research* 24 (February 1993), pp. 5–27.

6. Curt Bechler and Scott D. Johnson, "Leadership and Listening: A Study of Members' Perceptions," *Small Group Research* 26 (February 1995), pp. 77–85.

7. Lyman K. Steil, Larry L. Barker, and Kittie W. Watson, *Effective Listening: Key to Your Success* (Reading, MA: Addison-Wesley, 1983), pp. 21–22.

8. Kenneth N. Leone Cissna and Evelyn Sieburg, "Patterns of Intentional Confirmation and Disconfirmation," in *Bridges, Not Walls,* 4th ed., ed. John Stewart (New York: Random House, 1986), pp. 231–39.

9. Watson, "Listener Preferences," pp. 271–75.

10. Ibid., p. 270.

11. George R. Bach and Peter Wyden, *The Intimate Enemy* (New York: Avon, 1968).

12. David M. Berg, "A Descriptive Analysis of the Distribution and Duration of Themes Discussed by Task-Oriented Small Groups," *Speech Monographs* 34 (1967), pp. 172–75.

Chapter 4

1. Joseph A. DeVito, *The Communication Handbook: A Dictionary* (New York: Harper & Row, 1986).

2. Marshall S. Poole, David R. Siebold, and Robert D. McPhee, "Group Decision Making as a Structurational Process," *Quarterly Journal of Speech 71* (1985), pp. 74–102; and Marshall S. Poole, "Group Communication and the Structuring Process," in *Small Group Communication: A Reader,* 6th ed., ed. Robert S. Cathcart and Larry A. Samovar (Dubuque, IA: Wm. C. Brown, 1992), pp. 147–57.

3. Meredith May, "Talkin' off the Hizzle with Homeys," *The San Francisco Chronicle,* April 29, 2001, pp. A1, A17.

4. Ibid. p. A17. (You can purchase the *Berkeley High Slang Dictionary* for $5 by contacting Rick Ayres at *rickilene@igc.org.*)

5. Dale G. Leathers, "Process Disruption and Measurement: Small Group Communication," *Quarterly Journal of Speech 55* (1969), pp. 288–98.

6. This example is a modification of a case where a Fresno, California high school student was suspended from school for using "nigga" to greet a friend on school grounds.

7. Ray L. Birdwhistell, lecture at Nebraska Psychiatric Institute, Omaha, Nebraska, May 11, 1972.

8. Sandra Ketrow, "Nonverbal Aspects of Group Communication," in *The Handbook of Group Communication Theory & Research,* ed. Lawrence R. Frey (Thousand Oaks, CA: Sage, 1999), pp. 251–87.

9. Ibid.

10. Edward T. Hall, *The Silent Language* (Garden City, NJ: Doubleday, 1959).

11. Ketrow, "Nonverbal Aspects of Group Communication."

12. Ibid.

13. Ibid.

14. P. Eckman, P. Ellsworth, and W. V. Friesen, *Emotion in the Human Face: Guidelines for Research and an Integration of Findings* (New York: Pergamon, 1971).

15. A. E. Scheffler, "Quasi-Courtship Behavior in Psychotherapy," *Psychiatry 28* (1965), pp. 245–56.

16. Edward A. Mabry, "Developmental Aspects of Nonverbal Behavior in Small Group Settings," *Small Group Behavior 20* (1989), pp. 190–202.

17. Martin Remland, "Developing Leadership Skills in Nonverbal Communication: A Situational Perspective," *Journal of Business Communication* 3 (1981), pp. 17–29.

18. Judee K. Burgoon and Thomas Saine, *The Unknown Dialogue: An Introduction to Nonverbal Communication* (Boston: Houghton Mifflin, 1978).

19. Joel D. Davitz and Lois Davitz, "Nonverbal Vocal Communication of Feelings," *Journal of Communication* 11 (1961), pp. 81–86.

20. Ketrow, "Nonverbal Aspects of Group Communication."

21. R. G. Harper, A. N. Weins, and J. D. Matarazzo, *Nonverbal Communication: The State of the Art* (New York: Wiley, 1978).

22. Hall, *The Silent Language,* pp. 175–76.

23. Ketrow, "Nonverbal Aspects of Group Communication."

24. Ibid.

25. S. R. Hiltz and M. Turoff, "Virtual Meetings: Computer Conferencing and Distributed Group Support," in *Computer Augmented Teamwork: A Guided Tour,* eds. R. P. Bostrom, R. T. Watson, and S. T. Kinney (New York: Van Nostrand Reinhold, 1992), pp. 67–85.

26. Sharon L. Murrell, "The Impact of Communicating through Computers," Unpublished doctoral dissertation, State University of New York at Stony Brook, 1983.

27. Everett M. Rogers, *Communication Technology: The New Media in Society* (New York: Free Press, 1986).

28. Ketrow, "Nonverbal Aspects of Group Communication."

29. Compiled from Larry L. Barker, Kathy J. Wahlers, Kittie W. Watson, and Robert J. Kibler, *Groups in Process: An Introduction to Small Group Communication,* 3rd ed. (Englewood Cliffs, NJ: Prentice Hall, 1987), p. 208, and Robert J. Johansen, J. Vallee, and K. Spangler, *Electronic Meetings: Technical Alternatives and Social Choices* (Reading, MA: Addison-Wesley, 1979), pp. 113–15.

Chapter 5

1. *Random House Dictionary of the English Language,* Unabridged, 2nd ed. (New York: Random House, Inc., 1987), p. 472.

2. Susan Jarboe, "Group Communication and Creativity Processes," Lawrence R. Frey, *The Handbook of Group Communication Theory & Research* (Thousand Oaks, CA: Sage, 1999), p. 336.

3. Jarboe, "Group Communication and Creativity Processes," pp. 336–41.

4. John J. Sosik, Bruce J. Avolio, and Surinder S. Kahai, "Inspiring Group Creativity: Comparing Anonymous and Identified Electronic Brainstorming," *Small Group Research* 29 (1998), pp. 3–31.

5. Jarboe, "Group Communication and Creativity Processes," pp. 341–47.

6. J. G. Rawlinson, *Creative Thinking and Brainstorming* (New York: Wiley, 1981).

7. Alex Osborn, *Applied Imagination,* rev. ed. (New York: Charles Scribner's Sons, 1957).

8. M. Basadur and R. Thompson, "Usefulness of the Ideation Principle of Extended Effort in Real World Professional and Managerial Problem Solving," *Journal of Creative Behavior* 20 (1982), pp. 23–34.

9. R. Brent Gallupe, Alan R. Dennis, William H. Cooper, Joseph S. Valacich, Lame M. Bastianum, and Jay F. Nunamaker, Jr., "Electronic Brainstorming and Group Size," *Academy of Management Journal* 35 (June 1992), pp. 350–70. See also Joseph S. Valacich, Alan R. Dennis, and T. Connolly, "Idea Generation in Computer-Based Groups: A New Ending to an Old Story," *Organizational Behavior and Human Decision Processes* 57 (1994), pp. 448–68.

10. Russell L. Ackoff and Elsa Vergara, "Creativity in Problem Solving and Planning," in *Handbook for Creative and Innovative Managers,* ed. Robert L. Kuhn (New York: McGraw-Hill, 1988), pp. 77–90.

11. Leslie Kaufman-Rosen, "Big Blue's Butterfly," *Newsweek,* March 20, 1995, p. 46.

12. Del Jones, "GE Leader Recalls 'Eureka' Moment: Being No. 1 Was Limiting Opportunity," *The Cincinnati Enquirer,* April 8, 2001, pp. D1–2.

13. R. L. Firestein, "Effects of Creative Problem-Solving Training on Communication Behaviors in Small Groups," *Small Group Research* 21 (1990), pp. 507–21.

14. For a clear review of these issues, see Dale E. Brashers, Mark Adkins, and Renee A. Meyers, "Argumentation and Computer-Mediated Group Decision-Making," in *Group Communication in Context,* ed. Lawrence R. Frey (Hillsdale, NJ: Lawrence Erlbaum Associates, 1994), pp. 263–82.

15. Dennis S. Gouran, Randy Y. Hirokawa, and Amy E. Martz, "A Critical Analysis of Factors Related to Decisional Processes Involved in the *Challenger* Disaster," *Central States Speech Journal* 37 (1986), pp. 119–35.

16. Brashers et al., "Argumentation and Computer-Mediated Group Decision-Making."

17. Richard Huseman, Glenn Ware, and Charles Gruner, "Critical Thinking, Reflective Thinking, and the Ability to Organize Ideas: A Multivariate Approach," *Journal of the American Forensic Association* 9 (1972), pp. 261–65.

18. M. Neil Browne and Stuart M. Keeley, *Asking the Right Questions: A Guide to Critical Thinking,* 3rd ed. (Englewood Cliffs, NJ: Prentice Hall, 1992), pp. 3–5.

19. Ibid., pp. 3–7.

20. Brashers et al., "Argumentation and Computer-Mediated Group Decision-Making," pp. 263–82.

21. Gouran et al., "A Critical Analysis of Factors Related to Decisional Processes Involved in the *Challenger* Disaster," p. 130.

22. Mark F. Stasson and Scott D. Bradshaw, "Explanations of Individual-Group Performance Differences: What Sort of 'Bonus' Can Be Gained Through Group Interaction?" *Small Group Research* 26 (May 1995), pp. 296–308.

23. For a more detailed description of and source for these GSS tools and their potential impact on group critical thinking, see Brashers et al., "Argumentation and Computer-Mediated Group Decision-Making."

Chapter 6

1. Jay Hall, "Decisions, Decisions, Decisions," *Psychology Today,* November 1971, pp. 51–54, 86–87; Jay Hall and W. H. Watson, "The Effects of a Normative Intervention on Decision-Making Performance," *Human Relations* 23 (1970), pp. 299–317; Irving L. Janis, *Groupthink: Psychological Studies of Policy Decisions and Fiascoes,* 2nd ed. (Boston: Houghton Mifflin, 1982); Randy Y. Hirokawa, "Consensus Group Decision-Making, Quality of Decision and Group Satisfaction: An Attempt to Sort Fact from Fiction," *Central States Speech Journal* 33 (1982), pp. 407–15; Lester Coch and J. R. P. French, Jr., "Overcoming Resistance to Change," *Human Relations* 1 (1948), pp. 512–32; and Myron W. Block and L. R. Hoffman, "The Effects of Valence of Solutions and Group Cohesiveness on Members' Commitment to Group Decisions," in *The Group Problem-Solving Process,* ed. L. Richard Hoffman (New York: Prager, 1979), p. 121.

2. Brant R. Burleson, Barbara J. Levine, and Wendy Samter, "Decision-Making Procedure and Decision Quality," *Human Communication Research* 10 (1984), pp. 557–74.

3. Hirokawa, "Consensus Group Decision-Making," pp. 407–15; Hirokawa, "Why Informed Groups Make Faulty Decisions: An Investigation of Possible Interaction-Based Explanations," *Small Group Behavior* 18 (1987), pp. 3–29; and Hirokawa, "Discussion Procedures and Decision-Making Performance: A Test of the Functional Perspective," *Human Communication Research* 12 (1985), pp. 203–24.

4. Carl E. Larson and Frank M. J. LaFasto, *TeamWork: What Must Go Right, What Can Go Wrong* (Newbury Park, CA: Sage, 1989), pp. 27–38.

5. John E. Dewey, *How We Think* (Boston: D.C. Heath, 1910).

6. Susan Jarboe, "Procedures for Enhancing Group Decision Making," in *Communication and Group Decision Making,* 2nd ed., eds. Randy Y. Hirokawa and Marshall Scott Poole (Thousand Oaks, CA: Sage, 1996), pp. 345–83.

7. Marshall S. Poole, "Decision Development in Small Groups II: A Study of Multiple Sequences in Decision Making," *Communication Monographs* 50 (1983), pp. 224–25, and "Decision Development in Small Groups III: A Multiple Sequence Model of Group Decision Development," *Communication Monographs* 50 (1983), pp. 321–41.

8. Randy Y. Hirokawa, "Group Communication and Decision-Making Performance: A Continued Test of the Functional Perspective," paper presented at the annual convention of the Speech Communication Association (Boston, 1987); Randy Y. Hirokawa and Kathryn M. Rost, "Effective Group Decision Making

in Organizations: Field Test of the Vigilant Interaction Theory," paper presented at the annual convention of the Speech Communication Association (Atlanta, 1991).

9. Elizabeth E. Graham, Michael J. Papa, and Mary B. McPherson, "An Applied Test of the Functional Communication Perspective of Small Group Decision Making," *Southern Communication Journal* 62 (Summer 1997), pp. 269–79.

10. Among these studies were John K. Brilhart and Lurene M. Jochem, "Effects of Different Patterns on Outcomes of Problem-Solving Discussion," *Journal of Applied Psychology* 48 (1964), pp. 175–79; Ovid L. Bayless, "An Alternative Model for Problem Solving Discussion," *Journal of Communication* 17 (1967), pp. 188–97; Carl E. Larson, "Forms of Analysis and Small Group Problem Solving," *Speech Monographs* 36 (1969), pp. 452–55; and Hirokawa, "Discussion Procedures and Decision-Making Performance."

11. Benjamin J. Broome and Luann Fulbright, "A Multistage Influence Model of Barriers to Group Problem Solving: A Participant-Generated Agenda for Small Group Research," *Small Group Research* 26 (February 1995), pp. 25–55.

12. Joseph A. Bonito, "An Information-Processing Approach to Participation in Small Groups," *Communication Research* 28 (June 2001), pp. 275–303; Michael G. Cruz, Franklin J. Boster, and Jose I. Rodriquez, "The Impact of Group Size and Proportion of Shared Information on the Exchange and Integration of Information in Groups," *Communication Research* 27 (June, 1997), pp. 291–313.

13. Michael E. Mayer, Kevin T. Sonoda, and William B. Gudykunst, "The Effect of Time Pressures and Type of Information on Decision Quality," *Southern Communication Journal* 62 (Summer 1997), pp. 280–92.

14. For example, see Sidney J. Parnes, "Effects of Extended Effort in Creative Problem Solving," *Journal of Educational Psychology* 52 (1961), pp. 117–22.

15. Graham, Papa, and McPherson, "An Applied Test of the Functional Communication Perspective of Small Group Decision Making."

16. For a more detailed description of these support systems, see Joseph E. McGrath and Andrea B. Hollingshead, *Groups Interacting with Technology* (Thousand Oaks, CA: Sage, 1994).

17. Leonard M. Jessup and Joseph S. Valacich, eds., *Group Support Systems: New Perspectives* (New York: Macmillan, 1993).

18. S. Opper and H. Fresko-Weiss, *Technology for Teams: Enhancing Productivity in Networked Organizations* (New York: Van Nostrand Reinhold, 1992).

19. Andrea B. Hollingshead, Joseph E. McGrath, and Kathleen M. O'Connor, "Group Task Performance and Communication Technology: A Longitudinal Study of Computer-Mediated versus Face-to-Face Work Groups," *Small Group Research* 24 (August 1993), pp. 307–33.

20. Izak Benbasat and Lai-Huat Lim, "The Effects of Group, Task, Context, and Technology Variables on the Usefulness of Group Support Systems: A Meta-Analysis of Experimental Studies," *Small Group Research* 24 (November 1993), pp. 430–62.

21. Poppy McLeod, "New Communication Technologies for Group Decision Making: Toward an Integrative Framework," in *Communication and Group Decision Making,* 2nd ed., eds. Randy Y. Hirokawa and Marshall Scott Poole (Thousand Oaks, CA: Sage, 1996), pp. 426–61.

22. Robert F. Bales, *Interaction Process Analysis* (Reading, MA: Addison-Wesley, 1950); Donald G. Ellis and B. Aubrey Fisher, *Small Group Decision Making: Communication and the Group Process,* 4th ed. (New York: McGraw-Hill, 1994); and Poole, "Decision Development in Small Groups II."

23. Ellis and Fisher, *Small Group Decision Making,* pp. 144–57.

24. Poole, "Decision Development in Small Groups II."

25. David R. Siebold, "Making Meetings More Successful: Plans, Formats, and Procedures for Group Problem Solving," in *Small Group Communication: A Reader,* 5th ed., eds. Robert S. Cathcart and Larry A. Samovar (Dubuque, IA: Wm. C. Brown, 1988), pp. 219–20.

Chapter 7

1. The terms *primary* and *secondary* tension were first used by Ernest G. Bormann; elaboration of the concepts may be found in Bormann, *Discussion and Group Methods: Theory and Practice,* 2nd ed. (New York: Harper & Row, 1975), pp. 181–90.

2. Robert F. Bales, "The Equilibrium Problem in Small Groups," in *Working Papers in the Theory of Action,* eds. Talcott Parsons, Robert F. Bales, and Edward A. Shils (New York: Free Press, 1953), pp. 111–61.

3. Joseph B. Walther and Judee K. Burgoon, "Relational Communication in Computer-Mediated Interaction," *Human Communication Research* 19 (1992), pp. 50–88.

4. Carolyn M. Anderson, Bruce L. Riddle, and Mathew M. Martin, "Socialization Processes in Groups," in *Handbook of Group Communication Theory & Research,* ed. Lawrence R. Frey (Thousand Oaks, CA: Sage, 1999), pp. 139–63.

5. Ibid., p. 142.

6. Ibid.

7. Ibid.

8. Joann Keyton, *Group Communication* (Mountain View, CA: Mayfield, 1999), p. 115.

9. Anderson et al., p. 147.

10. Ibid., p. 148.

11. Ibid., p. 149.

12. Stewart Sigman, "The Applicability of the Concept of Recruitment to the Communication Study of a Nursing Home: An Ethnographic Case Study," *International Journal of Aging and Human Development* 22 (1985–86), pp. 215–33. See also Melanie Booth-Butterfield, Stephen Booth-Butterfield, and Jolene Koester, "The Function of Uncertainty Reduction in Alleviating Primary Tension in Small Groups," *Communication Research Reports* 5 (1988), pp. 146–53.

13. Anderson et al., p. 151

14. K.E.W. Morrison, "Information Usefulness and Acquisition During Organizational Encounter," *Management Communication Quarterly* 9 (1995), pp. 131–55.

15. Anderson et al., p. 152.

16. Ibid., p. 164.

17. Joann Keyton, "Group Termination: Completing the Study of Group Development," *Small Group Research* 24 (1993), pp. 84–100.

18. Michael Z. Hackman and Craig E. Johnson, *Leadership: A Communication Perspective* (Prospect Heights, IL: Waveland Press, 1991), p. 11.

19. John R. P. French and Bertram Raven, "The Bases of Social Power," in *Group Dynamics: Research and Theory,* 3rd ed., eds. Dorwin Cartwright and Alvin Zander (New York: Harper & Row, 1968), pp. 259–69.

20. Ernest G. Bormann, *Discussion and Group Methods: Theory and Practice,* 2nd ed. (New York: Harper & Row, 1975), pp. 253–69; and John C. Geier, "A Trait Approach to the Study of Leadership in Small Groups," *Journal of Communication* 17 (1967), pp. 316–23.

21. Katherine W. Hawkins, "Effects of Gender and Communication Content on Leadership Emergence in Small Task-Oriented Groups," *Small Group Research* 26 (May 1995), pp. 234–49.

22. Judith A. Kolb, "Are We Still Stereotyping Leadership? A Look at Gender and Other Predictors of Leader Emergence," *Small Group Research* 28 (1997), pp. 370–93.

23. Susan B. Shimanoff and Mercilee M. Jenkins, "Leadership and Gender: Challenging Assumptions and Recognizing Resources," in *Small Group Communication: Theory and Practice,* 7th ed., eds. Robert S. Cathcart, Larry A. Samovar, and Linda Henman (Madison, WI: Brown & Benchmark, 1996), pp. 327–44.

24. Stephanie Zimmerman, "Social Cognition and Evaluations of Health Care Team Communication Effectiveness," *Western Journal of Communication* 58 (Spring 1994), pp. 116–41.

25. Daniel Feldman, "Development and Enforcement of Group Norms," *Academy of Management Review* 9 (1984), pp. 47–53.

26. Stanley Schacter, "Deviation, Rejection, and Communication," *Journal of Abnormal and Social Psychology* 46 (1951), pp. 190–207, and Harold Leavitt, *Managerial Psychology,* 2nd ed. (Chicago: University of Chicago Press, 1964), pp. 270–74.

27. Ronald R. Sims, "Linking Groupthink to Unethical Behavior in Organizations," *Journal of Business Ethics* 11 (September 1992), pp. 651–62.

28. Katherine W. Hawkins and Bryant P. Fillion, "Perceived Communication Skill Needs for Work Groups," *Communication Research Reports* 16 (Spring 1999), pp. 167–74.

29. Carl E. Larson and Frank M. J. LaFasto, *TeamWork: What Must Go Right, What Can Go Wrong* (Newbury Park, CA: Sage, 1989).

30. M. E. Johnson and J. G. Fortman, "Internal Structure of the Gross Cohesiveness Scale," *Small Group Behavior* 19 (February 1988), pp. 187–96.

31. C. N. Greene, "Cohesion and Productivity in Work Groups," *Small Group Behavior* 21 (February 1989), pp. 221–25.

32. Brian Mullen, Tara Anthony, Eduardo Salas, and James E. Driskell, "Group Cohesiveness and Quality of Decision Making: An Integration of Tests of the Groupthink Hypothesis," *Small Group Research* 25 (May 1995), pp. 189–204.

33. Claus W. Langfred, "Is Group Cohesiveness a Double-Edged Sword? An Investigation on the Effects of Cohesiveness on Performance," *Small Group Research* 29 (1996), pp. 124–43.

34. Jack R. Gibb, "Defensive Communication," *Journal of Communication* 11 (1961), pp. 141–48.

Chapter 8

1. G. M. Parker, *Team Players and Teamwork: The New Competitive Business Strategy* (San Francisco: Jossey-Bass, 1990), and R. A. Eisenstat, "Fairfield Systems Group," in *Groups That Work and Those That Don't,* ed. J. R. Hackman (San Francisco: Jossey-Bass, 1990), pp. 171–81.

2. Robert Freed Bales, *Personality and Interpersonal Behavior* (New York: Holt, Rinehart & Winston, 1970).

3. Dirk Scheerhorn and Patricia Geist, "Social Dynamics in Groups," in *Managing Group Life,* eds. Lawrence R. Frey and J. Kevin Barge (Boston: Houghton Mifflin Company, 1997), pp. 80–103.

4. Carolyn M. Anderson and Matthew M. Martin, "The Effects of Communication Motives, Interaction Involvement, and Loneliness on Satisfaction: A Model of Small Groups," *Small Group Research* 26 (February 1995), pp. 118–37.

5. William F. Owen, "Metaphor Analysis of Cohesiveness in Small Discussion Groups," *Small Group Behavior* 16 (1985), pp. 415–26.

6. David A. Kolb, *Experiential Learning: Experience as the Source of Learning and Development* (Englewood Cliffs, NJ: Prentice Hall, 1984).

7. Synthesized from Isabel Briggs Myers, *Introduction to Type: A Description of the Theory and Application of the Myers-Briggs Type Indicator* (Palo Alto, CA: Consulting Psychologists Press, 1987); Otto Kroeger and Janet A. Thuesen, *Type Talk: The 16 Personality Types That Determine How We Live, Love, and Work* (New York: Dell Publishing, 1988); Otto Kroeger with Janet A. Thuesen, *Type Talk at Work: How the 16 Personality Types Determine Your Success on the Job* (New York: Dell Publishing, 1992); and Paul D. Tieger and Barbara Barron-Tieger, *Nurture by Nature: Understand Your Child's Personality Type—And Become a Better Parent* (Boston: Little, Brown and Company, 1997), pp. 5–62.

8. The following information about culture is synthesized from a number of sources, including Edward T. Hall, *Beyond Culture* (New York: Anchor Press, 1977); Geert Hofstede, *Culture's Consequences: International Differences in Work-Related Values* (Beverly Hills, CA: Sage Publications, 1980); William B. Gudykunst and Stella Ting-Toomey, *Culture and Interpersonal Communcation* (Newbury Park, CA: Sage Publications, 1988); Myron Lustig and Jolene Koester, *Interpersonal Competence: Interpersonal Communication Across Cultures* (New York: HarperCollins College Publishers, 1993); and Myron W. Lustig and Laura L. Casotta, "Comparing Group Communication Across Culture: Leadership, Conformity, and Discussion Procedures," in *Small Group Communication: A Reader,* 6th ed., eds. Robert S. Cathcart and Larry A. Samovar (Dubuque, IA: Wm. C. Brown Publishers, 1992), pp. 393–404.

9. Min-Sun Kim and William F. Sharkey, "Independent and Interdependent Construals of Self: Explaining Cultural Patterns of Interpersonal Communication in Multicultural Organizational Settings," *Communication Quarterly* 43 (Winter 1995), pp. 20–38.

10. The following information is synthesized from several sources, including Lea P. Stewart, Alan D. Stewart, Sheryl A. Friedley, and Pamela J. Cooper, *Communication between the Sexes,* 2nd ed. (Scottsdale, AZ: Gorsuch Scarisbrick, Publishers, 1990), pp. 43–114; Anthony Mulac, Pamela Gibbons, and Stewart Fujiyama, "Male/Female Language Differences Viewed from an Inter-Cultural Perspective: Gender as Culture," paper presented at the Speech Communication Association Annual Convention (November 1990), Chicago; Daniel N. Maltz and Ruth A. Borker, "A Cultural Approach to Male–Female Miscommunication," in *Language and Social Identity,* ed. John J. Gumperz (Cambridge: Cambridge University Press, 1982), pp. 195–216; and Deborah Tannen, *You Just Don't Understand: Women and Men in Conversation* (New York: Ballantine Books, 1990).

11. This information is synthesized from Michael L. Hecht, Mary Jane Collier, and Sidney A. Ribeau, *African American Communication: Ethnic Identity and Cultural Interpretation,* vol. 2, Language and Language Behaviors series (Newbury Park, CA: Sage Publications, 1993), especially Chap. 3, pp. 82–113, and Anita K. Foeman and Gary Pressley, "Ethnic Culture and Corporate Culture: Using Black Styles in Organizations," *Communication Quarterly* 35 (Fall 1987), pp. 293–307.

12. Rebecca Leonard and Don C. Locke, "Communication Stereotypes: Is Interracial Communication Possible?" *Journal of Black Studies* 23 (March 1993), pp. 332–43.

13. Mark P. Orbe, "Remember, It's Always Whites' Ball: Descriptions of African American Male Communication," *Communication Quarterly* 35 (Fall 1987), pp. 293–307.

14. C. Kirchmeyer and A. Cohen, "Multicultural Groups: Their Performance and Reactions with Constructive Conflict," *Group & Organization Management* 17 (1992), pp. 153–70, and C. Kirchmeyer, "Multicultural Task Groups: An Account of the Low Contribution Level of Minorities," *Small Group Research* 24 (February 1993), pp. 127–48.

15. This information is taken primarily from Rick Hicks and Kathy Hicks, *Boomers, Xers, and Other Strangers: Understanding the Generational Differences that Divide Us* (Wheaton, IL: Tyndale House Publishers, 1999), especially pp. 229–353. Other sources of information include Morris E. Massey, *The People Puzzle: Understanding Yourself and Others* (Reston, VA: Reston Publishing Company, 1979), and Don Tapscott, *Growing Up Digital: The Rise of the Net Generation* (New York: McGraw-Hill, 1998).

16. Warren E. Watson, Kumar Kamalesh, and Larry K. Michaelson, "Cultural Diversity's Impact on Interaction Process and Performance: Comparing Homogeneous and Diverse Task Groups," *Academy of Management Journal* 36 (1993), pp. 590–602, and Leisa D. Sargent and Christina Sue-Chan, "Does Diversity Affect Group Efficacy? The Intervening Role of Cohesion and Task Interdependence," *Small Group Research* 32 (August 2001), pp. 426–50.

17. Ernest G. Bormann, "Symbolic Convergence Theory and Communication in Group Decision Making," in *Communication and Group Decision Making*, 2nd ed., eds. Randy Y. Hirokawa and M. Scott Poole (Thousand Oaks, CA: Sage Publications, 1996), pp. 81–113.

18. Catherine Cobb Morocco, "Development and Function of Group Metaphor," *Journal for the Theory of Social Behavior* 9 (1979), pp. 15–27.

19. Bormann, "Symbolic Convergence," pp. 229–30.

20. Complete information on constructing a SYMLOG diagram, along with an abbreviated explanation of SYMLOG theory, may be found in a workbook, R. F. Bales, *SYMLOG Case Study Kit* (New York: The Free Press, 1980). An even more simplified explanation of SYMLOG theory and method for constructing a diagram may be found in Joann Keyton, "Coding Communication in Decision-Making Groups," in *Managing Group Life: Communicating in Decision-Making Groups* (Boston: Houghton Mifflin Company, 1997), pp. 236–69. For readers who are interested in details of both the theory and methodology, we refer them to R. F. Bales and Stephen P. Cohen, *SYMLOG: A System for the Multiple-Level Observation of Groups* (New York: The Free Press, 1979).

21. Richard V. Polley, SYMLOG computer software, Lewis and Clark University, Portland, OR.

Chapter 9

1. Kathleen M. O'Connor, Deborah H. Gruenfeld, and Joseph E. McGrath, "The Experience and Effects of Conflict in Continuing Work Groups," *Small Group Research* 24 (August 1993), pp. 363–82.

2. The information about the Bay of Pigs invasion is taken from Irving L. Janis, *Groupthink: Psychological Studies of Policy Decisions and Fiascoes,* 2nd ed. (Boston: Houghton Mifflin, 1983), pp. 14–47.

3. D. Cole, "Meetings that Make Sense," *Psychology Today* (May 1989), pp. 14–15.

4. Janis, *Groupthink,* pp. 14–47

5. Brian Mullen, Tara Anthony, Eduardo Salas, and James E. Driskell, "Group Cohesiveness and Quality of Decision Making: An Integration of the Groupthink Hypothesis," *Small Group Research* 25 (May 1994), pp. 189–204.

6. Irving L. Janis and Leon Mann, *Decision Making: A Psychological Analysis of Conflict, Choice, and Commitment* (New York: Free Press, 1977).

7. Mark Schittekatte and Alain Van Niel, "Effects of Partially Shared Information and Awareness of Unshared Information on Information Sampling," *Small Group Research* 27 (1996), pp. 431–49.

8. Janis and Mann, *Decision Making.*

9. Charles R. Franz and K. Gregory Jin, "The Structure of Group Conflict in a Collaborative Work Group During Information Systems Development," *Journal of Applied Communication Research* 23 (1995), pp. 108–27.

10. R. Spears and M. Leah, "Panacea or Panopticon? The Hidden Power in Computer-Mediated Communication," *Communication Research* 21 (1994), pp. 427–59.

11. Kenneth Thomas, "Conflict and Conflict Management," in *Handbook of Industrial and Organizational Psychology,* ed. Marvin Dunnette (Chicago: Rand McNally, 1976), pp. 890–934.

12. Hal Witteman, "Analyzing Interpersonal Conflict: Nature of Awareness, Type of Initiating Event, Situational Perceptions, and Management Styles," *Western Journal of Communication* 56 (Summer 1992), pp. 248–80.

13. Victor D. Wall and Linda L. Nolan, "Small Group Conflict: A Look at Equity, Satisfaction, and Styles of Conflict Management," *Small Group Behavior* 18 (1987), pp. 188–211.

14. Renee Meyers and Dale Brashers, "Influence Processes in Group Interaction," *The Handbook of Group Communication Theory and Research,* ed. Lawrence Frey (Thousand Oaks, CA: Sage, 1999), pp. 288–312.

15. Victor D. Wall, Gloria J. Galanes, and Susan B. Love, "Small Task-Oriented Groups: Conflict, Conflict Management, Satisfaction, and Decision Quality," *Small Group Behavior* 18 (1987), pp. 31–55.

16. Arie W. Kruglanski and Donna M. Webster, "Group Members' Reactions to Opinion Deviates and Conformists at Varying Degrees of Proximity to Decision Deadline and of Environmental Noise," *Journal of Personality and Social Psychology* 61 (1991), pp. 212–26.

17. Rick Garlick and Paul A. Mongeau, "Argument Quality and Group Member Status as Determinants of Attitudinal Minority Influence," *Western Journal of Communication* 57 (Summer 1993), pp. 289–308.

18. Lisa J. Gebhart and Renee A. Meyers, "Subgroup Influence in Decision-Making Groups: Examining Consistency from a Communication Perspective," *Small Group Research* 26 (May 1995), pp. 147–68.

19. Dale Brashers and Renee Meyers, "Tag-team Argument and Group Decision Making: A Preliminary Investigation," *Spheres of Argument: Proceedings of the Sixth Speech Communication Association/American Forensics Association Conference on Argumentation,* ed. Bruce Gronbeck (Annandale, VA: Speech Communication Association, 1989), pp. 542–50.

20. Gebhart and Meyers, "Subgroup Influence."

21. James B. Thomas, Reuben R. McDaniel, Jr., and Michael J. Dooris, "Strategic Issue Analysis: NGT and Decision Analysis for Resolving Strategic Issues," *Journal of Applied Behavioral Science* 25 (May 1989), pp. 189–201.

22. Roger Fisher and William Ury, *Getting to Yes: Negotiating Agreement Without Giving In* (New York: Penguin Books, 1983).

Chapter 10

1. Ralph M. Stogdill, Carrol L. Shartle, Willis L. Scott, Alvin E. Coons, and William E. Jaynes, *A Predictive Study of Administrative Work Patterns* (Columbus: The Ohio State University, Bureau of Business Research, 1956); Ralph M. Stogdill and Alvin E. Coons, eds., *Leader Behavior: Its Description and Measurement* (Columbus: The Ohio State University, Bureau of Business Research, 1957); and Robert Blake and Jane Mouton, *The Managerial Grid* (Houston: Gulf, 1964).

2. Michael Z. Hackman and Craig E. Johnson, *Leadership: A Communication Perspective* (Prospect Heights, IL: Waveland Press, 1991), pp. 26–27.

3. Ibid., p. 27.

4. John Gastil, "A Meta-Analytic Review of the Productivity and Satisfaction of Democratic and Autocratic Leadership," *Small Group Research* 25 (August 1994), pp. 384–410, and John Gastil, *Democracy in Small Groups* (Philadelphia: New Society Publishers, 1993).

5. William C. Schutz, "The Leader as Completer," in *Small Group Communication: A Reader,* 3rd ed., eds. Robert S. Cathcart and Larry A. Samovar (Dubuque, IA: Wm C. Brown, 1979), pp. 454–60.

6. Fred Fiedler, *A Theory of Leadership Effectiveness* (New York: McGraw-Hill, 1967).

7. Paul Hersey and Kenneth H. Blanchard, *Management of Organizational Behavior,* 4th ed. (Englewood Cliffs, NJ: Prentice Hall, 1982).

8. Gastil, "A Meta-Analytic Review," p. 403.

9. J. Kevin Barge, "Leadership as Medium: A Leaderless Group Discussion Model," *Communication Quarterly* 37 (Fall 1989), pp. 237–47.

10. Much of the following information is discussed in detail in John K. Brilhart and Gloria J. Galanes, *Effective Group Discussion,* 8th ed. (Madison, WI: Brown & Benchmark, 1995), pp. 177–202.

11. Carl E. Larson and Frank M. J. LaFasto, *TeamWork: What Must Go Right, What Can Go Wrong* (Newbury Park, CA: Sage, 1989), pp. 27–33.

12. Katherine W. Hawkins, "Effects of Gender and Communication Content on Leadership Emergence in Small Task-Oriented Groups," *Small Group Research* 26 (May 1995), pp. 234–49.

13. Larson and LaFasto, *TeamWork,* especially chaps. 6, 9, and 10.

14. P. H. Andrews and R. T. Herschel, *Organizational Communication: Empowerment in a Technological Society* (Boston: Houghton Mifflin, 1996).

15. Michael Z. Hackman and Craig E. Johnson, *Leadership: A Communication Perspective* (Prospect Heights, IL: Waveland Press, 1991).

Chapter 11

1. *Spectra,* IX (December 1973), n.p.

2. George Kennedy (trans.), *Aristotle, On Rhetoric* (New York: Oxford, 1991), p. 181.

3. Jane Blankenship, *A Sense of Style* (Belmont, CA: Dickenson, 1968), p. 12.

4. Ibid., p. 41.

5. Karyn Rybacki and Donald Rybacki, *Communication Criticism: Approaches and Genres* (Belmont, CA: Wadsworth, 1991), p. 40.

Appendix

1. Stanley Seashore, *Group Cohesiveness in the Industrial Work Group* (Ann Arbor: University of Michigan Institute for Social Research, 1954).

2. Dean C. Barnlund and Franklyn S. Haiman, *The Dynamics of Discussion* (Boston: Houghton Mifflin, 1960), pp. 401–4

BIBLIOGRAPHY

Chapter 1

Brilhart, John K., and Gloria J. Galanes. *Effective Group Discussion.* 10th ed. New York: McGraw-Hill, 2001.

Keyton, Joann. "Relational Communication in Groups." In *The Handbook of Group Communication Theory & Research,* ed. Lawrence R. Frey. Thousand Oaks, CA: Sage, 1999, pp. 192–224.

Shaw, Marvin E. *Group Dynamics: The Psychology of Small Group Behavior.* 3rd ed. New York: McGraw-Hill, 1981.

Chapter 2

Fisher, Aubrey, and Donald Ellis. *Small Group Decision Making: Communication and the Group Process.* 4th ed. New York: McGraw-Hill, 1994.

Katz, Daniel, and Robert Kahn. *The Social Psychology of Organizations.* 2nd ed. New York: Wiley, 1978.

Von Bertalanffy, Ludwig. *General Systems Theory: Foundations, Development, Applications.* New York: Braziller, 1968.

Chapter 3

Brilhart, John K., and Gloria J. Galanes. *Effective Group Discussion.* 10th ed. New York: McGraw-Hill, 2001, chaps. 3 and 5.

Cathcart, Robert S.; Larry A. Samovar; and Linda Henman, eds. *Small Group Communication: Theory & Practice.* 7th ed. Madison, WI: Brown & Benchmark, 1996, sections 5 and 6.

Gudykunst, William B. *Bridging Differences: Effective Intergroup Communication.* Newbury Park, CA: Sage, 1991.

King, Stephen W. "The Nature of Communication." In *Small Group Communication: A Reader.* 5th ed., eds. Robert S. Cathcart and Larry A. Samovar. Dubuque, IA: Wm. C. Brown, 1988.

Steil, Lyman K., and Larry Barker. *Effective Listening: Key to Your Success.* Reading, MA: Addison-Wesley, 1983.

Watzlawick, Paul; Janet A. Beavin; and Don D. Jackson. *The Pragmatics of Human Communication.* New York: Norton, 1967.

Chapter 4

Anderson, Peter A. "Nonverbal Communication in the Small Group." In *Small Group Communication: A Reader.* 6th ed., eds. Robert S. Cathcart and Larry A. Samovar. Dubuque, IA: Wm. C. Brown, 1992, pp. 272–86.

Brilhart, John K., and Gloria J. Galanes. *Effective Group Discussion.* 10th ed. New York: McGraw-Hill, 2001, chaps. 3, 4, and 5.

Burgoon, Judee K. "Spatial Relationships in Small Groups." In *Small Group Communication: Theory & Practice.* 7th ed., eds. Robert S. Cathcart, Larry A. Samovar, and Linda Henman. Madison, WI: Brown & Benchmark, 1996, pp. 241–53.

Ketrow, Sandra. "Nonverbal Aspects of Group Communication." In *The Handbook of Group Communication Theory & Research,* ed. Lawrence R. Frey. Thousand Oaks, CA: Sage, 1999, pp. 251–87.

Chapter 5

Beyer, Barry K. *Practical Strategies for the Teaching of Thinking.* Boston: Allyn & Bacon, 1987.

Browne, M. Neil, and Stuart M. Keeley. *Asking the Right Questions: A Guide to Critical Thinking.* 5th ed. Englewood Cliffs, NJ: Prentice Hall, 1998.

Campbell, Stephen K. *Flaws and Fallacies in Statistical Thinking.* Englewood Cliffs, NJ: Prentice Hall, 1974.

Ehninger, Douglas, and Wayne Brockriede. *Decision by Debate.* 2nd ed. New York: Harper & Row, 1978.

Jarboe, Susan. "Group Communication and Creativity Processes." And Keyton, Joann. "Relational Communication in Groups." In *The Handbook of Group Communication Theory & Research,* ed. Lawrence R. Frey. Thousand Oaks, CA: Sage, 1999.

Neimark, Edith D. *Adventures in Thinking.* San Diego: Harcourt Brace Jovanovich, 1987.

Raths, Louis E.; Selma Wasserman; Arthur Jonas; and Arnold Rothstein. *Teaching for Thinking: Theory, Strategies, and Activities for the Classroom.* 2nd ed. New York: Teachers College, Columbia University, 1986.

Chapter 6

Broome, Benjamin J., and Luann Fulbright. "A Multistage Influence Model of Barriers to Group Problem Solving: A Participant-Generated Agenda for Small Group Research." *Small Group Research* 26 (February 1995), pp. 25–55.

Dewey, John. *How We Think.* Boston: D.C. Heath, 1910.

Hirokawa, Randy Y. "Discussion Procedures and Decision-Making Performance: A Test of the Functional Perspective." *Human Communication Research* 12 (1985), pp. 203–24.

Larson, Carl E., and Frank M. J. LaFasto. *TeamWork: What Must Go Right, What Can Go Wrong.* Newbury Park, CA: Sage, 1989.

Maier, Norman R. F. *Problem Solving and Creativity in Individuals and Groups.* Belmont, CA: Brooks/Cole, 1970.

McGrath, Joseph E., and Andrea B. Hollingshead. *Groups Interacting with Technology.* Thousand Oaks, CA: Sage, 1994.

Chapter 7

Anderson, Carolyn N.; Bruce L. Riddle; and Matthew M. Martin. "Socialization Processes in Groups." In *The Handbook of Group Communication Theory & Research,* ed. Lawrence R. Frey. Thousand Oaks, CA: Sage, 1999, pp. 139–166.

Bormann, Ernest G. *Discussion and Group Methods: Theory and Practice.* 2nd ed. New York: Harper & Row, 1975, chaps. 8 and 9.

Brilhart, John K., and Gloria J. Galanes. *Effective Group Discussion.* 10th ed. New York: McGraw-Hill, 2001, chaps. 7 and 8.

Fisher, B. Aubrey, and Donald G. Ellis. *Small Group Decision Making.* 3rd ed. New York: McGraw-Hill, 1990, chap. 6.

Chapter 8

Bales, Robert Freed, and Stephen P. Cohen. *SYMLOG: A System for the Multiple-Level Observation of Groups.* New York: The Free Press, 1979.

Hecht, Michael L.; Mary Jane Collier; and Sidney A. Ribeau. *African American Communication: Ethnic Identity and Cultural Interpretation,* vol. 2. Language and Language Behaviors series, Newbury Park, CA: Sage Publications, 1993, especially chap. 3.

Hicks, Rick, and Kathy Hicks. *Boomers, Xers, and Other Strangers: Understanding the Generational Differences that Divide Us.* Wheaton, IL: Tyndale House Publishers, 1999.

Kolb, David. *Experiential Learning: Experience as the Source of Learning and Development.* Englewood Cliffs, NJ: Prentice Hall, 1984.

Kroeger, Otto, with Janet A. Thuesen. *Type Talk at Work: How the 16 Personality Types Determine Your Success on the Job.* New York: Dell Publishing, 1992.

Lustig, Myron W., and Laura L. Cassotta. "Comparing Group Communication across Cultures: Leadership, Conformity, and Discussion Processes." In *Small Group Communication: A Reader.* 6th ed., eds. Robert S. Cathcart and Larry A. Samovar. Dubuque, IA: Wm. C. Brown Publishers, 1992, pp. 382–92.

Stewart, Lea P.; Alan D. Stewart; Sheryl A. Friedley; and Pamela J. Cooper. *Communication Between the Sexes: Sex Differences and Sex-Role Stereotypes.* 2nd ed. Scottsdale, AZ: Gorsuch Scarisbrick, Publishers, 1990, in particular, chaps. 2, 3, and 4.

Tannen, Deborah. *You Just Don't Understand: Women and Men in Conversation.* New York: Ballantine Books, 1990.

Chapter 9

Fisher, Roger, and Scott Brown. *Getting Together: Building a Relationship That Gets to Yes.* Boston: Houghton Mifflin, 1988.

Fisher, Roger, and William Ury. *Getting to Yes: Negotiating Agreement Without Giving In.* New York: Penguin Books, 1983.

Janis, Irving L. *Groupthink: Psychological Studies of Policy Decisions and Fiascoes.* 2nd ed. Boston: Houghton Mifflin, 1983.

Meyers, Renee, and Dale Brashers. "Influence Processes in Group Interaction." In *The Handbook of Group Communication Theory and Research,* ed. Lawrence Frey. Thousand Oaks, CA: Sage, 1999, pp. 288–312.

Thomas, Kenneth W. "Conflict and Conflict Management." In *Handbook of Industrial and Organizational Psychology,* ed. Marvin Dinette. Chicago: Rand McNally, 1976.

Chapter 10

Brilhart, John K., and Gloria J. Galanes. *Effective Group Discussion.* 10th ed. New York, McGraw-Hill, 2001, chap. 10.

Cathcart, Robert S.; Larry A. Samovar; and Linda D. Henman. *Small Group Communication: Theory & Practice.* 7th ed. Madison, WI: Brown & Benchmark, 1996, section 7.

Larson, Carl E., and Frank M. J. LaFasto. *TeamWork: What Must Go Right, What Can Go Wrong.* Newbury Park, CA: Sage, 1989.

Robert, Henry M. *Robert's Rules of Order Revised.* Glenview, IL: Scott, Foresman, 1981.

Tropman, John E. *Effective Meetings.* Beverly Hills, CA: Sage, 1980.

Chapter 11

Blankenship, Jane. *A Sense of Style.* Belmont, CA: Dickenson, 1968.

Gronbeck, Bruce; Kathleen German; Douglas Ehninger; and Alan Monroe. *Principles of Speech Communication.* New York: Longman, 1998.

Hasling, Jack. *The Audience, The Speaker, The Message.* Boston: McGraw-Hill, 1998.

Lucas, Stephen. *The Art of Public Speaking.* Boston: McGraw-Hill, 1998.

Rybacki, Karyn, and Donald Rybacki. *Communication Criticism: Approaches and Genres.* Belmont, CA: Wadsworth, 1991.